Frommer's®

FIFTH EDITION

NYC
Free &
dirt cheap

WILEY

John Wiley & Sons, Inc.

Published by:

John Wiley & Sons, Inc.

111 River St.
Hoboken, NJ 07030-5774

ISBN: 978-1-118-36901-2 (paper); 978-1-118-51765-9 (ebk); 978-1-118-51763-5 (ebk)

Editor: Kathleen Warnock
Production Editor: Michael Brumitt with M. Faunette Johnston
Cartographer: Roberta Stockwell
Photo Editor: Alden Gewirtz
Production by Wiley Indianapolis Composition Services
Interior design by Melissa Auciello-Brogan
Photo on p. 1 by Elinor Stible, p. 4 & p. 46 by Cherie Cincilla, p. 2, 80, 180, 222 by Alden Gewirtz, p. 136 & p. 296 by Shayna Marchese, and p. 318 by Justin Appenzeller.

For information on our other products and services or to obtain technical support, please contact our Customer Care Department within the U.S. at 877/762-2974, outside the U.S. at 317/572-3993, or fax 317/572-4002.

Wiley also publishes its books in a variety of electronic formats. Some content that appears in print may not be available in electronic formats.

Manufactured in the United States of America

CONTENTS

LIST OF MAPS

About the Author

Ethan Wolff is a fourth-generation New Yorker. How he happened to grow up in Virginia is a complete mystery to him. He lives with his wife and daughter in Brooklyn.

Acknowledgments

Thanks to John Vorwald, who came up with the idea for this book and shepherded it through development; to Kathleen Warnock for her stellar editing; and to Stephanie Wolff, Evelyn Grollman, Anna Sandler, and Elroy Wolff for pitching in. Apologies to everyone who has had to put up with my cheapness over the years. It was all just research.

—Ethan Wolff

How to Contact Us

In researching this book, we discovered many wonderful places—hotels, restaurants, shops, and more. We're sure you'll find others. Please tell us about them, so we can share the information with your fellow travelers in upcoming editions. If you were disappointed with a recommendation, we'd love to know that, too. Please write to:

Frommer's NYC Free & Dirt Cheap, 5th Edition
John Wiley & Sons, Inc. • 111 River St. • Hoboken, NJ 07030-5774
frommersfeedback@wiley.com

Advisory & Disclaimer

Please be advised that travel information is subject to change at any time—and this is especially true of prices. We therefore suggest that you write or call ahead for confirmation when making your travel plans. The authors, editors, and publisher cannot be held responsible for the experiences of readers while traveling. Your safety is important to us, however, so we encourage you to stay alert and be aware of your surroundings. Keep a close eye on cameras, purses, and wallets, all favorite targets of thieves and pickpockets.

Free & Dirt Cheap Icons & Abbreviations

We use **four feature icons** that point you to the great deals, in-the-know advice, and unique experiences that separate urban adventurers from tourists. Throughout the book, look for:

FREE   Events, attractions, or experiences that cost no more than your time and a swipe of your Metrocard.

FINE PRINT   The unspoken conditions or necessary preparations to experience certain free and dirt cheap events.

★   The best free and dirt cheap events, dining, shopping, living, and exploring in the city.

   Special events worth marking in your calendar.

Travel Resources at Frommers.com

Frommer's travel resources don't end with this guide. Frommer's website, **www.frommers.com**, has travel information on more than 4,000 destinations. We update features regularly, giving you access to the most current trip-planning information and the best airfare, lodging, and car-rental bargains. You can also listen to podcasts, connect with other Frommers.com members through our active-reader forums, share your travel photos, read blogs from guidebook editors and fellow travelers, and much more.

If you have Patience (and Fortitude) you can seek out many of the finer things in NYC for little or no cost.

THE BEST THINGS IN LIFE ARE FREE

It's no secret that NYC costs are out of control. Great Recession or no, there remain plenty of local prices steep enough to make a Park Avenue plutocrat wince. We've got $275 plates of pasta (with white truffles at Nello), $295 burgers (served on a gold-dusted bun at Serendipity 3), and $1,000 omelets (lobster and caviar from Norma's at the Parker Meridian). For more prosaic tastes, New York City will serve you a $12 cup of coffee (Café Grumpy), a $26 cocktail (Jimmy at the James New York), or a $36 salad (the Cobb at Michael's).

Extremes aside, prices are up all across the city. The subway has gone to $2.25, accompanied by cutbacks in service. Slices follow fares, and the average piece of pizza is approaching $2.50. Even the price of the humble bagel has jumped over 65% in recent years. The national housing market may be in the tank, but you'd never know it in Manhattan. One-point-five million covers your average price tag. If you opt to rent instead, $2,569 is your going rate. For a *studio* in Manhattan. So, in a town with $12 coffees and $1,000 plates of eggs, where an apartment that would make a convict feel claustrophobic costs a million and a half dollars, a book about living on the cheap must be a pretty slim volume, right?

Wrong.

New York takes a lot of pride in being the cultural capital of the world, and to maintain that reputation we let many of the goods go for free. Art, music, dance, and drama can all be found for simply the price of showing up, and there's plenty of it to go around. When I visit another city and see that they're putting on a production of alfresco Shakespeare I think, "How sweet." This book lists *eight* of them. We've got another dozen or so spots that host free outdoor films. Over 40 cultural institutions are always free, and most of our top-tier museums set aside several hours a week where you pay what you wish to enter. The best work of the world's emerging artists hangs in our galleries, which never charge for entry. New York's libraries circulate thousands of books, videos, and albums, in addition to offering us free films, classes, and lectures that add up to 38,000 giveaways a year. From La MaMa to the MoMA, you don't need to be a millionaire to cash in on great culture here.

When it comes time to eat, New Yorkers are blessed with incredible ethnic food, which also doubles as some of the city's cheapest. Chinatown serves up savory dumplings for a buck, sesame pancake sandwiches for $2.25, and four-course buffets for $4. My favorite New York tacos are only $3 a pop, and for $4.50 you can dig into humanity's greatest achievement, the *bánh mì* sandwich.

Between these pages, I show you how to catch a free cruise through New York Harbor to the city's most scenic picnic grounds, on top of dirt cheap walking tours covering downtown to DUMBO to the Atlantic Ocean. I give you some great cheap date ideas, like First Saturdays in Brooklyn, the Rubin Museum of Art's Cabaret Cinema, and a whole passel of restaurants that will have you eating well without draining your wallet. I also reveal some of the city's secret delights, like George

Washington's desk, a Dutch house from around 1675, and the original Winnie-the-Pooh.

In the post-9/11 era, tourists and locals alike may be appreciating the city in new ways, but it's easy to forget that New York is not an inevitability; it's a rare phenomenon. Taking advantage of all the amazing resources is practically a civic duty. When you catch on with a big New York giveaway, you get the bonus of free camaraderie. There's nothing better than sharing the knowledge that you're in on something amazing, like a band playing its heart out in front of sunset on the Hudson, or the group spirit of a Bryant Park film, or the feeling of wending your way out of Central Park after a world-class Shakespeare in the Park production. Even everyday moments can inspire. How many years has it been since Hollywood made a movie half as entertaining as a couple of hours sitting on the steps of the New York Public Library, or Federal Hall, or the Met?

These experiences are priceless—gifts bestowed by the city that can make parsimony feel like one of humanity's crowning virtues. Whether you've checked this book out of the library or picked it up from the discount bin, you should revel in your cheapness. What feels better than beating the system? Just because you don't have the cash flow for $50 cocktails doesn't mean New York has to feel like someone else's party. When you walk across the Brooklyn Bridge on a sunny afternoon, park yourself by the waters of the Temple of Dendur, or cruise past the Statue of Liberty, you own them as much as anyone else does. The city's great charm is that it's available to anybody, at any time.

For better and for worse, every day in New York is an adventure. Make the most of it, even if you're not sitting on a hoard of gold.

The National Museum of the American Indian is one of NYC's best-kept "free" secrets.

BEST OF THE FREE & DIRT CHEAP APPLE

New Yorkers are lucky in having a menu of freebies and cheapies in an expensive city. From Shakespeare in the Park to car-less drive-in movies to kayaking along the Hudson, there's a host of remarkable activities that can't be had in other cities at any price. Sleeping for cheap may be difficult, but there are some great exceptions. When it comes to stocking up, the Big Apple's big volumes make for unexpectedly great bargain-hunting. Add in cheap ethnic food and giveaway theater, and an urban adventurer can go far on very little. What follows is the best of the best.

1 Best Entertainment Bets

- 🏆 **Best Manhattan Parade:** New Yorkers are pros at assembling en masse. My favorite pageant is one of the city's most inclusive, the **Greenwich Village Halloween Parade,** with elaborate costumes and a healthy dose of gallows humor making the festive spirit infectious. See p. 21.

- 🏆 **Best Outer-Borough Parade:** As New York events become more and more commercialized, it's nice to have one occasion that's defiantly do-it-yourself. Coney Island's **Mermaid Parade** brings low-budget finery to the Atlantic shore. Classic cars serve as the chariots for a procession of mermaids and Neptunes who will never stand accused of being overdressed. See p. 303.

- 🏆 **Best Festival: Harlem Week** began as a single day 30 years ago and now stretches across the month of August. Film, jazz, and food festivals are among the highlights to be found along lovely brownstone blocks Uptown. See p. 19.

- **Best DIY Rock Show: Arlene's Grocery** (95 Stanton St.; ✆ **212/358-1633**) is the tri-state's best place to play rock star, with a live rock band to help you channel your inner Mick. See p. 272.

- **Best Cultural Center with Beer: Pete's Candy Store** (709 Lorimer St.; ✆ **718/302-3770**) does its part to keep Williamsburg elevated and enlightened, bringing in live music and readings. Spelling bees and quiz nights round out a full schedule of free diversions. See p. 277.

- **Best Bar Bands:** The former ballroom of the Brooklyn Academy of Music hosts **BAMcafé** (30 Lafayette Ave.; ✆ **718/636-4100**), for its free Friday and Saturday night music shows. The genres represented (rock, jazz, world, and R&B) are as diverse as Brooklyn itself. See p. 224.

- **Best Jazzy Venue:** Low-pretense Brooklyn meets Euro sophistication over pints of Hoegaarden at Williamsburg's **Zebulon** (258 Wythe Ave.; ✆ **718/218-6934**). Afrobeat, funk, and improv jazz can be heard here, most nights with no cover. See p. 235.

- **Best Summer Music Festival:** Every year **SummerStage** (Central Park; ✆ **212/360-2777**) channels music fans by the truckload into a small arena in the middle of Central Park. Though several shows are benefit performances with steep ticket prices, the calendar still offers names playing for free. See p. 247.

- **Best Summer Music Festival That's Not SummerStage:** The **Lincoln Center Out of Doors** (70 Lincoln Center Plaza; ✆ **212/546-2656**) festival presents hundreds of acts every August. The range is staggering, covering jazz, dance, opera, and everything in between. See p. 244.

- **Best Movie Screenings with a Roof:** Buy a membership at **MoMA** (11 W. 53rd St.; ✆ **212/708-9400**) and not only will you get free admission, you'll also have the run of the institution's three theaters. The fare is arty and never less than thought-provoking. For flicks 365 days a year, $85 is a bargain. See p. 160.

- **Best Movie Screenings Without a Roof:** Forty-Second Street welcomes movie fans with an eclectic selection during the **HBO Bryant Park Summer Film Festival** (✆ **212/512-5700**). The lawn fills up quickly, but that enhances the festive atmosphere. See p. 255.

- **Best Movie Screenings on a Roof:** On summer nights, God dims the overheads, and indie films play on rooftops (and in parks and schoolyards) across Brooklyn, Manhattan, and Queens. **Rooftop Films** (✆ **718/417-7362**) has fast become a local institution, with original, well-programmed fare. See p. 251.

- **Best Movie Date Night:** Friday nights the **Rubin Museum of Art** (150 W. 17th St.; ✆ **212/620-5000**) throws open its doors. You can tour Himalayan art for free, and for $7 you can treat yourself to a martini and a movie. The **Cabaret Cinema** series brings a selection of films, along with the occasional related celebrity, for just the price of a tipple or a snack at the bar. See p. 109.

- **Best Outdoor Summer Theater:** **Shakespeare in the Park** (✆ **212/539-8750**) hooks up thousands of New Yorkers with two great shows each summer (with top actors and directors). The Delacorte Theater in Central Park seems enchanted. See p. 260.

- **Best Outdoor Summer Theater That Isn't Shakespeare in the Park:** Energetic performances substitute for big names and big budgets in downtown's **Shakespeare in the Park(ing) Lot** (✆ **212/873-9050**). The setting couldn't be less formal, but somehow the troupe manages to cast its spell. See p. 261.

- **Best Free Dance:** Modern and experimental dance has a home during **Movement Research** at the Judson Church (55 Washington Sq. S.; ✆ **212/598-0551**). Dancers and choreographers vary, but the talent level stays high. The series seems to be getting better, especially now that the Judson Church has installed a new dance floor. See p. 271.

- **Best Comedy Troupe:** The founders of the **Upright Citizens Brigade** (307 W. 26th St.; ✆ **212/366-9176**) have gone on to movie and TV fame, but the institution's classes continue to crank out rapier wits. Improv nights here are cheap when they're not free, and the legendary *ASSSSCAT 3000* is not to be missed. See p. 275.

- **Best Readings in a Bookstore:** Recent years have not been kind to neighborhood booksellers, but Brooklyn's **Greenlight Bookstore** (686 Fulton St.; ✆ **718/246-0200**) is thriving. Their reading calendar is packed, with the likes of Jhumpa Lahiri, Matthew Modine, and Jeffrey Eugenides reading from their work. See p. 278.

- **Best Readings Outside of a Bookstore:** The great writerly look of **KGB Bar** (85 E. 4th St.; ✆ **212/505-3360**) is well matched by the great writers almost every night of the week. Enough quality words have been spilled beneath the Soviet-kitsch furnishings to publish KGB anthologies and a literary journal. See p. 281.

- **Best Bivalve and Brew Combo:** The charming West Village is not exactly cheap date territory. One exception is **Fish** (280 Bleecker St.; ✆ **212/727-2879**) where you can belly up to the bar for a half-dozen clams or oysters along with a PBR or glass of house wine. It's available at all times, and it's only $8. See p. 290.

- **Best Mix of Beautification and Intoxication:** Kitsch classic **Beauty Bar** (231 E. 14th St.; ✆ **212/539-1389**) has kicked off many a bachelorette party with their Martinis & Manicures happy hour. Just $10 (plus tip) covers both cocktails and cuticles. See p. 293.

2 Best Cheap Eats

- **Best Investment of $1 (Bagel):** New York exported the bagel to the four corners of America, but still has the best, and a buck will let you sample one at **Absolute Bagel** (2788 Broadway; ✆ **212/932-2052**). You can't make a better carb investment. See p. 74.

- **Best Investment of $1.95 (Hot Dog):** For cheap protein and quick bursts of patriotic fervor, New York's dogs can't be beat. **Gray's Papaya** (2090 Broadway; ✆ **212/799-0243;** other locations) is the best of the fruit-drink-and-wiener outlets, with flavorful grilled dogs that'll set you back less than $2. See p. 66.

- **Best Investment of $2.25 (Sesame Pancake):** The dumplings at **Vanessa's Dumpling House** (118a Eldridge St.; ✆ **212/625-8008**) are famous and a steal at four for $1. Less hyped but equally delicious are the sandwiches, which go gourmet by packing a big wedge of sesame pancake with fresh cilantro, carrot, and roast pork or beef. Upgrade to Peking duck for just 25¢ more. See p. 53.

- **Best Investment of $2.50 (Pizza Bread):** The pizza *bianca* at the **Sullivan St. Bakery** (533 W. 47th St.; ✆ **212/265-5580**) is closer to a piece of bread than a *Noo Yawk* slice, but it's long on old-world charm. Subtly flavored with rosemary and olive oil (no tomato or cheese), the dough manages to be simultaneously fluffy and chewy. See p. 73.

- **Best Investment of $3 (Tacos):** Served in a double layer of supple corn tortillas and topped with fresh tomatillo sauce, the tacos at **Zaragoza** (215 Ave. A; ✆ **212/780-9204**) burst with flavor. At just $3 for standouts like beef tongue and roast pork, they're the cheapest way to get south of the border without leaving NYC. See p. 58.

- **Best Investment of $4 (Buffet):** The competition between two Chinatown buffet restaurants has driven prices into the ground. An almost comical price of $4 covers four fresh, tasty Chinese entrees over rice at my favorite, **Yi Mei Gourmet Food** (51 Division St.; ✆ **212/925-1921**). See p. 53.

- **Best Investment of $4.50 (Sandwich):** For me, the *bánh mì* sandwich (pork pâté, pickled carrots, daikon, onion, and cilantro on a baguette) is more than just an ingenious blending of European and Asian flavors—it's one of the apexes of human civilization. You'll find my favorite at **Saigon Vietnamese Sandwich Deli** (369 Broome St.; ✆ **212/219-8341**). See p. 56.

- **Best Inexpensive Sit-Down Meal with Atmosphere:** Affordable Asian too often means overlit, dingy cafeteria settings. Not so at the Uptown oases of **Land Thai Kitchen,** with outposts in the west (450 Amsterdam Ave.; ✆ **212/501-8121**), and east (1565 Second Ave.; ✆ **212/439-1847**). Stylish, modern interiors make for great date atmospheres—enough that the spicy, fresh Thai food seems almost a lagniappe. See p. 75.

● **Best Burgers:** Although it doesn't have the long history of some of the competition, East Village bar **Royale** (331 W. 4th St.; ✆ **212/242-9502**) serves a classic burger. Big patties full of Black Angus flavor rest on brioche buns ($7), cooked to order and served fresh. The city's $18 rivals at the fancy-shmancy places don't even come close. See p. 58.

● **Best New York Slice:** First-time visitors to **Sal's & Carmine's Pizza** (2671 Broadway; ✆ **212/663-7651**), spurred to spontaneous compliments by the spectacular pies, can expect to hear back, "Well, where the hell you been this whole time?" One taste of the crispy crust and character-full sauce and you'll be asking yourself the same question. See p. 75.

3 Best Living Bets

● **Best Free School:** With college tuitions spiking endlessly upward, **Cooper Union** (Cooper Sq.; ✆ **212/353-4120**) is an anomaly: The 1,000 students get their education for exactly $0. The rest of us are invited in for exhibitions, readings, and lectures. See p. 145.

● **Best Free Smarts:** The **Graduate Center at the City University of New York (CUNY)** (365 Fifth Ave.; ✆ **212/817-8215**) keeps adults educated with a terrific selection of lectures, seminars, and panel discussions. Fees are reasonable, and big chunks of the program are on the house. See p. 146.

● **Best Gyms:** Stay thin without a fat wallet. For less than 28¢ a day, 49 rec centers can belong to you. The facilities of the **Department of Parks and Recreation** (✆ **311**) include tracks, weight rooms, dance studios, and boxing rings. For $150 a year ($50 more), you get access to the swimming pools, too. See p. 168.

● **Best Grooming:** Style-conscious New Yorkers flock to Bumble and bumble salon for the latest looks. Savvier souls sign up for the model calls at their school, **Bumble and bumble.University** (415 W. 13th St.; ✆ **866/7-BUMBLE** [728-6253]). If you're selected for the stylist training program, you'll get a free cut, a head full of product, and an invitation to call back in a few months to do it again. See p. 163.

- **Best Boat Ride:** Transform yourself into river traffic through the programs at the **Downtown Boathouse** (Pier 40, Pier 96, and at 72nd St.; www.downtownboathouse.org). They'll loan you a kayak and let you paddle around their West Wide piers. If you get your strength up, you'll be eligible for a longer ride into New York Harbor. See p. 145.

4 Best Shopping Bets

- **Best Thrift Shopping: Housing Works Thrift Shop** (143 W. 17th St.; ✆ **212/366-0820;** plus other locations) brings fashionable clothes and furniture down to prices real people can afford. The inventory is lightly used and quick to turn over, and the profits support a great cause (housing, services, and advocacy for people living with HIV and AIDS). See p. 190.

- **Best Museum Masquerading as a Thrift Store:** The prop shop operated by **Film Biz Recycling** (540 President St.; ✆ **347/384-2336**) contains a fascinating assemblage of obsolete phone, television, and office technology. Affordable prices make life easier for both set designers and folks looking to furnish apartments. See p. 205.

- **Best Department Store: Century 21** (22 Cortlandt St.; ✆ **212/227-9092**) is the Shakespeare in the Park of shopping—everybody knows about it, it's in great demand, and despite New Yorkers' high expectations it rarely comes up short. Amazing selection and equally amazing prices draw in the crowds 7 days a week. See p. 201.

- **Best Gourmet Food Shop for Tightwads:** Tracking down fancy fromage is not a difficult task in NYC, but to actually purchase a wedge without emptying your purse is another issue. Thank the cheese gods then for the **East Village Cheese Store** (40 Third Ave.; ✆ **212/477-2601**), which has a gigantic selection at humble prices. This is the ideal place for cocktail party hosts and hostesses to fortify themselves. See p. 208.

FREE New York's Top Five Best-Kept Free Secrets

1. Although most New Yorkers don't know it, Winnie-the-Pooh is a fellow citizen of the Big Apple. The original Pooh and his pals Piglet, Eeyore, Kanga, and Tigger have lived in Manhattan since 1947. Their latest home is nestled beneath a map of the Hundred Acre Wood at the **Stephen A. Schwarzman Building** (© 917/275-6975), the main branch of the New York Public Library. See p. 116.

2. Three gallery spaces at the **National Museum of the American Indian** (1 Bowling Green; © 212/514-3700) host well-curated exhibits of contemporary and historic Native American art. The building itself, a magnificent Beaux Arts custom house, is worthy of a visit of its own. See p. 96.

3. The **New York Earth Room** (141 Wooster St.; © 212/989-5566) is just that: 140 tons of soil hidden away in a SoHo loft. Even after multiple visits it's a completely unexpected sight, and a few whiffs of the earthy scent can be oddly rejuvenating. See p. 118.

4. For more than a hint of the natural world, light out for **Green-Wood Cemetery** (© 718/768-7300) in Brooklyn. Almost 500 acres of ancient trees and glacial ponds are interspersed with the graves of New York celebrities and Revolutionary War history. A colony of wild parrots adds a surreal final touch. See p. 130.

5. The former military base that is **Governors Island** (© 212/825-3045) opens up to the public in summer months, with picturesque free ferry rides through New York Harbor leading to the city's best picnic grounds. Programming has been quickly metastasizing—music, art, and a former Confederate prison have been added to the existing roster of historical tours. See p. 111.

5 Best Exploring Bets

● **Best Exhibits:** The main branch of the **Stephen A. Schwarzman Building** (Fifth Ave. and 42nd St.; © 917/275-6975), formerly the Humanities and Social Sciences Library, puts on terrific shows in the hushed interiors behind the lions. Rare editions and manuscripts are often on display, accompanied by thoughtful captions that make equally illuminating reading. This is also the home of the original Winnie-the-Pooh. See p. 116.

- **Best Tour:** The mayor and City Council have their offices in graceful **City Hall** (Broadway, at Murray St.; ✆ **212/788-2656**). An underpublicized free tour allows you to catch glimpses of NYC politicos, as well as the portraiture, architecture, and George Washington's desk. See p. 126.

- **Best New Museum Giveaway:** The Brooklyn Navy Yard welcomes the public with the recently constructed **BLDG 92** (63 Flushing Ave.; ✆ **718/907-5992**). An 1858 Marine Commandant's residence is integrated into a high-tech modern building, providing plenty of room to review the site's long shipbuilding history. See p. 89.

- **Best Art Museum: MoMA PS1** (22–25 Jackson Ave.; ✆ **718/784-2084**) puts on great art shows a stop away from Manhattan in Long Island City. The museum is housed in a conversion of a Renaissance Revival public school, and interior spaces have been redone to complement the cutting-edge art displayed here. Entrance is by suggested donation. See p. 113.

- **Best Dirt Cheap Date Night: First Saturdays** at the **Brooklyn Museum of Art** (200 Eastern Pkwy.; ✆ **718/638-5000**) are among the best parties of the year. You can generate conversation fodder at exhibits, films, and lectures. You'll also find live music, should all that talk lead to a little dancing. See p. 101.

- **Best Natural Oasis:** Visions of rhododendron valleys, waterfalls, and wetlands conjure up only one place in New York: the Bronx. If you've never seen the **New York Botanical Garden** (200th St. and Southern Blvd.; ✆ **718/817-8700**), you'll be amazed at the biological diversity. It might be the country's greatest public garden. See p. 131.

- **Best Place for Reflection:** The footprints of the World Trade Center towers are now filled with the largest man-made waterfalls in North America. A leafy plaza at the **9/11 Memorial** (Albany and Greenwich sts.; ✆ **212/266-5211**) provides the space and quiet to take in the scope of Ground Zero. See p. 96.

6 Best Sleeping Bets

- **Best Under-$35 Night in Manhattan:** The sleek lobby of the **Broadway Hotel & Hostel** (230 W. 101st St.; ✆ **212/865-7710**) belies the backpacker-friendly pricing. Unlike other local hostels, this one limits its dorm rooms to just two guests. Share a bunk room with a buddy and you'll be splitting an overnight bill of just $68. See p. 40.

- **Best Stay with Free Parking and Swimming Pool:** Enjoy interstate amenities right in the heart of the city at the **Travel Inn** (515 W. 42nd St.; ✆ **888/HOTEL58** [468-3558]). The sun deck, outdoor pool, and parking spaces all come for free. Doubles start at $125, which isn't all that much more than it would cost just to park. See p. 39.

- **Best Taste of West Village Brownstone Life:** The **Larchmont Hotel** (27 W. 11th St.; ✆ **212/989-9333**) has as prime a location as you could wish for at any price. The accommodations come with shared bathrooms, which knocks the rates down to affordable territory (a single can be as low as $90). See p. 31.

- **Best Taste of East Village Townhouse Life:** Avenue C may be party central these days, but the quirky themed rooms at **East Village Bed & Coffee** (110 Ave. C; ✆ **212/533-4175**) reflect the neighborhood's old-time arty charm. Soundproof windows in front ensure you get no more of nightlife than you want. Singles start at $120 and doubles aren't much more. See p. 26.

- **Best Taste of Single Room Occupancy Life:** Although a SRO cabin lacking in a ceiling is not for everybody, the **Bowery House** (220 Bowery; ✆ **212/837-2373**) offers a loving glimpse of a lost era. If you can handle earplugs and a shared bathroom, you'll score a great deal in the dead center of downtown. See p. 30.

- **Best Taste of Cotton Club–Era Harlem Life:** Don't be scared by the name; the **Harlem Flophouse** (242 W. 123rd St.; ✆ **212/662-0678**) isn't about mattresses on the floor, it's an homage to the musicians and artists who stayed here during the last Harlem Renaissance. Tasteful antiques add to the atmosphere of a restored 1890s row house, which hosts doubles for around $125 a night. See p. 41.

FREE & DIRT CHEAP CALENDAR OF EVENTS

New York knows how to throw a party. Throughout the year, you can find massive celebrations of ancient tribal affiliations, sexual orientations, and pagan holidays. Most of these celebrations come free.

In addition to the numbers listed below, NYC Visit, the city's convention and visitor's bureau, has the lowdown on most events (℅ 212/484-1222; www.nycvisit.com).

JANUARY

Midnight Run in Central Park `FREE`   For a saner New Year's night than the Times Square hell, one option is to hook up with the New York Road Runners Club. Their annual 4-mile Midnight Run takes costumed racers from 72nd Street to 102nd, and back around. The registration fee starts at $35 for Early Bird members, but if you don't feel the need to get winded in the small hours, you can enjoy the pre-run dancing, costume show, and fireworks for free. Dancing begins around 10pm and the parade starts an hour later. Gather near the Central Park Bandshell, south of the 72nd Street Transverse. ℅ **212/860-4455.** www.nyrr.org. Subway: B/C to 72nd St.; 6 to 68th St. Midnight December 31 (Jan 1).

Brooklyn New Year's Prospect Park `FREE`   There's no borough envy in Brooklyn as rival pyrotechnics welcome the new year above Prospect Park. Enjoy the fresh air as the embers cascade above the Grand Army Plaza at the stroke of midnight. Prime viewing areas include West Drive and along Prospect Park West, between Grand Army Plaza and 9th Street. As in Manhattan, there's a fun run, this one sponsored by NYCRUNS (www.nycruns.com) and carrying a registration fee of about $25. ℅ **718/965-8999.** www.prospectpark.org. Subway: 2/3 to Grand Army Plaza; B/Q to Seventh Ave. December 31 (Jan 1).

FEBRUARY

Chinese New Year `FREE`   Come February, Chinatown will be partying like it's 4711, in honor of the lunar new year. The annual parade sees a firecracker celebration and dragon and lion dancers winding through Mott, East Broadway, and the Bowery. ℅ **917/660-2402.** www.betterchinatown.com. Subway: J/N/Q/R/Z/6 to Canal St. Late January or early February.

MARCH

Saint Patrick's Day Parade `FREE` The green wave gathers momentum through Midtown and converges on Fifth Avenue, where 150,000 marchers (and at least that many spectators) celebrate Ireland's patron saint. Much of the crowd arrives well before the 11am start time. The entertainment continues with live music and drunken shenanigans at New York's thousand-plus Irish pubs. Wear green or risk pinchery. The parade runs from 44th up to 86th Street, right past Patrick's own cathedral. ✆ **718/231-4400.** http://nycstpatricksparade.org. Subway: E/M to Fifth Ave./53rd St. March 17 (Sat, Mar 16, in 2013).

APRIL

Easter Parade `FREE` People join and leave this Easter Sunday tradition as they please. Expect amazing hats and plenty of pastels. The stroll runs from 10am until 3 or 4pm, along Fifth Avenue between 49th and 57th streets. ✆ **212/484-1222.** Subway: E/M to Fifth Ave./53rd St.; B/D/F/M to 47th–50th sts./Rockefeller Center. Easter Sunday.

NFL Draft `FREE` The National Football League inaugurates its latest crop of millionaires at this 3-day fest. I enjoy the sight of fans converging on Radio City Music Hall, wearing the rainbow array of 32 different uniforms. Bracelets are distributed the night before, with the line opening at 10pm for midnight pick up (day 2 is less contested, and by the later rounds of day 3 you can skip the bracelet and head right for the "Carriage Door Entrance"). 1260 Sixth Ave., at 50th St. ✆ **212/247-4777.** www.radiocity.com. Subway: B/D/F/M to 47th–50th sts.–Rockefeller Center. Thursday to Saturday, late April.

MAY

Ninth Avenue International Food Festival `FREE` If some human in an obscure corner of the globe can call it lunch, odds are you can find it at this festival. Come mid-May, street-fair staples like Italian sausages and mozzarepa (cheese stuffed corn cakes) mingle with barbecued pigs, empanadas, and soy cupcakes from Ninth Avenue's indigenous roster. Don't miss hot-from-the-oven Greek pastries from Poseidon Bakery, between 44th and 45th streets. It runs on Ninth Avenue, from 42nd to 57th streets. ✆ **212/581-7029.**

www.ninthavenuefoodfestival.com. Subway: A/C/E/7 to 42nd St./ Port Authority. From noon to 5pm, Saturday and Sunday in mid-May.

New York Dance Parade `FREE`   From the cross-pollination of African and Irish tap dances in the Five Points slum to an impressive 20th-century run of ballet, ballrooms, and breakdancing, New York's dance legacy runs deep. In mid-May all of it goes on parade at once, a 6-hour affair with 10,000 dancers, many sporting elaborate getups. The parade boogies from 21st Street and Broadway down to St. Marks Place, where a wrap-up DanceFest goes off in Tompkins Square Park. Free lessons are thrown in as well. ✆ **267/350-9213.** www.danceparade.org. Saturday, mid-May, rain or shine.

Fleet Week `FREE`   One week a year, New Yorkers get nostalgic over the sight of thousands of sailors on the make in the port of Manhattan. Squint and pretend it's V-J Day. Along the West Side piers you can get an even closer look: Navy, Coast Guard, and Marine reps will let you tour some of the floating behemoths you spent all those tax dollars on. Demonstrations, tug of war competitions, and a ship parade are also on offer. ✆ **212/245-0072.** www. intrepidmuseum.org. Last week in May.

JUNE

Howl! Festival `FREE`   Though the East Village's legendary artistic past is increasingly obscured by layers of gentrifying paint, the first weekend in June sees a return of the old contrarian spirit. A group reading of Allen Ginsberg's "Howl" kicks things off, followed by drag shows and rock music and theater, all of it free. It's in Tompkins Square Park, Ave. A, between 7th and 10th streets. ✆ **212/466-6666.** www.howlfestival.com. Subway: L to First Ave.; 6 to Astor Place; N/R to 8th St. Early June.

Museum Mile Festival `FREE`   The classiest fair in New York sees Fifth Avenue closed to car traffic so 50,000 culture vultures can take in Manhattan's Gold Coast to the sounds of string quartets. Kids get live performances and special arts and crafts opportunities. Ten of the museums that give the mile its moniker offer free admissions. It's on Fifth Avenue, from 82nd to 110th streets. ✆ **212/606-2296.** www.museummilefestival.org. Subway: 4/5/6 to 86th St.; 6

to 77th, 96th, 103rd, or 110th St. From 6pm to 9pm, usually the second Tuesday in June.

LGBT Pride Week and March `FREE` The city bursts with Pride every June in a week that begins with rallies and protests and ends in a dance, fireworks, and a parade. Pride commemorates the June 27, 1969, Stonewall Rebellion, where gays and lesbians first stood against police harassment outside the Stonewall Inn in the West Village. Just standing on a street corner downtown can be almost as entertaining as the parade, especially the spectacle of drag queens teetering on high heels as they rush across multiple lanes of traffic. ✆ **212/807-7433.** www.nycpride.org. Mid- to late June.

Puerto Rico Day Parade `FREE` Fifth Avenue's staid character goes into remission for the Puerto Rico Day parade. There's salsa music and festive floats and millions of spectators lining the way. The parade has been running annually since 1958, and despite some ugly incidents, it remains a quality spectacle. It's on Fifth Avenue, from 44th to 79th streets. ✆ **718/401-0404.** www.nationalpuerto ricandayparade.org. From 11am to 5pm, the second Sunday in June.

Make Music New York! `FREE` The longest day of the year begets this citywide musical celebration. Inspired by the French *Fête de la Musique,* thousands of musicians take to the sidewalks of New York (as well as the parks, gardens, and clubs) to play for the sake of playing. Although only a few years old, this summer solstice event is quickly gathering momentum—enough to support a second fest on the winter solstice (Dec 21). Mohawk-sporters will not want to miss the offshoot Punk Island, a 50-band gig held on Governors Island. ✆ **917/779-9709.** www.makemusicny.org. June 21.

Mermaid Parade `FREE` This mobile freak show recalls the glory days of Coney Island. See p. 303 for more details. ✆ **718/372-5159.** www.coneyisland.com/mermaid.shtml. Subway: D/F/N/Q to Coney Island/Stillwell Ave.; then walk toward the Atlantic. Saturday, near the summer solstice, 2 to 6pm.

July

Fourth of July Fireworks `FREE` In New York's previous incarnation, you knew July 4th was coming because starting mid-June your sleep was interrupted by nightly amateur firework shows. With quality-of-life crackdowns, however, the Man has taken up a monopoly on the summer eye-candy. Fortunately, the Man does a nice job of blowing up stuff for our entertainment. Macy's explodes 120,000 shells into the air from barges that have lately been docked on the Hudson, much to coastal New Jersey's delight. The West Side Highway closes for the sake of spectators, but get there early—closures start 5 hours before showtime, with access blocks closed off as the highway fills. ✆ **212/494-2922.** www.macys.com. July 4.

August

Harlem Week `FREE`   Harlem Day was first celebrated in 1975, and over the subsequent 3 decades it has grown from a day to a week to over a month of cultural celebration. Auto shows, film festivals, Uptown Saturday Nite, and Harlem Day are among the 150-plus events. ✆ **212/862-8477.** www.harlemweek.com. Subway: B/C to 135th St.; 1 to 137th St. Late July to late August.

The Hong Kong Dragon Boat Festival in New York `FREE`   Dragon boats date back thousands of years, to races conducted during celebrations of the fifth lunar month of the Chinese calendar. The boats' appearance on Meadow Lake in Queens is a little more recent (1990), with a racing roster growing from four original teak specimens to dozens of sleek fiberglass models. Bands, craft demonstrations, theatrical and dance performances, and dumpling-eating contests augment the races. It all takes place in Flushing Meadows Park, Flushing, Queens. ✆ **718/767-1776.** www.hkdbf-ny.org. Subway: 7 to Mets/Willets Point; transfer to the special event bus. Saturday and Sunday, 9am to 5pm, usually in early August.

September

West Indian–American Day Parade `FREE`   New York's biggest parade takes place a long way from Fifth Avenue, along Eastern Parkway in Brooklyn. Two million revelers (yup, *2,000,000*) come together on Labor Day to move to Caribbean rhythms and dine on jerk chicken, oxtail, and *roti*. The route varies, but generally follows Eastern Parkway from Utica Avenue in Crown Heights down to the arch at Grand Army Plaza, and then Flatbush Avenue as far as

Empire Boulevard. ℭ **718/467-1797.** www.wiadca.com. Subway: 2/3 to Grand Army Plaza. From 11am to 6pm, Labor Day.

September Concert `FREE`   Under other circumstances, a day bringing hundreds of performers to dozens of venues in all five boroughs would be exciting, but the context of the September Concert is a somber one. To commemorate the World Trade Center attacks, the city fills with the healing sounds of music. Throughout September 11 (and a day or two on either side of it), find free sounds in cafes, bars, libraries, squares, and parks. There are multiple venues; check the website. ℭ **212/333-3399.** www.september concert.org. Around September 11.

The Feast of San Gennaro `FREE`   This is New York's oldest and biggest street fair—11 days of zeppole, pork *braciola,* and deep-fried Oreos in honor of the patron saint of Naples. Mulberry Street becomes an extremely narrow small-town carnival. There are rides for the kids, cannoli-eating contests for the adults, and an abusive clown in a dunking booth that's discomfiting for everybody. With the heavy emphasis on commerce and the beer-addled crowds, the fair gets old fairly quickly, although you can catch a passel of free concerts. It's on Mulberry Street, between Canal and Houston, with runoff on Hester and Grand. ℭ **212/768-9320.** www.sangennaro. org. Subway: N/R to Prince St.; 6 to Spring St. or Canal St. Starts the second Thursday in September, from 11:30am to 11:30pm (to midnight Fri–Sat).

OCTOBER

New York's Great Halloween Party `FREE`   The hobgoblins of little minds can be found in haunted sites across 40 of the city's back acres come Halloween. Central Park fills with excitable costumed children, looking for the perfect pumpkin among the 7,500 scattered among the straw at the Bethesda Fountain. Once the little demons have made their incisions they take the resulting jack-o'-lanterns north, to the Charles A. Dana Discovery Center, midpark at 110th Street. A parade is followed by an annual pumpkin sail, where the jack-o'-lanterns glow on the Harlem Meer as they float gently away. ℭ **212/860-1370.** www.centralparknyc.org. Subway: 6 to 68th or 77th St.; 1/2/3 or B/C to 72nd St. Saturday, a few days before Halloween (date varies).

Greenwich Village Halloween Parade `FREE` For many New Yorkers, every day feels like Halloween. Come late October, the last thing we need to wade through is another crowd of freaks. Fight this instinct, however, and you will enjoy New Yorkers' legendary gallows humor at the annual Halloween parade. This parade is one of New York's most participatory events (anyone costumed can join); no one will think any less of you for not being covered in body paint or latex, but you run the risk of feeling like you're in a wet-blanket minority. The parade runs up Sixth Avenue from Spring to 16th Street, from 7pm to 11pm. www.halloween-nyc.com. Subway: C/E to Spring St.; A/B/C/D/E/F/M to W. 4th St./Washington Sq.; F to 14th St.; L to Sixth Ave. October 31, with the coming of night.

`FREE` **A Brooklyn Christmas**

The big department stores offer the sidewalks plenty of entertainment with elaborate window displays, but for my money, New York's best free Christmas show is in Brooklyn. Homeowners from Bay Ridge to Bensonhurst run up the electric bills to bring bulb envy to their neighbors. Dyker Heights is "Christmas Central," with 100,000 tourists drawn every year to the blocks around 80th and 86th streets, between Tenth and Thirteenth avenues. Unbelievably elaborate choruses of mechanical Santas and snowmen compete to prove the lights are always brighter on the other side of the fence. Take the D to 79th Street or the R to 86th Street. Between Thanksgiving and New Year's.

NOVEMBER

The New York Marathon The race ends in Central Park near Tavern on the Green, where you can watch the survivors, adorned in the glory of heat-retaining silver blankets, as they walk it off. The race begins in the morning, with the elite runners getting off around 11am. © **212/423-2249.** www.ingnycmarathon.org. Subway (to Central Park): B/C to 72nd St. First Sunday in November.

Macy's Thanksgiving Day Parade `FREE` New York's favorite excuse for dragging bloated cartoon characters down the West Side comes with the Macy's Thanksgiving Day Parade Rocky, Bullwinkle, and Garfield join slightly less-inflated celebrities to march down Central Park West and Sixth Avenue from 77th Street to the Mothership (Macy's in Herald Sq.). *Tip:* Balloon fanatics can get a head start on the action the night before, when the balloons get their helium fixes on the broad sidewalks around the Natural History Museum from 3 to 10pm (it takes until about 5pm for the balloons to really start taking shape). ✆ **212/494-4495.** www.macys.com/parade. Subway: B/C to 72nd St., A/B/C/D/1 to Columbus Circle. From 9am to noon, Thanksgiving morning.

December

Lighting of the Christmas Tree at Rockefeller Center `FREE`   Professional ice-skaters make graceful turns, live music plays, and Hizzonner throws the switch on 30,000 bulbs strung along 5 miles of wire. Rock Center's overflow crowd, many of whom have been waiting for 4 or 5 hours, cheer with relief. Even for grinches like me, watching the tree come alive is a pretty cool moment, but they'd have to make the spruce levitate while spouting a fountain of $50 bills for me to want to weather that crowd twice. Better to come back at a more mellow time, especially if you can visit at dusk, when the tree is at its most quietly dramatic. ✆ **212/332-6868.** www.rockefellercenter.com. B/D/F/M to 47th–50th sts.–Rockefeller Center. From 7 to 9pm, the Wednesday after Thanksgiving.

Alternatives to the Rockefeller Center Tree Lighting `FREE`   It's not like Rock Center has the only Christmas tree in New York City. The **Winter Garden** at the World Financial Center sets 100,000 lights softly glowing. More elaborate rites can be found at **Lincoln Center**'s Christmas celebration, usually held on the Monday after Thanksgiving. A tree lighting supplements crafts booths and live music along Broadway from 61st to 68th streets. The crowds are a fraction of Rock Center's. World Financial Center. ✆ **212/945-0505.** www.worldfinancialcenter.com. Subway: 1/2/3 or A/C to Chambers St.; E to World Trade Center. Lincoln Center BID: ✆ **212/581-3774.** www.winterseve.org. Subway: 1 to 66th St./Lincoln Center.

Festival of Lights `FREE`   This skyscraping candle-holder (at 32 ft., it's the world's largest menorah) shines at sunset on the first night of Hanukkah, gaining another light on each of the following 7 days. It's in Grand Army Plaza on Fifth Avenue, at 59th Street. ✆ **917/287-7770.** Subway: N/Q/R to Fifth Ave.; F to 57th St. During Hanukkah.

New Year's Concert for Peace at the Cathedral of St. John the Divine FREE Leonard Bernstein inaugurated this event, and in the subsequent decades, it's become a candlelit legend. Pop stars like Judy Collins join opera greats and world-class conductors in headlining the bills. The best seats are reserved and come with steep price tags, but general seating is free. It's in the Cathedral of St. John the Divine. 1047 Amsterdam Ave., at 112th Street. ℂ **212/316-7490.** www.stjohndivine.org. Subway: 1/B/C to Cathedral Parkway/110th St. December 31, 7pm.

The striking Gershwin Hotel offers both individual rooms and (cheaper) dorm-style accommodations.

CHEAP SLEEPS

New York is the city that never sleeps. At these prices, who can afford to? The city plays host to some 48 million guests a year, and we'd be overcrowded even without them. Interested in a night at the Mandarin Oriental? An executive suite is a mere $2,950 a month. Err, *night*. Even the Holiday Inn Express by the Gowanus Canal in Brooklyn doesn't get much below $200 a night (and that's a good $50 off the overall city average). That said, there are plenty of ways to sleep for cheap in NYC. In the pages below, we'll show you nights at a boutique-style hostel for $35, doubles at some of the city's trendiest spots for less than $75 a person, and enough sub-$100 singles to get you through a major blowout with your spouse.

Shared bathrooms are one way to lower the price. Sacrificing views, elevators, and frills are others. Giving up on space is already a given; but you didn't come to New York City to hang out in your room, did you? Just because you're saving sawbucks doesn't mean you can't be in the thick of things—some of the city's best bargains come in prime locations. Time of year is the No. 1 factor in determining the price of your lodging. If you arrive in January or February, you'll find tons of options and be all but able to name your price. Sure, you'll be running into some weather, but you'll see an authentic New York, with folks getting back to their business after the December holidays. Those December holidays are about the worst time to visit, cost-wise, with hotels doubling their prices, and gouging guests the closer it gets to New Year's Eve. Summers are easier, as is the November gap between autumn leaves and Thanksgiving crowds. If your timing is right, you'll fare better on bidding sites like Priceline, which will release rooms at half the price of advertised "rack rates" (the prices I use in the listings below). You might also consider alternatives to conventional hotel rooms, like temporarily swapping your digs for a local's, renting an apartment, or even staying in the spare bedroom of a real, live New Yorker.

Note that price categories ("Under $150," "Under $100," and "Under $50") are determined according to the cheapest available rate and are rough guidelines. All accommodations are subject to additional city and state taxes of 14.75%, plus a $3.50 occupancy fee per room per night.

I hate to mention it, but we're dealing with bedbugs in New York City. If you're anxious, visit **www.bedbugregistry.com/metro/nyc** before you book. For more discussion on your options (from cheap to *luxe*), check out *Frommer's New York City For Dummies* and *Frommer's New York City*.

1 Lower East Side/East Village/SoHo

UNDER $150

East Village Bed & Coffee Although the area's becoming more of a destination for partying, this friendly town house retains a lot of downtown's old-time arty charm. Quirky one-off accommodations

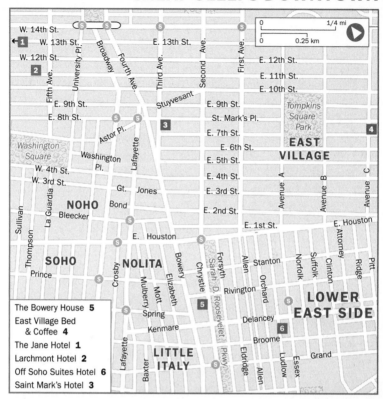

The Bowery House **5**
East Village Bed & Coffee **4**
The Jane Hotel **1**
Larchmont Hotel **2**
Off Soho Suites Hotel **6**
Saint Mark's Hotel **3**

range from the sunny French Room to the tiny van Gogh–accented Dutch Room. Singles start at $120 and they'll let you sleep four to a room for just $175. Bathrooms are shared and there's no elevator (the building is only three stories, so you won't have far to climb).

110 Ave. C, btw. 7th and 8th sts. ℭ **212/533-4175.** Fax 212/979-9743. www.bed andcoffee.com. 10 units, all with shared bathroom. $135–$155 double. AE, DC, MC, V. Subway: L to First Ave. **Amenities:** Common kitchens; Wi-Fi. In room: A/C.

Off Soho Suites Hotel If you're traveling with a posse, this converted tenement is a great option. Go for a suite, designed for two or four guests. The smaller iteration shares a bathroom and kitchen with the next suite; the larger has its own living room on top of a kitchen, bathroom, and master bedroom. The result is a set of spacious miniapartments, ideal for a group of friends (or a band gigging in one of the many nearby venues). Low season rates drop down as far as $299,

The Shadow Universe of Vacation Apartment Rentals

Given the scarcity of real estate in NYC, it makes sense that the city would develop a shadow universe of less-formal accommodations. My neighbors in Brooklyn rent out a spare room from time to time. It's just one way to close the gap between income and ungodly rents.

There are several ways to connect with nontraditional sleeping arrangements (I'd put you up at my place, but I can't risk my priceless collection of Hummel figurines). **Craigslist.org** is an obvious starting point. Watch out for poorly translated English and setups that sound too good to be true—because they *are*. Beyond short-term rentals, you can work out swaps where you trade time in your apartment for time in someone else's. A more formal version of this is **Home Exchange** (Ⓒ **310/798-3864;** www.homeexchange.com). As the name suggests, you're swapping houses (or maybe second houses), and the company claims that in 20 years they've never had vandalism, theft, or folks showing up to a vacant, wind-swept lot. Membership starts at $15.95 a month for 3 months, or $9.95 a month for a year; swaps are free.

If you want to stay in New York without putting up your own home, there are several services that help with rentals. Costs can be slightly higher than a Craigslist hookup, but it's nice to know your rental has been vetted and inspected. You may see places referred to as "bed-and-breakfasts," though they'll bear little relation to the hot-scones-and-Laura-Ashley-sheets variety. The use of the term reflects the 2010 New York State law that made unlicensed short-term rentals illegal. There's a very large exception for "hosted" accomodations (where the owner is in residence). Along with the new label, these "B&B" rooms now carry minimum stays, usually from 4 to 7 nights.

or around $75 per person if you have three fellow travelers. The staff is chill, and for exploring downtown neighborhoods you won't beat this off-Bowery location.

11 Rivington St., btw. Chrystie St. and the Bowery. Ⓒ **800/633-7646** or 212/979-9815. Fax 212/979-9801. www.offsoho.com. 38 units. $199 double with shared

NY Habitat (© 212/255-8018; www.nyhabitat.com) specializes in unhosted stays. They work with buildings that allow boarders, so you'll never have to stammer in a hallway and say that you're somebody's cousin. Much of their stock is corporate apartments, so digs can be bland, but there are a lot of large-size units (good for families or groups). A studio starts at $107 and a one-bedroom at $117, and prices go up from there. For both hosted and unhosted stays, **Affordable New York City** (© 212/533-4001; www.affordablenewyorkcity.com) has a large stock of Manhattan units. A shared bathroom setup runs $95 to $120, and a shared apartment with your own bathroom is $135 to $165. A studio apartment starts at $170. Another good list of rentals is carried by **City Sonnet** (© 212/614-3034; www.citysonnet.com). Manhattan hosted nights for one person run from $125 to $250, with a 5-night minimum. (Stays in Long Island City, Harlem, or Williamsburg tend to be less expensive.) Unhosted "artist's lofts" are available, but they're rented by the month.

One of the least expensive ways to hook up with a hosted stay is through **Airbnb** (© 855/424-7262; www.airbnb.com). This young company connects travelers with spare spaces. Users leave reviews, so you won't go into a stay blind—listings are rated across six categories, from accuracy to cleanliness to value. Checking over the site, you'll find longer-term sublets starting at $600 a month, and overnight stays beginning at around $50.

But then why pay for a hosted stay when you can have one for free? **CouchSurfing** (www.couchsurfing.org) is an organization dedicated to bringing the world closer, one couch (or spare bedroom) at a time. Membership costs nothing, and although availability in New York City is limited, there are plenty of connections to be made.

bathroom. AE, MC, V. Subway: J/Z to Bowery; F to Second Ave. **Amenities:** Fitness center. *In room:* A/C, TV, hair dryer, kitchenette, Wi-Fi.

Saint Mark's Hotel   This corner of the city is as youthful and bustling as New York gets. The young fare best here, not least because they won't be deterred by the walkup to the rooms. (They're also better primed to take advantage of the lively cheap eats right outside the door; see p. 60.) FINE PRINT No credit cards accepted, just cash or traveler's checks.

2 St. Marks Place, at Third Ave. ✆ **212/674-0100.** Fax 212/420-0854. www.stmarks hotel.net. 70 units. $102–$170 double. No credit cards. Subway: 6 to Astor Place; N/R to 8th St. **Amenities:** Restaurant; bar. *In room:* A/C, TV, Wi-Fi ($9.95).

UNDER $100

The Bowery House   The *louche* romance of the Bowery Bum is not for everybody, but if you'd like a glimpse of gritty New York history, these accommodations (ca. 1927), once called the Prince Hotel, have been lovingly restored. The cabins were used by returning World War II vets, which is reflected in the dog-tag door keys. I say "cabins," because these are something less than rooms—you'll get four walls and a lockable door, but nothing more than latticework for a ceiling. Combine the potential for noise with the small beds and it'll be easy to see why it's only $69 a night. Bathrooms are shared, stocked with Red Flower bath products and towels by Ralph Lauren.

220 Bowery, at Rivington St. ✆ **212/837-2373.** Fax 212/837-2370. www.thebowery house.com. 104 units. $129–$144 cabin for 2 with shared bathroom. AE, DC, MC, V. Subway: J/Z to Bowery; B/D to Grand St.; 6 to Spring St.; F to Second Ave. *In room:* A/C, Wi-Fi.

2 West Village

UNDER $150

The Jane Hotel   If you're looking for a mix of style and local color, the Jane's your place. This riverfront hotel was built in 1908 to house sailors, with tiny cabins reminiscent of seaboard quarters. A century later, the square footage isn't any bigger, but the closetlike interiors have been decked out with *luxe* wood, marble, and 300-count cotton sheets. Since bathrooms are shared for most rooms, prices are within the grasp of steerage passengers: $115 for singles, and $125 for bunk-bed cabins (add $10 for peak seasons; private bathroom accommodations start at $295). Previous to this incarnation, the Jane was a single room occupancy hotel, and the holdover tenants from that era add to the authenticity.

113 Jane St., at the West Side Hwy. ✆ **212/924-6700.** Fax 212/924-6705. www.the janenyc.com. 200 units. $125 cabin for 2. AE, DC, MC, V. Subway: A/C/E to 14th St.; L

to Eighth Ave. **Amenities:** Restaurant; bar; concierge. *In room:* A/C, TV, hair dryer, MP3 docking station, Wi-Fi.

Larchmont Hotel   Without laying out serious cash, it's pretty much impossible to get closer to brownstone Village life than this small, aging hotel. You will be sharing a bathroom, but you'll save a bundle: The small singles are $90 to $125, doubles run $119 to $145, and hefty queen-bed spaces are $149 to $165. (The higher end of the range comes on the weekends; prices include a continental breakfast.) If you book 4 nights in winter, they'll even throw in a fifth for free. It's hard to find a more central location than this, no matter how much money you're dropping.

27 W. 11th St., btw. Fifth and Sixth aves. ✆ **212/989-9333.** Fax 212/989-9496. www. larchmonthotel.com. 66 units. $119–$145 double. AE, MC, V. Subway: F/M to 14th St.; L to Sixth Ave. **Amenities:** Common kitchenette; Wi-Fi. *In room:* A/C, TV, hair dryer.

3 Chelsea/Flatiron/Union Square

UNDER $150

Chelsea Inn   Dual Queen Anne–style town houses from 1880 do the hosting at this central spot. Interiors are homey, with a feel more like an apartment than a hotel. There's no elevator, but staff will book you in a ground floor unit if stairs are an issue. Some units have shared bathrooms (it's a two-to-one ratio), but those rooms start at $89 a night for a single and $129 for a twin.

46 W. 17th St., btw. Fifth and Sixth aves. ✆ **800/640-6469** or 212/645-8989. Fax 212/ 645-1093. www.chelseainn.com. 26 units, 18 with private bathroom. $129–$199 double. Subway: F/M to 14th St.; L to Sixth Ave. *In room:* A/C, TV, fridge, hair dryer, Wi-Fi.

Chelsea Lodge   The town house blocks near the General Theological Seminary are as quaint as any in New York, and this unmarked brownstone will help you feel like a local traversing them. The building's original woodwork has been restored and the full-size beds are reasonably comfortable. Rooms have their own sinks and shower stalls, although toilets are shared out in the hallway. For that privation, you'll get a deep discount on a night in a prime location (a single is $134; double occupancy is only $10 more). FINE PRINT Tight quarters make this better for couples than shares.

318 W. 20th St., btw. Eighth and Ninth aves. ✆ **800/373-1116** or 212/243-4499. Fax 212/243-7852. www.chelsealodge.com. 22 units, all with semiprivate bathroom.

$144 double. AE, DC, DISC, MC, V. Subway: 1 to 18th St.; C/E to 23rd St. *In room:* A/C, TV, Wi-Fi.

Hotel 17   This Victorian-accented spot is a pocket of affordability between the East Village, Union Square, and Gramercy. Big with the Euro backpacking crew, there's a hostel-like energy, but the rooms are modern, and fresh off a recent renovation. Singles with shared baths go for as low as $79, and there are triples and quads (a low-season triple can be as cheap as $109). If the place looks familiar, perhaps you've seen it in Woody Allen's *Manhattan Murder Mystery*.

255 E. 17th St., btw. Second and Third aves. ℂ **212/475-2845.** Fax 212/677-8178. www.hotel17ny.com. 120 units. $89–$165 double with shared bathroom. MC, V. Subway: L to Third Ave. *In room:* A/C, TV, Wi-Fi.

UNDER $100

Chelsea International Hostel   You can't do much better location-wise than these typical hostel rooms clustered around a courtyard in the heart of Chelsea. International travelers love this well-managed place. It's $58 to $78 (depending on the season) per person for a two-bed dorm with a shared bathroom. A private double with its own bathroom starts at $165. Free Wi-Fi, continental breakfast, and linens are included, but bring your own towel.

251 W. 20th St., btw. Seventh and Eighth aves. ℂ **212/647-0010.** www.chelsea hostel.com. 288 dorm beds. $58–$78 per night. AE, DISC, MC, V. Subway: 1 to 18th St. **Amenities:** Shared kitchen; Wi-Fi.

Chelsea Star Hotel   The youthful focus of this small hostel is fitting given that Madonna lived here when she was 22. As it's on a busy corner, rooms can be noisy, but nothing out of line given the pricing. There's a lot of versatility here, with rooms ranging from coed dorm beds ($55–$60 a night, most with in-room bathrooms) to shared-bathroom singles ($129–$139) and doubles ($149–$159). If you're traveling with a posse, consider one of the apartment suites next door, which sleep four to six people ($209–$369).

300 W. 30th St., at Eighth Ave. ℂ **888/685-5319** or 646/402-6591. Fax 212/279-9018. www.starhotelny.com. 20 dorm beds. $55–$60 dorm, includes continental breakfast and tax. AE, DC, DISC, MC, V. Subway: A/C/E to 34th St./Penn Station. **Amenities:** Concierge. *In room:* A/C, Wi-Fi.

4 Midtown East

UNDER $150

Hotel 31   Like its southern cousin Hotel 17 (p. 32), there's not much that distinguishes this serviceable hotel besides low prices. Shared bathroom doubles start at $119, and private-bath accommodations begin at $155. You won't get those prices in the fall (U.N. folks take over pretty much the whole place then), but this is a great central location if you're in town at a down time.

120 E. 31st St., btw. Lexington Ave. and Park Ave. S. ✆ **212/685-3060.** Fax 212/532-1232. www.hotel31.com. 100 units. $119–$220 double with shared bathroom; $155–$220 double with private bathroom. AE, DC, MC, V. Subway: 6 to 33rd St. *In room:* A/C, TV, hair dryer, Wi-Fi.

The Pod Hotel   Big-time design meets small-time prices at this Midtown economy hotel. Supermodern rooms reflect a Scandinavian influence, with light wood and brushed metal. The latest electronics—LCD TVs, MP3 docking stations, and Wi-Fi—are all within easy reach, and you definitely won't feel overwhelmed by excesses of space. Bunk bed arrangements go for $79 in the low seasons, and a single with a shared bathroom starts at $75. FINE PRINT After January and February's doldrums pass, look for rates to more than double here. Spin-off location Pod 39 (145 E. 39th St.) offers similarly small rooms, but not much by way of bargains.

230 E. 51st St., btw. Second and Third aves. ✆ **800/742-5945** or 212/355-0300. Fax 212/755-5029. www.thepodhotel.com. 345 units, 152 with shared baths. $99–$299 double. AE, DC, MC, V. Subway: 6 to 51st St.; E/M to Lexington Ave./53rd St. **Amenities:** Bar; concierge. *In room:* A/C, TV, MP3 docking station, Wi-Fi.

Ramada Eastside   Ramada Inns originated in 1954 on Route 66, but like many folks, they've made an easy transition to Manhattan. The chain's East Side hotel is clean and functional, with cozy rooms distinguished by Tempur-Pedic DreamSpa mattresses. There's also free breakfast, Wi-Fi, and a tiny gym.

161 Lexington Ave., at 30th St. ✆ **800/567-7720** or 212/545-1800. Fax 212/679-9146. www.ramada.com. 101 units. $115–$300 double. AE, DC, MC, V. Subway: 6 to 28th St. **Amenities:** Breakfast room; fitness center. *In room:* A/C, TV, hair dryer, Wi-Fi.

Vanderbilt YMCA   The Y has sheltered many a newly minted New Yorker on the hunt for more permanent housing. For city visitors, low

CHEAP SLEEPS IN MIDTOWN

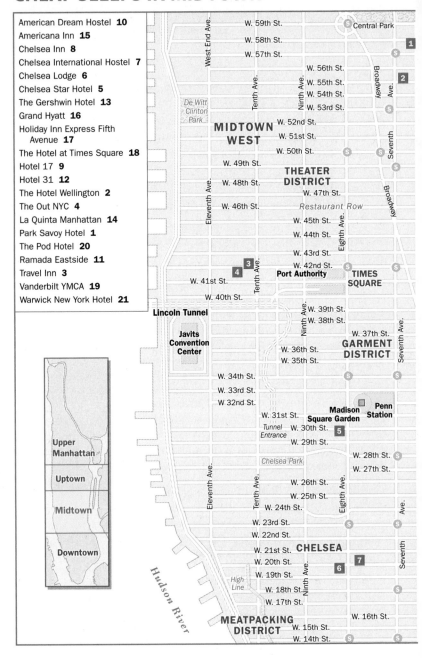

prices and free access to two swimming pools and a massive fitness center make this a tempting option. Digs are not exactly long on charm. Of the several city Ys, the Vanderbilt is the best managed, and $105 single room rates (shared bathrooms) are hard to beat in this central location.

224 E. 47th St., btw. Second and Third aves. ℭ **212/912-2500.** Fax 212/752-0210. www.ymcanyc.org. 370 units. $139 bunk bed double with shared bath; $160 private bath double. AE, MC, V. Subway: 4/5/6/7/S to 42nd St./Grand Central. **Amenities:** Gym; 2 pools. *In room:* A/C, TV, Wi-Fi.

UNDER $100

American Dream Hostel   The Barretto family lives out their American dream at this friendly Kips Bay hostel. The location is central, allowing easy walking access to the Flatiron District, East Village, and Midtown. Breakfast is included and it's much more than an afterthought (waffles are made fresh daily). A double with a shared bathroom is $120 on a weeknight and $150 for a weekend. Dorm arrangements are split into boys and girls, at $59 per night (add $10 on the weekends). FINE PRINT There's an age limit: over 30, and you're no longer eligible to sleep in the dorms.

168 E. 24th St., btw. Third and Lexington aves. ℭ **212/260-9779.** Fax 212/260-9944. www.americandreamhostel.com. 65 beds. $120–$150 bunk bed double with shared bath. AE, DISC, MC, V. Subway: 6 to 23rd St. **Amenities:** Kitchen. *In room:* A/C, TV, Wi-Fi.

The Gershwin Hotel   This hotel's design, arty flair, and central location would seem to put it out of budget reaches, but a semi-secret cache of dorm spaces makes it quite accessible. The six-person Fabuloso room starts at $44 a night per person (up to $64 at peak times), with a bathroom inside the room. Real rooms here start at about $180. FINE PRINT Linens are provided, but not lockers.

7 E. 27th St., btw. Madison and Fifth aves. ℭ **212/545-8000.** Fax 212/684-5546. www. gershwinhotel.com. 150 units, 60 dorm beds. $180–$339 double room. AE, MC, V. Subway: 6 or N/R to 28th St. **Amenities:** Bar; restaurant; babysitting. *In room:* A/C, TV, hair dryer, Wi-Fi.

5 Midtown West

UNDER $150

Americana Inn   The roadside motel-style name here signals the utilitarian accommodations. Despite a lack of frills, the place is clean and well-run, and pretty hard to beat for the price. Singles start at around

Doing Your Bidding

I'm a huge fan of **Priceline.com**. A quick perusal of their offerings pops up discounted rates on a bevy of New York bargain hotel mainstays (many of which I list here, albeit at slightly higher "rack rates"). But that's not the fun part. Outwitting the virtual auctioneer is where the action's at. Hotels, just like airlines, hate to see space go unsold. When underbooking beckons, they release swaths of rooms to price-slashers like Priceline (**Hotwire.com** is another good option for similar bargaining). You can easily pay 50%, or even 70%, off the regular published rate if you sync your bid up right. To get a little more insight into plausible ranges, check out **www.biddingfortravel.com**, which allows folks to trade notes on recent wins. There are usual suspects in the city, mostly hotels so large that they almost always end up releasing rooms to discounters. Places like the **Warwick New York Hotel** (65 W. 54th St.; ✆ **212/247-2700;** www.warwickhotelny.com), the **Hotel Wellington** (871 Seventh Ave.; ✆ **212/347-3900;** www.wellingtonhotel.com), **Holiday Inn Express Fifth Avenue** (15 W. 45th St.; ✆ **800/465-4329;** www.ichotelsgroup.com), and the **Grand Hyatt** (109 E. 42nd St.; ✆ **212/883-1234;** www.grandnewyork.hyatt.com) are frequent names on "congratulations, your bid was accepted" messages.

When you do get accepted, that's it; you're locked in and your credit card has been charged, so make sure you're ready to commit. On Priceline's site, New York is broken down into 11 areas, representing four boroughs. There are seven categories of hotel, from one-star economy to four-star deluxe. You can only make one bid every 24 hours per area, star level, and dates. "Matrix bidding" is a good workaround for that policy: It can get pretty complicated, but the basic plan is to make your first bid with only your main target neighborhood included. When your lowball gets negged, you can bid again at a slightly higher price without the 24-hour wait period, as long as you expand the area you're searching in. If that bid fails, you can expand and bid again. It'll take persistence, but the pillow will feel that much softer when you know you only paid a fraction of what your neighbor paid for his.

$125. There are sinks in the rooms, but bathrooms are shared for all units. The ratio is three or so rooms per bathroom. Ask for a room in the back, as there's street noise up front.

69 W. 38th St., at Sixth Ave. ✆ **888/HOTEL58** [468-3558] or 212/840-6700. Fax 212/840-1830. www.theamericaninn.com. 50 units, all with shared bathroom. $147–$160 double. AE, MC, V. Subway: B/D/F/M/N/Q/R to 34th St./Herald Sq. **Amenities:** Common kitchen. *In room:* A/C, TV, hair dryer (ask reception).

The Hotel at Times Square The savvy marketers at Apple Core have rebranded this former Super 8. It still has a chain feel, but remodeling has injected a little more style, and there's nothing generic about the building's ornate, bowed facade. The location is close to Rockefeller Center, and they throw in breakfast, too. Prices start at $110 for a single, but get pretty gouge-y at peak times.

59 W. 46th St., btw. Fifth and Sixth aves. ✆ **800/567-7720** or 212/719-2300. Fax 212/921-8929. www.applecorehotels.com. 209 units. $140–$370 double. AE, DC, MC, V. Subway: B/D/F/M to 47th–50th sts./Rockefeller Center. **Amenities:** Breakfast room; concierge; exercise room. *In room:* A/C, TV, hair dryer, Wi-Fi.

La Quinta Manhattan This chain hotel is in an ornate 1904 Beaux Arts building, although the street is so busy hardly anybody notices the architecture. Koreatown is a great neighborhood for affordable feasting, and the streets are lively but not as annoying as Times Square. Like its sibling "nyma" across the street, La Quinta is friendly and competent, and they throw in a free breakfast. Prices veer wildly depending on the time of year. There's a laid-back bar on the roof, with Empire State Building views.

17 W. 32nd St., btw. Fifth and Sixth aves. ✆ **800/567-7720** or 212/736-1600. www.applecorehotels.com. 182 units. $115–$440 double. Rates include continental breakfast. AE, DC, DISC, MC, V. Subway: B/D/F/M/N/Q/R to 34th St./Herald Sq. **Amenities:** Breakfast room; bar; concierge; exercise room. *In room:* A/C, TV w/pay movies and video games, Wi-Fi.

Park Savoy Hotel Most stays this close to Central Park come at a price (high). Somehow this hotel in the center of everything charges just $115 for a single with a private bathroom. Doubles are $150, and while rooms are small, they're plenty serviceable. (If you need more space, the Great Lawn is just a little ways away.)

158 W. 58th St., btw. Sixth and Seventh aves. ✆ **212/245-5755.** Fax 212/765-0668. www.parksavoyhotel.com. 80 units. $150 double; $115 single. AE, MC, V. Subway: N/Q/R or F to 57th St. *In room:* A/C, TV, Wi-Fi ($10).

Travel Inn   Despite a 42nd Street location, this hotel has some unusual amenities for Manhattan, like an outdoor pool, sun deck, and free parking. There's a chain hotel feel, but rooms are decent sized and a renovation has the place fully updated. It's a little west of the beaten path, but that's a good thing when it comes time to lay down your head in a city that never sleeps. Low-season doubles start at $125—heck, you could spend that much just parking.

515 W. 42nd St., near Tenth Ave. (✆ **888/HOTEL58** [468-3558], 800/869-4630, or 212/695-7171. Fax 212/967-5025. www.thetravelinnhotel.com. 160 units. $125–$400 double. AE, DC, DISC, MC, V. Subway: A/C/E/7 to 42nd St./Port Authority. **Amenities:** Coffee shop; fitness center; outdoor pool w/deck chairs and lifeguard in season; room service. *In room:* A/C, TV, hair dryer, Wi-Fi ($6).

UNDER $100

The Out NYC   This "straight-friendly urban resort" could as easily be described as a high-design gay compound. It's on the western fringe of Times Square, giving it access to major gay neighborhoods in Chelsea and Hell's Kitchen. Of course, with an on-site spa, sun deck, garden, lawn, restaurant, and nightclub, who needs the rest of the city? A regular room costs a pretty penny (doubles run about $350 a night), but if you're amenable to a roommate or three you can catch a great deal. "Sleep Share" accommodations are $99 a night. Four sleep in a room and split a bathroom, but the beds are full-size and there are privacy curtains and personal TVs. Although nominally "straight-friendly," don't expect any Tucker Max acolytes in the next bed over.

510 W. 42nd St., btw. Tenth and Eleventh aves. (✆ **212/947-2999.** Fax 212/947-2988. www.theoutnyc.com. 105 units, 8 sleep shares. $99 per dorm bed. AE, DC, DISC, MC, V. Subway: A/C/E/7 to 42nd St./Port Authority. **Amenities:** Restaurant; bar; concierge; fitness center. *In room:* A/C, TV, Wi-Fi.

6 Upper West Side

UNDER $150

Hotel Newton   An attentive, uniformed staff makes a warm welcome at this Uptown bargain spot. Rooms are on the large side (for the city), with firm beds and a rosy color scheme to match cherrywood furnishings. A standard double with a shared bath drops as low as $75 in the winter (it'll be double that at peak times). The range for a standard single with bathroom is $105 to $200.

CHEAP SLEEPS UPTOWN

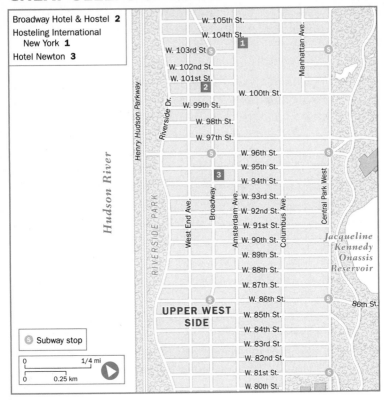

Broadway Hotel & Hostel **2**

Hosteling International
New York **1**

Hotel Newton **3**

W. 105th St.
W. 104th St.
W. 103rd St. ⑤ **1**
W. 102nd St.
W. 101st St.
2
W. 100th St.
W. 99th St.
W. 98th St.
W. 97th St.
W. 96th St. ⑤
W. 95th St.
3 W. 94th St.
W. 93rd St.
W. 92nd St.
W. 91st St.
W. 90th St.
W. 89th St.
W. 88th St.
W. 87th St.
W. 86th St. 86th St.
UPPER WEST SIDE W. 85th St.
W. 84th St.
W. 83rd St.
W. 82nd St.
W. 81st St.
W. 80th St.

Hudson River

Henry Hudson Parkway

Riverside Dr.

RIVERSIDE PARK

West End Ave.

Broadway

Amsterdam Ave.

Columbus Ave.

Central Park West

Manhattan Ave.

Jacqueline Kennedy Onassis Reservoir

⑤ Subway stop

0 ———— 1/4 mi
0 ———— 0.25 km

2528 Broadway, btw. 94th and 95th sts. ✆ **800/643-5553** or 212/678-6500. Fax 212/678-6758. www.thehotelnewton.com. 117 units. $105–$199 double with shared bathroom; $112–$285 double with private bathroom. AE, DC, DISC, MC, V. Subway: 1/2/3 to 96th St. **Amenities:** Room service. *In room:* A/C, TV, hair dryer, Wi-Fi ($4.95).

UNDER $50

Broadway Hotel & Hostel   The approach here is "boutique hostel," lending a cosmopolitan touch to backpacker-friendly rates. Sleek design and a social, international crowd mark the lobby and common space. Upstairs is a mix of hostel bunk beds and sedate private-bath rooms. The former is a great deal—there are only two berths to a room, meaning you can double up with a friend for $68 a night, or take a chance on a share for just $34. (At peak times, this price will double.) The communal bathrooms are clean and modern, and the hotel provides both linens and daily housekeeping.

230 W. 101st St., at Broadway. ✆ **212/865-7710.** Fax 212/865-2993. www.broadway hotelnyc.com. 60 dorm rooms, 50 doubles. $34–$60 per dorm bed; $78–$168 double with shared bathroom; $98–$178 double with private bathroom. AE, DC, DISC, MC, V. Subway: 1 to 103rd St. **Amenities:** Wi-Fi. *In room:* A/C, TV.

Hostelling International New York   The largest hostel in the U.S. occupies this block-long Victorian-Gothic edifice, built in 1883. With 624 beds, there's a lot of room at the inn, divided into male, female, and coed dorm spaces. Rooms sleep 6, 8, 10, or 12, with discounts for the larger spaces. A night starts at $30 and goes up to $45 for the dorms, with an extra $3 charged if you're not a member of Hostelling International (an annual membership can be purchased there for $28). With hundreds of youthful guests, there's a ton of social potential, some of it facilitated by the hostel. Free or inexpensive city tours run daily, and there are pub-crawls and nightclub visits at night. Linens and towels are provided.

891 Amsterdam Ave., btw. 103rd and 104th sts. ✆ **212/932-2300.** Fax 212/932-2574. www.hinewyork.org. 624 beds. $30–$49 per bed. AE, DC, MC, V. Subway: 1 to 103rd St. **Amenities:** Cafe; shared kitchen; Wi-Fi. *In room:* A/C.

7 Harlem

UNDER $150

Harlem Bed & Breakfast   "B&B" is probably pushing it as a designation, as this place is youthful and informal enough to pass for a hostel. The location is a classic 1896 brownstone in central Harlem, with some period details surviving inside. Of the 13 units, 10 have a shared bath, bringing prices for a single down as low as $75. If you're traveling in a group, a satellite location hooks up two-bedroom apartments and larger, starting at $395 a night.

54 W. 120th St., btw. Mt. Morris Park W. and Lenox Ave. ✆ **917/882-6222.** www. harlembedandbreakfast.com. 13 units, 10 with shared bathroom. $95–$395 double. AE, DISC, MC, V. Subway: 2/3 to 116th St. **Amenities:** Breakfast room. *In room:* A/C, TV, hair dryer, Wi-Fi.

Harlem Flophouse   Harlem is experiencing another renaissance, and if you'd like to spend the night a couple of blocks from Bill Clinton's office, this 1890s row house is a great pick. The flophouse name refers to the musicians and artists who crashed here back in the day. Rooms are comfortable, furnished with tasteful antiques. Bathrooms are shared between two rooms, and if you're booking in summer, keep in mind this place was built long before the advent of air-conditioning.

242 W. 123rd St., btw. Adam Clayton Powell and Frederick Douglass boulevards. ℭ**212/662-0678.** www.harlemflophouse.com. 4 rooms. $100 per room; $25–$35 for additional person; weekends $25 higher. MC, V. Subway: 2/3 or A/B/C/D to 125th St. *In room:* TV, Wi-Fi.

8 Brooklyn

UNDER $100

The New York Loft Hostel   Bushwick's blend of young, arty energy and rundown streets is about as close as you can get to the East Village of the '80s. (There's even an offshoot of the original Life Café immortalized in *Rent*.) An early-20th-century loft building hosts this hostel, with exposed brick walls and industrial-chic steel bunks. Rooms sleep up to 16, and a communal scene carries over to the backyard and the hot tub. Dorm beds start at $65 and include continental breakfast. On Wednesdays, Fridays, and Sundays, take advantage of free summer barbecues (free fondue in winter).

249 Varet St., btw. Bogart and White sts., Bushwick, Brooklyn. ℭ **800/780-5733** or 718/366-1351. www.nylofthostel.com. 80 dorm beds. $65–$40 dorm. Subway: L to Morgan Ave. **Amenities:** Shared kitchen; hot tub; Wi-Fi. *In room:* A/C.

ZIP112   Williamsburg's youthful nightlife scene more than rivals Manhattan's: You could spend an entire vacation in this part of Brooklyn and be thrilled with all your options for food, drink, music, and art. Manhattan is an easy trip on the L train. You'll also enjoy skyline views from the dorms and balcony. The dorm beds are female-only, from $50 to $70 a night (four beds to a room). Those traveling in twos can book the private double (shared bathroom). FINE PRINT Rooms are on the fifth floor; there's no elevator.

112 N. 6th St., btw. Berry St. and Wythe Ave., Williamsburg, Brooklyn. ℭ **347/403-0577.** www.zip112.com. 8 dorm beds, 1 double. $120–$150 double. Subway: L to Bedford Ave. **Amenities:** Shared kitchen. *In room:* A/C, hair dryer, Wi-Fi.

UNDER $50

NY Moore Hostel   If ever a ramshackle pizza joint could justify an accommodations selection, it's Bushwick's Roberta's. Artisanal

Nights Without Roofs in NYC

You can spend the night under the stars in New York City. Parks offer family camping nights in all five boroughs, even Manhattan (Central Park and Inwood Hill Nature Center do the hosting). Knowing that urbanites are light on tents and portable stoves, the city provides all the equipment save sleeping bags. They even throw in dinner, s'mores, and breakfast the next morning. It's all free, although you will have to get lucky with a lottery to nail down a space. Usually 30 spots are available for each camp night; the nights come on 30 different dates in summer, 6 nights per borough. Check with the Urban Park Rangers (**www.nycgovparks.org**) for exact times and dates, and register for the online lottery.

If you're looking to camp sans kids, there is one overnight spot in the city, at **Floyd Bennett Field** (✆ **718/338-3799;** www.recreation. gov). On the edge of Jamaica Bay, close to Riis Beach, this was NYC's first municipal airport. The site was decommissioned in 1971, with lush vegetation allowed to reclaim parts of the grounds. In addition to nature trails, you can check out historic aircraft, toy plane hobbyists, and communal gardens. There are 35 sites for year-round tent camping (another six sites are reserved for RVs). The rate is $20 per day, with a six-person capacity per site (toilet facilities are of the portable kind, and the showers are $10 at the Aviator Sports Center). You can access the park by taking the 2 or 5 train to Flatbush Avenue and then the Q35 bus.

Neapolitan pies in a post-industrial garage are worth a ride from Manhattan, or you could stay down the block at this brand-new hostel. Rooms are loftlike, with more light and space than you'd expect for the price. Choose from coed or female-only dorms (sharing a bathroom and six to eight beds) for $48 to $56 per night.

179 Moore St., btw. Bushwick Ave. and White St., Bushwick, Brooklyn. ✆ **347/227-8634.** Fax 347/464-4109. www.nymoorehostel.com. 56 beds. $48–$56 per bed. Subway: L to Morgan Ave. **Amenities:** Shared kitchen. *In room:* A/C, TV, Wi-Fi.

9 Queens

UNDER $150

The Brooqlyn Guest House   New Yorkers looking to save a little money light out for underpublicized neighborhoods like Ridgewood, on the Brooklyn-Queens border. This mom-and-pop town house, on a brick-paved block, provides more space, quiet, and amenities than you'll find at trendier addresses. Suites are long on style, taking a homey approach to modern design. Front porches provide a small-town feel, although Manhattan is just 15 minutes away on the L train. Two-bedroom suites are great for families or two couples to share, with nightly rates ranging from $120 to $250.

Ridgewood, Queens (address provided at booking). ✆ **646/820-0155.** www.the brooqlyn.com. 4 units. $120–$250 2- or 2½-bedroom suite. MC, V. Subway: L to Dekalb St. *In room:* A/C, TV, hair dryer, kitchen, MP3 docking station, Wi-Fi.

No-Tell Boatel

It ain't exactly Cunard, but this ramshackle compound in the Far Rock-aways will let you sleep on the water from just $55 a night. The **Boatel** (✆ **718/945-4500;** www.marina59.com) is a collection of abandoned power boats moored in Somerville Basin, with views toward Jamaica Bay. (There are also views of JFK air traffic, the projects, and a couple of wandering goats.) The whole thing is somewhat less than street legal, so that nightly rate is a "donation," put toward a visit to an "art installation." The vessels are artist-decorated, and movies and lectures make for communal entertainment in the evenings. You can choose from 16 berths ($55–$105 per night), most sleeping two to four, with room for more to come aboard. The emphasis is on adventure, not pampering. Pack a flashlight, a sleeping bag, and food for grilling. Open Wednesdays through Sundays, mid-May through October. Reserve early, as the cabins fill up quickly. 59-14 Beach Channel Dr., Far Rockaway, Queens. By subway, take the Far Rockaway/Mott Ave. branch of the A train to Beach 60th St.

Country Inn & Suites   This chain is less than quirky, but if you're on the hunt for cheap, clean, and comfy you could do worse. Rooms are nice sized, there's a fitness center, and breakfast is free. Although the surroundings aren't much to look at, Manhattan access is excellent from a selection of four subway lines.

40-34 Crescent St., btw. 40th and 41st aves., Long Island City, Queens. ✆ **718/729-0111.** Fax 718/729-0112. www.countryinns.com. 133 units. $127 -$150 double. AE, DC, DISC, MC, V. Subway: N/Q/7 to Queensboro Plaza; F to 21st St./Queensbridge. **Amenities:** Breakfast room; fitness room. *In room:* A/C, TV, hair dryer, Wi-Fi.

Verve Hotel   These boutique accommodations are made affordable by an industrial Queens location. Nearby subway lines make for a quick and easy trip into Manhattan. The larger suites are reasonably priced and come with hot tubs, and many rooms have skyline views. And, you get a free continental breakfast.

40–03 29th St., btw. 40th Rd. and 40th Ave., Long Island City, Queens. ✆ **718/786-4545.** Fax 718/786-4554. www.vervehotel.com. 87 units. $99–$189 double. AE, DC, DISC, MC, V. Subway: N/Q to 39th Ave. **Amenities:** Breakfast room; fitness room. *In room:* A/C, TV, hair dryer, Wi-Fi.

10 Staten Island

Fort Place Bed & Breakfast   St. George is a quick ferry trip from Manhattan, but its small-town scale feels worlds away. You can spend the night at this Civil War -era Victorian mansion. A mix of period details and vintage Deco furnishings provide character. The house is a short walk to the **Staten Island Yankees** (p. 285) and even closer to the Staten Island Ferry Terminal, where you can take a free ride across the harbor to Manhattan. Singles are just $85, and doubles $120, with shared bathrooms.

22 Fort Place, btw. Montgomery and Monroe aves., St. George, Staten Island. ✆ **718/772-2112.** www.fortplace.com. 5 rooms. $120 double. AE, MC, V. Subway: R to Whitehall St.; 1 to South Ferry, take the ferry to Staten Island and follow the signs. *In room:* A/C, TV, hair dryer on request, Wi-Fi.

The famous "Recession Special" at Gray's Papaya is a NYC classic.

CHEAP EATS

New Yorkers speak over 130 languages, and we eat at least that many different cuisines. Many of the ethnic superstars are hidden away in low-rent corners of the boroughs, but plenty of spectacular cheap eats can be found even in the high-rent districts of Manhattan. Being selective about price doesn't necessarily mean sacrificing quality. Some of my favorite cooking just happens to be some of the city's cheapest. The island tilts toward downtown when it comes to budget grazing—Chinatown and the East Village dominate. Across the rest of the city, Asian eateries offer the most for the least, with some solid backing from Latino and Indian contenders. Culinary trends of late have been favoring the low end, meaning new purveyors of cheap burgers, hot dogs, fried chicken, and pizza now dot the city. Lunch specials are a great way to sample the city's harvest with a minimal investment, but for all meals, I'm constantly surprised by how far $6 or $7 or even $3 can take me. Leave the Jacksons in the wallet and *bon appétit.*

1 Financial District

Bennie's Thai Café *THAI* This unprepossessing basement spot serves authentic Thai food that bursts with flavor. Worker bees stream in for the $6.45 lunch specials served over rice on weekdays from 11am to 3pm. Red, yellow, and green curries are the highlights. The dishes are pork, chicken, and beef, so vegetarians have to order off the regular menu. Helpfully, vegetarian entrees, including an awesome Pad Thai, average $8.95.

88 Fulton St., at Gold St. ℂ **212/587-8930.** www.benniesthaicafenyc.com. Mon–Fri 11am–9pm; Sat–Sun noon–9pm. Subway: A/C/J/Z/2/3/4/5 to Fulton St./Broadway Nassau.

Carl's Steaks *CHEESESTEAKS* City of Brotherly Shove transplants have long looked down their noses at New York's attempts at the cheesesteak. A slew of hopefuls have stepped up, but only Carl's delivers a sandwich with the potential to hold its own in Philly. The shaved sirloin melts on the tongue, while taut hoagie rolls make the meal substantial. American or provolone are options, but connoisseurs know Cheese Whiz is the only way to go. A steak sandwich is $6.75, with cheese $7.25; $2.50 for a side of fries.

79 Chambers St., btw. Broadway and Church St. ℂ **212/566-2828.** www.carlsteaks. com. Mon–Tues 11am–9:30pm; Wed–Fri 10:30am–9:30pm; Sat–Sun noon–9:30pm. Subway: A/C or 1/2/3 to Chambers St.; R to City Hall. Other location: *Midtown,* 507 Third Ave., at 34th St. ℂ **212/696-5336.** Subway: 6 to 33rd St.

L & L Hawaiian Barbecue *HAWAIIAN* For most New Yorkers, the *katsus, loco mocos,* and *lau lau* combos here will be unfamiliar. The tangy Asian-inflected flavors make quick converts, though. Plates come with creamy macaroni salad and scooped rice. Short ribs in black pepper sauce are $6.99; a mixed barbecue combo that could feed a family for a week is $10.59. (Manhattan is blessed with the only version of this franchise east of Texas.)

64 Fulton St., btw. Cliff and Gold sts. © **212/577-8888.** www.hawaiianbarbecue.com. Mon–Fri 10:30am–11pm; Sat–Sun 11am–11pm. Subway: A/C/J/Z/2/3/4/5 to Fulton St./Broadway Nassau.

2 Chinatown

Bánh Mì Saigon Bakery *VIETNAMESE*   If you ask me, *bánh mì* sandwiches are up there with penicillin as far as human achievements go. Layers of cilantro, carrot, cucumber, and a creamy dressing top a crusty baguette. Beyond the bread, French influence can also be found in the thinly sliced pâté that accompanies crumbled pork sausage in the classic version ($4.25 here). This purveyor's counter inside a jewelry shop reinforces the sense that anything this delicious must be illegal.

198 Grand St., btw. Mulberry and Mott sts. © **212/941-1541.** www.banhmisaigon nyc.com. Daily 8am–6pm. Subway: B/D to Grand St.; J/Z to Bowery.

Dragon Land Bakery *BAKERY*   Bakeries litter the landscape in Chinatown, most offering up fresh goods at ridiculous prices. The differences between any two shops are subtle, but Dragon Land does a particularly good job. In addition to baked goods, the mango- and green tea–flavored puddings are delicious. Prices range from $1 to $4.

125 Walker St., btw. Centre and Baxter sts. © **212/219-2012.** Daily 7:30am–8pm. Subway: J/N/Q/R/Z/6 to Canal St.

Hong Kong Station *CHINESE*   DIY soup-designing saves you money! Less labor-intensive than *shabu shabu,* Hong Kong Station does the work once you've selected a noodle, a broth, and fillings. Chinatown body parts (pig's blood, beef shank, and chicken gizzards) can be found, along with less adventuresome greens, tofu, and fish balls. Garlic and hot sauces top it all off, along with scallions and "parsley" (well, cilantro actually—somebody fire the translator). A noodle soup starts at $2, with toppings $1.45 each.

45 Bayard St., at Elizabeth St. © **212/233-0288.** www.hongkongstation.us. Sun–Thurs 7am–10:30pm; Fri–Sat 7am–11:30pm. Subway: J/N/R/Q/Z/6 to Canal St. Other location: 45 Division St., btw. Market and Catherine sts. © **212/966-9682.** Subway: F to E. Broadway; J/N/R/Q/Z/6 to Canal St.

Pho Grand *VIETNAMESE*   Pho Grand is a contender for the best Vietnamese food in the city, and it's just a little added bonus that it's

CHEAP EATS DOWNTOWN

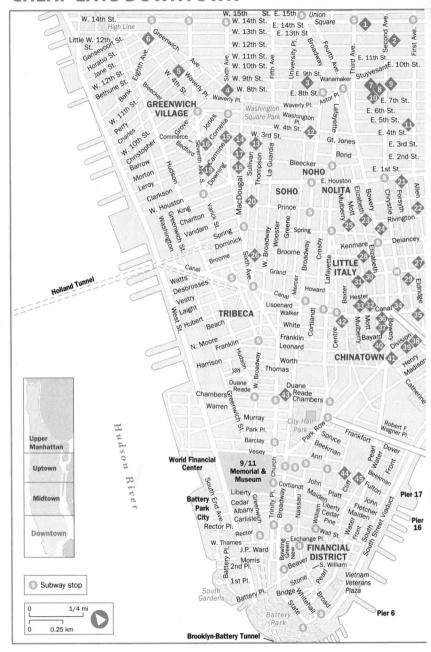

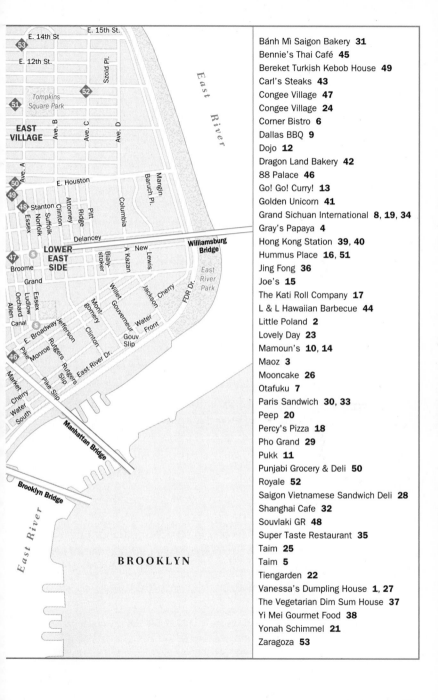

Bánh Mì Saigon Bakery **31**
Bennie's Thai Café **45**
Bereket Turkish Kebob House **49**
Carl's Steaks **43**
Congee Village **47**
Congee Village **24**
Corner Bistro **6**
Dallas BBQ **9**
Dojo **12**
Dragon Land Bakery **42**
88 Palace **46**
Go! Go! Curry! **13**
Golden Unicorn **41**
Grand Sichuan International **8, 19, 34**
Gray's Papaya **4**
Hong Kong Station **39, 40**
Hummus Place **16, 51**
Jing Fong **36**
Joe's **15**
The Kati Roll Company **17**
L & L Hawaiian Barbecue **44**
Little Poland **2**
Lovely Day **23**
Mamoun's **10, 14**
Maoz **3**
Mooncake **26**
Otafuku **7**
Paris Sandwich **30, 33**
Peep **20**
Percy's Pizza **18**
Pho Grand **29**
Pukk **11**
Punjabi Grocery & Deli **50**
Royale **52**
Saigon Vietnamese Sandwich Deli **28**
Shanghai Cafe **32**
Souvlaki GR **48**
Super Taste Restaurant **35**
Taim **25**
Taim **5**
Tiengarden **22**
Vanessa's Dumpling House **1, 27**
The Vegetarian Dim Sum House **37**
Yi Mei Gourmet Food **38**
Yonah Schimmel **21**
Zaragoza **53**

Some Deals on Dim Sum

A typical New York brunch is $20 to $30 per person, but you can feast like royalty for $10 to $15 a head at a Chinese brunch, or *dim sum*— Cantonese for "touch the heart," which refers to the small dishes that are usually pushed around on carts. You point to the dishes you want, the waitstaff stamps your card, you eat entirely more than you planned, and then marvel at how cheap the bill is. Fill up on everything from steamed pork buns, shrimp *shumai,* and fried taro balls (one of my favorites) to chicken feet and jellied pig's blood.

For the full effect, you'll want a large dining hall with the carts, and **Jing Fong,** 20 Elizabeth St. (📞 **212/964-5256**), is always a winner with my friends and family. Just dining in the cacophonous football field–size space along with dozens of Chinese families is an experience in itself. But the secret's out, and you may wait 30 minutes or more during weekend brunch hours. You'll have a similarly grand experience at **Golden Unicorn** (my Chinese friends prefer this place), 18 E. Broadway, at Catherine Street (📞 **212/941-0911**), though you'll pay a few bucks more per person. Prices hit rock bottom at **88 Palace,** 88 East Broadway, second floor (📞 **212/941-8886**), in the Chinese mall under the Manhattan Bridge. A huge feast including beers for three people came to $34 before tip. Even carnivores enjoy the **Vegetarian Dim Sum House** (📞 **212/577-7176**), at 24 Pell St., which does satisfying mock-meat versions of all the traditional dishes, minus the carts.

—*Stephen Bassman*

also among the cheapest. Huge bowls of rich, complex *pho* (beef noodle soup) are only $5.25. Vermicelli noodle and rice dishes come in under $6. Most entrees top out well before $10 and are routinely delicious. A lodgelike interior with wooden panels underscores the homey quality of the food.

277C Grand St., btw. Forsyth and Eldridge sts. 📞 **212/965-5366.** www.phograndny. com. Daily 10:30am–11pm. Subway: B/D to Grand St.

Shanghai Cafe *CHINESE*   Soup dumplings are one of the top draws in Chinatown, combining supple skins and a physics-defying broth.

Shanghai Cafe makes a specialty of the dish. Bamboo baskets come full of addictive steamed pork (eight for $4.95) or pork with crab (eight for $6.95) dumplings. The balance of the menu is tasty, too, with most dishes coming in under $10.

100 Mott St., btw. Canal and Hester sts. ✆ **212/966-3988.** www.shanghaicafenyc. com. Daily 11:30am–9pm. Subway: J/Z, N/Q, 6 to Canal St.

Super Taste Restaurant *CHINESE*   In the back of this bare-bones soup shop, you can see the noodle-maker at work, stretching dough as ritualistically as a pizza-maker. The noodles themselves are taut and flavorful, dunked into a rich beef broth that originated along the Silk Road. Soups average $5. Steamed dumplings with silky wrappings make a great side at $3.

26 Eldridge St., btw. Canal and Division sts. ✆ **212/625-1198.** Daily 10am–11pm. Subway: F to E. Broadway; B/D to Grand St.

Vanessa's Dumpling House *CHINESE/DUMPLINGS*   If they tripled their prices, this shop on the Lower East Side end of Chinatown would still be cheap. They offer an amazing $2.25 sandwich, a big wedge of sesame pancake with roasted beef or pork in a fresh cilantro and carrot dressing. Add 25¢ and go full-on gourmet with Peking duck. Dumplings make a great side, at four for $1 and cooked in a thick, flavorful wrapping. Soups start at $1 and buns at three for $1. A renovation doubled the size and made things less chaotic, with some tables for sit-down dining. FINE PRINT There are additional locations on 14th Street and in Williamsburg, but prices are slightly higher and the food's not quite as good.

118 Eldridge St., btw. Broome and Grand sts. ✆ **212/625-8008.** Daily 7:30am– 10:30pm. Subway: B/D to Grand St. Other locations: *East Village,* 220 E. 14th St., btw. Second and Third aves. ✆ **212/529-1329.** Subway: L to Third Ave. *Williamsburg, Brooklyn,* 310 Bedford Ave., btw. S. 1st and S. 2nd sts. ✆ **718/218-8806.** Subway: L to Bedford Ave.; J/M/Z to Marcy Ave.

Yi Mei Gourmet Food *CHINESE*   I'm all for capitalism if it means that two tasty buffets will set up side-by-side shops and battle it out for the cheapest, freshest food around. Yi Mei and its neighbor Golden Bowl both put out a dozen-plus daily entrees, from salt-and-pepper shrimp to century eggs to baby *bok choy*. Choose any four items and it's $4, and that includes a cup of soup (which resembles bathwater and should be skipped). Both restaurants are good, but for my (almost no) money, Yi Mei's got the edge.

51 Division St., btw. Market and Catherine sts. ✆ **212/925-1921.** Daily 7am–9pm. Subway: F to E. Broadway; J/N/Q/R/Z/6 to Canal St.

3 Lower East Side

Bereket Turkish Kebob House *TURKISH* The guys working here never got the memo that fast food doesn't require four-star taste. The $3.50 falafel is crispy, served in a flavorful pita with farm-fresh tomatoes and lettuce. The rest of the menu is even better. My own personal addiction is the *adana* kabob, a spicy blend of lamb and beef, available as a $6 pita sandwich.

187 E. Houston St., at Orchard St. ✆ **212/475-7700.** Daily 24 hr. Subway: F to Second Ave.

Congee Village *CHINESE* The Chinese–Disney–acid trip interior here has recently been scaled back, resulting in a marble and brick expanse that could *almost* pass for classy. The house specialty is congee, a hearty rice porridge that starts at $3.50 and comes in multiple combinations (I love the squid with ginger). For sharing, try the house special chicken, a banquet plate of garlicky delight at $9 for a half. Lunch specials, served over rice, average $4.25. [FINE PRINT] The original space is wildly popular; for shorter waits try the Bowery satellite. Ask to sit on the upper level.

100 Allen St., btw. Delancey and Broome sts. ✆ **212/941-1818.** www.congeevillage restaurants.com. Sun–Thurs 10:30am–12:30am; Fri–Sat 10:30am–2am. Subway: F to Delancey St.; J/M/Z to Essex St. Other location: *Bowery*, 207 Bowery, btw. Spring and Rivington sts. ✆ **212/766-2828.** Subway: J/Z to Bowery; 6 to Spring St.

Souvlaki GR *GREEK* If you're deferring your Greek island vacation until the euro zone stabilizes, this pocket of Mykonos makes a great stand-in. Flowers, whitewashed walls, and Mediterranean-blue accents provide a date-friendly atmosphere. A food-truck stint honed the cooking, perfecting savory chicken and pork ($4.50) skewers, packed into a moist flatbread pita. On the side, a fresh Greek salad is $7 and hand-cut fries are $4.

116 Stanton St., btw. Ludlow and Essex sts. ✆ **212/777-0116.** www.souvlakigr.com. Daily 11am–midnight. Subway: F to Delancey St.; J/M/Z to Essex St.

Tiengarden *VEGETARIAN* A mix of pencil-thin model types and local hard-core vegans frequent this quirky little storefront for some of the healthiest food around. The Chinese-inspired menu is prepared without dairy, onion, or garlic, but somehow manages to be packed with flavor. Prices have gone up some, but it's still cheap for such wholesome offerings—noodle dishes and oversize soups start at $9, and entrees hover around $11.

170 Allen St., btw. Stanton and Rivington sts. ℭ **212/388-1364.** www.tiengardener. com. Daily noon–10pm. Subway: F to Second Ave.; J/M/Z to Essex St.

Yonah Schimmel *KNISHES* The knish is a New York classic and can be found everywhere from delis to hot dog stands, but for the best in gut bombs, you have to go to the Lower East Side. Yonah Schimmel offers up flavors traditional (potato, mushroom, kasha) and sacrilegious (pizza), cooked with a generations-old recipe. For $3.50, it's hard to get more filled up. The rich cheese versions are less cost-conscious ($4), but equally delicious.

137 E. Houston St., btw. First and Second aves. ℭ **212/477-2858.** www.yonah schimmel.com. Mon–Thurs 9am–7pm; Fri–Sun 9am–11pm. Subway: F to Second Ave.

4 SoHo/NoLita

Lovely Day *JAPANESE/THAI* This little cafe is as hip as affordable gets, and they've bounced back from a fire. The menu features creative takes on Thai and Japanese dishes, with noodles coming in at $8.50. A plate of meat and pineapple fried rice is $8. Red or green curries and pineapple cashew plates are all under $10. The seasonings are a little on the sweet side, but the fun, bustling room quickly puts a diner in a forgiving mood.

196 Elizabeth St., btw. Prince and Spring sts. ℭ **212/925-3310.** Daily 11am–11pm. Subway: 6 to Spring St.

Mooncake *PAN-ASIAN* This family-run shop serves up fresh food with Asian accents. Portions are decent for such small prices. A pork chop sandwich with mango chutney is $8, as is a steak and pepper hero. For $1.50 more, you can get a salad bowl with lemongrass shrimp and Vietnamese-style vermicelli noodles. The biggest seller is the healthy miso-glazed salmon, a plate of which is $10.

28 Watts St., near Sixth Ave. ✆ **212/219-8888.** www.mooncakefoods.com. Mon–Sat 11am–11pm. Subway: A/C/E to Canal St. Other locations: *Midtown West,* 263 W. 30th St., btw. Seventh and Eighth aves. ✆ **212/268-2888.** Subway: 1/2/3 or A/C/E to Penn Station. *Midtown West,* 359 W. 54th St., btw. Eighth and Ninth aves. ✆ **212/262-9888.** Subway: N/Q/R to 57th St.

Paris Sandwich *VIETNAMESE* Fresh baguettes are the innovation here, cooked on-site and then transformed into hearty Vietnamese heroes ($4–$4.75). Although I prefer the *bánh mì* elsewhere, the grilled pork is spectacular, caramelly meat sunk deep into the pores of the bread. Cheap fresh-roasted Vietnamese coffee, soups, noodles, and curries are also for sale.

213 Grand St., btw. Elizabeth and Mott sts. ✆ **212/226-3828.** www.parissandwiches. com. Daily 9am–8pm. Subway: B/D to Grand St.; J/Z to Bowery. Other location: *Chinatown,* 113 Mott St., btw. Hester and Canal sts. ✆ **212/226-7221.** Subway: J/N/Q/R/Z/6 to Canal St.; B/D to Grand St.

Peep *THAI* Peep proves that an upscale, modern decor and central location don't require exorbitant prices. Dinners are reasonable ($11 Pad Thai and sautéed entrees), though the real deal comes at lunch. For $8 you get an appetizer and an entree, with a large selection of Thai favorites to pick through. Presentation is as attractive as the crowd. Though the neighborhood's discovered this place, it's usually not so crowded that you can't get a seat. FINE PRINT Don't miss the seemingly transparent bathrooms.

177 Prince St., btw. Sullivan and Thompson sts. ✆ **212/254-PEEP** (7337). www. peepsoho.net. Sun–Thurs 11am–midnight; Fri–Sat 11am–1am. Subway: C/E to Spring St.

Saigon Vietnamese Sandwich Deli *VIETNAMESE* The *bánh mì* craze is still raging on, but I am happy to be a slavish follower of fashion if it means spectacular sandwiches at ludicrously low prices. A recent spruce-up and expansion of this little takeaway shop has resulted in slightly raised prices, but the quality is up as well—substantial baguettes are packed dense with fresh, top-quality cilantro, radish, carrots, and homemade pâté. Just $4.50 covers the house special (there are a dozen or so sandwiches available in all).

369 Broome St., near Mott St. ✆ **212/219-8341.** www.vietnamese-sandwich.com. Daily 7am–7pm. Subway: J/Z to Bowery; B/D to Grand St.

5 East Village

Little Poland *DINER/POLISH* The old-time Eastern European flavor of the East Village is fading, but fortunately this greasy-spoon stalwart is hanging on. Some dozen hearty soups are less than $4 a bowl, and pirogi are eight for $8.25. For dinner, a breaded pork chop bigger than its serving plate is $10.95, and if you're in before noon, you can get a full array of breakfast specials (starting with two eggs, potatoes, toast, juice, and coffee for $4.25). If you can't fill your stomach here for $11, perhaps you should consider a career as a competitive eater.

200 Second Ave., btw. 12th and 13th sts. ☎ **212/777-9728.** Daily 7am–11pm. Subway: L to First or Third Ave.

Otafuku *JAPANESE* Ideal drunk food can be found at this tiny take-out in the East Village—though the sober will be equally sated. The dishes are hot, flavorful, filling, and decidedly odd. The mainstays are *okonomiyaki,* a pizza-shaped pancake fried up with shredded cabbage, bonito flakes, and a choice of meat; and *takoyaki,* dumplings made of batter and octopus, topped with some of the above pancake fixin's. At $3 to $8, everything's cheap and large enough to share. *Yakisoba* (fried noodles with squid and shrimp) is only $7. FINE PRINT This is sidewalk food. The place is the size of a closet, and aside from a bench in front, there's no seating.

236 E. 9th St., btw. Second and Third aves. ☎ **212/353-8503.** Mon–Thurs 1–10pm; Fri–Sat noon–11pm; Sun noon–10pm. Subway: 6 to Astor Place; N/R to 8th St.

Pukk *THAI* Don't be intimidated by the overdesigned interior (reclining Buddha encased in Lucite, anyone?) of this narrow neighborhood restaurant. The food here transcends trendiness to deliver inventive meat-free soups, curries, and tofu. Among the fake flesh, "duck" is the standout. Entrees and noodle dishes start at $7 (the spicy eggplant tofu comes in a huge, delicious portion), and two-course lunches are just $6.

71 First Ave., btw. 4th and 5th sts. ☎ **212/253-2741.** www.pukknyc.com. Sun–Thurs 11:30am–11pm; Fri–Sat 11:30am–midnight. Subway: F to Second Ave.

Punjabi Grocery & Deli *INDIAN* Local hipsters have discovered this Sikh taxi stand, which serves its dual constituencies with equal cordiality. Choose from six veggie entries, which are then microwaved and served over rice. Have two on a small plate for $3.50, or three over a

THE BEST DEALS ON ST. MARKS PLACE

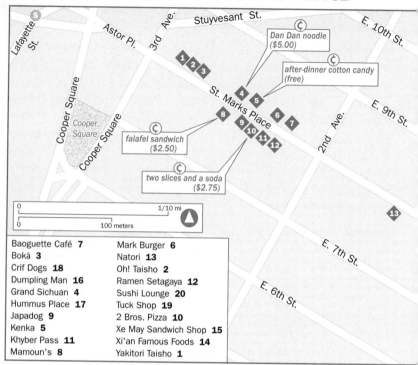

Dan Dan noodle ($5.00)

after-dinner cotton candy (free)

falafel sandwich ($2.50)

two slices and a soda ($2.75)

Baoguette Café **7**
Bokä **3**
Crif Dogs **18**
Dumpling Man **16**
Grand Sichuan **4**
Hummus Place **17**
Japadog **9**
Kenka **5**
Khyber Pass **11**
Mamoun's **8**
Mark Burger **6**
Natori **13**
Oh! Taisho **2**
Ramen Setagaya **12**
Sushi Lounge **20**
Tuck Shop **19**
2 Bros. Pizza **10**
Xe May Sandwich Shop **15**
Xi'an Famous Foods **14**
Yakitori Taisho **1**

big plate for $5.50. The food is fresh and spicy, and you can throw in two samosas for only $2.50 more.

114 E. 1st St., btw. First Ave. and Ave. A. ☏ **212/533-9048.** Daily 24 hr. Subway: F to Second Ave.

Royale *BURGERS*   Though it's short on history (and the TVs undermine its character), this bar's deft burger execution reflects the ambitions of a place targeting classic status. Big patties full of Black Angus flavor rest on brioche buns ($7), cooked to order and served fresh. (Add $1 for a "Royale with Cheese.") In the warmer months, the garden in back makes for a laid-back scene. To maximize your savings, come at happy hour (weeknights from 4–7pm) and enjoy two for one drafts and well drinks.

157 Ave. C, btw. 9th and 10th sts. ☏ **212/254-6600.** www.royalenyc.com. Sun–Thurs 4pm–2am; Fri–Sat 4pm–4am. Subway: L to First Ave.

Zaragoza *MEXICAN*   A renowned late-night fortification stop, this run-down deli's food tastes just as good *before* a 5-hour East Village bender. The handwritten menu shows off homemade delicacies, long

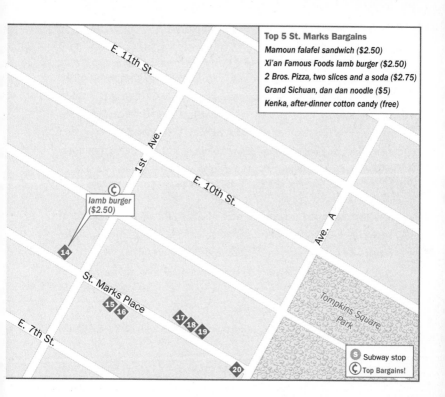

Top 5 St. Marks Bargains

Mamoun falafel sandwich ($2.50)
Xi'an Famous Foods lamb burger ($2.50)
2 Bros. Pizza, two slices and a soda ($2.75)
Grand Sichuan, dan dan noodle ($5)
Kenka, after-dinner cotton candy (free)

lamb burger
($2.50)

E. 11th St.
1st Ave.
E. 10th St.
Ave. A
St. Marks Place
E. 7th St.
Tompkins Square Park

ⓢ Subway stop
ⓒ Top Bargains!

on authenticity and short on price. Among the rotating selection of stewed meats, you can't go wrong with roast pork, chipotle chicken, *lengua* (beef tongue, but trust me), and the enchiladas, spiced with hints of pineapple. The friendly counter folk will stuff your meat of choice in a double corn tortilla and top it with an addictive tomatillo sauce for just $3. They also serve top-rate tostadas, tamales, and under-$10 entrees, all of which justify my somewhat obsessive relationship with this place.

215 Ave. A, btw. 13th and 14th sts. ⓒ **212/780-9204.** www.mexicanrestaurantnew york.com. Mon–Thurs 9:30am–midnight; Fri–Sat 9:30am–4am; Sun 11am–midnight. Cash only. Subway: L to First Ave.

6 West Village

Corner Bistro *AMERICAN/BURGERS* Inside this dark, worn West Village bar you'll find one of the best burgers in the city. The no-frills regular is $6.75, while $8 adds decadent layers of cheese, bacon, and

Meal Deal-ing on St. Marks Place

St. Marks Place runs from Avenue A (bookended by Tompkins Square Park) to Third Avenue (it turns into Astor Place there, before becoming 8th St.). Somehow in just 3 short blocks, there are more than five dozen restaurants. The combination of proximity, NYU-friendly pricing, and exotic and original cooking make this the city's best stretch for affordable, adventurous dining. Highlights follow, listed from west to east.

NORTH SIDE

Yakitori Taisho. This tavern's perennially overflowing crowds attest to the down-home goodness of the Japanese cooking. (Sister spot **Oh! Taisho** is two doors down.) ✆ **212/228-5086.** 5 St. Marks Place.

Bokā. Fine moderately priced Korean, but most folks are here for legendary BonChon Chicken—take your pick of spicy hot or garlicky soy. ✆ **212/228-2887.** 9 St. Marks Place.

Grand Sichuan. Best. Restaurant. Ever. See p. 65. 19–23 St. Marks Place.

Kenka. Perhaps the most transporting restaurant in New York, this rollicking *izakaya* is a teleporter right into a Japanese beer hall. Cheap eats, bright flavors, and free DIY cotton candy for dessert. ✆ **212/254-6363.** 25 St. Marks Place.

Mark Burger. Terrific sliders with a rich porterhouse, chuck, and short rib blend are just $2.50 each. ✆ **212/677-3132.** 33 St. Marks Place.

Baoguette Café. A "gourmet" spin on Asian street food, with some hits (classic *bánh mì*, $6.50) and some misses (bizarrely spiced catfish sandwich, $7.50). ✆ **212/460-9100.** 37 St. Marks Place.

Xi'an Famous Foods. The Flushing (Queens) favorite introduces New Yorkers to Silk Road–influenced Chinese cuisine. Lamb "burgers" equal instant New York classics. No phone. 81 St. Marks Place.

Hummus Place. Choose from three rich hummus platters. See p. 74. 109 St. Marks Place.

Crif Dogs. A favorite refueling spot with tasty hot dogs. An unassuming telephone booth leads to a hidden, pricey cocktail den. ✆ **212/614-2728.** 113 St. Marks Place.

Tuck Shop. This "canteen" specializes in savory, flaky pies, running from Aussie traditional to Thai-influenced gourmet ($6). ✆ **212/979-5200.** 115 St. Marks Place.

SOUTH SIDE

Mamoun's. Mamoun's $2.50 falafel is legendary. See p. 64. 22 St. Marks Place.

Japadog. This Vancouver mom-and-pop export puts creative takes on hot dogs inside superior buns. Signature Terimayo dogs (beef with teriyaki and Japanese mayonnaise) go for $6.25. ✆ **212/476-2324.** 30 St. Marks Place.

2 Bros. Pizza. Not the world's greatest pie, but at just $1 for a fresh slice, pretty hard to beat. ✆ **212/777-0600.** 32 St. Marks Place.

Khyber Pass. The decor here may be a little tired, but if you're looking to expand your palate, you'll find intriguing Afghan at moderate prices. ✆ **212/473-0989.** 34 St. Marks Place.

Ramen Setagaya. This is not the ramen you lived off of in college: Homemade broth combines clams, scallops, lemon peel, and pork for amazing, addictive soups ($10–$11.75 at dinner). ✆ **212/387-7959.** 34½ St. Marks Place.

Natori. Don't be deterred by the ragged exterior; the fish at this East Village pioneer is superfresh, and available until 7pm as an early bird special. ✆ **212/533-7711.** 58 St. Marks Place.

Xe May Sandwich Shop. Fresh ingredients and a generous heaping of meat make these the best *bánh mì* ($6–$6.50) around. Fusion fans can opt for $2.50 tacos. ✆ **212/388-1688.** 96 St. Marks Place.

Dumpling Man. Handmade numbers here start at $4.50 for six. ✆ **212/505-2121.** 100 St. Marks Place.

Sushi Lounge. Half-off sushi is the gimmick here, kicking in once you reach the $8 threshold. After 10pm beers and Japanese cocktails are also 50% off. ✆ **212/598-1188.** 132 St. Marks Place.

Street Meat & Greet: Carts & Trucks

Street carts are classic icons of New York City, although many still specialize in the hot dogs and Day-Glo-orange empanadas of Gotham's last incarnation. For a new city era, purveyors have gotten much more sophisticated, adding elaborate truck setups to the mix. There's even an annual award show, the Vendys (**www.streetvendor.org**), that recognizes the city's finest street meat artisans. You can also follow/find many of your favorite trucks via Facebook and Twitter.

The **Biryani Cart** (southwest corner, 46th St. and Sixth Ave.) won the '08 and '09 People's Choice Award for its fresh, flavorful Indian cuisine. Namesake chicken *biryani* is $6 for a huge portion, and *kati* rolls ($6 for two) are a Midtown cult favorite.

Just a half a block away is another crowd-pleaser, **Kim's Aunt Kitchen** (46th St., btw. Fifth and Sixth aves.). The awesome whiting sandwich (fish, fried on the spot) is just $4; order it on a hero with plenty of tartar and hot sauce.

The fast rise of Jeremy Lin has put Taiwan on New York's radar. For authentic Taiwanese cooking, check out the **Bian Dang** (**www.bian dangnyc.com**) truck, the successor to NYC Cravings. Two huge pieces of chicken, rice, and pickled veggies are $8. For the same price you can get the diabolically tasty fried pork chop, served with pork sauce! Check the website or Twitter feed, as the truck rotates between several parking spaces on the weekdays. (There's also a brick and mortar location, inside Koreatown's Food Gallery 32, see p. 71.)

For Korean on the move, check out the Mexican-inflected mashups served at the **Korilla BBQ** (**www.korillabbq.com**) truck. Taco trios

onions. This place is a well-guarded local secret, known only to you and the 10,000 other people waiting on line beside you at the bar. (Weekday afternoons are the least-crowded times.) A mug of beer to wash it down will only set you back $3.

331 W. 4th St., btw. Jane St. and Eighth Ave. ℂ **212/242-9502**. www.cornerbistrony. com. Mon–Sat 11:30am–4am; Sun noon–4am. Subway: 1/2/3 or A/C/E to 14th St.; L to Eighth Ave. Other location: *Long Island City, Queens*, 47-18 Vernon Blvd., at 47th Rd. ℂ **718/606-6500**. Subway: G to 21st St.; 7 to Vernon Blvd./Jackson Ave.

and burritos are on the bill ($7), stuffed with hearty *bulgogi* and six kinds of kimchi. Check Twitter or the interwebs for the truck's weekday lunch and dinner locations.

The city's most famous cart is **53rd and Sixth** (**www.53rdand6th. com**), named for the Midtown corner it holds down from 7pm until 5am. Tourists are regularly flummoxed by the length of the line (to say nothing of its 2,500-plus Yelp reviews), but it's no mystery to the regulars—the $6 platters and $4 sandwiches here combine flavorful chicken and a legendary white sauce with a recipe guarded more tightly than Fort Knox. (The daytime "imposter" cart on the same corner has become almost as good as the original.)

You can make a great ethnic eating adventure by touring Midtown carts, or head for Latin America via Brooklyn's **Red Hook Food Vendors** ★ (**www.redhookfoodvendors.com**). For decades, the local Latino population has been playing soccer at Red Hook park, and trucks have parked nearby to provide sustenance to players and fans (the season runs weekends May–Oct, 9am–9pm). My favorite truck (and I'm not alone, to judge by the line) is **Country Boys,** aka the Martinez Taco Truck, parked near the corner of Bay and Clinton streets. Homemade masa dough is the key to killer Pueblan-style huaraches ($6 for a huge one), and superfresh quesadillas and tacos are safe bets, too. If you want to taste the top prize winner at the 2009 Vendys, this is your truck. (Nearby **Solber Pupusas** took home the Vendy cup in 2011; one taste of their Salvadoran corn patties and you'll know why.)

Dojo *HEALTH/JAPANESE* As any NYU student will tell you, the cheapest sit-down meals can be found at Dojo. The menu is Japanese-inspired, but the restaurant serves a full array of healthy-ish food for reasonable fees. A soy burger goes for $4.25, salads start at $5.95, and a big plate of veggie don noodles is $5.95. Try the Japanese homemade ginger ale ($2)!

14 W. 4th St., btw. Broadway and Mercer St. ✆ **212/505-8934.** Mon–Thurs and Sun 11am–midnight; Fri–Sat 11am–1am. Subway: B/D/F/M to Broadway/Lafayette St.; 6 to Bleecker St.

Joe's *PIZZA* In the art of laying out consistently fresh slices, Joe's has it down (as it has since 1975). Village tourists, locals, and drunkards alike are drawn to the $2.75 beauties here, turned out piping hot from the gas-fired oven. Tangy sauce and thick cheese complement the character in the crust.

7 Carmine St., btw. Sixth Ave. and Bleecker St. ℭ **212/366-1182.** www.joespizzanyc. com. Daily 9am–5am. Subway: A/B/C/D/E/F/M to W. 4th St./Washington Sq.

Mamoun's *MIDDLE EASTERN/FALAFEL* This NYU favorite opened in 1971 and they've been so busy serving up Middle Eastern delicacies that they haven't had the chance to revise their prices much. At $2.50, the falafel sandwich is one of the city's best buys. The balls are small, dense, and packed with nutty flavor. Other veggie pitas, like the baba ghanouj, are also $2.50. The chicken kabob, a mix of savory, seared meat and lightly sweet tahini, is a highlight of the $5.50 meat sandwiches. Several competitors have hung their shingles on the block, but Mamoun's is still the best. Seating is limited; in nice weather Washington Square Park serves as Mamoun's back garden.

119 MacDougal St., btw. Minetta Lane and W. 3rd St. ℭ **212/674-8685.** www. mamouns.com. Daily 11am–5am. Subway: A/B/C/D/E/F/M to W. 4th St./Washington Sq. Other location: *East Village,* 22 St. Marks Place, btw. Second and Third aves. ℭ **212/387-7747.** Subway: 6 to Astor Place; N/R to 8th St.

Percy's Pizza *PIZZA* The advent of the 99¢ slice has been a boon for cheapskate dining in New York. Unfortunately, it's pretty clear how much you've invested at most cheap 'za shops. Not so Percy's, where a gas-fired grill knocks out pies that approach artisanal. A medium-thick crust is crispy on the bottom, supporting a slightly tangy sauce and a judicious cover of cheese. It's just a buck a slice, with fresh toppings like pepperoni just 50¢ more.

190 Bleecker St., btw. MacDougal St. and Sixth Ave. Sun–Thurs 11am–11pm; Fri–Sat 11am–5am. Subway: 1 to Houston St.; C/E to Spring St.; A/B/C/D/E/F/M to W. 4th St./ Washington Sq.

Taim *ISRAELI/FALAFEL* Though Taim takes a gourmet approach to its Middle Eastern cooking, it's barely reflected in the prices. Falafel is the specialty, balled into small, taut bites. The options include green, with mint, parsley, and cilantro; roasted red pepper; and *harissa,* a Tunisian version spiced up with paprika and garlic. A sandwich is $6.25 and comes with tahini and homemade hummus. Everything is

made fresh, justifying this carryout's name (Hebrew for "delicious").
FINE PRINT Seating is limited.

222 Waverly Place, btw. Perry and W. 11th sts. ℂ **212/691-1287.** www.taimfalafel.
com. Daily 11am–10pm. Subway: 1/2/3 to 14th St.

7 Chelsea/Union Square

Big Booty Bread Co. *BAKERY* All risk to expanding posteriors aside,
the $1.75 "cheese rock" is worthy of obsession. Like a dinner roll of
Olympian aspirations, the rock is taut on the outside, protecting a
savory, Latin-tinged *queso blanco* and yucca flour interior. Oven-
baked empanadas are huge and flavorful. Cupcake fans can gorge on
red velvet and *dulce de leche* cupcakes.

261 W. 23rd St., btw. Seventh and Eighth aves. ℂ **212/414-3056.** www.bigbooty
breadco.com. Mon–Fri 8am–8pm; Sat 8am–6pm. Subway: C/E or 1 to 23rd St.

Grand Sichuan International *CHINESE* Don't be fooled by the
average decor or below-average prices—this place serves the best
Chinese food in the city. The menu is large, but it's hard to make a
bad pick. Orange beef, sautéed string beans, and General Tso's
chicken are three common dishes that get reworked into Szechuan
gems. You can splurge on items such as the $16.95 smoked tea duck,
but if you limit your ordering to the many under-$10 entrees you
won't be disappointed. The soup dumplings ($5.75–$6.75) are legendary, and I am obsessed with the *dan dan* noodles ($4.50). Lunches
are not heavily attended, despite the $5.95 specials. At dinner, arrive
early or patient. FINE PRINT The other locations are good, but only St.
Marks brings the same magic as Chelsea.

229 Ninth Ave., at 24th St. ℂ **212/620-5200.** www.thegrandsichuan.com. Daily 11:30am–
11pm. Subway: C/E to 23rd St. Other locations: *East Village,* 19–23 St. Marks Place, btw.
Second and Third aves. ℂ **212/529-4800.** Subway: 6 to Astor Place; N/R to 8th St. *West
Village,* 15 Seventh Ave. S., btw. Carmine and Leroy sts. ℂ **212/645-0222.** Subway: 1 to
Houston St. *Midtown East,* 1049 Second Ave., btw. 55th and 56th sts. ℂ **212/355-5855.**
Subway: E/M to Lexington Ave./53rd St.; 4/5/6 to Lexington Ave./59th St. *Midtown West,*
368 W. 46th St., btw. Eighth and Ninth aves. ℂ **212/969-9001.** Subway: A/C/E/7 to 42nd
St./Port Authority. *Chinatown,* 125 Canal St., at Chrystie St. ℂ **212/625-9212.** Subway:
B/D to Grand St. *Bay Ridge, Brooklyn,* 8701 Fifth Ave., btw. 87th and 88th sts. ℂ **718/
680-8887.** Subway: R to 86th St. *Flushing, Queens,* 42–47 Main St., btw. Franklin and Blos-
som aves. ℂ **718/888-0553.** Subway: 7 to Main St./Flushing.

Hot Dog Days

Papayas and hot dogs aren't an intuitive combination, but the city hosts a heated rivalry over the best fruit and meat combos. Skeptics may argue that the difference between any two tube steaks is academic, but connoisseurs can parse subtle distinctions in density, texture, and taste. **Papaya King** was the original, but time has not been kind to this chain. Knockoff **Papaya Dog** holds down the middle of the pack, leaving **Gray's Papaya** as New York's top dog. The meat is flavorful, finished with a light char, and kept fresh thanks to quickly moving queues. Long live the recession—as long as Gray's continues to offer their Recession Special (two hot dogs and a drink for $4.95). FINE PRINT Standing room only here. 2090 Broadway, at 72nd St. ℂ **212/799-0243.** Daily 24 hr. Subway: 1/2/3 to 72nd St. Other location: *West Village*, 402 Sixth Ave., at 8th St. ℂ **212/260-3532.** Subway: A/B/C/D/E/F/M to W. 4th St./Washington Sq.

Kofoo *KOREAN* Where students congregate, cheap food follows. An F.I.T. clientele flocks to Kofoo, for a wide selection of Korean delights. *Kim bop,* Korean sushi, comes in 10 varieties, for $5.25 to $6.95. Korean rice classics including *bibim bop* and *jap chae* are $8 each. Fresh, crisp kimchi stands out. FINE PRINT There are just a couple of seats; most business is takeout.

334 Eighth Ave., btw. 26th and 27th sts. ℂ **212/675-5277.** Mon–Sat 11am–10pm. Subway: C/E to 23rd St.

La Taza de Oro *PUERTO RICAN* The daily specials at this classic greasy spoon make it easy to fill up. My favorites are *bacalao* (stewed codfish), *ropa vieja* ("old clothes"—a stew made with shredded beef), and *mofongo* (mashed fried plantains), which range from $6 to $8.50 and include knock-out rice and beans.

96 Eighth Ave., btw. 14th and 15th sts. ℂ212/243-9946. Mon–Sat 6am–10:30pm. Subway: A/C/E to 14th St.; L to Eighth Ave.

Maoz *FALAFEL* I've never understood how a little ball of shredded chickpea can come out tasting so meaty and delicious. Somehow falafel satisfies in a way other vegetables can't. (The deep-frying probably doesn't hurt.) Maoz makes some of the best falafel in town, and they'll let you customize your sandwich with toppings from their extensive salad bar. A sandwich, three toppings, and two sauces costs $5.25. Meal deals, which go over well will the local worker bees, are $7.75 to $9.95.

38 Union Sq. E., btw. 16th and 17th sts. *✆* **212/260-1988.** www.maozusa.com. Mon–Thurs 11am–11pm; Fri–Sat 11am–midnight; Sun 11am–10pm. Subway: L/N/Q/R/4/5/6 to 14th St./Union Sq. Other locations: *West Village,* 59 E. 8th St., btw. Broadway and University Place. *✆* **212/420-5999.** Subway: N/R to 8th St.; 6 to Astor Place. *Midtown West,* 558 Seventh Ave., at 40th St. *✆* **212/777-0820.** Subway: 1/2/3/7/N/Q/R/S to 42nd St./Times Sq. *Midtown West,* 683 Eighth Ave., btw. 43rd and 44th sts. *✆* **212/265-2315.** Subway: A/C/E/7 to Port Authority. *Upper West Side,* 2047 Broadway, btw. 70th and 71st sts. *✆* **212/362-2622.** Subway: 1/2/3 to 72nd St. *Upper West Side,* 2857 Broadway, btw. 110th and 111th sts. *✆* **212/222-6464.** Subway: 1 to 110th St.

Tebaya *CHICKEN WINGS*   All the way from Nagoya, Japan, comes this recipe for extraordinary chicken. I had no idea wings could taste this good. City of Buffalo, hang your head! The chicken is double fried to burn off the fat, and then basted in a savory garlic sauce. Ten pieces are $8.69. For your next Super Bowl party, volume discounts bring the price of each wing as low as 78¢. Japanese fast food items like teriyaki chicken sandwiches and fried potato cakes fill the rest of the menu. FINE PRINT Seating is limited.

144 W. 19th St., btw. Sixth and Seventh aves. *✆* **212/924-3335.** www.goojapan.com/newyork/index.html. Mon–Thurs 11:30am–10pm; Fri 11:30am–11pm; Sat noon–11pm; Sun noon–8:30pm. Subway: 1 to 18th St.

8 Midtown East

Bhojan *INDIAN*   When it comes to Indian, the East Village's Curry Row lags miles behind Midtown's Curry Hill. One of the best spots in the neighborhood is one of the newest, an elegant all-vegetarian paradise that highlights the cuisine of Gujarat and Punjab. "Thali" platters allow you to sample a range of delicacies, and they're just $9 for weekday lunches.

102 Lexington Ave., near 27th St. *✆* **212/213-9615.** www.bhojanny.com. Mon–Thurs 11:30am–10:30pm; Fri–Sat 11:30am–11pm; Sun 11:30am–10pm. Subway: 6 to 28th St.

Chennai Garden *INDIAN*   Vegetarians can relax in this Indian legend, as the long list of *dosai, utthappam,* and curries here doesn't contain a scrap of meat. Most entrees are under $10, and portions are substantial. Despite the prices, vibrant pink walls under subdued lighting make for a date-suitable atmosphere.

129 E. 27th St., btw. Park and Lexington aves. *✆* **212/689-1999.** www.orderchennaigarden.com. Mon–Fri 11:30am–3pm and 5–10pm; Sat–Sun noon–10pm. Subway: 6 to 28th St.

CHEAP EATS MIDTOWN

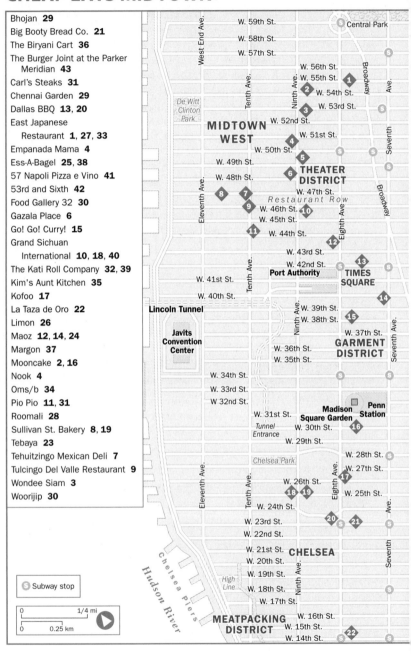

Bhojan **29**
Big Booty Bread Co. **21**
The Biryani Cart **36**
The Burger Joint at the Parker
    Meridian **43**
Carl's Steaks **31**
Chennai Garden **29**
Dallas BBQ **13, 20**
East Japanese
    Restaurant **1, 27, 33**
Empanada Mama **4**
Ess-A-Bagel **25, 38**
57 Napoli Pizza e Vino **41**
53rd and Sixth **42**
Food Gallery 32 **30**
Gazala Place **6**
Go! Go! Curry! **15**
Grand Sichuan
    International **10, 18, 40**
The Kati Roll Company **32, 39**
Kim's Aunt Kitchen **35**
Kofoo **17**
La Taza de Oro **22**
Limon **26**
Maoz **12, 14, 24**
Margon **37**
Mooncake **2, 16**
Nook **4**
Oms/b **34**
Pio Pio **11, 31**
Roomali **28**
Sullivan St. Bakery **8, 19**
Tebaya **23**
Tehuitzingo Mexican Deli **7**
Tulcingo Del Valle Restaurant **9**
Wondee Siam **3**
Woorijip **30**

Ⓢ Subway stop

0   1/4 mi
0   0.25 km

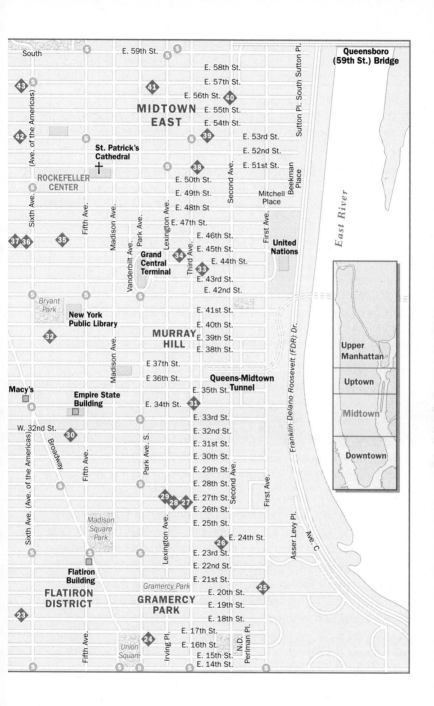

Ess-A-Bagel *BAGELS* The huge bagels here won't win any points with purists, but they make an already good deal even better at $1, or $2.75 with a huge helping of cream cheese. The bustling full-service shop has several tables for your savoring pleasure.

831 Third Ave., btw. 50th and 51st sts. ✆ **212/980-1010.** Mon–Fri 6am–9pm; Sat–Sun 6am–5pm. Subway: 6 to 51st St. Other location: *Gramercy,* 359 First Ave., at 21st St. ✆ **212/260-2252.** Subway: 6 to 23rd St.

57 Napoli Pizza e Vino *ITALIAN* I am a groupie for *pizzaiolo* Salvatore Olivella, having followed his classic Neapolitan pies from L'Asso to no. 28 to his latest wood-burning oven on 57th Street. Top-quality ingredients make for stellar pizzas, with tangy sauce topping well-structured, lightly singed crusts. Just $20 or so gets you a skateboard-shaped pizza that'll be hard for three people to finish. Take advantage of a rare slot of affordability on one of the city's toniest blocks, made possible only by the eccentric location, up a flight of stairs from C'est Bon Café.

120 E. 57th St., btw. Park and Lexington aves. ✆ **212/750-4586.** www.57napoli.com. Mon–Thurs 11am–11pm; Fri 11am–midnight; Sat 10am–midnight; Sun 10am–11pm. Subway: 4/5/6 or N/Q/R to 59th St./Lexington Ave.; E/M to 53rd St./Lexington Ave.

Oms/b *JAPANESE* This little shop frequented by Japanese expats puts rice balls together with whimsy and creativity. Strong flavors like burdock, wasabi shrimp, and plum are on offer, executed with artistic flair. More snacks than meals, balls start at only $1.50 apiece, with set menus starting at $7.25.

156 E. 45th St., btw. Third and Lexington aves. ✆ **212/922-9788.** www.riceball-omsb. com. Mon–Fri 8am–7:30pm; Sat 11:30am–5pm. Subway: 4/5/6/S to 42nd St./Grand Central.

Roomali *INDIAN* The *roti* here (an Indian pancake, give or take) is homemade daily, making a fresh foundation for a series of flavor-packed *kati* rolls. My favorite is the *achari* chicken, which is spicy and tangy and a deal at $6 (two for $11). *Aloo chana paneer* rolls, made with potatoes, chickpeas, and cheese are a great $5.50 option for vegetarians (two for $10). This Curry Hill shop does mostly takeout, but the small dining space is low-lit and pleasant.

97 Lexington Ave., at 27th St. ✆ **212/679-8900.** www.roomaliny.com. Daily noon–10pm. Subway: 6 to 28th St.

9 Midtown West

The Burger Joint at the Parker Meridian *BURGERS* One of the city's best burgers hides behind curtains inside the lobby of a fancy Midtown hotel. The Burger Joint is as unpretentious and inexpensive as its name, and the burger is a delicious instant classic, juicy and not too greasy. Buy one for $7, add 50¢ for cheese. ⌊FINE PRINT⌋ Though the entrance is hidden (look for the neon arrow by the check-in desk), the local business folk and tourist trade have discovered the place, and it's mobbed at lunch.

118 W. 57th St., btw. Sixth and Seventh aves. ✆ **212/245-5000.** www.parkermeridien. com/eat4.php. Sun–Thurs 11am–11:30pm; Fri–Sat 11am–midnight. Subway: N/Q/R or F to 57th St.

Empanada Mama *LATINO* This Queens transplant is a patty pro, offering up over two dozen takes on this humble Latin pocket. I prefer the tried and true to exotics like the Polish (kielbasa and sauerkraut) or the Elvis (peanut butter and bananas). Wheat-wrapped rascals hover around $2.50, and triangular corn flour versions are $2.40. Beef in the latter form is a "can't miss." A pleasant, colorful shop rounds out the experience, available 24/7.

763 Ninth Ave., btw. 51st and 52nd sts. ✆ **212/698-9008.** www.empmamanyc.com. Daily 24 hr. Subway: C/E to 50th St.

Food Gallery 32 *ASIAN* Koreatown's main drag already feels like a place you'd need a passport to get to, but this central food court takes the international effect up a notch. A clean, ultramodern interior welcomes you in for an array of Korean, Japanese, and Taiwanese delights. **Korea House** on the back left has generous bowls of *bibimbop* starting at $9. **Noodle 32** on the right serves up fresh pastas, starting with a $5.50 ramen. There's seating on three floors, with pagers to let you know when your order is ready.

11 W. 32nd St., btw. Broadway and Fifth Ave. ✆ **212/967-1678.** Daily 11am–midnight. Subway: B/D/F/M/N/Q/R to 34th St./Herald Sq.

Go! Go! Curry! *JAPANESE* You won't find a rainbow selection of curries here: This Japanese staple is a single brown gravy with a blend of sweet, spicy, and savory. Chicken or pork are optimal accompaniments, lightly breaded and sided with rice and shredded cabbage. Good-size "walk" portions are $7, and if the date has a *5* in it, you can add a topping like red pickle or egg for free.

273 W. 38th St., btw. Seventh and Eighth aves. ⓒ **212/730-5555.** www.gogocurry usa-ny.com. Daily 10:55am–9:55pm. Subway: A/C/E to 34th St./Penn Station. Other location: *West Village,* 231 Thompson St., btw. W. 3rd and Bleecker sts. ⓒ **212/505-2555.** Subway: A/B/C/D/E/F/M to W. 4th St./Washington Sq.

The Kati Roll Company *INDIAN* These aren't your bland Midtown deli wraps. Here, flaky, flavorful paratha bread envelops grilled meat and veggies that pop with exotic spicing. On the downside, the rolls ($3.50–$6.75) fall somewhere between snack and meal (but there's a discount when you buy two). Bollywood posters amplify the authenticity of a small, well-used space.

49 W. 39th St., btw. Fifth and Sixth aves. ⓒ **212/730-4280.** www.thekatirollcompany. com. Mon–Thurs 11am–11pm; Fri 11am–5am; Sat noon–5am; Sun noon–9pm. Subway: B/D/F/M to 42nd St.; 7 to Fifth Ave. Other locations: *West Village,* 99 MacDougal St., btw. Bleecker and W. 3rd sts. ⓒ **212/420-6517.** Subway: A/B/C/D/E/F/M to W. 4th St./Washington Sq.; 1 to Houston St. *Midtown East,* 229 E. 53rd St., btw. Second and Third aves. ⓒ **212/888-1700.** Subway: 6 to 51st St.; E/M to 53rd St./Lexington Ave.

Margon *CUBAN* This diner's delicious Caribbean fare, low prices, and location keep it packed with Midtown lunchers. Order a Cuban sandwich ($6.75), or choose from steam-table selections in the middle and to-go from the line in back. Chicken entrees are top sellers, served with rice and beans and just $8.75 for a plate.

136 W. 46th St., btw. Sixth and Seventh aves. ⓒ **212/354-5013.** https://margon restaurant.rapidorders.com. Mon–Fri 6am–4:45pm; Sat 7am–2:30pm. Subway: B/D/F/M to 47th–50th sts.–Rockefeller Center; N/Q/R to 49th St.

Pio Pio *PERUVIAN* The small corporate front desk here gives no indication of the cavernous bi-level dining room in back, finished in rustic wood and an intricate thatch of branches. Pio Pio has come a long way from its humble Queens storefront beginnings, but it still leans on its original specialty: golden rotisserie chicken marinated in Peruvian beer and a secret blend of spices. A whole chicken is just $16, or add avocado, rice, beans, and french fries with hot dogs (!) for a $36 Matador Combo feast, which is enough to put three people in a food coma. FINE PRINT This is a date-worthy spot for pretheater fuel-ups, although note that the rest of the menu is considerably pricier than the chicken specials.

604 Tenth Ave., btw. 43rd and 44th sts. ⓒ **212/459-2929.** www.piopionyc.com. Sun–Thurs 11am–11pm; Fri–Sat 11am–midnight. Subway: A/C/E/7 to Port Authority. Other locations: *Upper East Side,* 1746 First Ave., btw. 90th and 91st sts.

📞 **212/426-5800.** Subway: 4/5/6 to 86th St. *Upper West Side,* 702 Amsterdam Ave., at 94th St. 📞 **212/665-3000.** Subway: 1/2/3 to 96th St. *Midtown East,* 210 E. 34th St., btw. Second and Third aves. 📞 **212/481-0034.** Subway: 6 to 33rd St. Also 3 locations in Queens, and 1 in the Bronx.

Sullivan St. Bakery *BAKERY*   One of the best pizzas in town is the *bianca* at this upscale bakery. The bread is fluffy and lightly seasoned with rosemary, olive oil, and a little salt. It's an Old Country slice—rectangular instead of triangular and lacking red sauce—and it's served at an old economy price. Just $2.50 gets you a doughy length 4½ inches long.

533 W. 47th St., btw. Tenth and Eleventh aves. 📞 **212/265-5580.** www.sullivanstreet bakery.com. Mon–Sat 7:30am–7pm; Sun 7:30am–4pm. Subway: C/E to 50th St. Other location: *Chelsea,* 236 Ninth Ave., btw. 24th and 25th sts. 📞 **212/929-5900.** Subway: C/E to 23rd St.

Tehuitzingo Mexican Deli *MEXICAN*   A ramshackle counter area that could be a rest stop on a Mexican highway is the setting for this clandestine *taquería.* Über-authentic tacos are $2.50, generously piled with meat, from juicy pork *carnitas* to slow-cooked *lengua* to succulent chicken. Even better are the Mexican sandwiches, *tortas,* which are $6 meals unto themselves. The deli refrigerators stock Mexican beers, for refreshment on the side.

695 Tenth Ave., btw. 47th and 48th sts. 📞 **212/397-5956.** Daily 8am–11:30pm. Subway: C/E to 50th St.

Tulcingo Del Valle Restaurant *MEXICAN*   This mom-and-pop spot is as authentic as Tehuitzingo (see above), but with a sit-down scene. The specials board (mostly under $10) lists fresh-made entree platters, like chicken in a green pumpkinseed sauce. *Chilaquiles,* fried tortillas in red or green salsa, are a very tasty $6.95. I'm a fan of the tacos, especially the *carne asada,* at $2.75 a pop.

655 Tenth Ave., btw. 46th and 47th sts. 📞 **212/262-5510.** www.tulcingorestaurant. com. Mon–Sat 8am–10pm; Sun 10am–10pm.

Woorijip *KOREAN*   Korean delis are ubiquitous in New York, but most serve up bland, mainstream cafeteria fare. To find real Korean dishes, the destination is 32nd Street in Midtown, where a delicious by-the-pound deli is hidden among pricier Korean restaurants. *Bulgogi,* squid, tofu, jellyfish, Korean pancakes, and, of course, kim-chi, can be found on the serve-yourself buffet line ($6.99 per pound).

You can also get snacks and meals, like filling *kimbap* veggie rolls for under $5, and a $1 spicy bean sprout soup.

12 W. 32nd St., btw. Broadway and Fifth Ave. ✆ **212/244-1115.** Daily 8am–3am. Subway: B/D/F/M/N/Q/R to 34th St./Herald Sq.

10 Upper West Side

Absolute Bagel *BAGELS*   The absolutely fabulous bagels here are a little too puffy to be traditional, but the extra air doesn't hinder the taste. For $1.95 you get a bagel loaded with cream cheese. Opt for butter and it's just $1.25. Don't let the lines deter you—that's a reflection of the quality, and the cheerful staff works fast.

2788 Broadway, btw. 107th and 108th sts. ✆ **212/932-2052.** Daily 6am–9pm. Subway: 1 to 110th St.

Big Nick's Burger Joint/Pizza Joint *AMERICAN/BURGERS*   When your menu serves every dish ever thought of, you're bound to have a few items that seem a little overpriced. For the most part, though, this Upper West Side joint has great values on big portions. The options are endless—with burgers alone, there are over three dozen choices. It's $6.75 for the Big Nick and $9.75 for the heart-unfriendly Hollandaise and Canadian bacon Benedict Burger.

2175 Broadway, at 77th St. ✆ **212/362-9238.** www.bignicksnyc.com. Daily 24 hr. Subway: 1 to 79th St.

Hummus Place *MIDDLE EASTERN*   New York is known for dinner menus packed with just about every dish and combination imagined by humanity. There's something nice, however, about a place that specializes in one thing, especially when they do it so damn well. Imported white tahini is the key ingredient to the rich hummus served here. For around $8 you can have your choice of three versions: plain, with fava bean stew and egg, or with whole chickpeas. The somewhat expanded menu also offers *shakshuka,* a hearty Israeli tomato stew ($8.95) and falafel ($3.95).

305 Amsterdam Ave., btw. 74th and 75th sts. ✆ **212/799-3335.** www.hummusplace. com. Daily 10:30am–midnight. Subway: 1/2/3 to 72nd St. Other locations: *East Village,* 109 St. Marks Place, btw. First Ave. and Ave. A. ✆ **212/529-9198.** Subway: L to First Ave. *West Village,* 71 Seventh Ave. S., btw. Bleecker and Commerce sts. ✆ **212/924-2022.** Subway: 1 to Christopher St.; A/B/C/D/E/F/M to W. 4th St./Washington Sq. *Upper West Side,* 2608 Broadway, btw. 98th and 99th sts. ✆ **212/222-1554.** Subway: 1/2/3 to 96th St.

Land Thai Kitchen *THAI*   Mercer Kitchen alum David Bank presents the flavors of his native Bangkok inside the brick, tin, and mesh confines of this Uptown charmer. Seared mains from the wok top out at $13, while noodle dishes hover in the $11 to $12 range. The prix-fixe lunch, which includes papaya salad and basil and beef, proffers two courses for $9. FINE PRINT Small place plus rabid popularity equals potentially long waits (the Upper East Side spinoff takes reservations).

450 Amsterdam Ave., btw. 81st and 82nd sts. © **212/501-8121.** www.landthai kitchen.com. Mon–Thurs noon–10:30pm; Fri–Sat noon–11pm; Sun noon–10pm. Subway: 1 to 79th St.; B/C to 81st St. Other location: *Upper East Side,* 1565 Second Ave., btw. 81st and 82nd sts. © **212/439-1847.** Subway: 4/5/6 to 86th St.

Noche Mexicana *MEXICAN*   Authentic Mexican food was long a void in the New York gastronomic scene, but mom-and-pop places like Noche are rapidly raising standards. Choose a savory red or green salsa to top your enchilada platter ($10), or opt for a triple order of tamales ($8) or corn-tortilla chicken *chilaquiles* ($9). Tacos are excellent ($2.75 for most) and the wine is cheap, too.

842 Amsterdam Ave., at 101st St. © **212/662-6900.** www.noche-mexicana.com. Sun–Thurs 10am–11pm; Fri–Sat 10am–midnight. Subway: 1 to 103rd St.

Roti Roll Bombay Frankie *INDIAN*   A grill annexed to a bar and that's open until the wee hours, this place is a convenient spot to get your fortification during an UWS debauch. The specialty is *roti,* chewy wraps packed up with spicy fillings, approximating an Indian burrito. Egg ($3 each) and spiced potato with pea ($3.50 each) occupy the low end, working up to shrimp with sour cream and fenugreek ($7). Buy two and get a discount ($5 for the cheapest). And it's not just for a night out—it works equally well for lunch.

994 Amsterdam Ave., btw. 109th and 110th sts. © **212/666-1500.** Sun–Mon 11am–2am; Tues–Wed 11am–3am; Thurs–Sat 11am–4am. Subway: 1 to 110th St.

Sal's & Carmine's Pizza *PIZZA*   At your first taste of the pizza here, you will realize what your previous 10,000 New York slices were supposed to taste like. Creamy mozzarella syncs with a tangy sauce and crispy crust to achieve perfection. Although Sal has passed on, Carmine or a family member will be on hand to ensure both quality control and a curmudgeonly atmosphere. Each pie is a work of art and cannot be expected to endure a ride in a cardboard box: No delivery here. A regular slice is $3; add a buck for toppings.

CHEAP EATS UPTOWN

Absolute Bagel **1**
Big Nick's Burger Joint/Pizza Joint **9**
Choux Factory **19**
Dallas BBQ **12**, **15**
Delizia 73 Ristorante & Pizza **16**
East Japanese Restaurant **13**
Gray's Papaya **10**
Hummus Place **2**, **6**
Land Thai Kitchen **8**, **17**
Maoz **1**, **11**
Noche Mexicana **5**
Pio Pio **7**, **20**
Roti Roll Bombay Frankie **3**
Sal's & Carmine's Pizza **4**
Wa Jeal **18**
Yvonne Yvonne Jamaican Food Truck **14**

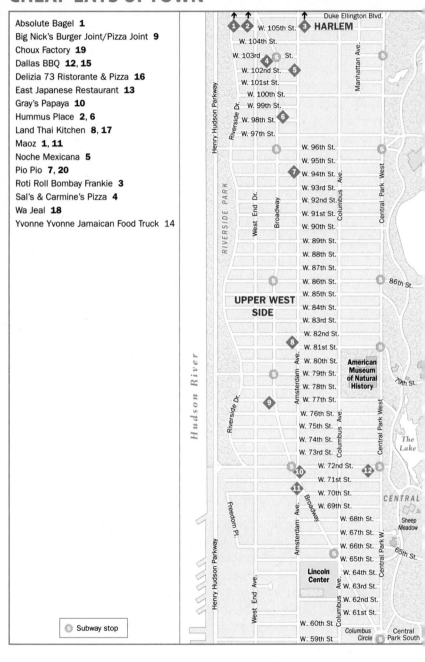

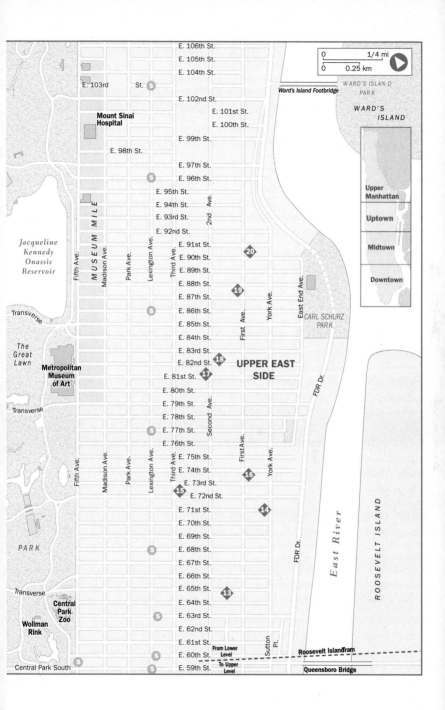

E. 106th St.
E. 105th St.
E. 104th St.
E. 103rd St. Ⓢ
E. 102nd St.
E. 101st St.
E. 100th St.
E. 99th St.
E. 98th St.
E. 97th St.
Ⓢ E. 96th St.
E. 95th St.
E. 94th St.
E. 93rd St.
E. 92nd St.
E. 91st St.
E. 90th St.
E. 89th St.
E. 88th St.
E. 87th St.
Ⓢ E. 86th St.
E. 85th St.
E. 84th St.
E. 83rd St.
E. 82nd St.
E. 81st St.
E. 80th St.
E. 79th St.
E. 78th St.
Ⓢ E. 77th St.
E. 76th St.
E. 75th St.
E. 74th St.
E. 73rd St.
E. 72nd St.
E. 71st St.
E. 70th St.
E. 69th St.
Ⓢ E. 68th St.
E. 67th St.
E. 66th St.
E. 65th St.
E. 64th St.
Ⓢ E. 63rd St.
E. 62nd St.
E. 61st St.
Ⓢ E. 60th St.
Ⓢ E. 59th St.

0   1/4 mi
0   0.25 km

WARD'S ISLAND PARK
Ward's Island Footbridge
WARD'S ISLAND

Upper Manhattan
Uptown
Midtown
Downtown

Mount Sinai Hospital

Jacqueline Kennedy Onassis Reservoir

MUSEUM MILE

Fifth Ave.
Madison Ave.
Park Ave.
Lexington Ave.
Third Ave.
2nd Ave.
Second Ave.
First Ave.
York Ave.
East End Ave.

Transverse

The Great Lawn

Metropolitan Museum of Art

Transverse

UPPER EAST SIDE

CARL SCHURZ PARK

FDR Dr.

East River

ROOSEVELT ISLAND

PARK

Transverse

Central Park Zoo

Wollman Rink

Central Park South

FDR Dr.

Sutton Pl.

From Lower Level
To Upper Level

Roosevelt IslandTram
Queensboro Bridge

⑳
⑲
⑱
⑰
⑯
⑮
⑭
⑬

77

2671 Broadway, btw. 101st and 102nd sts. ✆ **212/663-7651.** www.salandcarmine. com. Daily 11:30am–10pm. Subway: 1 to 103rd St.

11 Upper East Side

Dallas BBQ *BARBECUE* This local chain won't win any prizes for authenticity, but they do a decent take on comfort food. Ribs, pulled pork, and beef brisket highlight the menu, served in ample portions. For cheapskates, the early bird special is not to be missed—two full meals for $12.99. You'll get double soups, double servings of rotisserie chicken, cornbread, and potatoes or rice. It's as filling as New York gets for less than $6.50 a person. FINE PRINT The special varies from location to location, but generally it's available weekdays from 11am to noon, and again from 2 to 5pm; weekends 11am to 4pm; not available on holidays. Dine-in only.

1265 Third Ave., at 73rd St. ✆ **212/772-9393.** www.dallasbbq.com. Sun–Thurs 11am–midnight; Fri–Sat 11am–1am. Subway: 6 to 77th St. Other locations: *Chelsea,* 261 Eighth Ave., at 23rd St. ✆ **212/462-0001.** Subway: C/E to 23rd St. *Upper West Side,* 27 W. 72nd St., btw. Central Park W. and Columbus Ave. ✆ **212/873-2004.** Subway: B/C to 72nd St. *Washington Heights,* 3956 Broadway, at 166th St. ✆ **212/568-3700.** Subway: A/C/1 to 168th St. *East Village,* 132 Second Ave., at St. Marks Place. ✆ **212/777-5574.** Subway: 6 to Astor Place. *Times Square,* 241 W. 42nd St., btw. Seventh and Eighth aves. ✆ **212/221-9000.** Subway: 1/2/3/7/N/Q/R/S to 42nd St./Times Sq.; A/C/E to 42nd St./Port Authority. *The Bronx:* 281 W. Fordham Rd., at Cedar Ave. ✆ **718/220-2822.** Subway: 4 to Fordham Rd. *Brooklyn:* 180 Livingston St. ✆ **718/643-5700.** Subway: A/C/F/R to Jay St./Metro Tech; 2/3 to Hoyt St. *Queens:* 61-35 Junction Blvd., near 62nd Dr., at Rego Center. ✆ **718/592-9000.** Subway: M/R to 63rd Dr.-Rego Park.

East Japanese Restaurant *JAPANESE* This sit-down minichain was a New York pioneer in *yakitori,* or grilled skewers. The prices are moderate to begin with, but hit them at the right time and they get even better. Discounts and hours vary by location, but you're looking at deep cuts in skewers, sushi, and sashimi. Both lunch and dinner see great deals. My favorite is 66th Street; the Gramercy outlet (it has a sushi conveyor belt) is in decline.

354 E. 66th St., btw. First and Second aves. ✆ **212/734-5270.** Mon–Thurs noon–2:30pm and 5–10pm; Fri noon–2:30pm and 5–10:30pm; Sat 5–10:30pm; Sun 5–10pm. Subway: 6 to 68th St.; F to 63rd St. Other locations: *Midtown East,* 210 E. 44th St., near

Third Ave. ℭ **212/687-5075.** Subway: 4/5/6/7/S to Grand Central. Other locations: *Gramercy,* 366 Third Ave., btw. 26th and 27th sts. ℭ **212/889-2326.** Subway: 6 to 28th St. *Midtown West,* 253 W. 55th St., btw. Broadway and Eighth Ave. ℭ **212/581-2240.** Subway: N/Q/R to 57th St.

Eat Like the Rich: Upper East Side Bargains

The Upper East Side is a true cheap-eats challenge. After all, this is the playground of blue bloods and old money. Fortunately, the last few years has seen an influx of 20-somethings, due to relatively decent rents (for Manhattan). To satisfy this thriftier subsection of the 10021 ZIP Code, a number of affordable options are staking a claim.

I'm a fan of the **Yvonne Yvonne Jamaican Food Truck** (71st St. and York Ave.), home of silky braised oxtail ($6.50), and a Thursday $7 special of stewed peas and pig tails.

The chicken roll ($4.69) at **Delizia 73 Ristorante & Pizza** (1374 First Ave.; ℭ **212/517-8888**) is a hybrid meal of chicken parmigiana wrapped in pizza dough. Sweet marinara (for dipping) completes the picture; ask for it well done.

Sorry, Chinatown: For the best spicy sesame noodles in the city, head uptown to **Wa Jeal** (1588 Second Ave.; ℭ **212/396-3339**). A deft hand with the chili oil on top of springy noodles that have heft, along with vinegar and crisp scallions, cleaves through a creamy coating of peanut and oil. The result ($5.95) is spicy, sweet, salty, and sour—the best of Szechuan. The room's pretty, in dark wood and cream accents, and service is solid, as long as you wrangle your server.

For dessert? Go to the **Choux Factory** (1685 First Ave.; ℭ **212/289-2023**), with its rich cream puffs at just $2 a pop.

—Zachary Feldman

New York's many parks include the popular High Line, a repurposed elevated rail line that's become one of the most popular destinations in the city.

EXPLORING
NEW YORK

When it comes to culture, New Yorkers have so many amazing options it's probably inevitable that we start taking our bounty for granted. We sometimes forget that many of the world's great treasures have found their way to our island and its surrounding boroughs. New York is in a constant state of transformation, but a lot of history has survived, too, in houses, churches, and museums. Foundations and galleries protect New York's cutting-edge reputation, putting on thousands of risk-taking avant-garde art shows every year. What's most amazing, given the out-of-control nature of New York rents, is how easy it is to access these jewels on the cheap. Many museums let the public in for free, and many more either have pay-what-you-wish days or evenings or admission prices that are "suggested contributions." If it all seems overwhelming, you can get a professional to guide you through the cultural landscape: New York has a bushel of free tours as well. Just remember to get out there and take advantage—nothing lasts forever.

1 Museum Peace

Museum prices in New York are working their way skyward, with admission inflation running higher than even our outrageous movie tickets. Fifteen bucks seems to be the going price for big institutions, although the Guggenheim has ratcheted entry up to $22, and the MoMA will set you back a scandalous $25. It's a good thing that New York's cultural waters run deep. Below you'll find the gamut of (a) places that never charge, (b) places that have select times when the museum is free, and (c) museums that only suggest their admission prices—even the Whitney, Guggenheim, and MoMA will let you in for next to nothing if you time it right. Go and revel in NYC's embarrassment of cut-rate cultural riches.

ALWAYS FREE

American Folk Art Museum FREE After a decade rubbing shoulders with the MoMA in Midtown, this museum has returned to its original digs. Early American decoration is on permanent view, augmented by rotating exhibitions. Among the amazing oddball autodidacts here you'll find the world's largest collection of Henry Darger's art. Check out the free tours at 1pm on Tuesdays and Thursdays. (There's free music, too, with guitar performances at 2pm on Wed, singer-songwriters on Fri at 5:30pm.)

2 Lincoln Sq., Columbus Ave., btw. 65th and 66th sts., across from Lincoln Center. ✆ **212/595-9533.** www.folkartmuseum.org. Tues–Sat noon–7:30pm; Sun noon–6pm. Subway: 1 to 66th St.

Art Students League of New York Gallery FREE This independent art school, founded in 1875, is a New York legend. A host of big names started out here, including Norman Rockwell and Georgia O'Keeffe, who left behind work in the League's permanent collection. The galleries on the second floor exhibit portions of that collection along with art by current students, members, and other contemporaries.

EXPLORING DOWNTOWN

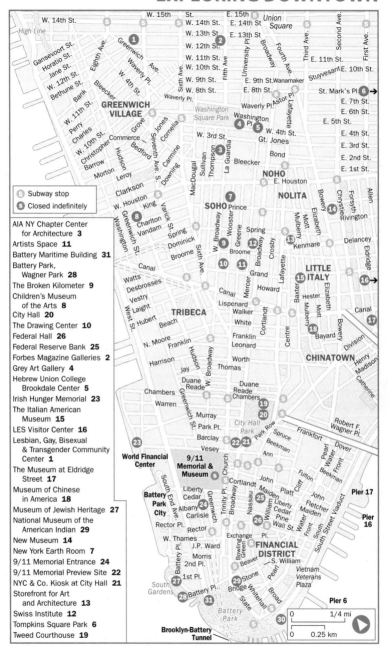

EXPLORING MIDTOWN

EXPLORING UPTOWN

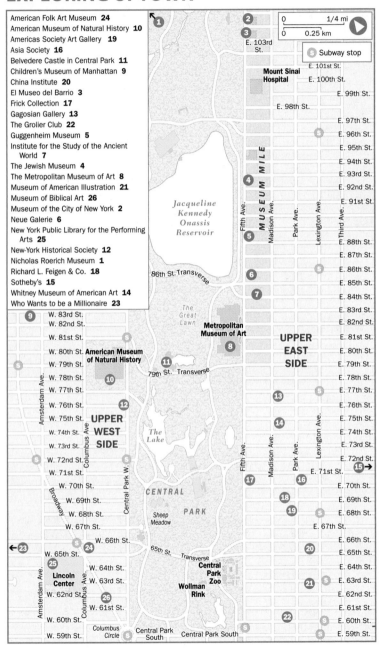

E. 103rd St.

Mount Sinai Hospital

E. 101st St.
E. 100th St.
E. 99th St.
E. 98th St.
E. 97th St.
E. 96th St.
E. 95th St.
E. 94th St.
E. 93rd St.
E. 92nd St.
E. 91st St.

Subway stop

0   1/4 mi
0   0.25 km

Jacqueline Kennedy Onassis Reservoir

MUSEUM MILE

Fifth Ave.
Madison Ave.
Park Ave.
Lexington Ave.
Third Ave.

E. 88th St.
E. 87th St.
86th St. Transverse
E. 86th St.
E. 85th St.
E. 84th St.
E. 83rd St.

The Great Lawn

Metropolitan Museum of Art

UPPER EAST SIDE

E. 82nd St.
E. 81st St.
E. 80th St.
E. 79th St.
E. 78th St.
E. 77th St.
E. 76th St.
E. 75th St.
E. 74th St.
E. 73rd St.
E. 72nd St.
E. 71st St.
E. 70th St.
E. 69th St.
E. 68th St.
E. 67th St.
E. 66th St.
E. 65th St.
E. 64th St.
E. 63rd St.
E. 62nd St.
E. 61st St.
E. 60th St.
E. 59th St.

W. 83rd St.
W. 82nd St.
W. 81st St.
W. 80th St. American Museum
of Natural History
W. 79th St.
W. 78th St.
W. 77th St.
W. 76th St.
W. 75th St.
W. 74th St.
W. 73rd St.
W. 72nd St.
W. 71st St.
W. 70th St.
W. 69th St.
W. 68th St.
W. 67th St.
W. 66th St.
W. 65th St.
W. 64th St.
W. 63rd St.
W. 62nd St.
W. 61st St.
W. 60th St.
W. 59th St.

79th St. Transverse

UPPER WEST SIDE

The Lake

Amsterdam Ave.
Columbus Ave.
Central Park W.
Broadway

CENTRAL PARK

Sheep Meadow

65th St. Transverse

Central Park Zoo
Wollman Rink

Lincoln Center

Columbus Circle
Central Park South
Central Park South

EXPLORING BROOKLYN

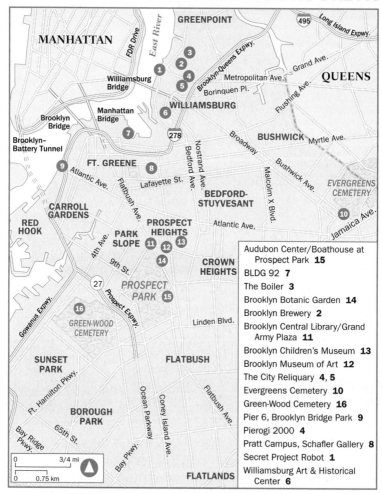

Audubon Center/Boathouse at Prospect Park **15**

BLDG 92 **7**

The Boiler **3**

Brooklyn Botanic Garden **14**

Brooklyn Brewery **2**

Brooklyn Central Library/Grand Army Plaza **11**

Brooklyn Children's Museum **13**

Brooklyn Museum of Art **12**

The City Reliquary **4, 5**

Evergreens Cemetery **10**

Green-Wood Cemetery **16**

Pier 6, Brooklyn Bridge Park **9**

Pierogi 2000 **4**

Pratt Campus, Schafler Gallery **8**

Secret Project Robot **1**

Williamsburg Art & Historical Center **6**

215 W. 57th St., btw. Broadway and Seventh Ave. ☎ **212/247-4510.** www.theart studentsleague.org. Mon–Fri 9am–8:30pm; Sat–Sun 9am–4:30pm (closed Sun Jan–Aug, closed at 3pm Sat Jan–May). Subway: N/Q/R to 57th St.; B/D/E to Seventh Ave.

Audubon Terrace   Broadway, between 155th and 156th streets, boasts a complex of educational and cultural institutions, housed around a central courtyard with an odd, oversize statue of El Cid. The sedate classical structures are completely unexpected in the middle of a colorful Harlem neighborhood, and few people make the trek this far north on the island.

EXPLORING QUEENS

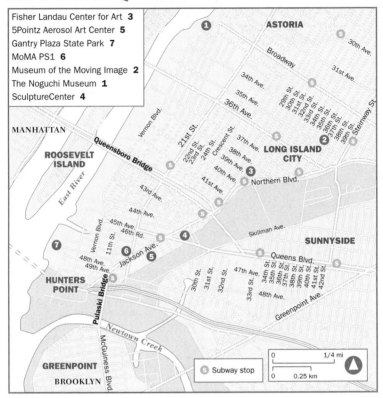

Fisher Landau Center for Art **3**
5Pointz Aerosol Art Center **5**
Gantry Plaza State Park **7**
MoMA PS1 **6**
Museum of the Moving Image **2**
The Noguchi Museum **1**
SculptureCenter **4**

As a result, Audubon Terrace has been hemorrhaging institutions at a rapid pace. All but the following two have flown south/downtown:

The Hispanic Society of America `FREE`   Hispanic treasures ranging from Bronze Age tools to Goya portraits, seemingly assembled at random, fill this intriguing, newly renovated museum. Free tours are offered every Saturday at 2pm. Don't miss the intricate marble chapel sculptures on the first floor and the gorgeous arabesque tiles upstairs.

Audubon Terrace, Broadway, btw. 155th and 156th sts. © **212/926-2234.** www. hispanicsociety.org. Tues–Sat 10am–4:30pm; Sun 1–4pm. Subway: 1 to 157th St.

American Academy of Arts and Letters `FREE`   This prestigious century-old organization extends membership to the cream of the nation's writers and artists. Exhibits in March and May highlight the works of these artists, as well as the recipients of Academy prizes.

Audubon Terrace, Broadway, btw. 155th and 156th sts. 🕿 **212/368-5900.** www.arts andletters.org. Open when exhibitions are up Thurs–Sun 1–4pm (closed Fri–Sun during holiday weekends). Subway: 1 to 157th St.

Austrian Cultural Forum `FREE`   The architecture of the Austrian Cultural Forum has garnered more eyebrows raised than critical praise. I find the exterior ominous, like a dagger looming over the street. The interior is more attractive, sleek, if somewhat cold. Austrian- and European-themed shows rotate through the five-level gallery, and there are regular film and music programs. `FINE PRINT` Events are free, but many require advance reservations.

11 E. 52nd St., btw. Fifth and Madison aves. 🕿 **212/319-5300.** www.acfny.org. Daily 10am–6pm. Subway: E/M to Fifth Ave./53rd St.

BLDG 92 `FREE`   The history of the Navy Yard is simultaneously the history of Brooklyn and America, giving this small museum unexpectedly broad appeal. A timeline in the main exhibit space walks you through the yard's highlights, spanning a century and a half of ironclads, steamships, and aircraft carriers. The structure itself is intriguing, a genteel 1858 Marine Commandant's residence with an environmentally friendly modern building artfully grafted onto it. On the fourth floor, find a pleasant terrace and gourmet canteen eats (artisanal grilled cheese, $5).

63 Flushing Ave., at Carlton Ave., Brooklyn. 🕿 **718/907-5992.** www.bldg92.org. Wed–Sun noon–6pm; select Mon holidays. Subway: A/C to High St./Brooklyn Bridge; F to York St.; G to Clinton-Washington aves. Also free weekend shuttle from Jay and Willloughby sts.

Bronx Museum of the Arts `FREE`   This hulk of modernity plunked amid the Art Deco restraint of the Grand Concourse puts on adventurous shows. Most of the artists exhibited here have logged time as Boogie Down residents. If not, they'll represent some aspect of New York's cultural diversity. In celebration of a 40th birthday, the museum recently dropped its suggested admission to become full-time free.

1040 Grand Concourse, at 165th St., the Bronx. 🕿 **718/681-6000.** www.bronx museum.org. Thurs and Sat–Sun 11am–6pm; Fri 11am–8pm. Subway: B/D/4 to 161st St./Yankee Stadium.

Carnegie Hall `FREE`   The Rose Museum recounts the practice, practice, practice it takes to get to this storied music hall. A chronology and memorabilia are on view, in addition to temporary exhibits on Carnegie legends such as the Gershwins, Maria Callas, and Leonard Bernstein.

154 W. 57th St., 2nd floor, btw. Sixth and Seventh aves. ✆ **212/903-9629.** www. carnegiehall.org. Daily 11am–4:30pm, and to Stern Auditorium and Perelman Stage ticket holders during evening concerts. Closed July 1–Sept 14. Subway: A/B/C/D/1 to 59th St.–Columbus Circle; N/Q/R to 57th St./Seventh Ave.

Center for Jewish History `FREE`   This multifloor center hosts several simultaneous exhibitions, from photo shows to manuscripts to paintings, most documenting Jewish contributions to American society. Artifacts are well lit, and exhibit notes are informative without running on too long. Pass through the metal detector and get a badge at the front desk. Everything is free except for the Yeshiva University Museum galleries, which are $8 (although they're free on Mon and Wed nights, and Fri middays).

15 W. 16th St., btw. Fifth and Sixth aves. ✆ **212/294-8301.** www.cjh.org. *Reading Room,* Mon 9:30am–7:30pm; Tues–Thurs 9:30am–5:30pm; Fri 9:30am–1:30pm; Sun 11am–4pm. *Genealogy Institute,* Mon 9:30am–7:30pm; Tues–Thurs 9:30am–5:30pm; Fri 9:30am–1:30pm; Sun 11am–4pm. *Yeshiva University Museum,* Mon 5–8pm (free after 5pm); Sun, Tues, and Thurs 11am–5pm; Wed 11am–8pm (free after 5pm); Fri 11am–2:30pm (free). *All other galleries,* Mon and Wed 9:30am–8pm; Tues and Thurs 9:30am–5pm; Fri 9:30am–3pm; Sun 11am–5pm. Subway: L/N/Q/R/4/5/6 to 14th St./ Union Sq.; F/M to 14th St.; L to Sixth Ave.

The Chancellor Robert R. Livingston Masonic Library of Grand Lodge `FREE`   The museum front room of the Masons' library is adorned with several display cases. Most artifacts are of limited interest to non-Masons, although there is a grandfather clock that watched over George Washington's visits to a Yorktown, Virginia, lodge. More interesting are the tours of the larger building, which show off colorful, immaculate meeting rooms and a ballroom whose design was lifted for the *Titanic.* No appointment is necessary; a greeter will meet you by the rear elevators.

71 W. 23rd St. (rear elevators to the 14th floor), btw. Fifth and Sixth aves. ✆ **212/337-6620.** www.nymasoniclibrary.org. Tours Mon–Sat 10:30am–2:15pm. Library Mon and Wed–Fri 8:30am–4:30pm; Tues noon–8pm. Subway: F/M or N/R to 23rd St.

Derfner Judaica Museum `FREE`   The Hebrew Home at Riverdale hosts this newly expanded display of historic Judaica, which ranges from *mezuzot* to Persian ivory paintings to miniature folk-art arks. More recent treasures are interspersed as well, like an Israeli copper Hanukkah lamp, and a painting by Zygmunt Menkes. A sculpture garden and Hudson views further sweeten the pot for a jaunt to the Bronx.

FREE Back in the High Line Again

Tenth Avenue once carried the nickname "Death Avenue" because of the ground-level rail lines that cut a swath of destruction through the residential streets. During the Depression, $150 million was spent to get the trains aboveground, only to have the entire system rendered obsolete by the Eisenhower Interstate Highway System. The tracks were abandoned in 1980 and all but a couple dozen blocks through Chelsea and the Meatpacking District were dismantled. In 2009, a spruced-up version of those tracks was unveiled as a city park. Nine access points lead to the exquisitely landscaped blocks of the **High Line,** an elevated oasis wedged among creaky warehouses and the major glitz of the Standard Hotel. To get an expert's gloss on it, check out the free **Tuesday night tours,** which run at 6:30pm every season but winter. Public art and stargazing are among the park's bonus attractions. I recommend a sunset visit—the Hudson is bathed in color, and up on the tracks you have the feeling of being on a floating island, somehow removed from the city even as you're right in the stylish heart of it. From Gansevoort to 30th sts., near Tenth Ave. ✆ **212/500-6035.** www.thehighline.org. Subway to south entrance: A/C/E to 14th St.; L to Eighth Ave.

5901 Palisade Ave., Riverdale, the Bronx. ✆ **718/581-1000.** www.hebrewhome.org. Sun–Thurs 10:30am–4:30pm. Subway: 1 to 242nd St.–Van Cortlandt Park.

Federal Hall National Memorial FREE   A former U.S. custom house, this columned Wall Street museum now recounts the long and storied history of its site. The renovated building offers free weekday guided tours on the hour, from 10am to 3pm (no tour at noon). See p. 313 in chapter 8 for a full review.

26 Wall St., at Nassau St. ✆ **212/825-6888.** www.nps.gov/feha. Mon–Fri 9am–5pm. Subway: 2/3/4/5 to Wall St.

Federal Reserve Bank FREE   In addition to the gallery of the **American Numismatic Society** (p. 312) on the ground floor, advance sign-up will give you the chance to glimpse a little of the building. It's basically a tour of a bank: a bank with the largest gold cache in the world, but still a bank. Along the way you'll see two short videos, one weirdly defensive about the employees of the currency-processing division, and one weirdly defensive about the employees who work with the gold. Five stories beneath the street you'll get to see the vault itself, which resembles a gym locker room, except with some $200 billion in gold shimmering behind the bars. As a reward for your attention, they'll give you $1,000 in cash. Shredded cash. FINE PRINT Call 1 to 2 weeks in advance to reserve a space.

33 Liberty St., btw. William and Nassau sts. ℂ **212/720-6130**. www.newyorkfed.org. Tours weekdays 11:15am, noon, 1:15, 2:30, 3:15, and 4pm (they last about an hour). Subway: A/C/J/Z/2/3/4/5 to Fulton St./Broadway Nassau.

Fisher Landau Center for Art FREE   Few New Yorkers know about the 25,000-square-foot exhibition and study center inside this converted Queens industrial space. The pristine galleries display painting, sculpture, and photography from 1960 to the present, including works by the likes of Agnes Martin, Robert Rauschenberg, and Cy Twombly. You'll find three floors of viewing pleasure. You'll also delight in the cultlike glazed eyes of security guards who relay your every move via walkie-talkies.

38–27 30th St., btw. 38th and 39th aves. ℂ **718/937-0727**. www.flcart.org. Thurs–Mon noon–5pm. Subway: N/Q to 39th Ave.

5Pointz Aerosol Art Center FREE   The subways of the '70s were moving galleries for graffiti, which became a New York trademark. The trains may be sanitized now, but aerosol art lives on. A huge expanse of factory walls near PS1 serves as a canvas for an ever-evolving collection of spray-painted glory. Hip-hop luminaries are among the pilgrims making the trip to this open-air "institute of higher burnin'."

45–46 Davis St., at Jackson Ave. www.5ptz.com. Sat–Sun noon–7pm; other times by appointment. Subway: E/G/M/7 to Court Sq.

Forbes Magazine Galleries FREE   Magazine magnate Malcolm Forbes's galleries once approximated what a 10-year-old boy with unlimited financial means would think to collect. Unfortunately, the model boats, toy soldiers, and Monopoly boards are now gone. In their place you'll find art galleries (Sabina Forbes II was recently represented), a jewelry gallery, and a potpourri category presented in the Carrère Gallery.

62 Fifth Ave., at 12th St. ℂ **212/206-5548**. www.forbesgalleries.com. Tues–Wed and Fri–Sat 10am–4pm. Subway: L/N/Q/R/4/5/6 to 14th St./Union Sq.

Franklin D. Roosevelt Four Freedoms Park FREE   FDR's 1941 State of the Union speech provides the inspiration for this long-in-the-making memorial. Architect Louis I. Kahn's elegant design tapers 120 little-leaf linden trees down to an East River landing where the freedoms themselves (of speech and worship, from fear and want) are carved in granite. The memorial's location on the southern tip of Roosevelt Island also affords close-ups of the ruins of the 1856 Renwick Smallpox Hospital.

Southern tip Roosevelt Island. © **212/204-8831.** www.fdrfourfreedomspark.org. Daily sunrise–sunset. Subway: F to Roosevelt Island; Roosevelt Island Tram (p. 115).

General Grant National Memorial FREE   Manhattan is home to the nation's largest mausoleum, the graceful 1897 structure that houses the remains of General Ulysses S. Grant. (For punch-line sticklers, Mrs. Julia Grant is interred here as well.) The hushed interior conveys peaceful repose. There's a small on-site museum where you'll be surprised to discover the huge deal Grant's funeral was in New York. The tomb itself was once a popular attraction, but tourists have found more pressing enticements, and the memorial feels secluded, nearly forgotten. Free talks are given at 11:15am, 1:15, and 3:15pm daily.

Riverside Dr., at 122nd St. © **212/666-1640.** www.nps.gov/gegr. Daily 9am–5pm. Subway: 1 to 125th St.

Hall of Fame for Great Americans FREE   You'd think a gigantic monument designed by Stanford White, with tablets by Tiffany Studios, memorializing American heroes like Mark Twain, Abe Lincoln, and Susan B. Anthony would be a major draw, but this oddball attraction is sadly overlooked. The distant location, on the Bronx Community College campus, might be part of the problem. If you're in the area, stop by, because the open colonnade with its 102 bronze busts and classical architecture is a wonderful surprise.

Hall of Fame Terrace, 181st St. and University Ave., the Bronx. © **718/289-5161.** www.bcc.cuny.edu/halloffame. $2 suggested donation. Daily 10am–5pm. Subway: 4 to 183rd St.

Hamilton Grange National Memorial FREE   Federalist Paper author and first secretary of the treasury Alexander Hamilton started construction on his Federal-style country home in 1800. Harlem is not so country anymore, but the National Park Service recently moved the house around the corner to St. Nicholas Park, which better reflects the structure's origins nestled among the hills and trees of a vanished

Harlem. (Fittingly, the current site was within the boundary of Hamilton's original 32-acre estate.) FINE PRINT You can tour the period-furnished rooms with a ranger at 11am, noon, 1, 2, and 4pm; remaining hours are set aside for self-guided visits.

414 W. 141st St., btw. Convent and St. Nicholas aves. ℂ **646/548-2310.** www.nps. gov/hagr. Wed–Sun 9am–5pm. Subway: 1 to 137th St.; A/B/C/D to 145th St.

Hebrew Union College–Jewish Institute of Religion Museum FREE Multiple galleries display assorted Judaica along with contemporary artwork of a Jewish bent. The historical exhibits are particularly interesting, like explorations of the Albanian Muslim rescuers of the Holocaust, or the internment of Mayor LaGuardia's Jewish sister at Ravensbrück. Shows change regularly, with 8 to 10 moving through each year. FINE PRINT A photo ID is required to enter.

1 W. 4th St., btw. Broadway and Mercer St. ℂ **212/824-2205.** www.huc.edu/museums/ ny. Mon–Thurs 9am–5pm; Fri 9am–3pm; selected Sun 10am–2pm. Subway: N/R to 8th St.; 6 to Astor Place.

Institute for the Study of the Ancient World FREE The two galleries here are dedicated to thoughtful exhibits that bring alive eras you may not realize existed. I was astounded by the Kazakh gold work at the recent Nomads and Networks show, which also included a 2,000-year-old embroidered saddle, a wooden pillow, and a bong. Scholarly texts provide insight into the objects.

15 E. 84th St., btw. Madison and Fifth aves. ℂ **212/992-7800.** www.isaw.nyu.edu. Tues–Sun 11am–6pm; Fri 11am–8pm. Subway: 4/5/6 to 86th St.

Irish Hunger Memorial FREE This large-scale sculpture on the downtown Hudson waterfront memorializes the Irish famine of 1845 to 1852. The center of the installation is a famine-era cottage moved stone by stone from the old country, resting on a field of blackthorn and heather. Take the path to the memorial's top and watch it open up to sublime views of the Statue of Liberty and Ellis Island.

Vesey St. and North End Ave. ℂ **212/967-9700.** www.batteryparkcity.org. Daily 6am–1am. Subway: 1/2/3 or A/C to Chambers St.

Lesbian, Gay, Bisexual & Transgender Community Center Museum FREE This isn't really a museum per se, but a community center that puts up exhibits in its hallways. There's a lot of erotic art, along with the occasional historical perspective, like an encapsulation of a San Francisco public library archive. The real gem in this building is the mural *Once Upon a Time,* painted by Keith Haring in a second-floor bathroom. Converted to a meeting room, this space pulsates with life thanks to a spectacular, salacious mural created by Haring shortly before his death.

208 W. 13th St., btw. Seventh and Greenwich aves. ⓒ **212/620-7310.** www.gay center.org. Lobby Mon–Fri 9am–10pm; Sat 11am–10pm; Sun 11am–9pm. Subway: 1/2/3 or F/M to 14th St.; L to Sixth Ave.

Madame Alexander Heritage Gallery `FREE`   Immigrant daughter and lifelong New Yorker Madame Beatrice Alexander Behrman pioneered doll-making. Her version of *Gone With the Wind*'s Scarlett was the first doll to be based on a pop culture character. More on the story can be found in the Harlem headquarters, with its displays of photos, advertising, and, of course, dolls. Over 600 fill the display cases. You can catch a free guided tour of the gallery and the showroom every 90 minutes on weekdays, starting at 10am and concluding with a final tour at 4pm. If you get nervous around a lot of kids, steer clear.

615 W. 131st St., 6th floor, btw. Broadway and Twelfth Ave. ⓒ **212/283-5900,** ext. 7299. www.madamealexander.com. Mon–Fri 9am–5pm. Subway: 1 to 125th St.

The Museum at FIT `FREE`   This museum on the campus of the Fashion Institute of Technology is long on historic style, specializing in the 20th century. For contemporary looks, student shows are surprisingly sophisticated. Other rotating exhibits display items from the special collections, like accessories, sketches, or a mourning robe (ca. 1870).

The southwest corner of Seventh Ave., at 27th St. ⓒ **212/217-4558.** www.fitnyc.edu. Tues–Fri noon–8pm; Sat 10am–5pm. Subway: 1 to 28th St.

Museum of American Illustration `FREE`   Illustrators never seem to get their proper respect as visual artists, constantly upstaged by those showoff painters and photographers. The two galleries maintained by the Society of Illustrators strive to remedy that situation. Contest winners and works of Society members can be found on the walls, along with classics from the permanent collection (the Society was formed in 1901, so there's a lot to fall back on). Exhibits change frequently.

128 E. 63rd St., btw. Park and Lexington aves. ⓒ **212/838-2560.** www.society illustrators.org. Tues 10am–8pm; Wed–Fri 10am–5pm; Sat noon–4pm. Subway: N/Q/R to Fifth Ave.; F to Lexington Ave./63rd St.

Museum of Biblical Art   With its de rigueur acronym, MOBIA makes a game effort to fit in with its museum brethren in the heart of New Gomorrah. Exhibition subjects have ranged from oil lamps of the Holy Land to soldiers' Bibles.

1865 Broadway, at W. 61st St. ℂ **212/408-1500.** www.mobia.org. Tues–Wed and Fri–Sun 10am–6pm; Thurs 10am–8pm. Subway: A/B/C/D/1 to 59th St./Columbus Circle.

National Museum of the American Indian `FREE` Housing Native American treasures in a former arm of the federal government seems a bit of a cruel irony, but the overall effect here is of reverence for endangered arts. This Smithsonian branch augments its exhibits with films and videos; check the schedule at **www.nativenetworks.si.edu**. There's programming for kids, too, including storybook readings and workshops. Everything is free, though craft workshops can have material fees. Some events require reservations. See also p. 314.

1 Bowling Green, btw. State and Whitehall sts. ℂ **212/514-3700.** www.american indian.si.edu. Daily 10am–5pm; Thurs until 8pm. Subway: 4/5 to Bowling Green; 1 to South Ferry.

Nicholas Roerich Museum `FREE` One of New York's least-known museums showcases the Russian scholar and painter Nicholas Roerich. A genteel Riverside Drive town house holds three floors of galleries, cluttered with Roerich's paintings. The images favor Russian icons and Himalayan landscapes, executed with bright colors and stylized lines. Objects gathered in Roerich's Asian explorations are scattered throughout the museum, and a subtle spiritual air pervades. The museum's motto, *Pax Cultura* (Peace through Culture), gets expressed in a full schedule of free concerts and poetry readings. Music generally plays Sundays at 5pm; check online for additional dates and times.

319 W. 107th St., btw. Riverside Dr. and Broadway. ℂ **212/864-7752.** www.roerich. org. Tues–Fri noon–5pm; Sat–Sun 2–5pm. Subway: 1 to 110th St.

9/11 Memorial `FREE` Having to endure the rigors of a security checkpoint only heightens the contrast of quiet and calm you experience on this memorial's leafy plaza. Two austere squares mark the footprints of the World Trade Center towers, with water flowing into dark center boxes whose depths can't quite be plumbed. Watching the cascade (these are the largest man-made waterfalls in North America), it's hard not to think of the iconic images of the towers' collapse. Names incised on the outer rim reflect the cross section of New York that bore the brunt of the attacks, nowhere more poignant than when you see a name appended "and her unborn child." I recommend a dusk visit, when the crowds have eased, and the subdued lighting lends itself to reflection. FINE PRINT Advance passes are required, and easily reserved online for free. Limited same-day passes are distributed at the 9/11 Memorial Preview Site (20 Vesey St., at Church St.); the NYC & Co. kiosk at City Hall; and the NY Water Taxi booth at the South Street Seaport.

Albany and Greenwich sts. ℂ **212/266-5211.** www.911memorial.org. Daily 10am–6pm, extended to 8pm Mar–Oct; last entry 1 hr. before close. Subway: A/C/J/Z/2/3/4/5 to Fulton St./Broadway Nassau; 2/3 to Park Place; E to World Trade Center; R or 1 to Rector St.

Onassis Cultural Center `FREE`   Aristotle Onassis—or as most of us know him, Mr. Jackie O.—was the man behind this Midtown institution, which supports Hellenic art and culture. Winding stairs in the middle of the Olympic Tower atrium's south side lead to a warren of galleries with unexpected waterfall views. Samples from Byzantium show off the flat faces of a world before linear perspective was invented. Modern Greek efforts can often be found here as well. On the lobby floor, a long-term display shows off rare casts of Parthenon marbles.

The Olympic Tower atrium, 641 Fifth Ave., entrance just east of Fifth on 51st or 52nd sts. ℂ **212/486-4448.** www.onassisusa.org. Mon–Sat 10am–6pm. Subway: E/M to Fifth Ave./53rd St.

Pratt Galleries `FREE`   The fruits of Pratt Institute's prestigious arts and design programs can be found in the galleries the school runs. Current student shows are mixed in with alumni and faculty exhibitions, as well as those of other artistic innovators.

144 W. 14th St., btw. Sixth and Seventh aves. ℂ **212/647-7778.** www.pratt.edu. Tues–Sat 11am–6pm. Subway: 1/2/3 and F/M to 14th St.; L to Sixth Ave. Other location: *Schafler Gallery, Pratt campus,* 200 Willoughby Ave., Ft. Greene, Brooklyn. ℂ **718/636-3517.** Mon–Fri 9am–5pm. Subway: G to Clinton–Washington aves.

Scandinavia House `FREE`   The Midtown headquarters of the Nordic Center in America is as stylish as the northern nations that spawned it. A third-floor gallery hosts contemporary art from the Norse nations, interspersed with historical material, like recent shows on Swedish actress Greta Garbo and Swedish diplomat Raoul Wallenberg.

58 Park Ave., btw. 37th and 38th sts. ℂ **212/879-9779.** www.scandinaviahouse.org. Tues–Sat noon–6pm. In summer, call ahead for schedule changes. Subway: 4/5/6/7/S to 42nd St./Grand Central; 6 to 33rd St.

Sony Wonder Technology Lab `FREE`   Sony sucks in new generations of technology addicts with this four-level supermodern demonstration center, which was recently overhauled. Kids can try their

`FREE` Broadway Stars

Given the city's endemic light pollution, it would seem that whoever came up with the idea of building an observatory in Manhattan wasn't totally clear on the concept. Amazingly, however, some celestial sights do seep through our glowing night skies. On a Columbia University rooftop you can see for yourself. Select nights during the school year, professors and graduate students gloss the stars at the historic Rutherfurd Observatory, starting off with a lecture and slideshow. There are also family nights for kids ages 6 to 10. The price for all this isn't astronomical—it's totally free. **Pupin Physics Laboratory,** 550 W. 120th St., btw. Broadway and Amsterdam Ave. Follow the signs to the lecture hall. ℭ **212/854-1976,** www.astro.columbia.edu. Subway: 1 to 116th St./Columbia University. After sunset and weather permitting, of course (lecture and slideshow go rain or shine). For a more informal look at the heavens, check out **Stargazing on the High Line,** a Tuesday night progam hosted by the Amateur Astronomers Association of New York. Come dusk, high-powered telescopes train on stars, planets, and the Moon. On the High Line, btw. Little W. 12th and 14th sts. ℭ **212/206-9922.** www.thehighline.org. Subway: A/C/E to 14th St.; L to Eighth Ave. Free, weather permitting.

hands at robotics, medical imaging, and video game design, among other expensive toys. Free movies round out the stimuli; see p. 248 in chapter 7. FINE PRINT Tickets are free, but are required. A few walk-up tickets are distributed, but the better way to go is with an advance reservation, made between 7 days and 3 months in advance.

550 Madison Ave., at 56th St. ℭ **212/833-8100.** www.sonywondertechlab.com. Tues–Sat 9:30am–5:30pm; last entrance 30 min. before closing. Subway: E/M to Fifth Ave./53rd St.; 4/5/6/N/Q/R to Lexington Ave./59th St.

Storefront for Art and Architecture `FREE` Designed with odd panels that expand into the street, this idiosyncratic institution does a lot with its very narrow space. Always intelligent exhibits explore architecture, art, and design.

97 Kenmare St., btw. Mulberry St. and Cleveland Place, near Lafayette St. ℭ **212/431-5795.** www.storefrontnews.org. Tues–Sat 11am–6pm. Subway: 6 to Spring St.; N/R to Prince St.

Theodore Roosevelt Birthplace `FREE`   An asthmatic son of a prominent New York family, Theodore Roosevelt transformed himself into a
symbol of fortitude, becoming a rancher, a soldier, a governor, and
eventually the only New York City native elected president. His original birthplace was demolished in 1916, but 3 years later friends and
family built a replica town house on the site. Period pieces, the major-
ity of which belonged to the Roosevelts, fill the stately rooms. Take one
of the informative hourly tours and you'll learn Eleanor Roosevelt's
maiden name (it was Roosevelt), the origins of the teddy bear, and that
T. R. survived the loss of his wife and mother on the same day.

28 E. 20th St., btw. Broadway and Park Ave. S. ℂ **212/260-1616.** www.nps.gov/thrb.
Tues–Sat 9am–5pm (tours hourly 10am–4pm). Subway: N/R or 6 to 23rd St.

Tibet House U.S. `FREE`   This blah apartment house seems an
unlikely place for inspiring Tibetan art, but the second floor holds a
vibrant collection of paintings, sculptures, and artifacts. The art is
intricate and the quiet rooms encourage lingering. A large gallery
space hosts rotating shows with a Tibetan angle. FINE PRINT There's a
donation box for goodwill offerings; $5 is suggested.

22 W. 15th St., 2nd floor, btw. Fifth and Sixth aves. ℂ **212/807-0563.** www.tibet
house.org. Mon–Fri noon–5pm. Subway: L/N/Q/R/4/5/6 to 14th St./Union Sq.

United Nations Visitors' Center `FREE`   This is it, the literal capital of
the world. After going through the security line, which moves with all
the efficiency and enthusiasm of an American airport's, you'll enter
the Visitors' Lobby. Built in 1950, it's a little dated but still impressive.
Multiple U.N.–related art exhibits fill the space. For $16 you can take
a full tour of the building, but for cheaper thrills, the Headquarters
Park is a worthy diversion. Sculpture is scattered across a grassy
expanse built on a scale rarely found in Manhattan.

First Ave. at 46th St. ℂ **212/963-4475.** www.un.org. Mon–Fri 9am–5:30pm (entrance
closes at 4:45pm); Sat–Sun 10am–4:15pm; closed weekends Jan–Feb. Subway: 4/5/6
or 7 to Grand Central.

SOMETIMES FREE

Several museums that won't give up their goods for free full-time do
set aside special hours and days where you can pay what you wish.
Beware the last free day before an exhibition ends, though. More than
a few procrastinators call New York home, and you'll find them gathered en masse for final free windows of opportunity.

Sometimes Free or Pay-What-You-Wish Museums

Monday/ Tuesday	Wednesday	Thursday	Friday	Saturday	Sunday
The Museum at Eldridge Street (Mon 10am–5pm)	Museum of Jewish Heritage: A Living Memorial to the Holocaust (Wed 4–8pm)	Brooklyn Children's Museum (Third Thurs 4–7pm)	Children's Museum of Manhattan (First Fri 5–8pm)	Brooklyn Children's Museum (Second Sat 10–11am)	Brooklyn Children's Museum (Second Sun 10–11am)
China Institute (Tues 6–8pm)		Children's Museum of the Arts (Thurs 4–6pm)	International Center of Photography (Fri 5–8pm)	Brooklyn Museum of Art (First Sat 5–11pm)	Frick Collection (Sun 11am–1pm)
		China Institute (Thurs 6–8pm)	Japan Society (Fri 6–9pm)	El Museo del Barrio (Third Sat 11am–8:30pm)	New York Hall of Science (Sun 10–11am, Sept–June)
		Museum of Arts and Design (Thurs 6–9pm)	The Morgan Library & Museum (Fri 7–9pm)	Guggenheim Museum (Sat 5:45–7:45pm)	Museum of Biblical Art (Sun 10am–6pm)
		Museum of Chinese in America (Thurs 11am–9pm)	Museum of Modern Art/MoMA (Fri 4–8pm)	The Jewish Museum (Sat 11am–5:45pm)	The Studio Museum in Harlem (Sun noon–6pm)
		New Museum (Thurs 7–9pm)	Museum of the Moving Image (Fri 4–8pm)		
			Neue Galerie (First Fri 6–8pm)		
			The New York Aquarium (Fri 3pm–close)		
			New York Hall of Science (Fri 2–5pm, Sept–June)		
			New-York Historical Society (Fri 6–8pm)		
			The Noguchi Museum (First Fri 10am–5pm)		
			The Rubin Museum of Art (Fri 6–10pm)		
			Whitney Museum of American Art (Fri 6–9pm)		

Asia Society   John D. Rockefeller III founded the Asia Society in the mid-1950s to encourage cultural exchanges and understanding between Asians and Americans. The newly renovated headquarters building has beautiful galleries, showing off parts of Rockefeller's collection in addition to rotating exhibits. The interior architecture is impressive, especially the sleek staircase that looks like a snake's skeleton wandering up the floors.

725 Park Ave., at 70th St. ✆ **212/288-6400.** www.asiasociety.org. Regular admission $10; free Fri 6–9pm Sept–June. Tues–Sun 11am–6pm; Fri 11am–9pm, except July 1 to Labor Day, when museum closes 6pm Fri. Subway: 6 to 68th St./Hunter College.

Brooklyn Museum of Art   One of the largest art museums in the United States, the Brooklyn Museum is as spruced up and thriving as the borough that hosts it. With a glorious new entryway, remodeled exhibitions, and a building with over half a million square feet, there are several days' worth of exploring to be done here. The Egyptian collection is world-class and beautifully displayed, with informative, well-written notes accompanying each object. My favorites are the fourth floor's period rooms. Don't miss the **Jan Schenck House,** a

FREE Date Night: Target First Saturdays at the Brooklyn Museum

One of New York's best cheap date opportunities comes once a month at the Brooklyn Museum. Every first Saturday, the museum transforms itself into a house party on a massive scale. The crowd is more diverse than the U.N. General Assembly, with a dizzying range of ages, cultures, and styles represented. The museum keeps most of its galleries open for your perusal. When you run low on witty commentary, distractions like films and lectures beckon. Dance performances can be found, too, or if the date is going particularly well, you might let your feet work the floor yourself. The live music tends to be upbeat and very danceable. There's no charge for any of this, and nobody hits you up for a donation. The night is so festive that your date may not even notice just how cheap it's been. See the Brooklyn Museum review above for the address and subway directions. Some attractions require tickets which, although free, may require standing on line.

touch of Dutch in old Breuckelen that somehow survived on the edge of Jamaica Bay from 1675 to 1952.

200 Eastern Pkwy., at Washington Ave., Brooklyn. *C* **718/638-5000.** www.brooklyn museum.org. Suggested admission $12; free 1st Sat of the month 5–11pm. Wed and Fri 11am–6pm; Thurs 11am–10pm; 1st Sat of the month 11am–11pm; each Sat thereafter and Sun 11am–6pm. Subway: 2/3 to Eastern Pkwy./Brooklyn Museum.

China Institute A scholarly approach informs the exhibits at this 85-year-old culture and arts center. Two small, square galleries bookend the reception area and display traditional Chinese art, with beautifully crafted examples of calligraphy, painting, architecture, and textile work.

125 E. 65th St., btw. Park and Lexington aves. *C* **212/744-8181.** www.chinainstitute. org. Regular admission $7; free Tues and Thurs 6–8pm. Daily 10am–5pm (Tues, Thurs to 8pm). Subway: 6 to 68th St./Hunter College.

El Museo del Barrio A school classroom display was the genesis for this Museum Mile institution, the only museum in the United States dedicated to Puerto Rican, Caribbean, and Latin American art. The artistic history of the region, from pre-Columbian origins to the present, is recounted in a permanent installation. Changing exhibitions cover contemporary subjects and artists.

1230 Fifth Ave., at 104th St. *C* **212/831-7272.** www.elmuseo.org. Suggested admission $9; free every 3rd Sat 11am–8:30pm. Tues–Sat 11am–6pm; Sun 1–5pm. Subway: 6 to 103rd St.

Frick Collection Coke (the stuff for steel, not the soda or the stimulant) was very, very good to Henry Clay Frick, who was a Gilded Age plutocrat by the age of 30. When it came time to decorate the walls of his Upper East Side palace, he looked to the likes of Titian, Vermeer, and Goya. Hank didn't skimp on the furniture or carpeting, either. Though there is a slightly musty quality to this place (it dates to 1914), the collection is undeniably impressive, and special exhibitions have garnered plenty of buzz.

1 E. 70th St., at Fifth Ave. *C* **212/288-0700.** www.frick.org. Regular admission $18; pay what you wish Sun 11am–1pm. Tues–Sat 10am–6pm; Sun 11am–5pm. Subway: 6 to 68th St./Hunter College.

Guggenheim Museum Artists complained bitterly about the curved walls that spiral up seven stories, but Frank Lloyd Wright knew what he was doing, and flat art mounts on the sides of the Guggie just fine.

You'll feel like you're climbing through a nautilus shell as you view the latest installation in the central atrium, recently the host of Cai Guo-Qiang's startling nine-car cascade. A tower alongside the spiral hosts a permanent collection stocked with Chagalls, Matisses, van Goghs, and Picassos. For a whole 120 minutes a week, on Saturday nights in the latest iteration of the program, the Guggenheim lets you poke around for free.

1071 Fifth Ave., at 88th St. © **212/423-3500.** www.guggenheim.org. Regular admission $22; pay what you wish Sat 5:45–7:45pm (last ticket issued at 7:15pm). Fri and Sun–Wed 10am–5:45pm; Sat 10am–7:45pm. Subway: 4/5/6 to 86th St.

International Center of Photography   The ICP does a good job of balancing photography's past and future, with daguerreotypes and digital receiving as much wall time as classic b&w street photographers of the '50s and '60s. Usually three separate exhibitions are up at any given time, except when the museum's two floors are turned over to a larger survey like contemporary African work, or the **ICP Triennial,** which showcases the best new photography.

1133 Sixth Ave., at 43rd St. © **212/857-0000.** www.icp.org. Regular admission $12; pay what you wish Fri 5–8pm. Tues–Wed and Sat–Sun 10am–6pm; Thurs–Fri 10am–8pm. Subway: B/D/F/M to 42nd St.; 7 to Fifth Ave.

Japan Society   A waterfall trickling through a bamboo thicket welcomes you to this cultural institution near the U.N. The second floor has several rooms of galleries dedicated to Japanese art, ranging from classical Buddhist sculpture to photography to a spectacular recent exhibit of 19th-century lacquer masterworks.

333 E. 47th St., btw. First and Second aves. © **212/832-1155.** www.japansociety.org. Regular admission $12; free Fri 6–9pm. Tues–Thurs 11am–6pm; Fri 11am–9pm; Sat–Sun 11am–5pm. Subway: 4/5/6/7/S to 42nd St./Grand Central; 6 to 51st St.

The Jewish Museum   Four thousand years of Jewish history for this? Absolutely. A French Gothic château on the Upper East Side holds this remarkable collection, which chronicles the twists and turns of the Jewish experience, from a foundation stone of the third wall of Jerusalem to prints by Chagall. Lower floors handle temporary exhibits, like the terrific recent William Steig show.

1109 Fifth Ave., at 92nd St. © **212/423-3200.** www.thejewishmuseum.org. Regular admission $12; free Sat. Fri–Tues 11am–5:45pm; Thurs 11am–8pm. Subway: 4/5 to 86th St.; 6 to 96th St.

Cheapie Kid Stuff

Brooklyn Children's Museum The world's first children's museum has kept up with the times, with a newly renovated green building (there's even an indoor stream). The permanent collection is more than kids' play, with some 30,000 artifacts of natural and human history. 145 Brooklyn Ave., at St. Marks Ave. ℭ **718/735-4400.** www. brooklynkids.org. Regular admission $7.50, free every 3rd Thurs 4–7pm and first weekend of each month 2–5pm. Wed–Sun 10am–5pm (also open Tues in summer; check ahead as hours change to accommodate school schedules). Subway: C to Kingston Ave.; A/C to Nostrand Ave.

Children's Museum of Manhattan This uptown museum introduces kids to museum patronage before they can even walk. Toddlers can interact with giant talking dragons and play firetrucks, and there's a dedicated soft space for crawlers. Older kids learn through adventures with Dora and Diego, and the hands-on "City Splash" water exploration. 212 W. 83rd St., btw. Amsterdam Ave. and Broadway. ℭ **212/721-1223.** www.cmom.org. Regular admission $11, free 1st Fri of the month 5–8pm. Tues–Fri and Sun 10am–5pm (5–8pm 1st Fri); Sat 10am–7pm. Subway: 1 to 86th St.

Children's Museum of the Arts Kids have hands-on experiences with art at this sleek new incarnation of the CMA. The WEE Arts Studio is designed for toddlers, while older kids get creative in studios dedicated to disciplines like clay, media, sound, and fine art. There are three to four gallery shows every year, many showcasing art by kids. 103 Charlton St., btw. Hudson and Greenwich sts. ℭ **212/274-0986.** www.cmany.org. Regular admission $10, pay what you wish Thurs 4–6pm. Mon and Wed noon–5pm; Sat–Sun 10am–5pm; Thurs–Fri noon–6pm. Subway: 1 to Houston St.; C/E to Spring St.

The Morgan Library & Museum J. P. Morgan's collection of manuscripts, books, drawings, and prints has been housed in this McKim, Mead & White masterpiece since 1906. The building celebrated its centennial by doubling its public exhibition space with a glass-and-steel

Renzo Piano expansion. Lush original rooms are joined by two floors hosting exhibitions dedicated to photography, ancient cylinder seals, Bob Dylan ephemera, and the like.

225 Madison Ave., at 36th St. ℭ **212/685-0008.** www.themorgan.org. Regular admission $15 adults; free Fri 7–9pm. (McKim rooms are also free Tues 3–5pm and Sun 4–6pm.) Tues–Thurs 10:30am–5pm; Fri 10:30am–9pm; Sat 10am–6pm; Sun 11am–6pm. Subway: 6 to 33rd St.

Museum of Arts and Design   Craft design gets its 15 minutes inside the towering new home of this Midtown museum. Exhibits focus on emerging artists and new ideas of form, especially as the latter follows function. Clay, glass, wood, metal, and fiber are among the materials represented. For big spenders, the artisans on display often have their wares available in the shop.

2 Columbus Circle, btw. Broadway and Eighth Ave. ℭ **212/599-7777.** www.mad museum.org. Regular admission $15; pay what you wish Thurs after 6pm. Tues–Sat and Sun 11am–6pm; Thurs–Fri 11am–9pm. Subway: A/B/C/D/1 to 59th St./Columbus Circle.

Museum of Chinese in America   The Chinese-American population of New York City has more than doubled in the last 20 years, so it's no surprise MOCA left its original digs in a crumbling old public school for a new space six times as large. Maya Lin's design balances past and present, playing off the building's industrial history, most dramatically in the raw brick courtyard. A core exhibit on the Chinese-American Experience is supplemented by oral history projects, photo shows, and art installations.

215 Centre St., btw. Grand and Howard sts. ℭ **212/619-4785.** www.mocanyc.org. Regular admission $7; free Thurs. Mon and Fri 11am–5pm; Thurs 11am–9pm; Sat–Sun 10am–5pm. Subway: J/N/Q/R/Z/6 to Canal St.; B/D to Grand St.

The Museum at Eldridge Street   To look at the immaculate stained glass, carved wood, and starry ceilings inside this 1887 synagogue, you would never guess it spent decades on the verge of collapse. Guided tours are the way to go here, showing off the intricate restoration, along with a hidden snuff compartment and a massive central chandelier turned upside down when the building's lighting was converted from gas to electric. Mondays are free, although there is a *tzedakah* box if you'd like to leave a contribution (the fix-up cost some $20 million and took 20 years).

12 Eldridge St., btw. Canal and Division sts. ⓒ **212/219-0302.** www.eldridgestreet. org. Regular admission $10; free Mon. Sun–Thurs 10am–5pm; Fri 10am–3pm. Immigrant experience tours hourly 10am–4pm, architecture and preservation tours at 11:30am, 1:30pm, and 3:30pm. Subway: F to E. Broadway; B/D to Grand St.

Museum of Jewish Heritage: A Living Memorial to the Holocaust

This institution's unwieldy name reflects its dual callings as museum and memorial. The six-sided original building has a permanent exhibit that puts a human face on the Holocaust. A new wing houses ambitious temporary exhibits. The renovation also brought sculptor Andy Goldsworthy, who audaciously planted dwarf oak trees inside a series of boulders. This *Garden of Stones* has been growing for a decade now, and resonating as a living memorial. Although the museum charges admission most times, access to the Goldsworthy installation is always free.

36 Battery Place, near Little West St. ⓒ **646/437-4200.** www.mjhnyc.org. Regular admission $12; free Wed 4–8pm. Sun–Tues and Thurs 10am–5:45pm; Wed 10am–8pm; Fri 10am–5pm (closed 3pm during non–daylight saving time and on the eve of Jewish holidays). Subway: 4/5 to Bowling Green; R to Rector St.; 1 to South Ferry.

Museum of Modern Art (MoMA)

MoMA's nothing-left-to-chance makeover has resulted in a structure with the overall feel of a Fortune 500 headquarters. Of course, for $650 million, the finishes *should* look pretty damn nice. The stars of the permanent collection (Cézanne, Hesse, Mondrian) are joined by high-wattage temporary exhibitions. You'll pay through the nose for the privilege of wandering these sepulchral halls, except on Friday nights, which are free courtesy of Target and feature appallingly long lines. Is it just me, or could they have spent a little less on top-grade marble, and let the art be more accessible?

11 W. 53rd St., btw. Fifth and Sixth aves. ⓒ **212/708-9400.** www.moma.org. Regular admission $25; free Fri 4–8pm. Wed–Thurs and Sat–Mon 10:30am–5:30pm (until 8:30pm 1st Thurs of the month); Fri 10:30am–8pm. Subway: E/M to Fifth Ave./53rd St.

Museum of the Moving Image

Adolph Zukor opened Astoria Studios in 1920 and many of the new industry's early works were made there. The site still hosts television and film production, two activities that fuel this nearby institution's obsession. Exhibits trace the moving image's evolution from 19th-century optical toys through film cameras and television sets. If you spring for admission, you'll be entitled to see a film or two in one of the museum's brand-spanking-new theaters.

36-01 35th Ave., at 37th St., Astoria, Queens. ℂ **718/784-0077.** www.movingimage. us. Regular admission $12; free Fri 4–8pm (film screenings not included). Wed–Thurs 11am–5pm; Sat–Sun 11am–6:30pm; Fri 11am–8pm. Subway: M/R to Steinway St.

Neue Galerie The Galerie's 1914 brick-and-limestone mansion is one of the most elegant spots in the city. Ronald Lauder, a billionaire son of Estée Lauder (née Josephine Esther Mentzer of Corona, Queens), spent years adapting the interior to showcase 20th-century German and Austrian art and design. Upstairs in the two floors of galleries you'll find works by the likes of Gustav Klimt, Egon Schiele, Paul Klee, and Max Beckman. Admission is $20, but thanks to a Bloomberg grant, the first Friday of the month is free from 6 to 8pm. (The grant is renewed year to year, so check to make sure it's still running.) See also p. 248 for free films.

1048 Fifth Ave., at 86th St. ℂ **212/628-6200.** www.neuegalerie.org. Regular admission $20; free 1st Fri of the month 6–8pm. Thurs–Mon 11am–6pm; until 8pm 1st Fri of the month. Subway: 4/5/6 to 86th St.

New Museum "Maximum security" was my first thought when this gray hulk went up on the Bowery, and the caged-in ceiling of the foyer does little to dispel the prison vibe. That said, the free Thursday nights (take a ticket at the entrance and hop upstairs for three galleries of viewing pleasure) are fun, presenting contemporary artwork that's generally low-fi, playful, and international in scope. Families can take advantage of free programs for kids on the first Saturday of each month (advance registration is required).

235 Bowery, btw. Stanton and Prince sts. ℂ **212/219-1222.** www.newmuseum.org. Regular admission $14; free Thurs 7–9pm. Wed and Fri–Sun noon–6pm; Thurs 11am–9pm. Subway: F to Second Ave.; J/Z to Bowery.

The New York Aquarium Its origins at Castle Clinton in 1896 make this the oldest aquarium in the U.S., although its Coney Island facility has only been in operation since 1957. Some areas here could stand a spruce-up, but if you come with low expectations (and a passel of impressionable kids), you're sure to enjoy some quality shark, jellyfish, or otter face time. Regular admission is $14.95, but Fridays after 3pm it's pay what you wish, with a suggested contribution of $13.

Surf Ave. and W. 8th St., Coney Island, Brooklyn. ℂ **718/265-2663.** www.nyaquarium. com. Regular admission $14.95; pay what you wish Fri after 3pm. Spring and fall Mon–Fri 10am–5pm, until 5:30pm Sat–Sun and holidays; summer Mon–Fri 10am–6pm, until

7pm Sat–Sun and holidays; winter daily 10am–4:30pm. Subway: F/Q to W. 8th St./NY Aquarium.

New York Hall of Science Nominally a hall of science, this place is really a big playground. The exhibits are hands-on, letting kids get engulfed by a giant soap bubble, float on air in an antigravity mirror, and retrieve images from the depths of outer space. In summer the huge outdoor **Science Playground** provides jungle gyms, slides, see-saws, and spinners to help the physics medicine go down. FINE PRINT: It's an extra $6 for adults, $5 for students and seniors to play the Rocket Miniature Golf Course.

47–01 111th St., in Flushing Meadows–Corona Park, Queens. ✆ **718/699-0005.** www.nysci.org. Regular admission $11, plus $4 for the Science Playground; free Fri 2–5pm, Sun 10–11am (Sept 1–June 30 only). July–Aug Mon–Fri 9:30am–5pm, Sat-Sun 10am–6pm; Sept 1–June 30 Tues–Thurs 9:30am–2pm, Fri 9:30am–5pm, Sat–Sun 10am–6pm (closed Mon Sept 1–Mar 31). Subway: 7 to 111th St.

New-York Historical Society The hyphen is not a proofreading debacle—with its founding in 1804, this institution predates the streamlining of New York's spelling. They've got the bragging rights for the city's oldest museum, although a $65-million upgrade has it ready for the 21st century. Compelling temporary exhibits explore city history, joining a permanent collection stuffed with significant paintings, maps, tools, and a proposed New Amsterdam coat of arms that dates back to 1630.

170 Central Park W., at 77th St. ✆ **212/873-3400.** www.nyhistory.org. Regular admission $15; pay what you wish Fri 6–8pm. Tues–Thurs and Sat 10am–6pm; Fri 10am–8pm; Sun 11am–5pm. Subway: B/C to 81st St.; 1 to 79th St.

The Noguchi Museum Many New Yorkers have passed the Red Cube sculpture on lower Broadway, the stainless-steel plaque at the AP's headquarters in Rockefeller Center, and the sunken garden at the Chase Manhattan Bank Plaza, without realizing they're all by Japanese-American artist Isamu Noguchi. Noguchi's former home/studio shows off additional creativity in transforming a photo-engraving plant into a graceful oasis in the midst of industrial Queens. Renovated in 2004 and 2008, the museum features galleries of Noguchi's sculptural and architectural forms, and a tranquil birch-shaded sculpture garden.

9–01 33rd Rd., at Vernon Blvd., Long Island City, Queens. ✆ **718/204-7088.** www.noguchi.org. Regular admission $10; pay what you wish the 1st Fri of every month. Wed–Fri 10am–5pm; Sat–Sun 11am–6pm. Subway: N/Q to Broadway. Walk 8 blocks along Broadway toward the East River.

The Rubin Museum of Art New Yorkers finally got a Himalayan art museum when the Rubin opened up in 2004. A marble-and-steel spiral staircase, the focal point of the Barneys department store that was the previous tenant, winds through seven floors of painting, sculpture, and textiles. Thoughtful texts provide context for the bodhisattvas and mandalas on the walls. On Friday nights at 6:15 (except during the summer), when entry to the museum is free, you can catch a tour with a contemporary artist or curator and learn even more.

150 W. 17th St., btw. Sixth and Seventh aves. ✆ **212/620-5000.** www.rmanyc.org. Regular admission $10; free Fri 6–10pm. Mon and Thurs 11am–5pm; Wed 11am–7pm; Fri 11am–10pm; Sat–Sun 11am–6pm. Subway: 1/2/3 or F/M to 14th St.; L to Sixth Ave.

The Studio Museum in Harlem Dedicated to the art of African Americans, with a sideline on the African Diaspora, this small museum has gathered a terrific permanent collection. Exhibits rotate frequently and the calendar is packed with freebies. There are poetry readings, dance, forums, and open studios for the A-I-R program, which shows off the Artists in Residence that the Studio Museum helps support.

144 W. 125th St., btw. Lenox Ave. and Adam Clayton Powell Blvd. ✆ **212/864-4500.** www.studiomuseum.org. Suggested admission $7; free Sun. Thurs–Fri noon–9pm; Sat 10am–6pm; Sun noon–6pm. Subway: 2/3 to 125th St.

Whitney Museum of American Art Behind imposing Bauhaus walls on Madison Avenue lies a spectacular collection of 20th-century art. The Whitney is rich in Edward Hoppers, Louise Nevelsons, and Georgia O'Keeffes, and they're good about rotating the permanent collection through their upper galleries. Shows of contemporary artists on other floors tend to be rather cutting edge for a big Uptown institution. The legendary **Whitney Biannual**—love it or hate it (or both)—is the institution's biggest draw.

945 Madison Ave., at 75th St. ✆ **212/570-3676.** www.whitney.org. Regular admission $18; pay what you wish Fri after 6pm. Wed–Thurs and Sat–Sun 11am–6pm; Fri 1–9pm. Subway: 6 to 77th St.

SUGGESTED ADMISSIONS

Many New York institutions let in visitors on the basis of a "suggested admission." The price you have to pay isn't set in stone; it's set by the dictates of your own conscience. Before you decide how much to pony up, remember that you're already giving if you pay local taxes.

We working stiffs support the NYC Department of Cultural Affairs, the largest agency of its kind in the U.S. In 2012, the agency had $152 million set aside for expenses. The DCA helps fund dozens of local institutions, many of which are owned by the city (and by extension, you and me). Sometimes $1 seems like the right amount to be spending on one's own museum. That's not to say if you're flush you should be stiffing these institutions, which do spectacular work. If you've got a spare couple of bucks, by all means toss them in the hat.

American Museum of Natural History   It's easy to lose yourself within the 4-square-block walls of this legendary museum. Low-profile sections still have the dingy lighting and old-fashioned lettering of a few decades ago, but the big players received radical upgrades. Dinosaurs have been brought into the 21st century and $210 million has space-aged the Hayden Planetarium. With that big an outlay, the museum likes to see its full $19 admission when you come, although technically it's only a suggestion and you can pay what you wish.

Central Park W., btw. 77th and 81st sts. ✆ **212/769-5100** for information, or 769-5200 for tickets (tickets can also be ordered online, full-price only). www.amnh.org. Suggested admission $19. Space Show and museum admission together are $25, plus additional charges for IMAX movies and some of the special exhibitions. Daily 10am–5:45pm. Subway: B/C to 81st St.; 1 to 79th St.

The City Reliquary   This micro-museum is dedicated to the detritus of NYC, with an eye toward quirky collections like vintage thermoses and found snapshots. Recent renovations have brought the installation of the remains of a Brooklyn barber shop and a Chinatown newsstand. In addition to the storefront dime store and museum (entry is by a $5 suggested donation), there's a window display on nearby Grand Street, which was the institution's original inspiration.

370 Metropolitan Ave., btw. Havemeyer St. and Rev. Dr. Gardner C. Taylor Blvd., Williamsburg, Brooklyn. ✆ **718/782-4842**. www.cityreliquary.org. Suggested admission $5. Thurs–Sun noon–6pm. *Window display*, 307 Grand St., at Havemeyer St., Williamsburg, Brooklyn. Subway to both locations: L to Lorimer St.; G to Metropolitan Ave.

The Cloisters   On a picturesque Hudson cliffside, this Met subsidiary is a Frankenstein-esque amalgamation of medieval architecture: a Romanesque chapel, a 12th-century Spanish apse, and cloisters from five different monasteries. Tranquil gardens surround the site and enhance the sense that you're not just out of the city, you've dropped out of contemporary time altogether. If you've ever wondered why the

FREE Going to Governors Island

Native Americans called it *Pagganck* ("Nut Island"), the Dutch called it *Noten Eylant*, and until 1995 3,500 Coast Guard members and their families called it home. Today, the former military base that is Governors Island has been set aside for public use. During the summer, visitors can spend weekends wandering past abandoned mansions, forts, and bucolic parade grounds. It's all free, with a lovely ferry ride across New York Harbor thrown in as well. The breathtaking views make this New York's most ideal picnic spot. The island has totally been "discovered" and summer weekends offer a full slate of activities of all kinds for kids and adults, ranging from art exhibits to concerts to sports. You can bring your own bike to get around the island, or rent one when you arrive. Ferries run on the weekends and holiday Mondays, with departures from both the Brooklyn and Manhattan sides of the East River. A new tour of Castle Williams is also available, with the former fort and military prison open to the public for the first time in its 2-century history. The tour requires a (free) ticket, given out 1 hour before the tour; afternoon tours are often full, so plan to head over early. Manhattan ferry, Battery Maritime Bldg., 10 South St., btw. Broad and Whitehall sts. ✆ **212/825-3045.** www.nps.gov/gois. Subway: R to Whitehall St.; 1 to South Ferry. Brooklyn ferry, Pier 6, Brooklyn Bridge Park. East River at Atlantic Ave. Subway: R/2/3/4/5 to Court St./Borough Hall. Space on the ferries is limited, first-come, first-served.

Palisades in Jersey aren't more developed, it's because John D. Rockefeller, Jr., bought up all that land just to preserve this view.

99 Margaret Corbin Dr. (north end of Fort Tryon Park). ✆ **212/923-3700.** www.met museum.org. Suggested admission $25. Nov–Feb Tues–Sun 9:30am–4:45pm; Mar–Oct Tues–Sun 9:30am–5:15pm. Subway: A to 190th St., and then a 10-min. walk north along Margaret Corbin Dr., or pick up the M4 bus at the station (1 stop to Cloisters). Or take the M4 Madison Ave. to Fort Tryon Park–The Cloisters.

The Italian American Museum   This storefront museum doubles as a time machine: Exhibits are mounted amid the original teller windows of the circa-1885 Banca Stabile (don't miss the ancient vault in back).

This Old House: New York City Version

I find it amazing that anything lasts for long in NYC, especially old houses that don't do anything except clog up prime real estate. The **Historic House Trust** (📞 **212/360-8282;** www.historichousetrust.org) has information on 23 miraculously surviving dwellings, spread across all five boroughs. Admissions are usually under $5, which is not bad for the opportunity to travel back in time a century or two.

Dyckman Farmhouse Museum　The Dyckman family farmed upper Broadway for 2 centuries. Three generations called this original Dutch farmhouse home, and their descendents outfitted its museum incarnation with period pieces. In the garden you'll find an original smokehouse and a Revolutionary War–era Hessian hut. 4881 Broadway, at 204th St. 📞 **212/304-9422.** www.dyckmanfarmhouse.org. Admission $1. Fri–Sun 11am–5pm. Subway: A/1 to 207th St.

Edgar Allan Poe Cottage　That happy-go-lucky Virginian, Mr. Poe, moved to the Bronx in 1846, hoping that the country air would be good for his tubercular wife. She died just a few months later, and Poe himself checked out in 1849. Their final residence is now an anomaly among brick high-rises, with period furnishings and Poe exhibits inside. 2460 Grand Concourse, at E. Kingsbridge Rd. 📞 **718/881-8900.** www.bronxhistoricalsociety.org. Admission $5. Sat 10am–4pm; Sun 1–5pm. Subway: D/4 to Kingsbridge Rd.

The Morris-Jumel Mansion　One of Manhattan's coolest surprises is coming upon the grounds of the Morris-Jumel Mansion in the midst of monolithic Harlem apartment buildings. This genteel Palladian wonder is the oldest house in Manhattan, built in 1765 as a summer getaway. There isn't much land left on the plot, but what remains is pleasant to stroll around. You have to pay to enter the house, which provides a fascinating snapshot of its era (and of history: this was General Washington's headquarters for 2 months in 1776). *Tip:* Don't miss picturesque Sylvan Terrace across the street (just west of the mansion), one of the city's last blocks of wooden workers' row houses. 65 Jumel Terrace at 160th St., east of St. Nicholas Ave. 📞 **212/923-8008.** www.morrisjumel. org. Admission $5. Wed–Sun 10am–4pm. Subway: C to 163rd St.

A major expansion is imminent; in the meantime exhibits on topics like Garibaldi and the unification of Italy rotate through.

155 Mulberry St., at Grand St. ✆ **212/965-9000.** www.italianamericanmuseum.org. Suggested donation $5. Sat 11am–6pm; Sun noon–6pm. Subway: J/N/Q/R/Z/6 to Canal St.

The Metropolitan Museum of Art   On the Upper East Side, tucked away just off Central Park, you can find this undiscovered little gem of a collection. Allow yourself a good 10 minutes to see everything they've got. Yeah, well, the Met is the 800-pound gorilla of New York's museum scene, and it's not hiding from anybody. If it's not the greatest art museum in the world, it must be damn close, and it's all right there for the price of a suggested admission. Try not to miss the Studiolo from the Ducal Palace in Gubbio, the Monteleone Chariot, and the Temple of Dendur.

Fifth Ave., at 82nd St. ✆ **212/535-7710.** www.metmuseum.org. Suggested admission $25. Tues–Thurs and Sun 9:30am–5:30pm; Fri–Sat 9:30am–9pm; Mon 9:30am–5:30pm on select holidays only. Subway: 4/5/6 to 86th St.

MoMA PS1   School is out, replaced by art that's in, inside this 19th-century former public school. A gorgeous Renaissance Revival building hosts avant-garde shows rotating through the former classrooms. Formerly the P.S. 1 Contemporary Art Center, this MoMA offshoot does a terrific job of bringing fresh, intriguing art to Queens. Don't miss James Turrell's *Meeting* on the top floor, which frames the dusk sky in an extraordinary way.

22–25 Jackson Ave., Long Island City, Queens. ✆ **718/784-2084.** www.ps1.org. Suggested admission $10. Thurs–Mon noon–6pm. Subway: E/G/M/7 to Court Sq.

Museum of the City of New York   A gracious 1932 neo-Georgian mansion houses exhibits tracing NYC from the windmills of its Dutch colonial days up to its present status as the undisputed capital of the world. Lovely period rooms and a collection of theatrical memorabilia are highlights of the collection.

Fifth Ave., at 103rd St. ✆ **212/534-1672.** www.mcny.org. Suggested admission $10. Free if you work or live in East Harlem (tell the desk you're a neighbor). Daily 10am–6pm; select Sat extended to 8:30pm. Subway: 6 to 103rd St.

Queens Museum of Art   This museum has reproductions of Greek marbles and some nice Tiffany glass, but the real draw is *The Panorama of the City of New York,* the world's largest scale model. Every single building in the five boroughs is represented, in addition to every street and bridge, plus airplanes that take off and land at a tiny LaGuardia. The array was last updated in 1992, leaving the World Trade Center poignantly still standing at the tip of Manhattan. (Borrow binoculars from the gift shop to enjoy closer looks.) The Museum is in Corona Park, on the site of the 1964 World's Fair. Don't miss the nearby **Unisphere,** a highlight of the fair and the largest representation of Earth that we humans have cooked up yet. FINE PRINT Free tours of the museum are offered on Sundays at 2, 3, and 4pm.

Next to the Unisphere in Flushing Meadows–Corona Park, Queens. ✆ **718/592-9700.** www.queensmuseum.org. Suggested admission $5. Wed–Sun noon–6pm; Fri in July–Aug noon–8pm. Subway: 7 to Mets/Willets Point; follow signs through the park.

SculptureCenter Though this institution has been supporting and showcasing modern sculpture since 1928, its current home in a former Queens trolley repair shop can feel like a visit to a startup. Maya Lin's industrial-chic design is of the moment, but many of the touches are timeless. Ceilings soar 40 feet in the main room, and the basement project spaces are like minimalist catacombs. The rough edges haven't been disguised, but the overall effect is still refined, a perfect backdrop for the contemporary sculptures and installation art exhibited here. I love this place—it's a miniature version of what the Tate Modern in London should have been.

44–19 Purves St., off Jackson Ave., Long Island City, Queens. ✆ **718/361-1750.** www. sculpture-center.org. Thurs–Mon 11am–6pm. Suggested admission $5. Subway: E/M to Court Sq./23rd St.; G or 7 to 45th Rd./Court House Sq.

FREE EXHIBITS AT THE LIBRARIES

Free books are just the beginning with New York's libraries. In addition to **free classes** (p. 138) and **free films** (p. 248), Gothamites also get free exhibitions. The libraries really care about their material, which comes through in the impressively well-crafted displays. *Note:* The New York Public Library (Manhattan, the Bronx, and Staten Island), Brooklyn Public Library, and Queens Public Library are separate systems and require separate library cards.

Brooklyn Central Library FREE The galleries here present everything from painting to installation art to rare books. The works and the artists often have a local connection.

Moving Views

Straphangers get treated to a few spectacular scenes in exchange for their swipes. I love the 7 line as it approaches Manhattan from Queens. The track twists and turns like a slo-mo roller coaster with the Midtown skyline in the background. The J/M/Z ride across the Williamsburg Bridge has great views from windows north and south. The Manhattan Bridge gives B/D/N/Q riders dramatic East River vistas.

The most thrilling public transportation ride is the **Roosevelt Island Tram** (℘ **212/832-4555;** www.rioc.com). As you dangle in the air over the East River you get the East Side skyline, plus the U.N., plus great sightlines of the engineering marvels of the East River bridges. You also get the knowledge that one day in 2006 the tram stalled for hours, stranding passengers without much of an evacuation plan. (Accordingly, in 2010, the tram was shut down for a complete overhaul.) A frisson of actual danger comes free with the $2.25 one-way price (unlimited-plan Metrocards are accepted as well; you can also return via the F train's Roosevelt Island stop, just a few blocks away). The trip between 60th Street at Second Avenue and Roosevelt Island takes about 4 minutes. See p. 93 for information on exploring the new Four Freedoms Park on the island's southern tip. The tram operates daily 5:45am to 2:30am; until 3:30am on Fridays and Saturdays.

Grand Army Plaza. ℘ **718/230-2100.** www.brooklynpubliclibrary.org. Mon–Thurs 9am–9pm; Fri–Sat 10am–6pm; Sun 1–5pm. Subway: 2/3 to Grand Army Plaza.

New York Public Library for the Performing Arts FREE This library branch is a performance clearinghouse, conveniently located near the arts central that is Lincoln Center. Performing arts exhibitions can be found in the Donald and Mary Oenslager Gallery.

40 Lincoln Center Plaza, btw. 64th and 65th sts. ℘ **212/870-1630.** www.nypl.org. Tues–Wed and Fri–Sat noon–6pm; Mon and Thurs noon–8pm. Subway: 1 to 66th St.

Schomburg Center for Research in Black Culture FREE The massive collection of books and art gathered by bibliophile Arturo Alfonso Schomburg is housed at this research branch of the New York Public

Library. Thoughtful exhibits related to black culture rotate through, complemented by talks and performances. Call or check online for scheduling details.

515 Malcolm X Blvd., at Lenox Ave., btw. 135th and 136th sts. ℂ **212/491-2200.** www.nypl.org. Exhibition hours, Mon–Sat 10am–6pm. Subway: 2/3 to 135th St.

Stephen A. Schwarzman Building (Humanities and Social Sciences Library) `FREE` Many local fans of the writer A. A. Milne don't realize that Winnie-the-Pooh has been a fellow Manhattan resident for over half a century. Pooh and friends Piglet, Eeyore, Kanga, and Tigger are all on display here. These are Christopher's actual stuffed animals, instantly recognizable. They've held up pretty well for 90-year-olds, and they're nicely set near a mural of the Hundred Acre Wood. The other book- and manuscript-themed exhibits here (they've even got a Gutenberg Bible) are lovingly displayed and as well written as you'd expect from a library. See p. 128 for information on free tours.

Fifth Ave., at 42nd St. ℂ **917/275-6975.** www.nypl.org. General hours Mon and Thurs–Sat 10am–6pm; Tues–Wed 10am–8pm; Sun 1–5pm (closed Sun in summer); exhibitions may have shorter hours. Subway: B/D/F/M to 42nd St.; 7 to Fifth Ave.; 4/5/6/7/S to 42nd St./Grand Central.

2 Gallery Scene

Art galleries may be Gotham's greatest free cultural resource. Not only do these minimuseums provide us with works of inspiration, they also give us free booze and snacks at their openings. Don't be shy about barging into a show with million-dollar pieces. Gallery owners are almost as happy raising the profiles of their artists as they are closing a sale; both are essential for upping the prices of the work.

If you want invitations to openings, you have a couple of options. You can sign in when you visit a gallery and they'll keep you informed, or you can check online. **ArtCat.com** has an easy-to-read collection of the next week's openings, and **ArtSlant.com** will let you build your own lists of must-see shows. **Artcards.cc** is another good resource, with the added bonus of custom maps of the events you pick out. Typical gallery hours are Tuesday through Saturday from noon to 6pm, but check ahead, as times can vary. Summers can be pretty dead in the art world, and many galleries keep shorter hours, often closing on Saturdays. Many openings are on Thursday nights.

FREE Watching the Auction Action

Sure, you know all about New York's auction scene, the way you follow a stranger in, take an inconspicuous seat off to the side, and try to suppress a sneeze just as a gavel comes down to announce you're the proud owner of a $50,000 Ming vase. But there's more to New York auction houses than expensive misunderstandings and antitrust violations. Viewings and sale previews are excellent chances to treat upcoming lots as museum exhibits. The current top house is **Christie's,** at 20 Rockefeller Plaza, 49th Street between Fifth and Sixth avenues (© **212/636-2000;** www.christies.com). **Sotheby's** runs a close second on the Upper East Side, 1334 York Ave., at 72nd Street (© **212/606-7000;** www.sothebys.com). There are a couple of often-overlooked smaller houses that sell equally intriguing artifacts. **Swann Auction Galleries,** 104 E. 25th St., between Park Avenue South and Lexington Avenue (© **212/254-4710;** www.swanngalleries.com), has been around since 1941, with a focus on works on paper. **Bonhams & Butterfields** dates back to England and 1793, although its presence in New York is on a recent upswing. American art, Titanic artifacts, and natural history rarities have made their way through the spiffy headquarters at 580 Madison Ave., between 56th and 57th streets (© **212/644-9001;** www.bonhams.com).

Exhibition calendars for all houses are available online.

CHELSEA

New York's big-money art scene has put most of its eggs in one basket by clustering galleries between Tenth and Eleventh avenues. For the gallery fan, this means you can visit hundreds of shows without ever leaving **the lower West 20s.** The geography also rewards the serendipitous, allowing for quick pop-ins at randomly selected spaces. Not interested in a bunch of paint splotches on Brillo pads? Pop right back out. My favorite strategy is to write down some interesting-sounding shows from the listings and then hit a few of their unlisted neighbors. With floor after floor of galleries in the old warehouse buildings here, you're bound to find something of interest.

Subway: C/E to 23rd St.

FREE SoHo's Secret Installations

The **DIA Foundation for the Arts** (✆ **212/989-5566; www.diacenter. org**) maintains a pair of hidden galleries with eccentric conceptual works by Walter De Maria. Both galleries are open Wednesday to Sunday from noon to 6pm (closed 3–3:30pm).

New York Earth Room   Just like the name says, this is a room full of dirt. Really—140 tons of soil filling up a SoHo loft to a depth of almost 2 feet. It's an oddly compelling sight in the middle of the city, and the rich earthy scent is almost refreshing. 141 Wooster St., btw. Houston and Prince sts. www.earthroom.org.

The Broken Kilometer   A few blocks away you can find a gallery floor covered with orderly rows of solid brass rods. Placed end to end, the 500 rods would stretch exactly—yup, 1 kilometer. (Its sister piece, a sculpture with identical, unbroken brass rods buried vertically in the ground, is in Germany.) 393 West Broadway, btw. Spring and Broome sts. www.brokenkilometer.org.

David Zwirner FREE   One of many SoHo refugees, Zwirner shows a range of interesting, inventive art, usually from emerging artists. His Chelsea holdings cover three separate spaces on West 19th Street.

519, 525, and 533 W. 19th St., btw. Tenth Ave. and West St. ✆ **212/727-2070.** www.davidzwirner.com.

Gagosian Gallery FREE   Perhaps the heaviest hitter around, this gallery puts on major shows in a space large enough to accommodate sculptures by Richard Serra.

555 W. 24th St. and 522 W. 21st St., btw. Tenth and Eleventh aves. Other location: *Upper East Side,* 980 Madison Ave., btw. 76th and 77th sts. ✆ **212/741-1111.** www.gagosian.com.

Matthew Marks Gallery FREE   Matthew Marks has built a mini-empire in west Chelsea. His four galleries show top-tier painting, photography, and sculpture.

523 W. 24th St.; 502 W. 22nd St.; 522 W. 22nd St.; 526 W. 22nd St., btw. Tenth and Eleventh aves. ✆ **212/243-0200.** www.matthewmarks.com.

DOWNTOWN

In the early and mid-'80s, the headquarters of New York's avant-garde was the East Village. Tiny galleries dotted the landscape and helped break the era's big names. The stock market crash of '87 put an abrupt end to frivolous spending, and most of the galleries withered away. It's taken more than 2 decades, but galleries are just now returning. Throughout the **East Village** and **Lower East Side,** and even into **Chinatown,** storefront operations are coming to life. SoHo, conversely, continues to atrophy as an art scene. The galleries can't afford the rents, although a few top-rate institutions remain firmly embedded in the area.

Subway: *SoHo,* N/R to Prince St.; C/E to Spring St. *Lower East Side/Chinatown,* B/D to Grand St.; F to Delancey St.; J/M/Z to Essex St. *East Village,* F to Second Ave.

AIA New York Chapter Center for Architecture `FREE`   The exhibits here tend to be esoteric, geared more to the professional architect than the public at large. The space is interesting, however, with a nice layout. Beneath the ground floor is a side room that shows off the building's geothermal heating and cooling system: They drilled down deeper than the Empire State Building is high in order to make it work.

536 LaGuardia Place, btw. Bleecker and W. 3rd sts. ✆ **212/683-0023.** www.aiany.org.

Artists Space `FREE`   Young artists get exposure on the walls of this SoHo collective, which has been broadening horizons since 1972.

38 Greene St., 3rd floor, btw. Broome and Grand sts. ✆ **212/226-3970.** www.artists space.org.

The Drawing Center `FREE`   This downtown institution supports the often-overlooked discipline of drawing. Lectures and screenings, some of which are free, add to the "draw" at this newly expanded space.

35 Wooster St., btw. Broome and Grand sts. ✆ **212/219-2166.** www.drawingcenter.org.

Grey Art Gallery   This small gallery basically doubles as NYU's fine arts museum. There's nothing sophomoric about the visual art displayed here—rotating exhibitions are thoughtful and usually broadly scoped.

100 Washington Sq. E., btw. Washington Sq. S. and N. ✆ **212/998-6780.** www.nyu. edu/greyart. Suggested admission $3, not enforced.

Swiss Institute `FREE`   The artists shown here often have a Swiss connection. The recent move to a former Deitch Projects' space has brought a higher profile and a lot more square footage.

18 Wooster St., btw. Grand and Canal sts. ✆ **212/925-2035.** www.swissinstitute.net.

MIDTOWN/UPTOWN

With the avant-garde ensconced downtown and in Brooklyn, the galleries that breathe the rarified air of the Upper East Side tend toward the staid side. Art here is of a classic bent, though the definition of classic is pretty elastic these days. Expect to see master works ranging from the Renaissance to the last couple of decades. And if you thought the asking prices were wacky downtown, wait until you see these . . .

Subway: 6 to 68th St.; F to 63rd St.; N/Q/R or 4/5/6 to 59th St.

Americas Society Art Gallery `FREE`   The Americas, from Canada all the way down to Patagonia, are the focus of shows here.

680 Park Ave., at 68th St. ✆ **212/628-3200.** www.americas-society.org.

The Grolier Club `FREE`   This society shows off its love of books and graphic arts in galleries on two separate floors. Shows are free, as are some of the club's bibliophilic lectures.

47 E. 60th St., btw. Park and Madison aves. ✆ **212/838-6690.** www.grolierclub.org.

Hirschl & Adler Galleries `FREE`   After a quarter-century in a landmarked town house, this gallery recently decamped for expanded digs in the Crown Building. A dozen shows a year show off exquisite 18th- to 20th-century European and American painting and decorative arts.

730 Fifth Ave., btw. 56th and 57th sts. ✆ **212/535-8810.** www.hirschlandadler.com.

The Pace Gallery `FREE`   Modernism is the new classicism, and this successor to PaceWildenstein specializes in the best of it.

32 E. 57th St., btw. Fifth and Madison aves. ✆ **212/421-3292.** www.thepacegallery. com. Other locations: *Chelsea,* 534 W. 25th St., 510 W. 25th St., and 545 W. 22nd St., btw. Tenth and Eleventh aves. ✆ **212/929-7001.**

Richard L. Feigen & Co. `FREE`   Master works of the last few centuries are the focus here.

34 E. 69th St., btw. Park and Madison aves. ✆ **212/628-0700.** www.rlfeigen.com.

WILLIAMSBURG/BUSHWICK

Not so long ago, Williamsburg's orthodox Jewish population distributed petitions asking for help from above to stem the "plague of the artists" that encroaches on their community. There's been no immediate response from G-d, but I'd bet that the plague continues to rage for the foreseeable future, as artists flock to Brooklyn and overrun Bedford's hipster boundaries. Though it's still more DIY and low-budget than Manhattan's galleries, the scene here is catching up quickly. The only drawback is that the spaces are spread far apart, with recent attention paid to more far-flung Bushwick spaces. To make a full tour here, be prepared to trek some blocks. *Note:* Brooklyn galleries keep different hours from the Manhattan side; many are open from Friday to Monday, or weekends only.

Subway: L to Bedford Ave. or Lorimer St.; J/M/Z to Marcy Ave.; G to Metropolitan Ave.

Pierogi 2000 `FREE`   This small, well-established gallery hangs some of the best painting to be found in Brooklyn. Photo and installation work also go on display, often in the context of intriguing group shows. If you're in need of further visual stimuli, some 700 artists are browsable in the gallery's constantly evolving (and traveling) Flat Files collection.

177 N. 9th St., btw. Bedford and Driggs aves. © **718/599-2144.** www.pierogi2000. com. Tues–Sun 11am–6pm. Other location: *The Boiler,* 191 N. 14th St., btw. Nassau and Wythe aves. Thurs–Sun noon–6pm.

Secret Project Robot `FREE`   This gallery-slash–launching pad for live music and art-party events recently joined the Bushwick scene, settling on a benighted industrial block.

389 Melrose St., btw. Irving and Knickerbocker aves. © **917/860-8282.** www.secret projectrobot.org. Fri 6pm–midnight; Sat–Sun 2–8pm.

Williamsburg Art & Historical Center `FREE`   Housed in an amazing 1867 bank building, this community center is always good for an intriguing art exhibit or two.

135 Broadway, at Bedford St. © **718/486-7372.** www.wahcenter.net. Fri–Mon 1–6pm.

3 Open Studios & Art Fests

Run-down industrial neighborhoods beget artist populations, as the creatively minded come in for cheap, raw studio space. In the old days, a few neighbors would open their doors one weekend to show off their work to friends and floormates. With the explosion of New York's artist population, things have become more organized than the flier-on-a-lamppost invitation system. Several neighborhoods now offer full-blown arts festivals, with music, installations, theater, and gallery events supplementing open studios.

FREE *Mi Casa Es Su Casa:* **Open House New York**

New Yorkers obsess about real estate. As much time as we kill poring over the property blog **Curbed** (**www.curbed.com**), however, there's no substitute for actually poking around someone else's space in person. **Open House New York** opens the doors to some of the most mysterious spaces in the city. The first weekend in October brings New Yorkers access to envy-inducing private residences and awe-inspiring public structures. When else are you going to get a peek at the Richard Meier & Partners Model Museum, the Old Croton Aqueduct, or the grounds of the Roosevelt Island Smallpox Hospital? Locales (almost 200!) are scattered across all five boroughs, so you'll have to come up with a schedule or limit your targets. Reserve early (© **212/991-6470; www.ohny.org**), and note that some reservations come with a $5 fee.

Bushwick Open Studios (BOS) FREE   Bushwick is starting to feel a little like the old East Village, with a committed core of artistic pioneers and a coalescing sense of community. The studios are generally in old factories, with semilegal living quarters amid the canvases and installations. Beyond the voyeuristic pleasures of scoping out strangers' homes, there's free music and beer, and you get to see the art.

Bushwick, Brooklyn. www.artsinbushwick.org. Fri night performances; studios Sat–Sun noon–7pm. Subway: L to Morgan Ave., Montrose Ave., Jefferson St., or DeKalb Ave.; J/M/Z to Myrtle Ave., J to Gates Ave. or Flushing Ave.

Dumbo Arts Festival FREE   The city's preeminent arts fest belongs to DUMBO, where yupster incursions have yet to fully displace the artists whose studios fill these broad-shouldered warehouses. This is probably the best art crop in town, which may or may not be related to the inspiring Manhattan views you'll find through many an artist's window. The festival also features music, dance, video, and gallery extravaganzas, and most of it is free.

DUMBO, Brooklyn. © **718/488-8588.** www.dumboartsfestival.com. Usually the last weekend in Sept. Subway: F to York St.; A/C to High St.

Every Last Sunday on the Lower East Side FREE The "Bargain District" nickname has grown increasingly anachronistic as an influx of tony boutiques and restaurants has upped rents across my beloved LES. Plenty of galleries, studios, and performance spaces remain, and on the last Sunday of each month you can tour through them for free. The tours leave at 1pm, April through October.

Tour usually begins from LES Visitor Center at 54 Orchard St., btw. Grand and Hester sts. (✆ 212/226-9010. www.lowereastsideny.com. Apr–Oct last Sun of the month 1pm. Subway: J/M/Z to Essex St.; F to Delancey St.

Tribeca Open Artist Studio Tour FREE TriBeCa certainly doesn't qualify as a run-down neighborhood, so the 70 artist studios that open up for TOAST are a bit of a surprise. You'll also find free music and slide shows amid the tony condos. The event covers a long weekend in late April/early May.

From Canal south to Warren St., and Lafayette west to Greenwich St. www.toastart walk.com. Fri–Mon, check website for exact hours and locations. Subway: 1 to Franklin St.; A/C/E to Canal St.

Washington Square Outdoor Art Exhibit FREE This Depression-era idea for helping artists get their work out there is now safely into its ninth decade. Streets near Washington Square Park become a gigantic open-air art gallery, where you can browse through the works of some 200 artists and artisans. The show is juried, so even the crafts have standards to meet. Pick up a free map at the intersection of 8th Street and University.

Show covers University Place btw. 3rd and 12th sts., and spills over to Schwartz Plaza. (✆ 212/982-6255. www.washingtonsquareoutdoorartexhibit.org. Noon–6pm Sat–Mon on Memorial Day and Labor Day weekends; Sat–Sun the weekends following. Subway: N/R to 8th St.; A/B/C/D/E/F/M to W. 4th St./Washington Sq.

4 Free Tours

SPONSORED TOURS

New York's Business Improvement Districts (BIDs) started off as coalitions of local merchants who were mostly concerned with picking up trash and herding the homeless into neighborhoods without BIDs. Now fully established, BIDs have taken on cultural roles in their communities, sponsoring concerts and public art. Always eager to boost their 'hoods, a few offer free summer tours, some of which continue year-round. Though there's always something new to learn about New York, don't expect to hear many critical words about the neighborhood or its friendly, hardworking BID.

8th Street Walking Tour `FREE` Eighth Street and its East Village equivalent St. Marks Place are among the city's most colorful commercial strips. Get the inside dirt on the area's heritage, from Abe Lincoln to Jimi Hendrix, courtesy of the Village Alliance. Tours meet on the northwest corner of Second Avenue and St. Marks.

℗ **212/777-2173.** www.villagealliance.org. Late May through Sept select Sat 11:30am. Subway: N/R to 8th St.; 6 to Astor Place.

Flatiron District Walking Tour `FREE` The Flatiron Building (aka Burnham's Folly) is famous for its prowlike presence at the crossing of Broadway and Fifth Avenue. You'll learn all about it, and the neighborhood that borrows its name, on this 90-minute Sunday morning tour. Herman Melville, Edith Wharton, and O. Henry also play a part. Tours leave at 11am, rain or shine, all year long.

Meet at the William Seward statue on the corner of Madison Square Park, 23rd St. and Broadway. ℗ **212/741-2323.** www.flatironbid.org. Sun 11am. Subway: N/R to 23rd St.

Grand Central Partnership `FREE` Grand Central Terminal (not station—train lines end here) is as inspiring as public buildings get. A $175-million restoration has this 1913 Beaux Arts masterpiece looking better than ever. The full story of the building's architecture and history is recounted on a 90-minute tour that leaves from the atrium of 120 Park Ave., right across 42nd Street.

℗ **212/883-2420.** www.grandcentralpartnership.org. Fri 12:30pm. Subway: 4/5/6/7/S to 42nd St./Grand Central.

Orchard Street Bargain District Tour `FREE` The Lower East Side is a bottomless well of history and lore, a "modern-day Byzantium" in the words of novelist Richard Price. This tour focuses on the local commercial history. The first NYC district dedicated to discount retail, for decades the Jewish Lower East Side was the only place where you could shop on Sundays. Fittingly, that's the day this 3-hour tour runs, meeting at 11am in front of Katz's.

Meet up with the guide in front of Katz's Delicatessen, 205 E. Houston St., at Ludlow St. ℗ **866/224-0206** or 212/226-9010. www.lowereastsideny.com. Apr–Nov Sun 11am, rain or shine. Subway: F to Second Ave.

Times Square Exposé FREE   No one familiar with the seedy Times Square of legend would recognize the lounge chair scene there today. No doubt some character has been sacrificed, but at least we've got the tourists concentrated in a single location (and one that lets them feel right at home at that). The local BID shows its pride in its spruced-up streets every Friday at noon, touring past historic theaters and the ultramodern new additions to this storied nabe. Sign up at the NYC & Co Official Visitor Information Desk.

1560 Broadway, the east side of Seventh Ave., btw. 46th and 47th sts. ✆ **212/484-1222.** www.timessquarenyc.org. Fri noon, rain or shine. Subway: N/Q/R to 49th St.; 1/2/3/7/N/Q/R/S to 42nd St./Times Sq.

Union Square: Crossroads of New York Walking Tour FREE   Union Square Park opened in 1831, about the same time New York's wealthy reached this elevation on their inexorable climb uptown. The elegant neighborhood they created was soon steeped in culture, with an influx of theaters and concert halls. By World War I, the moneyed set had moved on and the area was in decline, except for Union Square itself, which remained a popular location for labor rallies and protests. Learn about the neighborhood's history Saturday afternoons at 2pm with Big Onion Walking Tours. Meet at the Lincoln statue on the north end of the park.

16th St. traverse, Union Sq. ✆ **212/517-1826.** www.unionsquarenyc.org. Sat 2pm. Subway: L/N/Q/R/4/5/6 to 14th St./Union Sq.

INDEPENDENT TOURS

Battery Park City FREE   Battery Park is justifiably proud of its beautiful landscaped grounds. With the parks restored to pre-9/11 showroom condition, the area is eager to show itself off. On select Wednesdays you'll find garden tours at 11am. Select weekend days in the warmer months, you can catch a public art tour that surveys the mixed bag of installations down here. There are also poetry and twilight nature walks. Check the website for exact times and hours.

✆ **212/267-9700.** www.bpcparks.org. Subway: R or 1 to Rector St.; 4/5 to Bowling Green.

Big Apple Greeter FREE   These New York boosters roll out the red carpet in an attempt to make their enthusiasm for the city infectious. Visitors can pick any neighborhood they like, and the greeters will find a knowledgeable volunteer to take them around for 2 to 4 hours.

It's free, and there's a no-tipping policy. FINE PRINT Reservations should be made 3 or 4 weeks ahead of time.

☎ **212/669-8159.** www.bigapplegreeter.org.

A Broader View: The African Presence in Early New York FREE Africans, both free and enslaved, had a big role in the development of New York City. This Ranger-led tour will tell you all about it, as you walk from Federal Hall to the African Burial Ground National Monument Memorial. Tours run Tuesdays and Thursdays at 10am; reservations are required. Plan on about 90 minutes (note that tours are suspended during the winter months).

Federal Hall, 26 Wall St., at Nassau St. ☎ **212/637-2019.** www.nps.gov/afbg. Tues and Thurs 10am. Subway: 2/3 or 4/5 to Wall St.; J/Z to Broad St.

Brooklyn Brewery FREE More of a lecture than a tour, this popular weekend event entails a visit to a room full of silver beer vats followed by a trip to the company store. Although the complimentary drink tokens have gone the way of Prohibition, there are tempting discounts when you buy your pints in bulk ($20 will get you five). Tours run Saturdays on the hour between 1 and 5pm and Sundays until 4pm. Doors open at noon. Friday nights you can enjoy the same beer discounts, and other weeknights $8 gets you a small-batch tour and a tasting for four house brews. Pizza delivery is encouraged, you'll find nearby Best Pizza (☎ **718/599-2210;** www.best.piz.za. com) worthy of the hubris suggested by its name.

79 N. 11th St., btw. Wyeth Ave. and Berry St. ☎ **718/486-7422.** www.brooklyn brewery.com. Subway: L to Bedford Ave.

Central Park Conservancy Walking Tours FREE Central Park's rich history and hidden nuggets are explored in these 60- to 90-minute walks. Themes range from landscaping to Revolutionary War sites to the rugged Ramble. Check the website because times, dates, and locations vary. The tours run frequently (some 10 times a week), year-round, in most any weather. Look out for the Conservatory Garden tours, which take you through Manhattan's most beautiful garden.

☎ **212/360-2726.** www.centralparknyc.org.

City Hall FREE When City Hall was finished in 1812, the builders didn't bother with marble and granite in the back, thinking cheaper sandstone would be good enough for a side that would face a bunch of hills and trees. Though the city has experienced a little bit of subsequent expansion, this small-scale building still houses offices of the mayor and city council. The underpublicized guided tour here takes you through a graceful rotunda and up to the Governor's Room, which has a priceless collection of portraits as well as a desk that was used by George Washington.

Broadway at Murray St. ✆ **212/788-2656.** www.nyc.gov/html/artcom/html/tours/tours.shtml. Reserve in advance for tours Thurs 10am (group tours available Mon–Wed and Fri at 10:30am). Subway: R to City Hall; 4/5/6 to Brooklyn Bridge/City Hall; J/Z to Chambers St.; 2/3 to Park Place.

Evergreens Cemetery Tour `FREE` This boneyard on the Brooklyn/Queens border seems to stretch forever. As the final resting place for over half a million people, it's a good thing there's ample space (225 acres to be exact). Rolling hills and vegetation galore make a lush contrast to the city. Guided walking tours are held on select Saturdays at around 11:15am, covering fascinating stories, like that of the businessman who moved into his late wife's mausoleum and spent the last decade of his life chatting and reading to her. Call or check online for a schedule and times.

1629 Bushwick Ave., at Conway St., Brooklyn. ✆ **718/455-5300.** www.theevergreens cemetery.com. Tours assemble at the main entrance, Bushwick Ave. and Conway St. Subway: A/C/J/L/Z to Broadway Junction.

Free Tours by Foot These energetic guides have so much confidence in their tours they're willing to give them away for free. (The assumption being you'll be jazzed enough by a Chinatown food tour or a walk around Greenwich Village that you'll throw a little something in the hat when it's done.) Tours run daily, and usually several are available to choose from. They've also recently inaugurated a Saturday bus tour, although that one costs $16 to reserve a seat, on top of whatever you feel like tipping. Reservations can be made online and are strongly recommended (tours do "sell out").

Locations vary. ✆ **646/450.6831.** www.freetoursbyfoot.com.

Grand Central Terminal On Wednesdays at half past noon, the Municipal Art Society, which helped save this commuter temple, offers an hour-and-a-half-long walking tour. They ask for a $10 donation, but there's no formal fee, just whatever you care to contribute. Meet at the information booth in the middle of the concourse, amid half an acre of gleaming Tennessee marble.

✆ **212/453-0050.** www.mas.org. Wed 12:30pm. 4/5/6/7/S to 42nd St./Grand Central.

Hey, I'm Walkin' Here! FREE These walks are for serious trekkers: Most cover more than 20 miles. The terrain is diverse, surveying scenic highlights of all five boroughs. Recent trips have targeted lesser-known destinations like the south shore of Staten Island, Morrisania, Prohibition Park, and Todt Hill.

www.burnsomedust.com.

Prospect Park Discover Nature Tours FREE Tours here lead into the wilds of Brooklyn, where you can see a newly rehabbed ravine, waterfalls, and Brooklyn's last forest. It's just like the Adirondacks—only with less driving, and better proximity to ethnic food when it's over. Discover tours run on Sundays at 3pm, with a break for winter. Meet at the Audubon Center (at the Boathouse), just inside the Lincoln Road/Ocean Avenue entrance. Check the website for other tour destinations, like the Lefferts Historic House.

⟨ **718/287-3400.** www.prospectpark.org. Subway: B/Q/S to Prospect Park.

Shorewalkers Shorewalkers sure know how to hoof it. This environmental walking group makes some huge treks around the city, usually keeping close to water. FINE PRINT Walks are free for members ($20 annual fee); donations are requested from visitors. Dates, times, and locations vary; call or check the website for specifics.

⟨ **212/330-7686.** www.shorewalkers.org.

Stephen A. Schwarzman Building (Humanities and Social Sciences Library) FREE This 1911 Beaux Arts classic is compelling enough from the outside, with its iconic stairs, and twin lion sentries (Fortitude and Patience). The interior is even more impressive. In addition to free exhibits (p. 116), the library offers daily guided tours. Tours meet Monday through Saturday at 11am and again at 2pm beside the information desk in Astor Hall; the Sunday tour is at 2pm only. When there's an exhibit at Gottesman Hall, you can get a separate tour. Meet Monday through Saturday at 12:30 and 2:30pm, and on Sunday at 3:30pm, at the entrance to the hall. FINE PRINT The library is closed Sundays in summer.

Fifth Ave., at 42nd St. ⟨ **917/275-6975.** www.nypl.org. Subway: B/D/F/M to 42nd St.; 7 to Fifth Ave.; 4/5/6/7/S to 42nd St./Grand Central.

Tweed Courthouse FREE Boss Tweed used this eponymous structure to fleece the city for millions (Tammany cohort Andrew Garvey, the "prince of plasterers," made a cool $133,187—in 1870 dollars—for just 2 days' work). Recently renovated, the building is a fascinating blend of architectural styles, with elaborate arches and brickwork. An octagonal skylight lets the sun pour in on the endless conferences conducted by the current tenant, the Board of Ed.

52 Chambers St., btw. Centre St. and Broadway. (C) **212/788-2656.** www.nyc.gov/html/artcom/html/tours/tours.shtml. Reserve in advance for tours Fri noon (group tours Tues at 10am). Subway: R to City Hall; 4/5/6 to Brooklyn Bridge/City Hall; J/Z to Chambers St.; 2/3 to Park Place.

Urban Park Rangers `FREE`   New Yorkers can have a tenuous connection to nature, which is a shame given all the green that's out there (we have more than twice the open space per capita of Tokyo, and three times that of Mumbai). Our local rangers stand by to get us out there, with free tours running in all five boroughs. A series of walks follow cultural and historical themes, from the Battle of Brooklyn to the Little Red Lighthouse. There's also a great set of hikes, from fitness to nature exploration, with night hikes and other opportunities to access places that are often off-limits. Schedules are available on the website.

Sites vary. (C) **311.** www.nycgovparks.org.

Urban Trail Conference `FREE`   A diverse selection of sites, from downtown Manhattan to the PepsiCo sculpture gardens in Purchase, New York, are toured by these intrepid trekkers. They ask for a $3 donation from nonmembers (a few events cost a little more), although first-timers get to walk for free. Big spenders can get a year's worth of activity by springing for the club's $10 annual dues (just $7 for your rookie season).

Phone numbers vary by tour guide. www.urbantrail.org.

5 Green Peace: Gardens

It's just not healthy for humans to go too long without a break from the concrete jungle. New York has some great parks, but the spaces there tend to be highly cultivated. Our community gardens are nice, too, but they're small and usually don't let the public in for more than a couple of hours a week. Botanical gardens are the best way to inhale fresh country air, and they're closer than you might think. Time your visit right, and they're also completely free.

FREE Parking It

Parks are among the city's best freebies, and we're fortunate to be in an era of expansion. Some 550 acres (!) of new parkland have opened up along the **piers near Chelsea.** The city did a gorgeous job with these urban beaches, including planting some actual slender-leaved vegetation called "grass." Across town, restoration continues on the **East River Park.** When it's finally completed, epic Brooklyn views will complement benches, ball fields, and a wide jogging path. Everyone knows about the great Manhattan views from the **Brooklyn Promenade,** but Queens has an equally impressive skyline vantage that many New Yorkers have never seen. The **Gantry Plaza State Park** in Long Island City is fitted with piers that jut out over the East River, facing the U.N. and Empire State Building, standing tall among Midtown's architectural jumble (and sinks to clean your catch, should you decide to cast a line into the East River). My favorite city spot for breathing country air is actually **Green-Wood Cemetery** (℅ **718/768-7300;** www.green-wood.com), on the south side of Park Slope. In addition to landscaped hills, venerable trees, glacial ponds, celebrity graves, and Revolutionary War history, your (free) price of admission also entitles you to the surreal sight of flocks of wild monk parrots, which have infiltrated the intricate Civil War–era front gate and surrounding grounds. For a dirt cheap meal afterwards, stop by the nearby **Sea Witch** (℅ **347/ 227-7166**), a neighborhood watering hole with killer cheeseburgers at just $5.50.

Brooklyn Botanic Garden Fifty-two acres of cherry trees, roses, formal gardens, and ponds in the heart of Brooklyn is nothing short of a miracle. This is the city's most popular botanic garden and it's spectacular almost year-round. April to early May are particularly worth noting, with the tulips poking out and the blossoms rioting. Don't miss the Fragrance Garden, designed for the blind, and one of the world's largest collections of bonsai. Free tours run on the weekends at 1pm with no reservations necessary, leaving from the brand-new Visitor Center. When the cherry blossoms are out, there are also free tours as part of the Hanami celebration. Regular admission is $10, but Tuesdays are free, as are Saturday mornings from 10am to noon. In winter, you can add Tuesday through Friday to the free list (mid-Nov to early March).

1000 Washington Ave., at Eastern Pkwy., Brooklyn. © **718/623-7200.** www.bbg.org. Tues–Fri 8am–6pm; Sat–Sun 10am–6pm; closes at 4:30pm Nov to mid-March. Open Mon holidays, except Labor Day. Subway: 2/3 to Eastern Pkwy./Brooklyn Museum; B/Q to Prospect Park; S to Botanic Garden.

New York Botanical Garden   Visions of the Bronx don't conjure up uncut forests, rhododendron valleys, waterfalls, ponds, and wetlands. But for over a century the Bronx has been home to one of America's premier public gardens. With over 250 acres of rolling hills and land-scaped gardens, if it's flora you can probably find it. Admission to the grounds is $10 ($20 gets you a tram tour and the run of everything), but all day Wednesday and Saturday morning from 10am to 11am you can get into the grounds for free.

200th St. and Southern Blvd., the Bronx. © **718/817-8700.** www.nybg.org. Tues–Sun and Mon holidays 10am–6pm; closes 5pm mid-Jan through Feb. Metro North (© 800/METRO-INFO [638-7646] or 212/532-4900) runs from Grand Central Terminal to the New York Botanical Garden station; it's a 20-min. ride. Subway: B/D/4 to Bed-ford Park, walk southeast on Bedford Park Blvd. 8 blocks.

Queens Botanical Garden   This little-known park is an oasis in the heart of busy Flushing. Formal gardens are joined by a 21-acre arboretum, plus rose, bee, and Victorian gardens. A gorgeous new visitor center, com-plete with environmentally friendly technology, opened in 2007. Spring is the natural time to visit—the entire garden is awash with color. Admis-sion is just $4, and that's waived from November through March. During the warmer months, entry is also free from 3 to 6pm Wednesdays and 4 to 6pm Sundays.

43–50 Main St., at Dahlia St., Flushing, Queens. © **718/886-3800.** www.queens botanical.org. Nov–Mar Tues–Sun 8am–4:30pm; Apr–Oct Tues–Sun 8am–6pm. Sub-way: 7 to Main St. Flushing.

Wave Hill   Some of the city's most gorgeous acreage can be found in Riverdale, in the Bronx, where Wave Hill's breathtaking views take in the panorama of the Hudson and the Palisades. Thousands of plant species are spread across the 28 acres here, originally the grounds of a private estate. The flora curious can educate themselves in the

carefully labeled herb and flower gardens. Horticultural, environmental, and forestry programs provide further edification. Regular
admission is $8, but the grounds are free from 9am to noon on Tues-
days (May–June and Sept–Oct) and Saturdays. In the off-peak months
(Nov–Apr, July, and Aug), it's free all day on Tuesday. Free garden
tours leave 2pm Sundays from the Perkins Visitor Center, and free gallery tours go Tuesdays and Saturdays at 1pm at the Glyndor Gallery.

675 W. 252nd St., at Independence Ave., the Bronx. ℂ **718/549-3200.** www.wavehill.
org. Mid-Mar through Oct Tues–Sun 9am–5:30pm; Nov to mid-Mar closes at 4:30pm.
Subway: 1 to 242nd St., pick up the free Wave Hill shuttle. Metro North (ℂ 212/532-
4900) from Grand Central to the Riverdale station; from there, it's a pleasant 5-block
walk to Wave Hill, or take the Wave Hill shuttle.

6 Zoo York

New York has plenty of fauna to go with its flora, though it isn't
always cheap to check out. The minizoos in the major Brooklyn,
Queens, and Manhattan parks charge $8 to $12 and the Bronx Zoo
asks for $16. Fortunately, there are alternatives. The Bronx has a "pay
what you wish" policy 1 day a week, and the city's parks are rich with
other opportunities for getting close to critters.

Bronx Zoo Wildlife Conservation Park   Yankee Stadium isn't the only
place in the Bronx where you can find thousands of animals running
wild in their natural habitat. The Bronx Zoo is the largest city zoo in the
country, and one of New York's greatest assets. Gibbons, snow leop-
ards, red pandas, Western lowland gorillas, okapi, and red river hogs
are just a few of the famous residents. With 265 acres to explore, it's
easy to wander away a full day here. For summer visits, try to get here
early or late, as the midday heat often finds the animals sleepy in their
enclosures. Admission is $16, but Wednesdays are on a contribution
basis (the suggested admission is the full price, but it's pay what you
wish). Additional charges ($3 or so) will apply for some exhibits.

185th St. and Southern Blvd. ℂ **718/367-1010.** www.bronxzoo.com. Nov–Mar daily
10am–4:30pm (extended hours for Holiday Lights late Nov to early Jan); Apr–Oct
Mon–Fri 10am–5pm, Sat–Sun 10am–5:30pm. Subway: 2/5 to E. Tremont Ave./West
Farms Sq., 2 to Pelham Pkwy. Also Metro North to Fordham Rd. (then Bx9 bus) and
the BxM11 express bus.

FREE BIRDS

A dearth of rest stops on the Eastern Seaboard makes New York parks essential for avian travelers. For better views of our most welcome tourists, visit three of our most accessible parks.

Bryant Park FREE This green patch in the city's center attracts not only vegetation-craving wage slaves, but a cross section of Northeast Seaboard birds. **Birding tours** cosponsored by the New York City Audubon Society (**www.nycaudubon.org**) begin at Heiskell Plaza, near the Sixth Avenue and 42nd Street entrance, Mondays from 8 to 9am and Thursdays from 5 to 6pm in April and May, and again in late September and October Thursdays from 8 to 9am. **Meet the Birds at Le Carrousel** provides entry to a more exotic avian crew. Every Tuesday from April to September between 11:30am and 2pm, you can interact with rescued parakeets, lovebirds, and other exotic fliers from the Arcadia Bird Sanctuary and Education Center.

© 212/768-4242. www.bryantpark.org. Subway: B/D/F/M to 42nd St.; 7 to Fifth Ave.

Central Park FREE Birdsong fills the thickets of the Ramble, an unexpectedly rural stretch of the park. You can take a closer look at the warbling set with a **kit** (a backpack with binoculars, reference materials, and a map) available from the Belvedere Castle. The kits are available Tuesday to Sunday from 10am to 4:30pm. Valid ID is required. Call ahead for reservations.

Mid-park at 79th St. © 212/772-0210. www.centralparknyc.org. Subway: B/C to 81st St.

FREE 🐶 Dog Days Afternoons

Being trapped in small, dark apartments is just as hard on dogs as it is on us. Fortunately for dogs, they have a release valve in the form of dog runs. The human and canine interactions make great free public theater. The **Tompkins Square** dog run, the city's first, is my favorite. Both the four-legged and two-legged regulars have a ton of character, and their friendships and rivalries are fascinating to observe. Don't miss the creative costumes of the **Dog Run Halloween Parade,** a 20-year tradition held at noon on the Sunday before Halloween. Tompkins Sq. Park, btw. 7th and 10th sts. and aves. A and B. **www.dogster.org**. Subway: 6 to Astor Place; F to Second Ave.

FREE A Midnight Elephant Walk

When the pachyderms of Ringling Brothers visit the Big Apple, they're coming off their Nassau Coliseum stand. Their train only gets them as far as the Long Island City yards. They can't exactly get a lift to the gig from a towncar, so they have to hoof it, through the Queens-Midtown Tunnel and down the streets of Manhattan. Watching the elephants emerge from the tunnel is an amazing spectacle. They walk in a file of trunks holding tails, with clown escorts all around. Often other hoofed beasts like zebras and camels come along for the stroll. The walk goes all the way to the elephants' 5-story ramp at Madison Square Garden, but the best scene is at the tunnel entrance around 37th Street between Second and Third aves. The crowd is fun-loving, with the freaks that events in Manhattan invariably bring out well-represented. The procession hits Manhattan around midnight. Whether you come for the spectacle or just to hiss the exploitation of animals, be sure to be on time because the whole thing goes surprisingly quickly. The elephant walk takes place at the beginning of the circus' annual stand (usually late March); check the weekly update on the website for the exact date and time. ℂ **212/465-6741.** www.ringling.com. Subway: 6 to 33rd. St.; A/C/E or 1/2/3 to 34th St.

Prospect Park FREE During spring's annual northward migration, hundreds of bird species pass through. To get some expert assistance in identifying the birdies, hook up with an introductory **bird-watching tour** (Sat noon–1:30pm). Tours leave from the boathouse, inside the Lincoln Road/Ocean Avenue entrance.

ℂ **718/287-3400.** www.prospectpark.org. Subway: B/Q/S to Prospect Park.

GO FISH

It's a fine line between standing along the shore like an idiot with a stick in your hands and going fishing, but kids love baiting up and casting in anyway. The city offers a few spots for gathering fodder for "the one that got away" tales.

Battery Park City `FREE`   Drop a line in the Hudson and see if you can pull up any three-eyed specimens. (Actually, the river's been mending remarkably in recent years, thanks to antipollution measures.) Bait and equipment are loaned out in Wagner Park. Sessions run from 10am to 2pm on select Saturdays. Look for free music and storytelling to accompany your angling.

© **212/267-9700.** www.bpcparks.org. Subway: R or 1 to Rector St.; 4/5 to Bowling Green.

Central Park `FREE`   Like the good New Yorkers they are, some 50,000 fish pack uncomplainingly into the confines of the Harlem Meer. You can try your hand at catching a bass, catfish, or bluegill with equipment loaned by the Charles A. Dana Discovery Center. Bait, pole, and instructions are provided. Note that it's strictly catch-and-release. Open Tuesday to Saturday 10am to 4pm (last pole goes out at 3pm) and Sunday 10am to 2pm (last pole out at 1pm), mid-April to mid-October. Valid photo ID is required.

Inside Central Park at 110th St., btw. Fifth and Lenox aves. © **212/860-1370.** www.centralparknyc.org. Subway: 2/3 to Central Park North.

Hudson River Park `FREE`   There's no dilemma whether to fish or cut bait here, as the **Big City Fishing** program takes care of the latter for you. Experienced anglers are on hand to offer advice, and the rods are free to borrow. Don't get too attached to your oyster toadfishes, flukes, or cunners, however, because everything is catch-and-release. Available summer Tuesdays through Fridays from 10am to 4:30pm, weather permitting.

Pier 84, the Hudson at W. 44th St. © **212/627-2020.** www.hudsonriverpark.org. Subway: A/C/E/7 to 42nd St./Port Authority.

The beautiful Reading Room of the New York Public Library is one of the free things in New York City that helps make everyday life enjoyable.

LOCAL LIVING

nybody who thinks it's easy to live in New York is sitting on a mountain of cash. You don't have to look any further than the housing market to find trouble. For the privilege of paying $1,800 a month to live in a noisy veal pen, chances are you'll be hit with a 15% broker's fee. Healthcare, health insurance, health clubs— just about everything can come with a huge price tag. Yet 8.2 million of us stay. The experience of being a New Yorker is too exciting and rich for us to complain (much) about the costs of living. We'd much rather talk about which neighborhood our apartment is in. Besides, the city presents plenty of free and cheap opportunities to improve your quality of life, from classes and lectures to grooming and recreation. Leases notwithstanding, it is quite possible to live large on small budgets in NYC.

1 Sense for Cents: Education

CLASSES, LECTURES & SEMINARS

Just walking the streets and riding the subways is all too often a learning experience in New York, but most of us have room for further development along less informal lines. A handful of classes and a nearly endless selection of lectures provide New Yorkers with educational opportunities left and right. Cooper Union looks the other way when it comes to tuition, and although other local institutions aren't quite so generous, most have programs open to the public for little or no charge.

Access Restricted FREE What began as an excuse to open up New York's glorious legal bastions to those of us who walk the line has expanded to providing entry to all manner of undertrafficked venues. The Lower Manhattan Cultural Council sponsors this series of free lectures, usually four themed events held in the spring months. The series is popular and space is limited, so make reservations as soon as you can (the RSVP goes live 8 days prior to each lecture).

Lower Manhattan Cultural Council, various locations. (C) **212/219-9401.** www. lmcc.net.

Battery Park City FREE In addition to giving us open space, landscaping, and music aplenty, Battery Park also helps boost our eyehand coordination. Three drawing classes are offered from early May to late October. Elements of Nature Drawing (Wed 11:30am–1:30pm), Drawing in the Park (Sat 10am–noon), and Figure al Fresco (Wed 2:30–4:30pm), are all led by an artist. (Alas, the figure in Figure al Fresco is clothed.) See later in this chapter for the eye-hand coordination covered by tai chi. Check the website for locations, usually Wagner Park and South Cove.

Battery Park City, along South End Ave., just west of West St. (C) **212/267-9700.** www. bpcparks.org. Subway: 1/2/3 or A/C to Chambers St.; 1 to Rector St. or South Ferry; 4/5 to Bowling Green.

BMCC Tribeca Performing Arts Center FREE This not-for-profit space brings in an array of jazz and pop performers. The concerts have standard (that is, pricey) ticket charges, but you can catch additional edification courtesy of the PAC's free humanities programs, which often run before shows. Documentary film footage and panel discussions (or Q&As) are the primary offerings; check the website for schedules.

199 Chambers St., btw. Greenwich St. and the West Side Hwy. ℂ **212/509-0300.** www.tribecapac.org. Subway: 1/2/3 or A/C to Chambers St.

Brooklyn Center for Media Education   The revolution may not be televised, but everything else will be. Check out the incredibly affordable classes at BRIC Arts. A 3-week basic editing course is $60, as is a 6-day graphic design intro. Basic Marketing Techniques and Introduction to Social Media are free, as are 2-hour orientations, which are prerequisites for some of the more advanced coursework. Get yourself certified as a community producer and you can use production equipment and facilities for free. An affiliated network (BCAT-TV) lets Brooklyn residents air programs, also for no cost. Start putting the free back in free speech by visiting the website and downloading a course catalog.

242 3rd St., btw. Third and Fourth aves., Park Slope, Brooklyn. ℂ **718/683-5645.** www.bricartsmedia.org. Subway: R to Union St.

Brooklyn Creative   Gallery and community space Rabbithole plays host to this low-cost educational center. Art and photography are the focus, with hands-on learning the main technique. Three-hour workshops start at $49, but the super bargain on the calendar falls under the title "5 Dollar Fridays." From 6:30 to 8pm on select Fridays, catch an introductory class on a topic like Photoshop basics or composition, for less than the cost of a pint of beer.

33 Washington St., btw. Water and Plymouth sts. ℂ **718/362–2394.** www.weare brooklyncreative.com. Subway: F to York St.

Columbia University FREE   New York City's member of the Ivy League has an impressive events calendar, with talks and colloquiums supplementing readings and musical performances. Topics range from esoteric science to less dry material ("My Life as an Undocumented Immigrant"). Venues vary, although Lerner Hall is a popular location, 2922 Broadway, at 115th Street. You should also check out the lectures in the **Cafés Columbia** series. Four categories of study (art, science, social science, and humanities) rotate through the

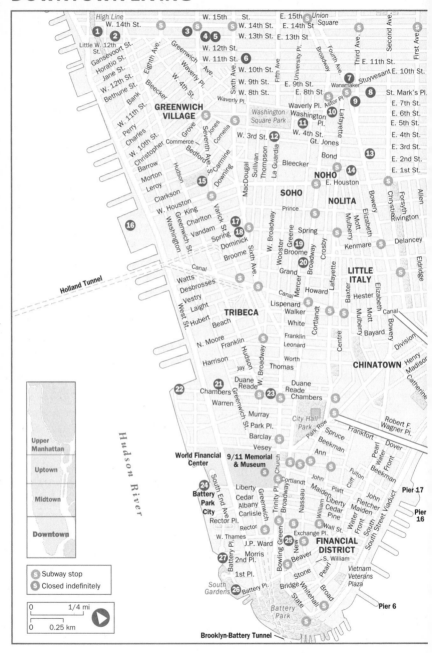

Upper Manhattan

Uptown

Midtown

Downtown

Ⓢ Subway stop
Ⓢ Closed indefinitely

| 0 | 1/4 mi |
| 0 | 0.25 km |

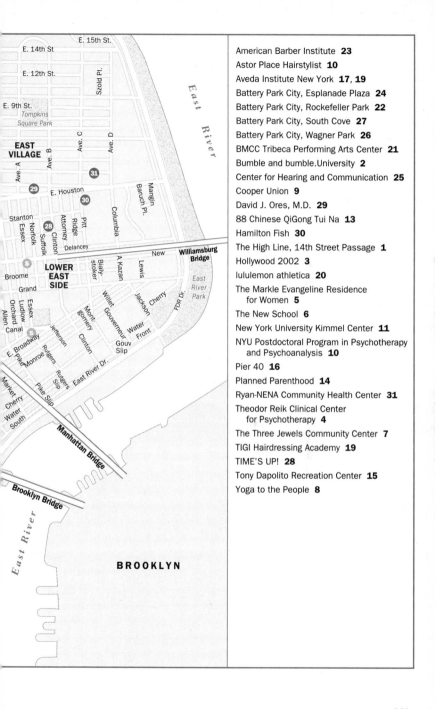

MIDTOWN LIVING

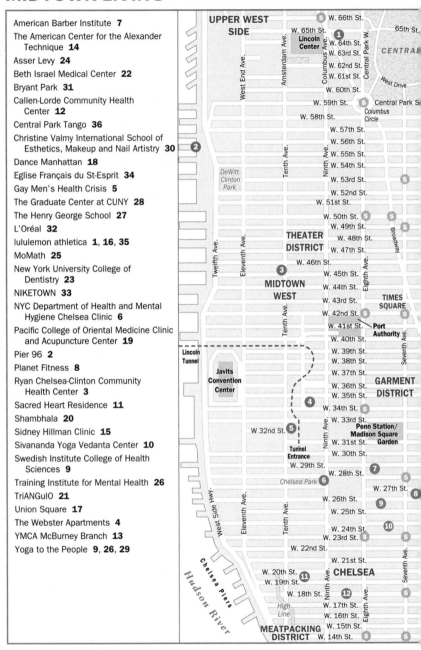

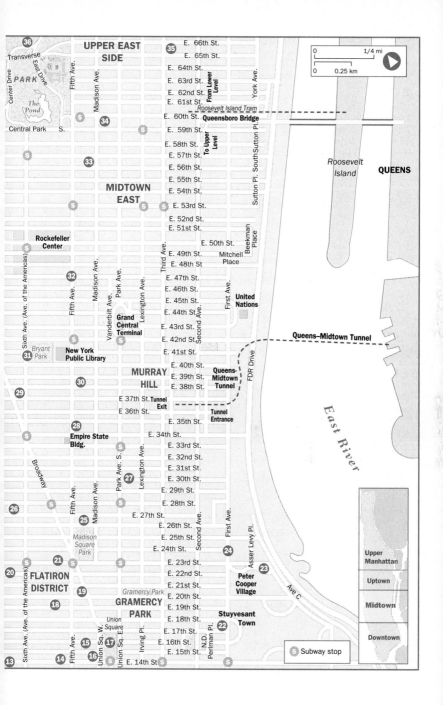

UPTOWN LIVING

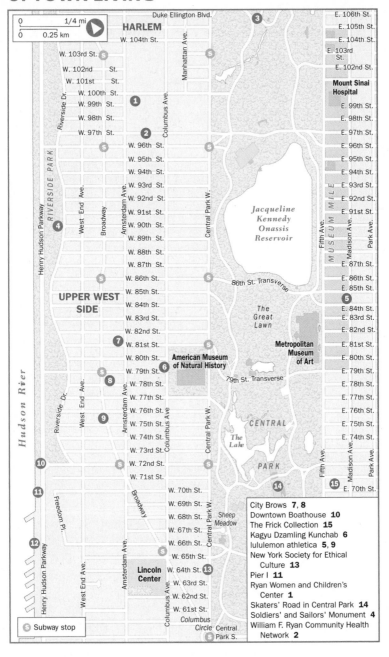

0 — 1/4 mi
0 — 0.25 km

HARLEM

Duke Ellington Blvd.

W. 104th St.
W. 103rd St. ⑤
W. 102nd St.
W. 101st St.
W. 100th St.
W. 99th St. ❶
W. 98th St.
W. 97th St. ❷
W. 96th St. ⑤
W. 95th St.
W. 94th St.
W. 93rd St.
W. 92nd St.
W. 91st St.
W. 90th St.
W. 89th St.
W. 88th St.
W. 87th St.
W. 86th St. ⑤
W. 85th St.

UPPER WEST SIDE

W. 84th St.
W. 83rd St.
W. 82nd St.
W. 81st St. ❼
W. 80th St.
W. 79th St. ⑤
W. 78th St.
W. 77th St.
W. 76th St.
W. 75th St.
W. 74th St.
W. 73rd St.
W. 72nd St. ⑤
W. 71st St.
W. 70th St.
W. 69th St.
W. 68th St.
W. 67th St.
W. 66th St.
W. 65th St.
W. 64th St. ⑬
W. 63rd St.
W. 62nd St.
W. 61st St.

Lincoln Center

Columbus Circle
Central Park S.

Riverside Dr.
RIVERSIDE PARK
Henry Hudson Parkway
West End Ave.
Broadway
Amsterdam Ave.
Columbus Ave.
Manhattan Ave.

Hudson River

Freedom Pl.
Henry Hudson Parkway
Amsterdam Ave.
West End Ave.
Riverside Dr.

❹ ⑤ ❽ ❾ ❿ ⑪ ⑫

Central Park W.

Jacqueline Kennedy Onassis Reservoir

86th St. Transverse

The Great Lawn

The Lake

CENTRAL

PARK

79th St. Transverse

American Museum of Natural History ❻

Metropolitan Museum of Art

MUSEUM MILE

Fifth Ave.
Madison Ave.
Park Ave.

Sheep Meadow

❸

E. 106th St.
E. 105th St.
E. 104th St.
E. 103rd St.
E. 102nd St.

Mount Sinai Hospital

E. 99th St.
E. 98th St.
E. 97th St.
E. 96th St. ⑤
E. 95th St.
E. 94th St.
E. 93rd St.
E. 92nd St.
E. 91st St.
E. 90th St.
E. 87th St.
E. 86th St.
E. 85th St. ⑤
E. 84th St.
E. 83rd St.
E. 82nd St.
E. 81st St.
E. 80th St.
E. 79th St.
E. 78th St.
E. 77th St.
E. 76th St.
E. 75th St.
E. 74th St.
E. 70th St. ⑮

❶❹ ⑮

Fifth Ave.
Madison Ave.
Park Ave.

City Brows **7**, **8**
Downtown Boathouse **10**
The Frick Collection **15**
Kagyu Dzamling Kunchab **6**
lululemon athletica **5**, **9**
New York Society for Ethical Culture **13**
Pier I **11**
Ryan Women and Children's Center **1**
Skaters' Road in Central Park **14**
Soldiers' and Sailors' Monument **4**
William F. Ryan Community Health Network **2**

⑤ Subway stop

PicNic Market & Café (© **212/222-8222;** www.picnicmarket.com) every Monday from 6 to 7pm. There's a $10 cover, but it includes a drink.

Main Campus, 2690 Broadway, entrance at 116th St. © **212/854-9724.** www.columbia.edu. Subway: 1 to 116th St.

Cooper Union `FREE` Self-made entrepreneur and inventor Peter Cooper founded the Cooper Union for the Advancement of Science and Art in 1857 to allow underprivileged talents to receive free education. The college's mission hasn't changed, and 1,000 students currently attend without tuition. Admission is based solely on merit, and competition is, as you'd expect, fierce. The public can take advantage of the institution in other ways, however. The **Saturday Outreach Program** (**www.saturdayoutreach.org**) helps high school students further themselves in the arts with free classes (even the materials fee is waived). Student exhibitions can be seen in free galleries, and free lectures are held in the Great Hall. Check online for an events calendar.

Cooper Sq., 8th St., btw. Bowery and Third Ave. © **212/353-4120.** www.cooper.edu. Subway: 6 to Astor Place; N/R to 8th St.

Downtown Boathouse `FREE` Every Wednesday night in summer, the boathouse offers kayaking classes free to the public. Most classes are held in the waters of Clinton Cove Park. Put your new knowledge to work by coming back to borrow a kayak (free; see "Rollin' on the Rivers," on p. 173). Classes start at 6pm, during the warmer months (Apr–Oct). `FINE PRINT` They'll be getting you in the water, so bring a bathing suit, and a lock if you want to make use of the changing room.

Pier 96, West Side Hwy. at 56th St. © **646/613-0375.** www.downtownboathouse.org. Subway: A/B/C/D/1 to 59th St./Columbus Circle.

Eglise Français du St-Esprit `FREE` This French-speaking Episcopal congregation has called New York home since 1628. French classes are a century-old tradition here, held before Sunday's Morning Prayer. The classes are free, at 10am every Sunday. Services start at 11:15am.

100 E. 60th St., btw. Madison and Park aves. © **212/838-5680.** www.stespritnyc.net. Subway: 4/5/6 or N/Q/R to 59th St.; F to Lexington Ave./63rd St.

Etsy Labs `FREE` The virtual DIY marketplace that is Etsy.com holds down a real-world address in DUMBO. Inside the Etsy Labs you can take advantage of free craft fests and lectures from technical aces on the coding side of crafting. Bring your own project and borrow some equipment and supplies, or learn from an expert (teacups, hats, and finger puppets have been items of attention in recent sessions). See the website for updated schedules. The **Church of Craft** (**www. churchofcraft.org**) also holds free creativity services the third Thursday of the month from 5 to 8pm.

55 Washington St., Ste. 712, btw. Water and Front sts. ℂ **718/855-7955.** www.etsy. com. Subway: F to York St.

The Frick Collection FREE   Inside the Gilded Age confines of this elegant art museum, you can catch Wednesday evening lectures. Subjects tend toward painterly subjects like Albrecht Dürer's hands and Goya's black paintings. A series called Artists, Poets, and Writers broadens the floor to include in-person luminaries like Frank Stella and analysis of immortals like Henry James. Lectures start at 6pm, with seating at 5:45pm. Don't arrive earlier than that, lest they have time to hit you up for the $18 admission fee.

1 E. 70th St., btw. Madison and Fifth aves. ℂ **212/288-0700.** www.frick.org. Subway: 6 to 68th St./Hunter College.

Gotham Writers' Workshop FREE   The Microsoft of NYC's writing programs, Gotham coaches up some 7,000 writers a year. You can sample the goods free at frequent 1-hour workshops. The events are held at the major bookstores around town (plus visits to Bryant Park), on topics like dialogue, travel writing, stand-up comedy, and Creative Writing 101. (Of course, you'll be encouraged to sign up for their weekly and intensive and online workshops, which do charge a fee.)

Various locations. ℂ **212-WRITERS** (974-8377). www.writingclasses.com.

The Graduate Center at the City University of New York FREE   Continuing ed lectures, seminars, and panel discussions can be found here, with more possibilities for finding cheap smarts than any other institution in the city. Titles run from "Jewish Ethics Under Pressure" to "Unzipping the Monster Dick: Deconstructing Ableist Penile Representations in Two Ethnic Homoerotic Magazines." Many events are free with seating on a first-come, first-served basis. Advance reservations can be made online. Also look for free lunchtime concerts on Thursdays at 1pm; several are followed by free master classes.

365 Fifth Ave., btw. 34th and 35th sts. ℂ **212/817-8215.** www.gc.cuny.edu. Subway: B/D/F/M/N/Q/R to 34th St./Herald Sq.; 6 to 33rd St.

The Henry George School `FREE`

Although Henry George is no longer a household name, in the 19th century his economics texts and lectures made him a major political player. His progressive ideas are still taught today, and in keeping with George's anti-privilege stance, the school that bears his name offers its programs free. Classes are available in English or Spanish, usually in the evenings. Teachings are based on George's championing of shifting tax burdens to land-owners. *Note:* Finishing the school's Fundamental Economics course is the prerequisite for most upper-level work. Those interested in samples of the material can attend the **Friday Evening Forum,** a free lecture series Fridays at 6:30pm.

121 E. 30th St., btw. Park and Lexington aves. ✆ **212/889-8020.** www.henry georgeschool.org. Subway: 6 to 28th St.

Math Encounters `FREE`

The city's newest museum is MoMath, an institution dedicated to expanding the horizons of arithmo-phobes and arithmophiles alike. An accompanying lecture series makes the discipline accessible, with topics like the math humor hidden in *The Simpsons* or the geometry of origami. Math Encounters is held at the Baruch College Conference Center (55 Lexington Ave. at 24th St.), with a move to the museum itself starting in February 2013. The lectures are usually offered the first Wednesday of the month; advanced reservations are recommended.

Where to Get Stuff Fixed (or Fix Other People's)

One of the city's more random institutions is **Proteus Gowanus,** a gallery and reading room that also hosts the world's only Gowanus Canal museum (the EPA recently bequeathed the official Superfund Site Sediment Sample). They have some great community programs, like a Wednesday night constrained-writing workshop (the Writhing Society, $5 suggested donation), and the **Fixers Collective (www. fixerscollective.org),** which gathers once a month on Thursday nights from 7 to 10pm. Pooled intelligence and a smattering of expertise get applied to the likes of busted bikes, fans, clocks, and umbrellas. If it'll fit through the door, it's eligible for some fiddling. Five dollar donations are happily accepted. 543 Union St., down the alley off Nevins St. ✆ **718/234-1572.** www. proteusgowanus.com. Proteus Gowanus gallery open Thurs–Fri 3–6pm; Sat–Sun noon–6pm.

MoMath, 11 E. 26th St., btw. Fifth and Madison aves. ℂ **212/542-0566.** www. momath.org. Subway: N/R or 6 to 23rd St.

MillionTreesNYC FREE   In an effort to green up the city (and maybe take a swipe at global warming while we're at it), the parks department is giving away a cool million trees. Unfortunately the ground rules—they must be planted on private property in one of the five boroughs—exclude a lot of New Yorkers. Even if the closest you've come to landowning is a half-dead jade plant in a windowsill, you can still take advantage of this program. Free classes are held all over town, on topics ranging from caring for a new tree to reforestation stewardship to the adoption of street trees.

Various locations. ℂ **212/333-2552.** www.milliontreesnyc.org.

The New School FREE   Though no longer so new (a 90th birthday celebration is already in the rear-view mirror), the New School stays up-to-date, and there's still a progressive edge to its programs. The calendar of free events is cluttered with readings, lectures, panel discussions, student films, and even investing seminars. Events are open to the public, with some requiring advance reservation; check online for a full calendar.

66 W. 12th St., btw. Fifth and Sixth aves. ℂ **212/229-5600.** www.newschool.edu. Subway: F/M to 14th St.; L to Sixth Ave.; L/N/Q/R/4/5/6 to 14th St./Union Sq.

New York Philosophy FREE   These monthly symposia are as much about conversations and cocktails as they are about the intricacies of metaphysical analysis. Convening in an Irish bar certainly doesn't detract from the sociability. Meet-ups are held monthly, usually 6 to 10pm on Tuesday, and are free with an online RSVP.

The Irish Rogue, 356 W. 44th St., btw. Eighth and Ninth aves. ℂ **212/445-0131.** www. nyphilosophy.com. Subway: A/C/E/7 to 42nd St./Port Authority.

New York Public Library FREE   It would be easier to list the classes *not* available for free at New York's public libraries than to mention all of the possibilities. Practical courses predominate, covering topics like writing, crafts, résumé updating, job searches, using the Internet, and the ins and outs of genealogical research. For a meta experience, you can also attend a self-directed class on how to take maximum advantage of library resources. The best way to get started is to go online and check out the options at your local branch.

For the Bronx, Manhattan, and Staten Island branches, log on to **www.nypl.org/branch**, or call ✆ **212/930-0800.** For the Queens Library, check **www.queenslibrary.org**, or call ✆ **718/990-0700.** In Brooklyn, log on to **www.brooklynpubliclibrary.org**, or you can call ✆ **718/230-2100.**

Every branch of the New York Public Library offers computers with free Internet, access to electronic databases, and Microsoft Office applications. Many branches also have computers loaded with multimedia CD-ROMs. You can focus on SimCity or ResumeMaker, depending on your level of job market optimism.

New York Society for Ethical Culture `FREE` For over 125 years now, this organization has been providing New Yorkers with humanist alternatives to organized religion. A liberal outlook is usually presented in the free lectures that are held here, as well as at the regular talks on Sunday mornings. Log on to the website for exact schedules.

2 W. 64th St., at Central Park West. ✆ **212/874-5210.** www.nysec.org. Subway: A/B/C/D/1 to 59th St./Columbus Circle.

New York University `FREE` The streets around Washington Square Park are dominated by NYU architecture and NYU students, and the community is invited to take advantage of this private university's resources. Lecture programs (the history of the Village, say), talks, and symposia can be found for free. Other events carry nominal admission charges, in the $2 to $5 range. The new Kimmel Center is a good place to start for tracking down free culture.

Kimmel Center, 60 Washington Sq. S., btw. LaGuardia Place and Thompson St. ✆ **212/998-4900.** www.nyu.edu or www.nyufreeandpublic.blogspot.com. Subway: A/B/C/D/E/F/M to W. 4th St./Washington Sq.

Open City Dialogue `FREE` It's difficult to scan the offerings of this bimonthly lecture series and not get immediately sucked in. If there's an overriding theme it's personal obsession, with recent forays into Civil War impersonators, the Amahuaca people, and visualizations of vibrations. Talks go every other Monday (or so) at 7:30pm in the backroom of Pete's Candy Store.

709 Lorimer St., btw. Frost and Richardson sts., Williamsburg, Brooklyn. ✆ **718/302-3770.** www.petescandystore.com. Subway: L to Lorimer St.; G to Metropolitan Ave.

Park Slope Food Coop `FREE` This Brooklyn cooperative keeps its community informed with lectures, demonstrations, and "Plow-to-Plate" film screenings. Topics here are left-leaning, concerning food, the environment, and timely advice about how not to be killed by eating beef. Everything is free, even to non-Coop members, although sometimes a small materials fee is added to food classes. Check online for the latest schedule. Classes and lectures are held on the second floor meeting room (which also hosts a periodic free clothes swap) unless otherwise noted. See p. 209 for info on shopping here.

782 Union St., btw. Sixth and Seventh aves., Park Slope, Brooklyn. ✆ **718/622-0560.** www.foodcoop.com. Subway: R to Union St.; 2/3 to Grand Army Plaza; B/Q to Seventh Ave.

Trade School `FREE`   That's trade as in barter, not line of work. The idealists at **OurGoods** (www.ourgoods.org) have taken their expertise in the sharing economy and applied it to education. Recent classes have covered embroidery, kite-making, and drafting a great OkCupid profile. For payment, keep your wallet in your purse. All classes work by trade, with fruit, craft supplies, and participation among the instruments of exchange. `FINE PRINT` Trade School is on the hunt for a permanent home, but in the meantime classes are held around the city; check the website for details.

Various locations. www.tradeschool.coop.

TANGO & NO CASH

Central Park Tango `FREE`   Under the Bard of Avon's watchful gaze, couples spin away Saturday nights here. Meet up at the south end of the Mall, right next to the Shakespeare statue. Tyros can take advantage of free classes, usually offered at 7:30pm. In inclement weather, dancers seek the shelter of the nearby Dairy. Otherwise it's alfresco under dusk skies, as they dance their ringlets to the whistling wind.

Central Park, enter around 65th St. ✆ **212/726-1111.** www.newyorktango.com. June–Sept Sat 6–9:30pm. Subway: F to Lexington Ave./63rd St.; 6 to 68th St./Hunter College; 1 to 66th St./Lincoln Center.

TriANGulO `FREE`   As a reflection of their confidence in tango's ability to hook new dancers, this studio throws in free beginner's workshops (usually the first Fri evening of the month, with the occasional Sun reprise). They also run specials for newbies, like $10 for any class. Check the website for dates and details.

135 W. 20th St., btw. Sixth and Seventh aves. ✆ **212/633-6445.** www.tangonyc.com. Subway: 1 to 18th St.; F/M to 23rd St.

FREE Dancing Days

If you're getting married, or have some other compelling reason to be interested in learning to dance, look into **Dance Manhattan.** The hustle and Carolina shag are among the offerings and you can get your feet wet for free at their monthly open houses. At 8pm, there's a lesson, half devoted to ballroom and the other to Latin dance. Lessons are followed by a party, and a performance after that. If you get hooked then and there, you'll be eligible for a discount on regular registration. 39 W. 19th St., fifth floor, btw. Fifth and Sixth aves. ℂ **212/807-0802.** www.dancemanhattan.com. Subway: N/R or F/M to 23rd St.

If the wedding has already taken place and nature has run its course, you may have children that need entertaining. Battery Park City hosts a series of **Family Dances** on Fridays and Saturdays during the summer, usually 6:30 to 8pm. This being New York, expect an international array of steps. West African, Swedish, and swing dancing are often on the bill. Neither children nor experience with West African, Swedish, or swing dance moves is required. Esplanade Plaza, Battery Park City, near South End Ave., just north of Albany St. ℂ **212/267-9700.** www.bpcparks.org. Subway: 1 or R to Rector St.; E to World Trade Center; 4/5 to Bowling Green.

If Battery Park's locale isn't idyllic enough for you, fox trot on up to **Riverside Park South** for sunset lessons. Summer Sundays provide the backdrop for a series of salsa, cha-cha, and bachata lessons taught by the **Piel Canela Dance & Music School.** There's some group steps, too, if you need a couple of bodies to hide behind—6 to 9pm. Pier 1, the Hudson at 70th St. ℂ **212/408-0219.** www.nycgovparks.org. Subway: 1/2/3 to 72nd St.

2 Health Sans Wealth

Sadly, far too many New Yorkers get by on a "just don't get sick" health plan. As many as one-fourth of us are uninsured, and medical fees aren't getting any cheaper. New healthcare legislation may soon change the insurance landscape (by 2014), but in the short term, folks of minimal means can be thankful for the sliding scale. Several community-minded organizations provide care at rates commensurate with an individual's income. If your take-home is low enough, you may also be eligible for subsidized insurance with an HMO. A good website to check out is that of the **Actors' Fund of America** (www. actorsfund.org). The fund has comprehensive listings for actors and artists who don't have the kinds of day jobs that throw in insurance and healthcare. If you're a documented entertainer, you can take advantage of the **Al Hirschfeld Free Health Clinic** (℃ **212/489-1939**). Civilians on small budgets can also look into the **Rock Dove Collective** (www.rockdovecollective.org), which matches up health practitioners with folks of a mutual aid mind. On the mental health front, **TherapySafetyNet** (www.therapysafetynet.org) connects a screened selection of psychologists and social workers with patients not covered by insurance plans. Affordable dentists, shrinks, and acupuncturists can also be tracked down for bodies on budgets.

HEALTH INSURANCE

Folks with cushy jobs can expect to see insurance on their laundry list of benefits. With more and more arts and media freelancers in the marketplace, however, it's easy to find oneself without coverage. The **Freelancers Union** and **Working Today** (℃ **800/856-9981;** www. freelancersunion.org) have combined to garner some of the bulk-rate buying power of a corporation. Even with a high deductible (like $10K high, ugh), the lowest you can go is $225 per month, and that's just for an individual. For $345 a month you can get a better deductible and copay arrangement, although it's still no bargain. The program is for artists and media types, leaving out our chef and waitress friends. **Healthy New York** is New York State's program for lower-income residents who earn too much for Medicaid. If you work and make less than $27,924 a year (individual) or $37,824 (couple), you may be able to take advantage of this plan. The premiums in Manhattan range from $227 to $330, without drug coverage, depending on which HMO you sign up with. High Deductible Health Plans and Health Savings Accounts are two other options. Log on to **www. healthyny.com** or call ℃ **866/HEALTHY-NY** (432-5849) for more info. Hopefully the Affordable Care Act, which is set to bring affordable insurance exchanges to the states by 2014, will bring costs down.

HEALTH CLINICS

New York's clinics tend to target specific constituencies. Though they may specialize in helping the indigent, or the HIV-positive, the clinics make it a policy not to discriminate against anyone. Even if you're uninsured, you can get some attention in places other than the city's emergency rooms. The **U.S. Department of Health and Human Resources** has a useful website (**www.hrsa.gov**) that will show you affordable health centers for any zip code.

Callen-Lorde Community Health Center   This primary care center caters to the LGBT (lesbian, gay, bisexual, transgender) community, but makes a point to be open to all. The general medicine and health and wellness programs are charged on a sliding scale.

356 W. 18th St., btw. Eighth and Ninth aves. © **212/271-7200.** www.callen-lorde.org. Subway: A/C/E to 14th St.; L to Eighth Ave.; 1 to 18th St.

David J. Ores, M.D.   Many a Lower East Sider, including your humble correspondent, is grateful to general practitioner Dr. Dave for his attentive care and humane prices. Dr. Dave's tiny clinic serves the neighborhood with a nod to the uninsured. Prices have crept up a little in recent years, but the scale still slides, and Dr. Dave always treats his patients fairly. Call first for an appointment.

189 E. 2nd St., btw. aves. A and B. © **212/353-3020.** www.davidjoresmd.org. Subway: F to Second Ave.; J/M/Z to Essex St.

Gay Men's Health Crisis   Dedicated to slowing the spread of HIV and to helping out those already affected, this organization offers a host of services for the HIV-positive community. Healthcare is provided on a sliding scale basis, and there are also workshops, seminars, and even free legal and tax services. STD and HIV testing is free as well. The GMHC Helpline is open for calls Tuesday 2 to 5pm, Wednesday from 10am to 2pm, and Friday from 2 until 6pm.

446 W. 33rd St., at Tenth Ave. © **800/AIDS-NYC** (243-7692). www.gmhc.org. For other information, the main office line is © 212/367-1000. Subway: A/C/E to 34th St./ Penn Station.

New York City Department of Health and Mental Hygiene FREE
The city operates 10 clinics in all five boroughs that offer free testing and treatment for STDs and HIV. They also follow up with no-cost counseling. Wait times can be on the long side, so show up before the clinic opens or bring a good book and make sure you've eaten. (The

same city department provides free lube and condoms, at locations across the city; they also connect smokers with cessation programs, most of which are free—check the website.)

Chelsea clinic, 303 Ninth Ave., at 28th St. ℭ 311 for hot line, or 212/427-5120. www. nyc.gov/html/doh. Mon–Fri 8:30am–3pm; some clinics extended to 3:30pm. Subway: C/E to 23rd St. Check the website for other locations throughout the city.

New York City Free Clinic `FREE`   NYU med students work with a professional at this Saturday morning clinic, where the homeless and the uninsured can get consultations, physicals, and other medical help. Advance appointments are required. If your chromosomes run XX, a new **Women's Health Free Clinic** may be suited to you, operating out of the same building. The Free Clinic website serves as an excellent clearinghouse for sliding scale and no-cost healthcare, too.

Inside the Sidney Hillman Clinic, 16 E. 16th St., btw. Union Sq. W. and Fifth Ave. ℭ 212/206-5200. www.med.nyu.edu/nycfreeclinic. Sat 9am–1pm. Subway: L/N/Q/R/4/5/6 to 14th St./Union Sq.

Planned Parenthood `FREE`   Free pregnancy tests are among the many reproductive-oriented services handled by this organization. Brooklyn, the Bronx, and Manhattan each have a clinic that can help out. Other services, including HIV counseling and assistance with STDs, have reasonable fees. Call the main number, ℭ **212/965-7000,** to schedule an appointment in any one of the clinics. `FINE PRINT` Hours are sometimes shorter than those listed below, call in advance to be sure.

Margaret Sanger Center, 26 Bleecker St., at Mott St. www.ppnyc.org. Mon–Tues 8am–4:30pm; Wed–Fri 8am–6:30pm; Sat 7:30am–4pm. Subway: 6 to Bleecker St.; B/D/F/M to Broadway/Lafayette St. *Borough Hall Center,* 44 Court St., 6th floor, btw. Remsen and Joralemon sts. Mon–Wed and Fri 8am–4:30pm; Thurs 8am–6:30pm; Sat 8am–4pm. Subway: 2/3/4/5 to Borough Hall; A/C/F/R to Jay St./Metro Tech. *Bronx Center,* 349 E. 149th St., at Courtland Ave. Tues, Wed, and Fri 8am–5pm; Thurs 8am–7pm; Sat 8:30am–4:30pm. Subway: 4 to 149th Ave.; 2/5 to Third Ave./149th St.

Ryan Center   The three associated Ryan clinics (on the Upper West Side, the Lower East Side, and in Midtown) provide a huge range of services, from HIV counseling to general medicine to mental health. Prices are set on a sliding scale. There is also a Harlem satellite and a women and children's center.

William F. Ryan Community Health Network, Clinic at 110 W. 97th St., btw. Columbus and Amsterdam aves. ℭ 212/749-1820. www.ryancenter.org. Subway: 1/2/3 or B/C to 96th St. *Ryan Women and Children's Center,* 801 Amsterdam Ave., at 99th St. ℭ 212/316-8300. Subway: 1/2/3 or B/C to 96th St. *Ryan-NENA Community Health*

FREE Frugal Legal

As a freelance writer, when I snap my fingers clients come running, tardy back pay in hand. Not everybody has the juice to ensure justice is always served, though, and for that we should be thankful for **Legal Services NYC** (☎ **646/442-3600;** www.legalservicesnyc.org), which keeps neighborhood offices in all five boroughs. The group provides free counsel on a range of issues, from employment, education, housing, family, and domestic violence to income tax and beyond. Families, children, seniors, people living under the poverty line, and folks with disabilities or HIV are the main constituency, although consumers and people protecting their communities are also supported.

The pro bono wing of the NYC bar association, the **City Bar Justice Center** (www.nycbar.org), also provides free help to low-income New Yorkers. For 15 years now, their Legal Hotline (☎ **212/626-7383**) has dispensed advice on civil legal issues from bankruptcy to housing law. The hotline runs weekdays from 9am to 1pm, with 3:30-to-5:30pm shifts on Tuesday and Thursday afternoons.

Artists have their own advocates in **Volunteer Lawyers for the Arts** (☎ **212/319-2787;** www.vlany.org), which makes pro bono placements for low-income creatives and nonprofits. During business hours you can get help via the Art Law Line (ext. 1 at the number above), which is staffed by lawyers and law students Monday through Friday from 10am to 6pm. Clinics provide free half-hour consultations, and there are many classes and workshops (some free) on the VLA calendar. An online browse through the current case list will convince you your troubles ain't so bad.

Center, 279 E. 3rd St., btw. aves. C and D. ☎ **212/477-8500.** Subway: F to Second Ave. All three clinics above open Mon and Thurs 8:30am–7pm; Tues, Wed, and Fri 8:30am–4:30pm; Sat 9:30am–1pm (except July–Aug; women and children's center closed Sat year-round). *Ryan Chelsea-Clinton Community Health Center,* 645 Tenth Ave., btw. 45th and 46th sts. ☎ **212/265-4500.** Mon, Tues, and Thurs 8:30am–7pm; Wed and Fri 8:30am–4:30pm; Sat 10am–2pm (except July–Aug). Subway: C/E to 50th St. *Thelma C. Davidson Adair/William F. Ryan Community Health Center,* 565 Manhattan Ave., btw. 123rd and 124th sts. ☎ **212/222-5221.** Mon–Fri 9am–5pm. Subway: A/B/C/D to 125th St.

DIRT CHEAP SHRINKS

Brief Psychotherapy Research Program   As signaled by the name, time efficiency is a major part of the program here. Depression, anxiety, and relationship and job troubles are the main areas of focus, treated with cognitive-behavioral techniques. A free diagnostic evaluation is followed by 30 1-hour sessions (smile for your close-up: The sessions are videotaped for program research and therapist supervision). A sliding scale runs $20 to $40 per visit, depending on income.

Beth Israel Medical Center, 317 E. 17th St., btw. First and Second aves. ℂ **212/420-3819.** www.brieftherapyprogram.com. Subway: L to First Ave.; L/N/Q/R/4/5/6 to 14th St./Union Sq.

National Psychological Association for Psychoanalysis   In an attempt to lessen the barriers to psychological treatment, this organization runs a referral service for affordable psychoanalysis and psychotherapy. Potential analysands whose income levels qualify can take advantage of sliding-scale fees that start at $35 per session.

Theodor Reik Clinical Center for Psychotherapy, 40 W. 13th St., btw. Fifth and Sixth aves. ℂ **212/262-5978.** www.npap.org. Subway: F/M to 14th St.; L to Sixth Ave.; L/N/Q/R/4/5/6 to 14th St./Union Sq.

NYU Postdoctoral Program in Psychotherapy and Psychoanalysis   As the largest psychoanalytic training program in the country, the range of techniques and treatments here is wide. You can help yourself while giving a postdoc the opportunity to practice on a real, live psyche (the training is excellent, and trainees are supervised by professors). There's a sliding scale, which gets very low for people with limited incomes—call for more information.

240 Greene St., 3rd floor, at Washington Place. ℂ **212/998-7890.** www.nyu.edu. Subway: N/R to 8th St.; 6 to Astor Place; A/B/C/D/E/F/M to W. 4th St./Washington Sq.

Training Institute for Mental Health   This institute, run by the University of the State of New York, trains psychiatric nurses, psychologists, and social workers. Get yourself sorted out while helping someone learn the field. Sliding scale fees go as low as $35 per session, with $30 the fee for an initial consultation. They also offer couples therapy, again on a sliding scale, with fees averaging $50 per session.

115 W. 27th St., btw. Sixth and Seventh aves. ℂ **212/627-8181.** www.timh.org. Subway: 1 or N/R to 28th St.

ACUPUNCTURE

Brooklyn Acupuncture Project The nonprofit Community Acupuncture Network strives to make treatment accessible. This member clinic in the South Slope works on a sliding scale and will do whatever they can to accommodate you, even if you're an income-less student. There's a $10 one-time registration fee, and then the scale starts at $25 per session. Don't let the pricing fool you—the clinic is serene and the care is highly professional.

530 Third Ave., btw. 12th and 13th sts. ✆ **718/369-0123.** www.brooklynacupuncture project.com. Mon–Fri 9am–8pm; Sat–Sun 11am–5pm. Subway: F/G/R to Fourth Ave./9th St.

Pacific College of Oriental Medicine Clinic and Acupuncture Center More and more people are seeking out Chinese herbs and medicine as an alternative to the escalating costs of Western medicine. This teaching clinic provides relatively inexpensive services, though the best bargains are for going under an intern's needles. Each session costs $45, with the eighth one free. Auricular treatments (acupuncture in the ear) for stress or to quit smoking are $12.

915 Broadway, 3rd floor, btw. 20th and 21st sts. ✆ **212/982-4600.** www.pacific college.edu. Mon–Thurs 9am–9pm; Fri–Sat 9am–5pm. Subway: N/R to 23rd St.

WorkSong Chinese Medicine Like the Brooklyn Acupuncture Project above, this neighborhood clinic is part of the Community Acupuncture Network. You'll be giving up a private room while you're waiting with your needles in, but for that minor cost you'll save plenty. Treatment follows the sliding scale, which runs $20 to $50 per session depending on your income. The practitioners here are very experienced and friendly as well.

88 Franklin St., btw. Calyer and Oak sts., Greenpoint, Brooklyn. ✆ **347/742-3834.** www.worksongacupuncture.com. Mon, Wed, and Fri 10am–7pm; Tues and Thurs 10am–8pm; Sat 10am–6pm. Subway: G to Greenpoint Ave.

DENTAL

Columbia University College of Dental Medicine You can get Ivy Leaguers to poke around your mouth for cheap. The students and residents at this popular teaching clinic are well-trained and fully supervised. With several eyes on your teeth, the visit will take longer than a trip to a private clinic, but you'll pay a lot less. A first visit, which includes an oral health screening and X-rays, is $85.

Columbia Presbyterian Medical Center, Vanderbilt Clinic, 622 W. 168th St., 7th floor, btw. Broadway and Fort Washington Ave. ✆ **212/305-6100.** www.dental.columbia. edu. Registration desk Mon–Fri 8:30am–5pm. Subway: 1/A/C to 168th St./Washington Heights.

New York City College of Technology   Student work makes for a seriously deep discount at the Dental Hygiene Clinic here. It will take a while—professors supervise the work and have to check it over before you're let out on your way—but the students here are working for a grade and tend to be thorough about cleaning your teeth. If you've got the time, the prices are amazing: a cleaning is only $10, and X-rays are only $15.

300 Jay St., 3rd floor, btw. Tech Place and Tillary St., Downtown Brooklyn. ✆ **718/260-5074.** www.citytech.cuny.edu. Subway: 2/3/4/5 to Borough Hall; A/C/F/R to Jay St./Metro Tech.

New York University College of Dentistry   NYU runs the largest dental college in the country and offers deep discounts on dental care. An initial appointment (which may require two visits) is $95 and covers a checkup, X-rays, and oral cancer screenings. For further work, the costs here are less than what they would be in a professional office (a cleaning is $70). FINE PRINT As your teeth are somebody's class work, expect to spend more time than you would in a private clinic.

345 E. 24th St., at First Ave., Clinic 1A. ✆ **212/998-9872.** www.nyu.edu/dental. Mon–Thurs 8:30am–8pm; Fri 8:30am–4pm. Subway: 6 to 23rd St.

ALEXANDER TECHNIQUE

The American Center for the Alexander Technique FREE   Tasmania-born thespian F. Matthias Alexander pioneered this enigmatic science, which seeks to retrain the body out of a lifetime of bad postural habits. To learn more, check out the free monthly demonstrations at this almost 50-year-old institution. They're held the first Monday of the month from 7 to 8:30pm. Seating is limited; call in advance to reserve a spot. Should you wish to follow up afterward, third-year students at the center need volunteers to work on. An eight-session course comes with an $80 fee, but you'll be treated under the supervision of a senior faculty member; for less formal training sessions, the base cost is between free and $25.

39 W. 14th St., Room 507, btw. Fifth and Sixth aves. ✆ **212/633-2229.** www.acatnyc. org. Subway: F/M to 14th St.; L to Sixth Ave.; N/Q/R/4/5/6 to 14th St./Union Sq.

3 In the Housing

What would New Yorkers have to talk about if we weren't complaining about our living arrangements? Or, for a lucky few of us, bragging about them? I, for example, pay $264 a month for my rent-stabilized four-bedroom with stunning views of the East River, Paris, and Cairo. The sad fact is, even as the economy only jogs along, NYC rental rates and housing prices remain firmly in the realm of the absurd. One concept we learn all too well in New York is that of the "relative bargain." For those not easily discouraged, however, a couple of resources can help a home-seeker get ahead.

For hotels, hostels, and other short-term digs, see Chapter 2, "Cheap Sleeps."

NO-FEE RENTALS

Broker's fees, the 10% to 15% surcharge slapped on by the realtor who tours you around a series of spaces that are way too small and more than you can afford anyway, are the painful cost of renting in NYC. You can beat the system by contacting landlords directly, through their classifieds in the *Voice* and *Times,* and through their websites. It takes some legwork, but if your need for housing isn't urgent, it's the way to go. If you know a specific building you're interested in, try to talk to the super. They'll know what units might be available soon. Patient perusal of Craigslist may be the best bet of all.

MIXED INCOME DIGS

In an effort to keep neighborhoods from becoming entirely monolithic, the city offers tax breaks to developers who are willing to set aside a certain number of units for middle- and low-income residents. As with everything else, the key is persistence. Waiting lists can be long and your lottery odds can be slim, but every time you make the effort to apply you tilt the playing field in your favor.

Department of Housing Preservation & Development This city agency connects buyers and sellers. The website lists lotteries for subsidized housing purchases, which will give you the keys to your own door at a substantially reduced cost. You'll have to meet income eligibility thresholds, and the property will have to be your primary residence. Most housing is in lower-income neighborhoods, often in outer reaches of the outer boroughs. Right now the pickings are pretty slim, but check the website for future apartment availability. There's also a lottery list for rental apartments, which are available way below market rates if you're lucky enough to have your application selected.

ⓒ **311.** For purchases, www.nyc.gov/html/hpd/html/buyers/lotteries.shtml; rentals www.nyc.gov/html/hpd/html/apartment/lotteries.shtml.

Mitchell-Lama Housing Companies MacNeil Mitchell and Alfred Lama's program has been around since 1955, offering housing to New Yorkers with lower-end incomes. You can choose from 97 city-sponsored buildings and 19 cosponsored by the federal government. Rents are highly subsidized, but the application process is cumbersome and not every building has an open waiting list (you'll also have to meet certain income requirements). To get a PDF file listing buildings with open lists, log on to **www.nyc.gov/html/hpd/downloads/pdf/ML-waiting-Lists-Status.pdf**. Each building requires a separate application. There are also state-administered units, which can be found at **www.nyshcr.org/Apps/hsgdevls/hsgdevls.asp**. For general information, call ⓒ **212/863-6500** for city units, or ⓒ **866/463-7753** for state units.

New York City Housing Development Corporation The city promotes several mixed-income new developments in the five boroughs. The **80/20** program is fairly common. Twenty percent of a building is rented at below-market rates to people who earn significantly less than the neighborhood's median income. You have to apply directly to the developer and the process takes a while, but if you get in, you'll score a deal. In many cases, you can move up in income brackets without jeopardizing your cheap rent (or cheap purchase—the

---

FREE **Renters' Assurance**

Despite the incursions of the open market in recent years, there remain over one million regulated apartments in NYC. The **Metropolitan Council on Housing** (**www.metcouncil.net**) has spent the last 50 years fighting for the rights of renters, and the preservation of affordable housing. It's an uphill battle against the big-money powers that be, but individuals can arm themselves with knowledge. The Met Council Hot Line provides information on tenant rights and dispenses advice. Call ⓒ **212/979-0611** on Monday, Wednesday, and Friday afternoons between 1:30 and 5pm for help. Check the website for neighborhood-specific assistance (they list a dozen-plus groups).

same program also offers apartments for sale). Note that the buildings involved are usually in developing neighborhoods, not in the city's trendiest zip codes. Log on to **www.nychdc.com** for a full list of HDC-financed sites, or call ✆ **212/227-5500.**

WOMEN'S RESIDENCES

Members of the fairer sex can also take advantage of the cheap accommodations offered by women's residences. These throwbacks to a more genteel era generally don't allow gentleman callers above the parlor levels, nor do they permit boozing (some residences even have curfews). However, rates are lower than New York's multigender hotels, and for newcomers to the city, it's a great way to make friends.

The Markle Evangeline Residence for Women   Built by the Salvation Army, the Markle has been providing women with a viable alternative to the New York housing mire for 80 years. The rules are predictably strict—no alcohol, no smoking, no men under 55 inside—and the rooms will never be described as spacious, but a resident gets free Wi-Fi and two squares a day. A great location on top of access to a TV room, computer labs, a rooftop garden, and organized social activities help justify the somewhat high rates. *Note:* More communal souls can save cash by opting for shared doubles or quads. Two references, an application, and a security deposit of $1,210 to $1,650 are required for long-term stays. Residency is open to women between the ages of 18 and 50.

123 W. 13th St., btw. Sixth and Seventh aves. ✆ **212/242-2400.** www.themarkle.org. Long-term monthly (minimum 90 days): $1,620–$1,735 single; $1450–$1,615 double; $1,180–$1,230 quad. 280 beds. Facilities: Private bathroom; in-room phone; 24-hr. security; maid service (once a week); roof garden; computer lab; TV lounge; laundry. Subway: 1/2/3 or F/M to 14th St.; L to Sixth Ave.

Sacred Heart Residence   In a historic brownstone right across from the General Theological Seminary, this Chelsea boarding house holds down a prime location (Jack Kerouac wrote the third draft of *On the Road* just up the block). The Congregation of San Jose de la Montana administers the building, providing temporary lodging for women 18 to 30 years old. You'll need to apply in advance and put down a $50 reservation, and there's a curfew (11pm on weeknights, midnight on the weekends). Rent is due in advance, $350 a week, which includes weekday breakfasts and dinners. Bathrooms are shared. FINE PRINT Reception is closed on the weekends, so plan a weekday arrival.

432 W. 20th St., btw. Ninth and Tenth aves. *©* **212/929-5790.** www.sacredheart residence.com. 28 rooms. Single or share of double, $350 weekly. Two meals a day on weekdays. Subway: C/E to 23rd St.

The Webster Apartments One of Macy's major shareholders gave a little back to working women by endowing this Midtown residence. Interns and working students pay only $285 a week, and employed women are charged by a sliding scale that tops out at $315 a week. If you're here on business (and female), it's just $85 a night, with a 3-night minimum. Bathrooms are in the hallway, but sharing has its advantages when it comes to enjoying the large walled garden and rooftop plot. You need to fill out an application to get in (the average stay is about 3 months).

419 W. 34th St., btw. Ninth and Tenth aves. *©* **212/967-9000.** www.webster apartments.org. 373 rooms. Single rooms: $285–$315 weekly, shared bathrooms, breakfast and dinner included. Facilities: Roof garden; TV lounge; maid service (once a week); laundry. Subway: A/C/E to 34th St./Penn Station.

4 Beauty & Massage

HAIR TODAY

NYC's hirsute astute take advantage of salon training sessions. Both students and pros need live heads to demonstrate on, and in exchange for your modeling, they'll provide all kinds of services for little or no money. Though there's no guarantee you'll get an expert cut, a lot of salon students in New York have the scissor skills to eclipse the masters. In addition to cuts, coloring services are sometimes available. Some salons want to look you over first (it helps if you've got a sympathetic face and a surplus of hair begging for a snipping), but generally it's pretty easy to get your grooming on the house. *Note:* Many salons need models, but not all like to advertise it. If you've got your eye on a prohibitively expensive spot, give them a call and see if they can use you. For a great online source, check out **www.salonapprentice.com**, which lists dozens of volunteer hair model opportunities every week.

SALON STYLINGS

Aveda Institute New York The popular environmentally conscious spa Aveda offers up its many services at deep discounts if you go through the students at the institute. Haircuts, coloring, blowouts, perms, facials, and waxing are all available. The prices aren't dirt cheap ($20 for a cut and simple style, $20 for a 30-min facial), but they're relative bargains compared to the rest of the neighborhood. If you want to model for a student, you can find free cuts and deeply discounted coloring at both the institute and at Aveda Academy classes.

Institute, 233 Spring St., btw. Sixth Ave. and Varick St. ✆ **212/807-1492.** www.aveda instituteny.com. Subway: C/E to Spring St. *Academy,* 20 Vandam St., btw. Sixth Ave. and Varick St. ✆ **212/524-2401.** www.avedaadvancedacademy.com. Subway: C/E to Spring St.; 1 to Houston St.

Bumble and bumble.University `FREE` 🖼 With classic New York perversity, the Meatpacking District has morphed into the city's trendiest district. Bumble and bumble's salon is right in the thick of things, but you can partake of their services for no money down. Bb. U's stylist training program puts on model calls for heads of hair deemed worthy in preevaluation (fill out the form online to wangle your invitation). If you make it through, they'll fuss over you for 2 hours or so, leaving you with a new cut and style. Once you're in the program, you can stay tapped into the gravy train with a follow-up every 3 or 4 months. (If you make the cut for cuts, you'll also be eligible for free color work.) You must be willing to get more than a trim, though they'll consult with you first to figure out what works. Tips aren't even necessary.

415 W. 13th St., 6th floor, btw. Ninth Ave. and Washington St. ✆ **866/7-BUMBLE** (728-6253). www.bbmodelproject.com. Subway: A/C/E to 14th St.; L to Eighth Ave.

Christine Valmy International School of Esthetics, Makeup and Nail Artistry What you give up in experience, you gain in price here. Facials are a great deal. Instructors do the supervising while students do the work. A full hour and a half facial ($38 on Sat and weeknights) is only $27 if you come in between 9:30am and 3:30pm on a weekday. Call a week ahead for an appointment.

437 Fifth Ave., btw. 38th and 39th sts. ✆ **212/779-7800.** www.christinevalmy.com. Subway: 7 to Fifth Ave.; 6 to 33rd St.

L'Oréal `FREE` If you want first dibs on the latest L'Oréal products, sign up with their Consumer Expressions Research Center. Participants get free gift bags of products at the end of their home trials, although the test products themselves have to be returned lest they fall into enemy hands. You'll also score a guest pass to shop at the L'Oréal company store, where beauty products (including the ever-popular Kiehl's) are offered at a big discount.

575 Fifth Ave., 3rd floor, at 47th St. ✆ **212/984-4164.** www.cercny.com. Subway: B/D/ F/M to 47th–50th sts./Rockefeller Center.

The Dealin' Barbers of Cheap Street

Barber colleges offer cut-rate cuts. The level of experience varies from student to student, so I don't recommend going for anything too tricky. In fact, you might limit these visits to summertime—when hair grows back quickest.

American Barber Institute Haircuts are only $6.99, though you'll have to sign a waiver before going under the shears. (The same price will get you a facial massage.) 252 W. 29th St., btw. Seventh and Eighth aves. ℂ **212/290-2289.** www.americanbarberinstitute.com. Subway: 1 to 28th St. Other location: 113 Chambers St., btw. Church St. and W. Broadway. ℂ **212/227-6353.** www.abitribeca.com. Subway: A/C or 1/2/3 to Chambers St.

You can get cheap cuts from pros, too. The cuts will run you a bit more, but you can rest easier knowing the scissors are in experienced hands.

Astor Place Hairstylist This family-run basement lair offers a vast array of barbers and hairstylists. Cuts are professional, and a lot more stylish than you might expect for $14. (Astor Place has had charge of my locks for years, and I look like a million bucks.) 2 Astor Place, btw. Broadway and Lafayette St. ℂ **212/475-9854.** www.astorplacehairnyc. com. Subway: N/R to 8th St.; 6 to Astor Place.

Hollywood 2002 Prime West Village real estate doesn't prevent this amiable shop from delivering a host of affordable crops. A men's cut will cost $12, and the barbers here take their time to make sure it's right. 204 W. 14th St., btw. Seventh and Eighth aves. ℂ **212/741-9680.** Subway: 1/2/3 or A/C/E to 14th St.; L to Eighth Ave.

TIGI Hairdressing Academy FREE Complementary and complimentary cuts and colors are on offer at this international school. The model call goes out every Wednesday night from 5 to 6:30pm. If they like your locks (they're on the prowl for stylish ladies and gents ages 18 to 35), you'll be invited back for a class the next week. Classes are usually held Sunday to Wednesday in the mornings. FINE PRINT You should be open to changing up your style with a new cut or color.

466 Broome St., 2nd floor, btw. Mercer and Greene sts. ℂ **212/702-9771.** www. tigistore.com. Subway: A/C/E or J/N/R/ Q/Z/6 to Canal St.

UNBEATEN BROWS

City Brows For shaping up your eyebrows, you won't find a quicker or more precise crew than the one here. Just $8 covers your choice of threading or waxing, with a sculptor's eye applied to shaping. A full range of salon services are also available, running from a $5 upper-lip wax or thread all the way to $50 herbal facials.

2202 Broadway, btw. 78th and 79th sts. ℂ **212/362-1500.** www.citybrows.com. Subway: 1 to 79th St. Other locations: *Upper West Side,* 2265 Broadway, btw. 81st and 82nd sts. ℂ **212/362-8500.** Subway: 1 to 79th St. *Washington Heights,* 1403 St. Nicholas Ave., btw. 180th and 181st sts. ℂ **212/568-5800.** Subway: 1 to 181st St.

INSTANT MASSAGING

Swedish Institute College of Health Sciences Swedish massage has been around for a couple of centuries now, but you don't need to travel all the way to Stockholm to improve your circulation. Since its founding in 1916, this institution has dedicated itself to natural approaches to health, which it makes available to the

Qigong Show

The methods offered by Chinatown's massage joints are as varied as the neighborhood itself. Everything from shiatsu to reflexology to my personal favorite, *qigong,* is available (and you don't even need to get all the way to Chinatown to enjoy them). *Qigong,* one of the world's oldest methods of healing, is the root of many popular forms of massage therapy. At **88 Chinese QiGong Tui Na,** trained therapists with startlingly strong hands will expertly knead your knotted muscles until you're ready to weep with relief. The space is bare bones but clean, with curtains and shoulder-height walls for privacy, and soothing Zen-like music tinkling in the background. The cost is $42 an hour, which leaves some room for much-appreciated tipping. 329 Bowery, btw. 2nd and 3rd sts., basement level. ℂ **212/ 260-7829.** Daily 11am–10pm. Subway: 6 to Bleecker St.; B/D/ F/M to Broadway/Lafayette St.
—Stephanie Wolff

public at reduced rates. You'll be worked on by a student, but they're very well-trained. Two clinical programs are offered, stress-reduction (for the healthy) and therapeutic massage (for people with medical conditions). The former program provides eight 1-hour sessions for $240, and the latter is 12 hours in 12 weeks for $360. Both programs are very popular, so registration is by mail only, with the form available on the website.

226 W. 26th St., btw. Seventh and Eighth aves. ℂ **212/924-5900.** www.swedish institute.edu. Subway: 1 to 28th St.

5 Recreation in the City

BIKE GANGS

Biking makes a virtue of New York's hard paved surfaces, turning our miles of roadway into recreational opportunities. One of the best ways to take advantage is by banding up with fellow riders. If you're not yet of the wheeled class, consider checking out **Recycle-A-Bicycle.** This nonprofit sells refurbished rides at low prices from two retail locations (p. 206). **Bike and Roll** (ℂ 212/260-0400; www.bikenew yorkcity.com) holds down prime locations for picking up rentals. A full day of basic-bike pedaling is $25 on Governors Island, and $34 to $44 in parks around Brooklyn and Manhattan. (The weekly rate of $130 is more cost-effective.) Even cheaper wheels come from **Citi Bike** (www.citibikenyc.com), a new program designed for short-ride access all across the city, which was set to premiere in the spring of 2012, then summer of 2012, but as of press time still hadn't kicked off. As we went to press, the yet-again-revised date for the rollout was March 2013! (We'll believe it when we see it.) There are supposed to be 7,000 self-serve bikes scattered around 420 city stations. To keep bike hoarding to a minimum, there's no additional charge for rides of 30 minutes or less. (Keep the bike an extra half-hour and it's $2.50 to $4, depending on your membership level; any longer than that and the penalty gets pretty stiff pretty quick.) Access passes run from 24 hours ($9.95) to 7 days ($25) to a full year ($95, or just a tad more than a quarter a day). The one catch is that you've got to tool around town with the Citibank logo on your ride. At least on a bike, it's easy to pass for a member of the 99%.

Fast and Fab   Whether you're a fast rider or a fabulous rider, or both, this LGBT biking group will welcome you. Annual membership is $30 ($20 if you join after May 1, and only $10 after Sept 1), but it'll get you invites to a series of rides around the city and out of town (say, a day trip to DIA Beacon). Intermediate cyclists are the target group. Meals and socializing often follow the rides.

ℂ **212/567-7160.** www.fastnfab.org.

Five Borough Bicycle Club `FREE`
This friendly club hosts a slew of day trips in and around the city. Beaches, the Bronx greenways, and Woodlawn Cemetery are among the attractions. The club runs some great tune-ups (as long as 90 miles) leading up to the 100 miles of the annual Montauk Century ride in May. Registration for day rides isn't necessary; just show up with water and wheels (the trip is free except for lunch money). A year's dues to join the club aren't particularly onerous at $20.

☎ **347/688-2925.** www.5bbc.org.

TIME'S UP! `FREE` 📝 This environmental group sponsors several well-organized rides. The most well known is **Critical Mass,** held on the last Friday of every month and taking place simultaneously in over 300 cities worldwide. The ride is designed to raise conscious-

`FREE` **Warriors, Come Out to Play**

"Geek Olympics" is probably an unfair way of summarizing the **Come Out & Play** street game festival. Technology does lend a major hand, with laptops and cellphones performing various tracking functions, but the event is more about playful use of public space than Internet addicts blinking their eyes against the harsh imposition of daylight. Urban minigolf, human Pong, and citywide scavenger hunts are among the draws, which fill a long weekend, usually in July. Check **www.comeoutandplay.org** for a schedule of games, or to volunteer one of your own. ☎ **646/807-8131;** various locations.

ness about environmental alternatives and biker rights. It's fun for sidewalk spectators, too, who can watch every kind of bike and bike-rider pedal past to a chorus of perversely gratifying taxi horns. The route varies, usually starting from the north side of Union Square (the Brooklyn version goes off the second Fri of the month from Grand Army Plaza). TIME'S UP! also hosts rides on tri-state rural routes, but the best trip to the country comes on the first Friday of the month. The **Central Park Moonlight Ride** shows off the water and trees and general tranquillity of the park at night. With guides riding point and taking up the rear, it's a safe and leisurely pedal. Rollerbladers with at least intermediate skills are welcome, too. The ride meets at 10pm at the southwest corner of Central Park, across from Columbus Circle. The trip is around 10 miles and runs all 12 months of the year. A Prospect Park Moonlight Ride has also been added, leaving from Grand Army Plaza on the second Saturday of the month at 9pm. TIME'S UP! is on the hunt for permanent headquarters, but you can take advantage of bike repair workshops and classes at their temporary spaces in Williamsburg and on the Lower East Side. All events are free, although as a volunteer-run organization, donations are cheerfully accepted.

156 Rivington St., btw. Suffolk and Clinton sts. ℂ **212/802-8222.** www.times-up.org. Subway: F to Delancey St.; J/M/Z to Essex St. Other location: *Williamsburg, Brooklyn,* 99 S. 6th St., btw. Bedford Ave. and Berry St. Subway: J/M/Z to Marcy Ave.; L to Bedford Ave.

GYM NEIGHBORS

When hauling groceries and laundry up to your sixth-floor walk-up is no longer exercise regimen enough, it's time to hit a gym. The cheapest choice by far is signing up with the Department of Parks and Recreation, though other options that don't much exceed $1 a day are available. If you want to shop around first, the website **www.gymsearch.net** has free coupons and guest passes for gyms around the region. It's free, but you have to register your contact info. If you want an even larger sampling of what's available around NYC, look into the PassBooks put together by the **American Health & Fitness Alliance** (ℂ **212/808-0765;** www.health-fitness.org). It costs $85, but free passes for health clubs (up to 1 month in some instances), classes, and training sessions tally up to $3,500. There are also similar versions for yoga and Pilates.

Department of Parks and Recreation   On top of playing fields and courts, the city also runs 49 recreation centers spread across all five boroughs. The amenity list is long and varied, including indoor and outdoor tracks, weight rooms, dance studios, and boxing rings. All of this can be yours for $100 a year. If you want to join a center with an indoor pool, it's an additional $50. (For seniors age 62 and over, it's only $25 a year with or without pools, and for under-18s, it's all free.) Many centers also offer classes in Pilates, aerobics, karate, kickboxing, wrestling, swimming, and the like. Some centers even have personal trainers. Usually an extra fee applies for classes, say $60 for a 10-class session. If you want to sample the goods, check out **BeFit-NYC Free First Mondays,** which provides classes and equipment at no charge (a few classes may carry a nominal fee). Other days of the week, catch the **Shape Up NYC** program, which offers free fitness classes around the city. Although scenes vary from rec center to rec center, generally city-run facilities are family-friendly and community oriented—look elsewhere if you're in the market for a meat market.

ℂ **311.** www.nycgovparks.org.

Planet Fitness   This gym chain has long held down spots across the four outer boroughs, but its Manhattan presence is new as of 2012, in the form of a sparkling three-story gym. As with the other locations, prices are rock bottom. A $30 annual fee plus $10 a month is all it takes to join, with classes and fitness sessions thrown in for free. Pony up $20 per month (plus a $39 annual fee) and you'll have a "Black Card," providing access to all 500 Planet Fitness gyms. At prices like these, the floors can get crowded, but the Chelsea location eases things with 24-hour access on the weekdays.

158 W. 27th St., btw. Sixth and Seventh aves. © **212/268-2501.** www.planetfitness. com. Subway: N/R to 28th St.

YMCA of Greater New York   The Y (© **212/630-9600;** www.ymca nyc.org) runs 24 health and wellness centers in the five boroughs. The facilities vary from site to site, but the general roster includes gyms, pools, racquetball and handball courts, aerobics studios, exercise machines, steam rooms, and saunas. (There's also cheap lodging at some locations; see p. 33). Fees vary. There are reduced fees available for seniors and families, and you should inquire about income-based reductions. The state-of-the-art facility is the new McBurney location (125 W. 14th St., btw. Sixth and Seventh aves.; F/M or L to Sixth Ave./14th St., or 1/2/3 to 14th St.; © **212/912-2300**). A 1-year membership to McBurney is $1,116, plus the $125 initiation fee. To get fit at a less central location is a much better deal—the Greenpoint YMCA (99 Meserole Ave., btw. Leonard St. and Manhattan Ave.; G to Nassau Ave. or Greenpoint Ave.; © **718/389-3700**) is only $648 for a year, with an $80 initiation fee. For a citywide YMCA pass, which allows access to every center, it's $125 to join and $97 a month after that.

CHEAP SKATES

Citi Pond at Bryant Park `FREE`   Frank J. Zamboni's brainchild smoothes the ice on this ingenious use of Bryant Park's center. Surrounded by the boutique stalls of the Holiday Shops, the ice-skating rink has a European small-town feel. Thanks to the bottomless pockets of Citi, skating is free, though folks whose skates are hanging by their laces in their parents' garages will have to plunk down $14 per session for rentals. The rink is open from late October through late February.

Bryant Park, btw. W. 40th and 42nd sts., along Sixth Ave. © **866/221-5157.** www. citipondatbryantpark.com. Daily 8am–10pm; until midnight Fri–Sat. Subway: B/D/ F/M to 42nd St.; 7 to Fifth Ave.

Lasker Rink This rink on the north side of Central Park is half the price of its fellow-park cousin (Trump Wollman). Adults can cut figure eights for just $6.75, with rental skates tossed in for $6. It also tends to be a lot less crowded up here.

Central Park, enter at 110th St., btw. Lenox and Fifth aves. ✆ **212/439-6900.** www.laskerrink.com. Mon and Wed–Thurs 10am–3:45pm; Tues 10am–3:30pm and 8–10pm; Fri 10am–5:15pm and 7–11pm; Sat 1–11pm; Sun 12:30–4:30pm. Subway: 2/3 to 110th St./Central Park North.

Riverbank State Park One of only two state-run parks in Manhattan, Riverbank is skating on thin ice thanks to perennial budget mismanagement in Albany. Hopefully the rink will survive. An arching roof provides some protection from the elements and crowds are blissfully moderate. Standard admission is $5 and it's $6 to rent skates. In summer, the rink turns to unbladed skating, with admission just $1.50, and roller skate rentals going for $6.

679 Riverside Dr., at 145th St. ✆ **212/694-3642.** www.nysparks.state.ny.us. Ice skating Fri 6–9pm; Sat–Sun 1–4pm and 6–9pm. Subway: 1 to 145th St.

POOLING RESOURCES

It costs $150 a year to use the city's indoor pools (see "Gym Neighbors," above), but if you're a frequent crawler, the price turns out to be pretty reasonable. In summer, you'll find 54 outdoor pools across the city (with no admission fee). The indoor pools stay open year-round (unless they're superseded by an on-site outdoor pool), but the outdoor ones are summer-only. Late June to Labor Day is the usual season, and you will find many, many kids taking advantage. General hours of operation are 11am to 3pm and 4 to 7pm; call individual pools for more information. Some pools set aside early morning and evening hours for lap swimming. In addition to city pools (**www.nyc govparks.org**), the state runs an Olympic-size natatorium in Manhattan. Local favorites include:

Asser Levy FREE An indoor and outdoor pool make this a great year-round swimming destination.

E. 23rd St. and Asser Levy Place, near the FDR Dr. ✆ **212/447-2020.** Subway: 6 to 23rd St.

Astoria Park Pool FREE This is one of the largest (designed to hold some 2,000 swimmers) and most famous pools in the country. Built in 1936 through the WPA, it features stunning skyline and bridge views. This outdoor pool is only open in the summer.

FREE NYC's All Skate

The Dead Road (aka Skaters' Road) in Central Park is one of my favorite spots in the city for a workout (well, an eyeball workout to be accurate). Watching dozens of expert roller skaters and bladers dancing and spinning to a jamming disco beat is a hypnotic sight. Some of the regulars have been rolling together for more than 2 decades and the skill level is very high, but if you're halfway competent you shouldn't feel intimidated. The scene is friendly and inclusive, so strap on some wheels and jump in. Even for nonskaters, this event is a highlight of the park. The DJs are great, especially now that the city has relented on its antibeat campaign. (In 1995, music was temporarily banned from the park so skaters wore Walkmen all tuned to the same radio channel, creating a surreal silent choreography.) The outdoor roller disco is in session from 2:45 to 6:45pm most Saturdays, Sundays, and national holidays between mid-April and October. For specifics about dates and DJs, check the **Central Park Dance Skater's Association**'s website (**www.cpdsa.org**). The Skate Circle on Skaters' Road is in the middle of the park, between 69th and 70th streets, just a little southwest of the Bethesda Fountain.

If skating in a boogielicious roller inferno is a little daunting, find safety in numbers with **Wednesday Night Skate** (**www.weskateny.org**). New York's biggest skating event wheels away from Union Square Park every Wednesday night. The routes vary from week to week, but generally you'll get to see a few miles' worth of NYC, say up Park Avenue, into Central Park, and back on over to Times Square. The event usually lasts 2 hours. The flock meets at the south end of Union Square Park at 7:45pm, from April through October. Helmets and wrist guards are required.

Astoria Park, 19th St. at 23rd Dr., Astoria, Queens. © **718/626-8620.** Subway: N/Q to Astoria–Ditmars Blvd.

Floating Pool FREE   A decommissioned river barge in Morgan City, Louisiana, provided the raw material for this popular freebie. Some 50,000 swim fans visited during 2007's inaugural year, when the pool was parked in the shadow of the Brooklyn Bridge. Barretto Point

Park in the Bronx currently holds the facility, although a floating pool can always change its coordinates. Check online to confirm its current whereabouts.

www.floatingpool.org.

Hamilton Fish FREE Despite its enormous size, this Lower East Side outdoor pool fills up quickly. Kids from the neighborhood splash while parents relax in the spacious adjoining plaza.

128 Pitt St., btw. E. Houston and Stanton sts. ℭ **212/387-7687.** Subway: F to Second Ave.; J/M/Z to Essex St.

McCarren Park FREE After a long stint as a music venue, this Depression-era pool has been restored to its liquid origins. The fix cost $50 million, but it brought thousands of smiles to Greenpoint and Williamsburg (as well as reports of misbehavior that required police attention). We'll see if that's under control by the pool's second summer in operation.

Lorimer St. at Bedford Ave. ℭ **718/965-6580.** Subway: G to Nassau Ave.; L to Bedford Ave.

Metropolitan Pool FREE Williamsburg is kept buoyant through cold weather at the indoor Met Pool, which still gleams from a recent multimillion-dollar renovation.

261 Bedford Ave., at Metropolitan Ave. ℭ **718/599-5707.** Subway: L to Bedford Ave.

Riverbank State Park FREE This 28-acre park on the Hudson ably disguises its foundation, which is a wastewater treatment plant. The indoor pool is run by the state, which charges $2 per visit ($3 for morning lap swim sessions), or $30 for a 1-month lap swimming pass.

679 Riverside Dr., at 145th St. ℭ **212/694-3666.** www.nysparks.state.ny.us. Pool general hours (adult swimming is limited; check in advance) Mon–Fri 6:30am–8:15pm; Sat–Sun 6:30am–6pm. Subway: 1 to 145th St.

Tony Dapolito Recreation Center FREE Another pool with both indoor and outdoor bases covered, this rec center is a West Village fave.

1 Clarkson St., btw. Seventh Ave. S. and Hudson St. ℭ **212/242-5228.** Outdoor pool July–Aug, indoor pool Sept–June. Subway: A/B/C/D/E/F/M to W. 4th St./Washington Sq.

RUN-ON SENTENCES

NIKETOWN New York Running Club FREE One of the nicest things about running is you can just go do it, with only a little thought to

weather and equipment. Still, it never hurts having some bonus moti-
vation and a little expertise. Nike sponsors this running program,
which takes Central Park runs Tuesday and Thursday evenings at
6:30pm, and Saturday mornings at 9am. You can get coaching, give
some shoes a tryout, and afterward refresh yourself with complimentary drinks and power bars.

6 E. 57th St., btw. Fifth and Madison aves. ℭ **212/891-6453.** Subway: N/Q/R to Fifth
Ave.; F to 57th St.

ROLLIN' ON THE RIVERS

New York's waterways were once great recreational resources, but
years of environmental laxity made much of the local liquid too toxic
to touch. A handful of groups are trying to speed along the rivers'
rebounds with giveaways along the shore. The East River, Hudson,
and Gowanus are all available for seaworthy (or at least sea-curious)
New Yorkers. If you can swim, you're eligible to take advantage.

Brooklyn Bridge Park `FREE`   The landscaping along Brooklyn's new
East River parkways holds its own against the spectacular Manhattan
skyline across the water. To take in the sights by kayak, check out the
free program offered by the boathouse here. The voyages are first-
come, first-served, aboard 20 recently purchased kayaks, from early
June to mid-September. In addition to all-day Saturday, every other
Thursday provides an opportunity for some after-work paddling.

Brooklyn Bridge Park, near Pier 2, Orange St. and the East River. ℭ **718/802-0603.**
www.bbpboathouse.org. Subway: 2/3 to Clark St.; A/C to High St.

Downtown Boathouse `FREE`   Out of the goodness of their hearts
(and a desire to promote the Hudson as a recreational outlet), this
group loans out kayaks and equipment all summer long. Some 50,000
people get out on the river between mid-May and mid-October. The
trips are limited to 20 minutes in protected areas near three west-side
piers, but if you show up a few times and get into shape, you'll be
eligible for an extended paddle from Pier 96 into New York Harbor.
This spectacular field trip lasts 3 hours, with unbelievable views all
the way. Potential paddlers gather before 8am and wait to have names
picked from a hat. On a nice day you've got about a 50/50 chance of
going, though you can increase your odds by arriving on a day with
cloud cover. The long-trip season runs mid-June to mid-September
(call ℭ **646/613-0740** to check the daily status; in really lousy weather
the kayaks stay docked). The Hudson is cleaner than it's been for

decades, so getting splashed here and there no longer requires immediate hospitalization. Yay.

Pier 96, Clinton Cove Park, West Side Hwy., at 56th St. www.downtownboathouse.
org. Sat–Sun and holidays 9am–6pm; July–Aug Mon–Fri 5–7pm. Subway: A/B/C/D/1
to 59th St./Columbus Circle. *Pier 40,* at Houston St. and the Hudson. Sat–Sun and
holidays 9am–6pm; Thurs 5–7pm. Subway: 1 to Houston St.; A/C/E to Canal St. *Riverside Park,* 72nd St., at the Hudson. Sat–Sun and holidays 10am–5pm. Subway: 1/2/3
to 72nd St.

The Gowanus Dredgers Canoe Club `FREE`   The Gowanus Canal is in
a transitional phase between being the butt of jokes and serving as a
genteel Brooklyn natural resource. A canoe trip here still leans toward
the former, providing a surreal float through what is mostly a forgotten
industrial wasteland. Self-guided map tours and boats to take them with
are available from late March through the end of October. Pick up is
near 2nd Street and Bond Street in Brooklyn, but check the calendar for
availability details first. For landlubbers, the Dredgers also offer free
bike tours. There's no charge for any of these programs, but as this is a
grassroots organization, every little bit of generosity helps.

Carroll Gardens, Brooklyn. ✆ **718/243-0849.** www.gowanuscanal.org. Wed 6–8pm;
Sat 1–5pm. Subway: F/G to Smith/9th St.

Inwood Canoe Club   The oldest club of its kind in NYC, with seven
Olympians among its alumni, the ICC kindly opens its doors on summer Sundays to neophyte paddlers. Public sessions run from 10am to
noon, with kayaks, life vests, and paddles included. The setting near
the George Washington Bridge is spectacular and the cost is minimal
($4, which goes straight to the insurance company).

Just south of the Dyckman Marina, walk west from Dyckman St. ✆ 212/463-7740.
www.inwoodcanoeclub.com. Sun 10am–noon. Subway: A or 1 to Dyckman St.

LIC Community Boathouse `FREE`   The East River (it's not really a river;
it's a tidal strait) is open to experienced and newbie paddlers alike. A
walk-up program runs Saturdays from 1 to 5pm or so (depending on the
tides), providing 20 minutes of skyline and water admiring on the Queens
waterfront at Halletts Cove. Making a request online (space permitting)
will get you onto a more elaborate trip, say a sunset tour, or a visit to
Brooklyn Bridge Park or Hellgate. The shore may be industrial, but as a
tidal strait the possibilities of porpoise and whale sightings are greater
than they are on the Hudson. The walk-up season runs select Saturdays
from late May to early October, weather permitting.

Hallets Cove walk-up program, 31-05 Vernon Blvd., at 31st Ave., Astoria, Queens. ✆ **718/228-9214.** www.licboathouse.org. Check the calendar for trip schedules. Subway: N/Q to Broadway.

Red Hook Boaters FREE   Native red clay (*Roode Hoek* in Dutch) is the origin of the name of this Brooklyn outlier, which is rapidly gentrifying thanks to the IKEA and a host of restaurants and bars. One great way to explore the area is with the Red Hook Boaters, a group dedicated to maintaining local waterfront access and raising aquatic awareness. Their free programs offer canoes and kayaks for 15- to 20-minute runs into the protected area near Louis Valentino, Jr. Park and Pier. In return, they ask that you pitch in with beach cleanup before or after (gloves, trash bags, and life jackets are provided, in addition to boats). When you've logged some time as a volunteer, you can join in on an open-water tour of Governors Island, Brooklyn Bridge Park, or the Buttermilk Channel. Walk-up kayaking runs Sunday afternoons from late May to early October, and Thursday evenings from mid-June until mid-August.

The beach at Louis Valentino, Jr. Park and Pier, Red Hook, Brooklyn, near Coffey and Ferris sts. ✆ **917/676-6458.** www.redhookboaters.org. Sun 1–5pm; Thurs 6–8pm. Subway: F/G to Smith/9th St.

Village Community Boathouse FREE   The rowboats known as Whitehall gigs used to flourish on New York Harbor, but human-powered boat travel has mostly gone the way of the U.S. shipping industry. To get a glimpse of what waterfront life was like (and to take advantage of fresh air and nice views), join up with the free rides this community organization hosts. You'll be captained by an experienced coxswain as you ply the waters near Pier 40, which is not so far from Whitehall Street, where the boats were once manufactured. The season runs April to November, with free boatbuilding sessions in the winter.

Pier 40, at Houston St. and the Hudson. ✆ **212/229-2059.** www.villagecommunity boathouse.org. Tues and Thurs 5:30pm–dusk; Sun noon–3pm. Subway: 1 to Houston St.; A/C/E to Canal St.

OMMM MY GOODNESS: MEDITATION

In a town so loud it can be hard to hear one's own thoughts, the contrast of a quiet meditation space can be startling. Though just about any house of worship in the city will suffice, sometimes it's nice to get a little guidance for inner journeying.

Kagyu Dzamling Kunchab This Tibetan organization brings the East to the West (side), with a traditional Dharma practice led by an ordained lama. Wednesday nights are open to the public for meditation, followed by a Buddhist teaching and Chenrezi practice. The evenings run from 6:30 to 8:30pm, but you can stay for as much of it as you'd like. The suggested donation is $10, which is tax deductible.

410 Columbus Ave., btw. 79th and 80th sts. ✆ **212/989-5989.** www.kdk-nyc.org. Subway: B/C to 81st St.; 1 to 79th St.

Shambhala `FREE` Two lovely meditation rooms host the open meditations offered by this Tibetan Buddhist group. Beginners can learn more at weekly lessons, Wednesdays at 6pm and Sundays at noon. When you've got some seasoning, come back for public sittings and evening chants on weeknights at 5:30pm and Sundays from 9am to noon. Every Tuesday night at 7pm is the weekly dharma gathering, which is a half-hour of group meditation followed by a talk, a discussion, and a reception. Suggested donation for Tuesday evenings is $5, $10 for meditation lessons. Public sittings are free.

118 W. 22nd St., 6th floor, btw. Sixth and Seventh aves. ✆ **212/675-6544.** www. ny.shambhala.org. Subway: 1 or F/M to 23rd St.

The Three Jewels Community Center `FREE` To further the teachings of the Buddha, this organization offers a lot of free programs. In conjunction with the Asian Classics Institute, you can find a wide range of classes, many of which are suited to beginners. There are also meditation sessions, with on-hand instructors. The main loft near Astor Place houses a combination dharma, yoga, meditation, and outreach center. Check the calendar for the latest schedule (some offerings do come with a charge, like the $12 suggested donation for yoga).

61 Fourth Ave., 3rd floor, btw. 9th and 10th sts. ✆ **212/475-6650.** www.threejewels. org. Subway: 6 to Astor Place; N/R to 8th St.

Zen Center of New York City Discover what one hand clapping sounds like at this Zen center in Brooklyn. Contributions are requested to participate in the meditation sessions (generally $3–$5), held Wednesdays through Sundays. If you're new to *zazen,* you can attend an introductory session on a Sunday morning. Sessions start at 9:15am and last around 3 hours. Admission is by a suggested contribution of $5.

500 State St., btw. Nevins St. and Third Ave., Boerum Hill, Brooklyn. ✆ **718/875-8229.** www.mro.org/firelotus. Subway: B/D/N/Q/R/2/3/4/5 to Atlantic Ave./Pacific St.; 4/5 to Nevins St.; A/C/G to Hoyt-Schermerhorn.

YOGA, TAI CHI & MORE

Tai chi has been slow to gather momentum as a trend, but yoga is well entrenched as the aerobics of the new millennium. Classes in these practices are surprisingly easy to find in New York parks, along with similar forms of fitness. You can also find studios to work on your downward-facing dog for not too much scratch. It's a good idea to wear comfortable clothing for these classes, and bring a mat or towel for yoga in the parks.

Battery Park City `FREE`   From 8:30 to 9:30am on most Fridays in summer (and into fall) you can get a master's guidance in tai chi at Battery Park's Esplanade Plaza (at the end of Liberty St.). No experience necessary. The season runs early May through October.

Battery Park City, along South End Ave., just west of West St. ℂ **212/267-9700.** www.bpcparks.org. Subway: 1/2/3 or A/C to Chambers St.; 1 to Rector St. or South Ferry; 4/5 to Bowling Green.

Brooklyn Bridge Park `FREE`   Torso stabilization is the goal here, in classes led by a fitness guru. The technique is Pilates mat work, and all skill levels are welcome. Registration begins at 6:30pm on Tuesdays from mid-June to mid-September. The class starts at 7pm, and space is limited. Check the website for information on Monday morning yoga, Sunday afternoon Zumba, and Friday evening belly dance and hip-hop dance aerobics. The Pilates are held on the Empire Fulton Ferry Boardwalk (moving to a tent in the Tobacco Warehouse in case of rain); most other fitness classes are at Pier 1.

Empire Fulton Ferry Boardwalk, near Old Dock St. and the East River. ℂ **718/802-0603.** www.brooklynbridgepark.org. Subway: F to York St.; A/C to High St. *Pier 1, the East River at Old Fulton St.* Subway: 2/3 to Clark St.; A/C to High St.

Bryant Park `FREE`   Bryant Park loans its central location to a host of activities, most notably Tuesday and Thursday morning **tai chi** classes. The class is taught from 7:30 to 8:30am, May through September, so you can focus your energy before punching the clock. If you're new to the practice, **World Tai Chi Day** might be the thing for you. On the last Saturday in April, Bryant Park is the site of a day of classes and demonstrations. Thursday evenings (6–7pm) May through September are dedicated to **yoga.** You can salute the setting sun and improve your flexibility from the southwest corner of the lawn (mats are provided). Morning people can catch the Tuesday yoga class from 10 to 11am. As an added bonus, you can take a **knitting class** (ℂ **212/787-5896**) on

Tuesday afternoons between 1:30 and 3pm in summer; yarn and needles are provided, and you might want to preregister over the phone. Been on the fence about taking up **fencing?** Let the Manhattan Fencing Center tip the scales in favor of passés with their free beginner lessons from 1 to 2pm Tuesdays, April through June.

Bryant Park, btw. 41st and 42nd sts., and Fifth and Sixth aves. ℂ **212/768-4242.** www.bryantpark.org. Subway: B/D/F/M to 42nd St.; 7 to Fifth Ave.

Dharma Yoga Brooklyn   Receiving through giving is the economic plan for this Park Slope newcomer. A second-floor studio hosts meditation, chanting, workshops, and classical yoga. The cost? That's up to you—sessions are by donation, with a $5 minimum requested.

82 Sixth Ave., 2nd floor, at St. Marks Ave., Park Slope, Brooklyn. ℂ **718/395-7632.** www.dharmayogabrooklyn.com. Subway: 2/3 to Bergen St.; B/Q to Seventh Ave.

lululemon athletica `FREE`   This Vancouver-born apparel store puts the free back in free-spirited with complimentary Sunday morning classes. Stop by any of the six locations for an hour of prime posture edjimication—usually yoga, but also branching out into Pilates and CrossFit training. They'll even let you borrow a mat (although if you choose to gear up, you won't have far to go). There are also free night-time Central Park **jogging** sessions ("the Run Club"), and **yoga** in Bryant Park (p. 177). Class times vary; check online for the latest.

1928 Broadway, at 64th St. ℂ **212/712-1767.** www.lululemon.com. Subway: 1 to 66th St./Lincoln Center. Other locations: *Upper West Side,* 2139 Broadway, btw. 75th and 76th sts. Subway: 1 to 79th St. *Upper East Side,* 1127 Third Ave., at 66th St. ℂ **212/755-5019.** Subway: F to 63rd St./Lexington Ave.; 6 to 68th St./Hunter College. *Upper East Side,* 1146 Madison Ave., at 85th St. ℂ **212/452-1909.** Subway: 4/5/6 to 86th St. *Union Square,* 15 Union Square W., btw. 14th and 15th sts. ℂ **212/675-5286.** Subway: L/N/Q/R/4/5/6 to Union Sq. *Soho,* 481 Broadway btw. Broome and Grand sts. ℂ **212/334-8276.** Subway: 6 to Spring St.; J/N/Q/R/Z/6 to Canal St. *Park Slope, Brooklyn, showroom,* 472 Bergen St., btw. Flatbush and Fifth aves. ℂ **718/636-6298.** Subway: 2/3 to Bergen St.

Prospect Park `FREE`   The Park Slope yoga studio Bend & Bloom teams up with lululemon to offer Thursday night yoga in Prospect Park. The sessions run for a twilit hour (7–8pm), with instructors representing several of the Slope's favorite studios, from May through early September.

Prospect Park, Grand Army Plaza entrance. ℂ **347/987-3162.** www.bendandbloom.com. Subway: 2/3 to Grand Army Plaza; B/Q to Seventh Ave.

Riverside Park South `FREE` Riverside Park stretches down a 4-mile strip of the Hudson broad enough to accommodate 267 acres. Wellness classes are offered at multiple points every summer, usually Zumba and yoga at **West Harlem Piers Park,** and tai chi at the **Soldiers' and Sailors' Monument.** Check the website for the latest schedule.

West Harlem Piers Park, 125th St. at Marginal St., at the Hudson. © **212/408-0219.** www.riversideparkfund.org. Subway: 1 to 125th St. *Soldiers' and Sailors' Monument,* 89th St. at Riverside Dr. Subway: 1 to 86th St.; 1/2/3 to 96th St.

Sivananda Yoga Vedanta Center `FREE` Once a month this yoga center introduces the community to their practice via an open house. The day begins at 10:30am with a lecture and demonstration, followed by a trial class, a vegetarian meal, and finally an introduction to meditation. If you don't have your own mat, bring a towel to place over one of their mats. The first or second Saturday of the month.

243 W. 24th St., btw. Seventh and Eighth aves. © **212/255-4560.** www.sivananda. org/ny. Subway: C/E or 1 to 23rd St.

Yoga to the People As the name suggests, this organization seeks to return yoga to its grassroots origins. Power vinyasa flow classes are taught in the St. Marks studio for a suggested donation of $10, but nobody tracks it—the people pay what they can. Classes run 7 days a week, with two special candlelit sessions on Sunday nights. You can also find traditional hot yoga classes ($8) at the 26th and 27th Street studios; hot yoga ($7) and hot vinyasa ($5) at 38th Street; and power vinyasa flow ($10 suggested donation) and hot yoga ($8) in Brooklyn.

12 St. Marks Place, btw. Second and Third aves. © **917/573-YOGA** (9642). www.yoga tothepeople.com. Subway: 6 to Astor Place; N/R to 8th St. *Chelsea,* 250 W. 26th St., 3rd floor, btw. Seventh and Eighth aves. Subway: C/E or 1 to 23rd St. *Chelsea,* 115 W. 27th St., 3rd floor, btw. Sixth and Seventh aves. Subway: 1 or N/R to 28th St. *Midtown,* 1017 Sixth Ave., at 38th St. Subway: B/D/F/M to 42nd St.; 7 to Fifth Ave. *Williamsburg, Brooklyn,* 211 N. 11th St., btw. Roebling St. and Driggs Ave. Subway: L to Bedford Ave.

Chinatown, with stores like Pearl River Market, is one of the destinations where you can find unique (and inexpensive) items for yourself or to give as gifts.

SHOPPING

The last time my country friend came to visit, I noticed him limping around with a broken shoelace. I immediately tried to steer him into the nearest drugstore, but he resisted, telling me he didn't want to be slammed with those "big-city shoelace prices."

I still chuckle at this story when I'm scoring some crazy deal in the heart of the city. The volume advantage that eight million citizens provide can't be touched out in the sticks. Clothes, electronics, furniture, food, and, yes, even shoelaces, are available here for a fraction of their price in the hinterlands. Plus Gotham's refined taste is great news for the cost-conscious when it comes time for gowns and coffee tables to begin their second and third lives. New York thrift stores, flea markets, and curbside trash piles are all treasure-troves for the patient and sharp-eyed, meaning savvy New Yorkers can finish off their cheap shopping lists better than anybody else in the U.S. of A. Which is helpful when your rent bill ensures you're living on a shoestring.

1 Dirt Cheap Shopping Zones

I'll never understand why New York stores of similar stripe all jam themselves into the same neighborhoods. The Bowery is dotted with restaurant supply shops, and then suddenly every storefront is dedicated to lighting. Lampshade shops gather on nearby side streets. Whatever the initial cause, the effect of the single-product density is bargaining power galore for the consumer. Don't like the price? Walk next door and see if you can do a little better.

DOWNTOWN
THE FINANCIAL DISTRICT
Come lunchtime downtown, the streets fill with workers scurrying around the cheap shopping outlets. **Fulton, Nassau,** and **Chambers** streets are big destinations, although there isn't anything here that can't be found in other places in the city. The two exceptions to that rule are the city's best electronics and best clothes stores, both near City Hall (see "Shekels & Chains: Department Stores" and "Electronics," later in this chapter).

Subway: A/C/J/Z/2/3/4/5 to Fulton St./Broadway Nassau; R to City Hall; 4/5/6 to Brooklyn Bridge/City Hall.

CHINATOWN
A trip to Chinatown can feel like a visit to a foreign country, with prices that are only a fraction of what's charged across the border. Although the days of easy access to knockoff Oakley sunglasses and Kate Spade bags are gone (the city has cracked down on counterfeiting), this is still the city's premier bargain destination. **Division Street and East Broadway** don't attract many tourists, but locals take advantage of the abundance of cheap apartment-ware shops, where good prices on appliances, furniture, knickknacks, and hardware can be found.

Subway: A/C/E/J/N/R/Q/Z/6 to Canal St.

NoLita & the East Village

NoLita and the East Village are stylish boutique playgrounds. As such, bargains can be hard to find. The good news is that low—if not dirt cheap—prices on haute couture can still be tracked down, if you put in the legwork. NoLita's **Elizabeth, Mott, and Mulberry streets** (btw. Houston and Prince) are dotted with an ever-increasing number of fashionable stops, including one of the city's best consignment stores (see "Designer Consignment Stores," later in this chapter). In the Village, **East 9th Street,** between Second Avenue and Avenue A, is home to a slew of up-and-coming local fashion designers—great for window shopping, if nothing else—and loads of small gift shops.

Subway: N/R to Prince St.; 6 to Spring St.; F to Second Ave.; J/Z to Bowery.

The Lower East Side

Holdover street signs designate the chunk of Manhattan south of Houston and east of the Bowery as the "Bargain District." You can still find fabric, bedding, and some clothing, but expensive boutiques and trendy restaurants are crowding the bargains out. The state of flux makes it fun to visit, especially on Sundays. **Orchard Street** closes to traffic **between Delancey and Houston streets,** and vendors lay out cheap goods on tabletops, in the spirit of the pushcarts that were once ubiquitous. In warmer months you may also get a free band, fashion show, or pickle festival. Many shopkeepers will bargain, if that's in your skill set. Little hipster shops have infiltrated Orchard and can also be found scattered around **Ludlow and Stanton** and other nearby streets. Much cheaper goods are available off **Delancey and Clinton streets,** which have a few holdout 99¢ stores and bargain-bin housewares.

Subway: F to Delancey St.; J/M/Z to Essex St.

On Broadway

The stretches of **Broadway between Bleecker and Canal streets** are a fashion runway for New York youth. With cheap stores abounding, the streets stay packed until nightfall. Though it's sometimes semiderisively referred to as the "Cheap Sneaker District," lower Broadway has a great selection of hip and affordable jeans, sweats, jackets, and, yes, sneakers. The area's traffic flow has only increased with the opening of a Bloomingdale's satellite and the high-profile addition has yet to price out its cut-rate neighbors.

Subway: B/D/F/M to Broadway/Lafayette St.; 6 to Spring St.; N/R to Prince St.

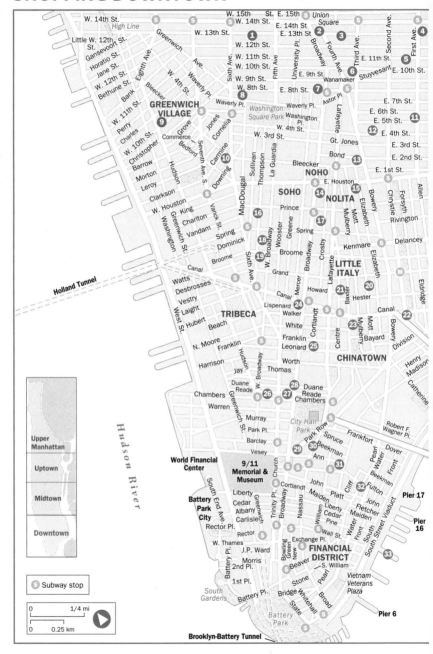

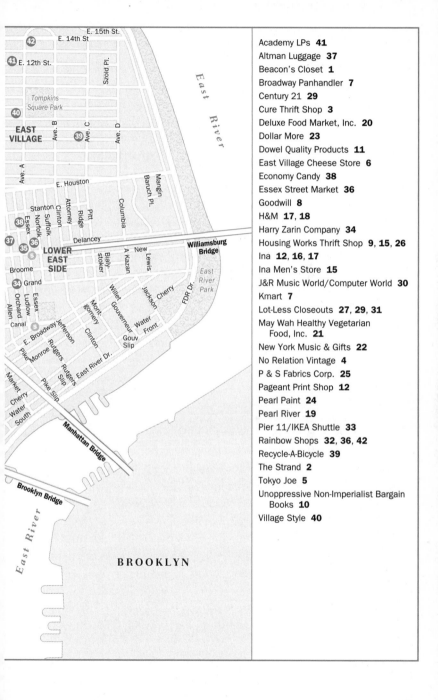

CHELSEA

Proximity to Fifth Avenue's deep purses helped propel Chelsea's stretches of **Sixth Avenue and Broadway** to the top of Manhattan's shopping heap in the late 19th century. The fancy folk eventually moved uptown and the department stores followed, but not before leaving behind some lovely cast-iron architecture. Big discount chains have moved in, including a popular Old Navy, and a couple of good thrift stops on **17th Street between Fifth and Sixth avenues.**

Subway: L to Sixth Ave.; F/M to 23rd St.

GRAMERCY

The residential enclave of Gramercy, sandwiched between hectic Midtown and East Village streets, is often overlooked as a shopping destination. That's great news for thrift aficionados, who can take advantage of less competition. Gramercy's almost total lack of hipster cred makes the cool clothing, furniture, and collectibles somewhat easier to come by than the East Village and NoLita. The shops along **23rd street between Second and Third avenues** are well stocked, and the goods are priced low enough that they're continually flowing. For my money, this is the best place in the city to bargain hunt for thrift threads.

Subway: 6 to 23rd St.

MIDTOWN

THE GARMENT DISTRICT

The huge old buildings in **the 30s between Madison and Eighth avenues** still bear faded advertisements for the furriers and milliners whose shops and factories filled the lofts here. Although much of the manufacturing has moved, the garment trade is still active in ground-floor showrooms. Most are wholesale only, particularly the stretch on **Broadway that runs into the 20s.** A few places are open to the retail public. Toward the west, Penn Station is a hub for light rail and subway trains, and the streets nearby are a natural mecca for shoppers. Several big discounters are stationed here, as is the largest store in the world, Macy's. For garment shopping, however, downtown is a better bet.

Subway: B/D/F/M/N/Q/R to 34th St./Herald Sq.; 1/2/3 or A/C/E to 34th St./Penn Station.

UPTOWN

Clustered on the Upper West and Upper East sides are some of the highest per capita incomes in the world. The big chains and department stores that cater to those lofty budgets dominate the local retail trade, though a few exceptions exist for discerning shoppers. For high-end fashions at low-end prices, the consignment shops on **Madison and Amsterdam avenues** are some of the best in the city.

Subway: 1/2/3 to 72nd St.; B/C to 72nd St.; 4/5/6 to 86th St.

2 Dirt Cheap Threads & More

DIRT CHIC

Used clothing falls into two categories in New York, "thrift" and "vintage." In a thrift shop you'll have to sort through racks of junk to find that one perfect shirt, but it won't set you back more than a few bucks. A good vintage proprietor will do the editing for you, but you'll pay for access to his or her good taste. For the trendiest items—like a '70s rock concert T-shirt—a couple of holes in the sleeve may not lower the $90 price tag. Uptown consignment shops will sell you a Chanel suit at a fraction of the original cost, but that's still going to be a several-hundred-dollar commitment. My favorites are shops that split the difference between thrift and vintage, selling used stuff that's still got some life left in it, but not at budget-busting prices. Many of the city's thrift shops are charitable nonprofits, so not only will you be getting a bargain, you'll also be helping out a worthy cause.

Note: Clothing isn't the only reason we tightwads love thrift stores. Most of the shops listed below also stock an impressive variety of used furniture, jewelry, electronics, books, records, and even art.

LORD HAVE GRAMERCY: CHEAP SHOPPING ON (& JUST OFF) 23RD STREET

My favorite shopping cluster is 23rd Street, near Third Avenue. Gramercy is prosperous enough to ensure high quality levels for hand-me-down goods, and a lack of hipster competition in these parts makes the racks less pawed-through. In addition to the stores below, there are also a **Salvation Army** (208 E. 23rd St.) and a **Cauz for Pawz** (212 E. 23rd St.) thrift shop, although I don't like either of them nearly as much as the places below.

SHOPPING IN MIDTOWN

Academy Records and CDs **19**
Adorama **18**
Angel Street Thrift Shop **12**
B&H **10**
Bideawee **39**
Book-Off **44**
City Opera Thrift Shop **28**
Clothingline/SSS **5**
Cosmetic Market **38**
Dave's **17**
DSW **6, 23**
Fishs Eddy **22**
The Garage **16**
Goodwill **27, 30**
Gray Line Linen **3**
H&M **9, 21, 36, 42, 46, 47**
Hell's Kitchen Flea Market **4**
Housing Works Thrift Shop **1, 15, 25**
Ina **11**
Jack's 99-Cent Stores **34, 41, 45**
Joe Fresh **7, 20, 43**
Kmart **8**
Loehmann's **13**
Furnish Green **33**
Macy's **35**
Metropolitan Pavilion **15**
Rags-A-GoGo **14**
Rainbow Shops **37, 40**
Starbright Floral Design **32**
Toys "R" Us **2**
Trader Joe's **24, 39**
The Vintage Thrift Shop **26**
West 25th Street Market **31**

City Opera Thrift Shop Locals sing the praises of this shop, with its balconies full of deals on art, books, and bric-a-brac. Furniture prices are excellent. Costumey looks dominate the clothing selection, including pieces that appear to have just left the stage. 222 E. 23rd St., btw. Second and Third aves. ✆ **212/684-5344.** www.nycopera.com. Subway: 6 to 23rd St.

Goodwill The style quota in these stores tends to be pretty low, with racks full of the fashion miscues of the last couple of decades. However, there's tons to look at, it's very well organized, and it's in a lot better shape than at the Salvation Army. Plus, when you do find your diamond in the rough you won't pay much for it. (If it were easy all the time, the big scores wouldn't be nearly as thrilling, right?) 220 E. 23rd St., btw. Second and Third aves. ✆ **212/447-7270.** www.goodwillny.org. Subway: 6 to 23rd St. Other Manhattan locations: *West Village,* 44 W. 8th St., btw. MacDougal St. and Sixth Ave. Subway: A/B/C/D/E/F/M to W. 4th St./Washington Sq. *Chelsea,* 103 W. 25th St., near Sixth Ave. ✆ **646/638-1725.** Subway: 1 or F/M to 23rd St. *Upper West Side,* 217 W. 79th St., btw. Broadway and Amsterdam Ave. ✆ **212/874-5050**. Subway: 1 to 79th St. *Washington Heights,* 512 W. 181st St., at Audubon St. ✆ **212/923-7910.** Subway: 1 to 181st St. *Upper East Side,* 1704 Second Ave., btw. 88th and 89th sts. ✆ **212/831-1830.** Subway: 4/5/6 to 86th St. *Harlem,* 2196 Fifth Ave., at 135th St. ✆ **212/862-0020.** Subway: 2/3 to Lenox Ave. *East Harlem,* 2231 Third Ave., btw. 121st and 122nd sts. ✆ **212/410-0973.** Subway: 4/5/6 to 125th St. Other locations in Brooklyn, Queens, and the Bronx.

Housing Works Thrift Shop Housing Works has the city's best thrift shops, with a constant stream of quality donations. Designer names often pop up on the clothes racks, and the jewelry shelves are filled with intriguing items. The real draw, however, is the furniture. Although the premium pieces end up in those gorgeously arrayed store windows (they're up for grabs in silent auctions), many a well-preserved table or chair finds its way to the sales floor. Housing Works is a nonprofit whose mission is to work with people with HIV/AIDS, and the homeless. Proceeds from these stores pay for almost 25% of the group's operating budget. 157 E. 23rd St., btw. Third and Lexington aves. ✆ **212/529-5955.** www.housingworks.org. Subway: 6 to 23rd St. Other locations: *Chelsea,* 143 W. 17th St., btw. Sixth and Seventh aves. ✆ **212/366-0820.** Subway: 1 to 18th St.; F/M to 14th St.; L to Sixth Ave. *Upper East Side,* 202 E. 77th St., btw. Second and Third aves. ✆ **212/772-8461.** Subway: 6 to 77th St. *Upper East Side,* 1730 Second Ave., at 90th St. ✆ **212/722-8306.** Subway: 4/5/6 to 86th St. *Upper West Side,* 306

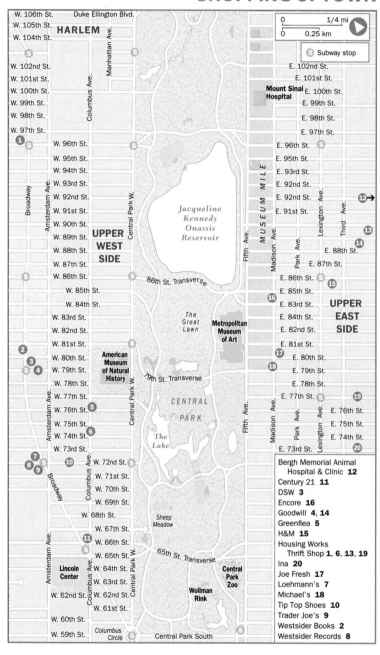

W. 106th St.   Duke Ellington Blvd.
W. 105th St.   **HARLEM**
W. 104th St.

0   1/4 mi
0   0.25 km

Ⓢ Subway stop

W. 102nd St.   E. 102nd St.
W. 101st St.   E. 101st St.
W. 100th St.   **Mount Sinai** E. 100th St.
W. 99th St.   **Hospital**   E. 99th St.
W. 98th St.   E. 98th St.
W. 97th St.   E. 97th St.
❶
W. 96th St.   E. 96th St.
W. 95th St.   E. 95th St.
W. 94th St.   E. 93rd St.
W. 93rd St.   E. 92nd St.
W. 92nd St.   E. 92nd St. ⑫→
W. 91st St.   *Jacqueline*   E. 91st St.
W. 90th St.   *Kennedy*   ⑬
W. 89th St.   *Onassis*
UPPER   *Reservoir*   ⑭
W. 88th St.   E. 88th St.
WEST
W. 87th St.   E. 87th St.
SIDE
W. 86th St.   E. 86th St. ⑮
               86th St. Transverse
W. 85th St.   E. 85th St.
W. 84th St.   E. 83rd St. ⑯
                                                        UPPER
W. 83rd St.   *The*   E. 84th St. **EAST**
W. 82nd St.   *Great*   **Metropolitan** E. 82nd St. **SIDE**
               Lawn   **Museum**
W. 81st St.   **of Art**   E. 81st St.
❷
W. 80th St.   **American**   E. 80th St. ⑰
❸   **Museum**
Ⓢ❹ W. 79th St. **of Natural**   E. 79th St. ⑱
               History
W. 78th St.   E. 78th St.
W. 77th St.   E. 77th St. Ⓢ ⑲
❺ W. 76th St.   E. 76th St.
W. 75th St.   *CENTRAL*   E. 75th St.
❻ W. 74th St.   E. 74th St.
W. 73rd St.   *PARK*   E. 73rd St. ⑳
❼ ❿ W. 72nd St. Ⓢ *The*
❽   *Lake*
❾ W. 71st St.
W. 70th St.
W. 69th St.
W. 68th St.   *Sheep*
              Meadow
❿
⑪ W. 66th St.
Ⓢ W. 65th St.
              65th St. Transverse
Lincoln   **Central**
Center   W. 64th St.   **Park**
W. 63rd St.   **Zoo**
W. 62nd St. W. 62nd St. **Wollman**
W. 61st St.   **Rink**
W. 60th St.
W. 59th St. *Columbus*   Central Park South
             Circle

Bergh Memorial Animal
   Hospital & Clinic **12**
Century 21 **11**
DSW **3**
Encore **16**
Goodwill **4, 14**
Greenflea **5**
H&M **15**
Housing Works
   Thrift Shop **1, 6, 13, 19**
Ina **20**
Joe Fresh **17**
Loehmann's **7**
Michael's **18**
Tip Top Shoes **10**
Trader Joe's **9**
Westsider Books **2**
Westsider Records **8**

191

Columbus Ave., btw. 74th and 75th sts. ✆ **212/579-7566.** Subway: B/C to 72nd St. *Upper West Side,* 2569 Broadway, btw. 96th and 97th sts. ✆ **212/222-3550.** Subway: 1/2/3 to 96th St. *West Village,* 245 W. 10th St., btw. Hudson and Bleecker sts. ✆ **212/352-1618.** Subway: 1 to Christopher St. *Hell's Kitchen,* 732 Ninth Ave., btw. 49th and 50th sts. ✆ **646/963-2665.** Subway: C/E to 50th St. *SoHo,* 130 Crosby St., at Jersey St. ✆ **646/786-1200.** Subway: B/D/F/M to Broadway/Lafayette St.; N/R to Prince St.; 6 to Spring St. *TriBeCa,* 119 Chambers St., btw. W. Broadway and Church St. ✆ **212/732-0584.** Subway: 1/2/3 or A/C to Chambers St. *Brooklyn Heights, Brooklyn,* 122 Montague St., at Henry St. ✆ **718/237-0521.** Subway: R/2/3/4/5 to Court St./ Borough Hall. *Park Slope, Brooklyn,* 266 Fifth Ave., at Garfield Place. ✆ **718/636-2271.** Subway: R to Union St.

The Vintage Thrift Shop   Most items here are in good enough shape to make this feel more like a boutique than a thrift shop. Vintage glasses, glassware, prints, clothes, and more can be found, with a certain amount of self-awareness evident in the pricing. There isn't room for much furniture, but what's here is priced to sell. 286 Third Ave., btw. 22nd and 23rd sts. ✆ **212/871-0777.** www.vintagethriftshop.org. Subway: 6 to 23rd St.

ELSEWHERE

Angel Street Thrift Shop   Angel Street does an impressive job of keeping its recycled goods *au courant.* The clothes are in good shape and most don't scream "bought at a thrift shop." Some unused ringers like sealed sheets and electronics sneak into the bric-a-brac and bedding sections. 118 W. 17th St., btw. Sixth and Seventh aves. ✆ **212/229-0546.** www.angelstreetthrift.org. Subway: 1 to 18th St.; F/M to 14th St.; L to Sixth Ave.

Beacon's Closet   Hipsters delight in the well-stocked palaces of the three locations of Beacon's Closet. As a clothing exchange, this store buys garments off its customers, with no appointment necessary. Clean out your closet and turn it into cash. Pick up 20% more by getting paid off in store credit and putting all those newly empty hangers to immediate use. The stores can be picky about what they'll take, but that just makes for a better selection for shoppers. All three locations have extensive collections of stylish clothes and shoes, although the high quality begets somewhat higher prices. 10 W. 13th St., btw. Fifth and Sixth aves. ✆ **917/261-4863.** www.beaconscloset.com. Subway: L/N/Q/R/4/5/6 to 14th St./Union Sq. Other locations: *Park Slope, Brooklyn,* 92 Fifth Ave., at Warren St. ✆ **718/230-1630.** Subway: R to Union St. *Williamsburg, Brooklyn,* 88 N. 11th St., btw. Berry St. and Wythe Ave. ✆ **718/486-0816.** Subway: L to Bedford Ave.

Finds & Relations

Just don't call it a thrift store: The East Village's **No Relation Vintage** prides itself on well-preserved *vintage* picks spread out amid row upon row of $10 duds. NYU kids and tourists ransack the rapidly changing stock for armfuls of soft horsehide jackets, glittery '60s party looks, '70s prairie dresses, button-downs, jerseys, and screen-printed T's. As a bonus, they'll let you reach even further back with low-priced furs from the '50s. Women plunder purses and round-toe heels while guys who fondly remember America's awkward years score Air Jordans and Levis E jean jackets. (To the dismay of the staff, this is also the official source for hideous Christmas sweaters.) The near-limitless stock makes squeezing into the shoebox-size dressing room and the smell of form-aldehyde worth it. I crave high-quality vintage dresses, but with their explosive popularity, most surrounding boutiques mark their buys up too much. Here I can dress myself head to toe for $30 and avoid being a walking fresh-from-the-East-Village-boutique cliché. 204 First Ave., btw. 12th and 13th sts. ✆ **212/228-5201.** www.ltrainvintage.com. Subway: L to First Ave. For sibling vintage retailers, see p. 187.

—Ashley Hoffman

Cure Thrift Shop   The cure in the name is for diabetes, which affects the founder, along with 24 million other Americans. While you're helping a worthy cause, help yourself to deals on furniture and high fashion. Designer dresses start at little more than $10, and skirts and scarves can be found for $5 or less. Students, seniors, diabetics, fol-lowers of the shop's Tumblr, and the shop's Facebook friends lower their clothing tabs by a further 15% Mondays through Wednesdays. 111 E. 12th St., btw. Third and Fourth aves. ✆ **212/505-7467.** www.curethriftshop.com. Subway: L/N/Q/R/4/5/6 to 14th St./Union Sq.; L to Third Ave.

Rags-A-GoGo   It's a rare thrift/vintage shop that hits the trifecta of good selection, good condition, and good prices the way RAGG does. This Chelsea charmer succeeds with rack after rack of cool pants, T's, sweatshirts, and button-downs. Dusty stuffed animals survey the scene, increasing the atmosphere of quirkiness essential to a good thrifting trip. 218 W. 14th St., btw. Seventh and Eighth aves. ℭ **646/486-4011.** www.rags-a-gogo.com. Subway: 1/2/3 or A/C/E to 14th St.; L to Eighth Ave.

Thames & Bocker Ample cheap warehouse space was the fertilizer for Bushwick's recent rise. The 6,000-square-foot ground floor of OfficeOps gets put to good use with rack after rack of affordable hipster boots, belts, shoes, jackets, plaid pants, and T's. 57 Thames St., enter at Knickerbocker Ave. ℭ **718/497-1331.** www.lepointvalue.com. Subway: L to Morgan Ave.

Unique Thrift Store Fulton Mall in downtown Brooklyn has long been an affordable shopping magnet (there are over 230 stores here, including a Gap Outlet). My favorite is this low-priced envoy of a Minnesota thrift chain. In the basement you'll find rack after rack of women's clothes, on top of $2.49 hardcover books (paperbacks go for a buck less). Upstairs is men's and children's. It's all well organized and the clothing is in good shape, if not always representing the height of style. There's a lot of acreage here, so block out some time. 408 Fulton Mall, btw. Gallatin Place and Bridge St. ℭ **718/643-1825.** www.imunique. com. Subway: 2/3 to Hoyt St.; A/C/F/R to Jay St./Metro Tech. Other locations: *Jamaica, Queens,* 161-20 Jamaica Ave., btw. 161st and 162nd sts. ℭ **347/901-5750.** Subway: E/J/Z to Jamaica Center-Parsons/Archer. *Kingsbridge, Bronx,* 218 W. 234th St., btw. Kingsbridge Ave. and Broadway. ℭ **718/548-1190.** Subway: 1 to 231st St.

The Urban Jungle Vintage/Thrift Warehouse A love of vintage that approaches the level of fetish imbues this massive Bushwick space. You can find accessories and art on top of the usual sneaker, T, housedress, and leather jacket suspects. Prices are good and the selection goes nigh on forever. The same holds true for the sibling locations of this minichain, which go by various names (see p. 193 above for No Relation). 118 Knickerbocker Ave., btw. Thames St. and Flushing Ave. ℭ **718/497-1331.** www.urbanjunglevintage.wordpress.com. Subway: L to Morgan Ave. Other locations: *Village Style,* 111 E. 7th St., btw. First Ave. and Ave. A. ℭ **212/260-6390.** www.villagestyleny.com. *Vice Versa,* 550 Fifth Ave., at 15th St., Park Slope, Brooklyn. Subway: R to Prospect Ave. *Vice Versa,* 241 Bedford Ave., btw. N. 3rd and N. 4th sts., Williamsburg, Brooklyn. ℭ **718/782-8847.** www.viceversavintage.com. Subway: L to Bedford Ave. *Atlantic Attic,* 771 Metropolitan Ave., btw. Humboldt St. and Graham Ave., Williamsburg, Brooklyn. ℭ **718/218-8670.** www.atlantisattic.blogspot.com. Subway: L to Graham Ave.

Designer Consignment Stores

It's not that hard to look like a million bucks in NYC, even if your clothes budget tops out at a much lower number. New York's best consignment shops carry loads of pre-owned, vintage, and overstock garments in near-showroom condition. The duds are by no means dirt cheap, but for the high end of design, the prices are as low as they come.

★ **Encore**   For resale women's wear, the Upper East Side is the place to be. Encore is the best of the best, chock-full of big, big names on two floors. A lot of it cost a fortune the first time around and it's still not cheap, but periodic sales can bring luxury into reach. Some of Jackie O's wardrobe made its curtain call here (which says a lot about the store's demographic). 1132 Madison Ave., btw. 84th and 85th sts., 2nd floor. © **212/879-2850.** www.encoreresale.com. Subway: 4/5/6 to 86th St.

Ina   When *Sex and the City*'s wardrobe department sold off its leftovers, of course it turned to Ina. This designer consignment shop carries the height of style, including the likes of Halston, Prada, and Daryl K. The racks are filled with both vintage and current items, and they're always in excellent shape. Shoes and accessories are here as well, and everything is marked way, way down (though outside of the sales, it's still not cheap). Men can get in on the action at the coed Chelsea and NoHo locations, or gents-only 19 Prince. *NoLita,* 21 Prince St., btw. Mott and Elizabeth sts. © **212/334-9048.** www.inanyc.com. Subway: 6 to Spring St.; N/R to Prince St. Other locations: *NoHo,* 15 Bleecker St., btw. Lafayette St. and Bowery. © **212/228-8511.** Subway: 6 to Bleecker St.; B/D/F/M to Broadway/ Lafayette St. *SoHo,* 101 Thompson St., btw. Prince and Spring sts. © **212/941-4757.** Subway: C/E to Spring St. *Men's store,* 19 Prince St., btw. Mott and Elizabeth sts. © **212/334-2210.** Subway: 6 to Spring St.; N/R to Prince St. Chelsea, 207 W. 18th St., btw. Seventh and Eighth aves. Subway: 1 to 18th St. *Uptown,* 208 E. 73rd St., btw. Second and Third aves. © **212/249-0014.** Subway: 6 to 77th St.

Michael's   Designer wear for women is the focus of this much-loved two-story consignment boutique. The names are familiar—Chanel, YSL, Prada, and Gucci—but the prices are barely recognizable. As pickers, they're very careful, making sure no rips or stains make it onto the floor. 1041 Madison Ave., 2nd floor, btw. 79th and 80th sts. © **212/737-7273.** www.michaelsconsignment.com. Subway: 6 to 77th St.

Tokyo Joe   When hipsters need the good stuff, they turn straight to this designer consignment shop. Cramped quarters can make for tough browsing, but the clothes themselves are in excellent shape. Don't miss the big section of lightly used and new shoes, going for a fraction of their cost Uptown. 334 E. 11th St., btw. First and Second aves. ℭ **212/473-0724.** Subway: L to First Ave.

OTHER TRES CHEAP FASHIONS

Dave's   Since 1963, this family-run shop has been outfitting New Yorkers for construction work, rough weather, and denim-clad nights on the town. Brands with ample blue-collar cred are well-represented (Carhartt, Dickies, Redwing), and the Levi's selection is close to exhaustive. Outgoing staff will help you navigate the store and the cash register will treat you kindly, with prices often 30% off the nearby Levi's store. 581 Sixth Ave., btw. 16th and 17th Sts. ℭ **212/989-6444.** www.davesnewyork.com. Subway: F/M to 14th St.; L to Sixth Ave.

H&M   Swedish discounter Hennes & Mauritz knocks off the latest styles at low, low prices. They specialize in hip looks for adults, and as such they're a big hit with the teens. Durability is not the greatest, though it is about what you'd expect for these prices. 1328 Broadway, at 34th St. ℭ **646/473-1165.** www.hm.com. Subway: B/D/F/M/N/Q/R to 34th St./Herald Sq.; 1/2/3 to 34th St./Penn Station. Other locations: *Midtown,* 640 Fifth Ave., at 51st St. ℭ **212/489-0390.** Subway: E/M to Fifth Ave. *Times Square,* 505 Fifth Ave., at 42nd St. ℭ **212/661-7012.** Subway: 1/2/3/7/N/Q/R/S to 42nd St./Times Sq. *Flatiron,* 111 Fifth Ave., at 18th St. ℭ **212/539-1741.** Subway: L/N/Q/R/4/5/6 to 14th St./Union Sq. *SoHo,* 558 Broadway, btw. Prince and Spring sts. ℭ **212/343-2722.** Subway: N/R to Prince St.; 6 to Spring St. *SoHo,* 515 Broadway, btw. Spring and Broome sts. ℭ **212/965-8975.** Subway: 6 to Spring St.; N/R to Prince St. *Midtown,* 731 Lexington Ave., at 59th St. ℭ **212/935-6781.** Subway: 4/5/6 or N/Q/R to 59th St./Lexington Ave. *Herald Square,* 435 Seventh Ave., btw. 33rd and 34th sts. ℭ **212/643-6955.** Subway: B/D/F/M/N/Q/R to 34th St./Herald Sq.; 1/2/3 to 34th St./Penn Station. *Upper East Side,* 150 E. 86th St., at Lexington Ave. ℭ **212/289-1724.** Subway: 4/5/6 to 86th St. *Harlem,* 125 W. 125th St., at Lenox Ave. ℭ **212/665-8300.** Subway: 2/3 to 125th St.

Joe Fresh   The pop of bright colors here is a reminder that this Canadian chain started out selling clothes from inside grocery stores. Some designs can be clunky, but generally this place is like a fashion-forward Old Navy. Close-outs offer good discounts, on top of $10 T's and four-packs of socks for $8. 510 Fifth Ave., at 43rd St. ℭ **212/764-1730.** www.joefresh.com. Subway: B/D/F/M to 42nd St.; 7 to Fifth Ave. Other locations:

Union Square, 110 Fifth Ave., btw. 16th and 17th sts. ☏ **212/366-0960.** Subway: L/N/Q/R/4/5/6 to 14th St./Union Sq. *Herald Square,* 215 W. 34th St., btw. Seventh and Eighth Aves. ☏ **212/643-1666.** Subway: B/D/F/M/N/Q/R to 34th St./Herald Sq.; 1/2/3 to 34th St./Penn Station. *Upper East Side,* 1055 Madison Ave., btw. 80th and 81st sts. ☏ **212/472-1505.** Subway: 6 to 77th St.

Loehmann's When the original Barneys faltered, longtime discount fave Loehmann's was quick to fill much of the square footage. Casual wear comes in at one-third to two-thirds off the department-store prices, and you can reel in even deeper discounts on the likes of Donna Karan and Versace inside the "Back Room." Great prices for women's shoes, too, and there's an underpublicized men's floor. 101 Seventh Ave., btw. 16th and 17th sts. ☏ **212/352-0856.** www.loehmanns.com. Subway: 1 to 18th St. Other location: *Upper West Side,* 2101 Broadway, at 73rd St. ☏ **212/882-9990.** Subway: 1/2/3 to 72nd St.

Rainbow Shops When the new women's and girl's clothing lines come out, Rainbow wastes no time in coming up with affordable copies. Urban styles predominate, with the target audience well under 25. They have shoes and accessories, lots of plus sizes, and you won't have to part with a pot of gold. ⌈FINE PRINT⌋ Durability is not the greatest here, so if you find something you like think about getting more than one. 110–114 Delancey St., btw. Essex and Ludlow sts. ☏ **212/254-7058.** www.rainbowshops.com. Subway: F to Delancey St.; J/M/Z to Essex St. Other locations: *East Village,* 504 E. 14th St., btw. aves. A and B. ☏ **212/677-6391.** *Harlem,* 308 W. 125th St., btw. Manhattan Ave. and Frederick Douglass Blvd. ☏ **212/864-5707.** Subway: A/B/C/D to 125th St. *Harlem,* 160 E. 125th St., at Lexington Ave. ☏ **212/410-5798.** Subway: 4/5/6 to 125th St. *Herald Square,* 380 Fifth Ave., btw. 35th and 36th sts. ☏ **212/947-0837.** Subway: B/D/F/M/N/Q/R to 34th St./Herald Sq. *Financial District,* 40 Fulton St., at Pearl St. ☏ **212/346-0865.** Subway: A/C/J/Z/2/3/4/5 to Fulton St./Broadway Nassau. *Midtown East,* 270 Madison Ave., btw. 39th and 40th sts. ☏ **212/532-1041.** Subway: 4/5/6/7/S to 42nd St./Grand Central. *Washington Heights,* 610 W. 181st St., btw. Wadsworth and St. Nicholas aves. ☏ **212/928-1969.** Subway: 1 to 181st St. Many locations in Brooklyn, too.

SHOE INS & OUTS

All the miles New Yorkers log as pedestrians help explain the occasional obsessive bent applied to our shoe shopping. My favorite footwear cluster can be found downtown. **Lower Broadway from East 4th Street down to Canal** has some great options, often doubled up with cheap jean retailers. NYU undergrads haunt this part of the city, and prices tend to accommodate student budgets.

DSW   This chain came all the way from Ohio to liberate New Yorkers from high shoe prices. Their warehouse-style megastores are packed with recent releases. Special sale areas have the best buys, with markdowns exceeding 75%. Ladies in particular will have to exhibit patience, as their selection goes on forever. 40 E. 14th St., 3rd floor, btw. University Place and Broadway. ℂ **212/674-2146.** www.dswshoe.com. Subway: L/N/Q/R/4/5/6 to 14th St./Union Sq. Other locations: *Midtown,* 213 W. 34th St., btw. Seventh and Eighth aves. ℂ **212/967-9703.** Subway: 1/2/3 or A/C/E to 34th St./Penn Station. *Upper West Side,* 2222 Broadway, btw. 79th and 80th sts. Subway: 1 to 79th St. *Downtown Brooklyn,* 139 Flatbush Ave., at Atlantic Ave. ℂ **718/789-6973.** Subway: B/D/N/Q/R/2/3/4/5 to Atlantic Ave./Pacific St.

Shoe Mania   This popular discount store has a wide-ranging selection, putting Kenneth Coles sole to sole with Doc Martens, Birkenstocks, and Mephistos. Whether you go for style or comfort, you'll find a good price on it here. 853 Broadway, at 14th St. ℂ **212/253-8744.** www.shoemania.com. Subway: L/N/Q/R/4/5/6 to 14th St./Union Sq. Other locations: *Midtown,* 331 Madison Ave., btw. 42nd and 43rd sts. ℂ **212/557-6627.** Subway: 4/5/6/7/S to 42nd St./Grand Central. *SoHo,* 654 Broadway, at Bond St. ℂ **212/673-0904.** Subway: 6 to Bleecker St.; B/D/F/M to Broadway/Lafayette St.

Tip Top Shoes   This Uptown shop is tops for walking shoes, which are essential equipment in New York. Rockport, Mephisto, and Ecco are among the brands represented here, sold at reasonable prices. They also carry shoes of a less practical nature for those who prefer form to function. Staff is knowledgeable, if a little harried by the frenetic pace of business here. 155 W. 72nd St., btw. Broadway and Columbus Ave. ℂ **800/WALKING** (925-5464) or 212/787-4960. www.tiptopshoes.com. Subway: 1/2/3 to 72nd St.

3 Flea New York

New Yorkers seeking free stimuli can certainly do worse than whiling away a few hours at a flea market. The rows of tables function as touchable museums, and the sheer width and breadth of stuff is stunning. Prices for goods are generally not as cheap as they should be, given the low-overhead locales, but there are ways to tip the scales in your favor. Sunday, as closing time approaches, the last thing a dealer wants to do is reload that half-ton armoire back into the truck.

Likewise, a sudden rain can make parting with a wooden antique or a suede jacket more sweetness than sorrow. Use the elements to your advantage when it's time to haggle.

Brooklyn Flea `FREE` This upbeat Fort Greene market has scored one of the nicest slices of real estate in the borough: the Deco wonderland inside the Williamsburgh Savings Bank's former lobby. More than 100 vendors lay out affordable clothing, crafts, vinyl, vintage jewelry, and architectural salvage. An even bigger draw here is the food—Korean hot dogs and Salvadorian *papusas* are just two of the cheap eat possibilities. (There's an all-food spinoff of the Flea called **Smorgasburg,** held on the Williamsburg waterfront during warm-weather Sat.) April through November, the market runs outdoors from

Come Sale Away

When out-of-towners marvel that anyone would pay what's printed on a New York price tag, they aren't taking into account that most locals never pay full retail prices. The key to dirt cheap shopping in the Big Apple is timing the sales. Seasons' ends, like just before back-to-school and just after Christmas, are routinely great for bargain hunters. Buy your sundresses and air conditioners in August, and wait until February to pick up that new winter coat. If your tastes run to vintage or barely used, try looking around in January, when a fresh crop of nonreturnable gift fails get consigned. My favorite Web sources for sale info are: **www.nymag.com/sales**, **www.ny.racked.com**, **www.thechoosybeggar.com**, and **www.topbutton.com**.

Another great New York feature is the sample sale. Fashion designers can't sell just everything they lay their scissors to. Sample outfits made specially for store buyers end up sitting on a rack, along with canceled orders, overstock, and items whose day in the fashion sun has come and gone. In addition to the Internet sources above, check in at www. clothingline.com. **Clothingline/SSS Sales** (✆ **212/947-8748**) has 20 years' experience running sample sales for a host of huge names like rag & bone, J. Crew, and Calypso. Days of the week and hours vary; usually opens 10 or 11am. 261 W. 36th St., 2nd floor, btw. Seventh and Eighth aves. Subway: 1/2/3 or A/C/E to 34th St./Penn Station.

10am to 5pm at Bishop Loughlin Memorial High on Saturdays, and on the Smorgasburg location on Sundays. The rest of the year it's at the bank both weekend days. 1 Hanson Place, at Flatbush Ave. www.brooklyn flea.com. Subway: B/D/N/Q/R/2/3/4/5 to Atlantic Ave./Pacific St. Other locations: *Ft. Greene*, 176 Lafayette Ave., btw. Clermont and Vanderbilt aves. Subway: G to Clinton/Washington aves., C to Lafayette Ave. *Williamsburg*, East River waterfront near Kent Ave., btw. N. 6th and N. 7th sts. Subway: L to Bedford Ave.

The Garage `FREE`   Imagine a series of yard sales jammed right on top of each other and you'll have an idea of the scene at the Garage. They've got lots of art, loose photos, and other oddball junk. Prices are higher than at its siblings (Hell's Kitchen and W. 25th St.), but it's still fun to browse. Two floors, open Saturdays and Sundays from 9am to 5pm. 112 W. 25th St., btw. Sixth and Seventh aves. © **212/243-5343.** www.hells kitchenfleamarket.com. Subway: F/M or 1 to 23rd St.

Greenflea `FREE`   This bustling indoor/outdoor Upper West Side fair is a favorite way to spend a Sunday afternoon. The antiques tend to be priced fairly, marginalized as they are by dealers offering less-inspired contemporary imports, crafts, and clothes. The latter also line the nearby strip of Columbus Avenue. Open 10am to 5:30pm, until 5:45pm April to October. 100 W. 77th St., at Columbus Ave. © **212/239-3025.** www.greenfleamarkets.com. Subway: B/C to 72nd St.; 1 to 79th St.

Hell's Kitchen Flea Market `FREE`   Though it hasn't quite caught up with its dearly departed predecessor in Chelsea, this is still the flea scene to beat in the city. Over 150 vendors bring vibrancy to a dingy strip behind the Port Authority. Prices are within the same stratosphere as you'd find on a suburban lawn. Open weekends, 9am to 5pm, weather permitting. 39th St., btw. Ninth and Tenth aves. © **212/243-5343.** www.hellskitchenfleamarket.com. Subway: A/C/E/7 to 42nd St./Port Authority.

West 25th Street Market `FREE`   This churchyard fair is conveniently close to the Garage. Some 125 vendors pack the space with good retro/antique picks, including clothes and art. Open weekends, 9am to 5pm. 29–37 W. 25th St., btw. Broadway and Sixth Ave. © **212/243-5343.** www. hellskitchenfleamarket.com. Subway: F/M or N/R to 23rd St.

4 Shekels & Chains: Department Stores

New York traditionally makes it hard for big franchises and chains to survive. The city is competitive to an extreme and there just isn't enough profit margin to pay a bunch of middle-management salaries.

FREE Take an Unböring Trip to IKEA

Escape from Manhattan Island, courtesy of **IKEA,** the Swedish-born affordable style haven. Red Hook, Brooklyn, is IKEA's first foray into New York City proper, and it's spectacular. In addition to the goods indoors (crazy cheap, and some it doesn't even look that way), there's a sprawling 6-acre esplanade with amazing harbor views behind the store. Should you need a break from the action, a bustling in-store cafeteria serves inexpensive food (including Swedish meatballs, of course).

It costs $5 to ride the **New York Water Taxi** (© 212/742-1969; www.nywatertaxi.com), leaving weekdays from Pier 11 on the East River end of Wall Street every 40 minutes between 2 and 7:40pm. The outbound trip is worth a $5 credit on an IKEA purchase of $10 or more, and that same purchase receipt will get you a free ride back. Weekends are completely free without even the $10 purchase obligation. 1 Beard St., at Otsego St., Red Hook, Brooklyn. © **718/246-IKEA.** See **www.ikea.com/us/en/store/brooklyn** for the full shuttle bus route via Park Slope.

For the Elizabeth, New Jersey, mothership, there's a bus from Port Authority. Unfortunately the bus only runs on weekends, and weekends at IKEA are *insane.* Take the Academy Bus, Gate #5, in the lower concourse, Port Authority, Eighth Avenue at 42nd Street. Buses (round-trip only) leave every half-hour between 10am and 2:30pm and return from Jersey every half-hour between noon and 6pm. The trip takes about 30 minutes each way (© **908/289-4488;** www.ikea-usa.com). *Note:* The bus can accommodate your new possessions on the ride back, as long as they're not too big to carry.

Though there are a few chains sprinkled through these pages, for the most part I avoid the national retailers. They don't give you enough bang for your buck.

Century 21   Nearly destroyed on 9/11, Century 21 has risen from the ashes to reclaim its place as the top clothes-shopping destination in the city. Fancy labels are fully represented here, sans the fancy prices. Expect designer goods at less than half the cost they carry in other department stores. There are great deals on sunglasses, linens, and housewares, too. Euro-fueled shopping euphoria has made this

Shopping Brooklyn Sidewalks

Take a tour of Brownstone Brooklyn and along with the tree-lined streets and historic architecture, you can also enjoy a favorite local tradition: stoop giveaways and weekend sales. The egalitarian spirit of Brooklyn is nowhere more alive than along the borough's sidewalks and iron railings, where cramped living spaces get unburdened. Books are the most common find. Brooklyn reads, and when it's done, it enjoys nothing more than setting that book out on the stoop for the next person. If it has a still-cold glass of iced tea next to it, maybe assume they just stepped inside, but otherwise, the tome is yours.

Furniture is another easy acquisition, especially the night before trash pickups. It's a mystery to me why anyone shops at the Red Hook IKEA when you can regularly find almost-new Björkuddens and easily repaired Liatorps. (With the bedbug issues plaguing New York, it might be best to pass over upholstered pieces, though.) If you're willing to part with a buck or two, you can also find fine pickings at weekend stoop sales. Treat it as an experiment in sociology and economics, trying to fathom why a Cobble Hill corporate lawyer whose hourly rate is $450 would choose to spend an entire beautiful Saturday outside on the stoop for a total take of $86 from unopened wedding gifts and last year's scuba equipment. Actually, who cares, as long as you can make off with the Tiffany keychain still in the box for $3, or the kids' massive LEGO hoard for just a couple of bucks more. Most of what doesn't sell will end up curbside or draped over the railing, joining the virtuous cycle of Brooklyn's recycling tradition. If a more curated approach is your style, stop by my shop, **Fork & Pencil** (p. 205), for all your railroad piston mold, 19th-century Japanese erotica, and royal Coldstream Guards coat needs.

—*Alex Grabcheski*

place mobbed even beyond peak lunch and weekend times, but recently extended hours (9pm or later) have helped. Don't be too intimidated by the long lines for the women's dressing room; the queue moves quickly. 22 Cortlandt St., btw. Broadway and Church St. ✆ **212/227-9092.** www.c21stores.com. Subway: E to World Trade Center; A/C/

J/Z/2/3/4/5 to Fulton St./Broadway Nassau; R to Cortlandt St.; 1 to Rector St. Other locations: *Upper West Side,* 1972 Broadway, at 66th St. ✆ **212/518-2121.** Subway: 1 to 66th St. *Bay Ridge, Brooklyn,* 472 86th St., btw. Fourth and Fifth aves. ✆ **718/748-3266.** Subway: R to 86th St. *Rego Park, Queens,* 61-01 Junction Blvd., at 62nd Dr. ✆ **718/699-2121.** Subway: M/R to 63rd Dr./Rego Park.

Jack's 99-Cent Stores   If you think a dollar doesn't get you far in the big city, you don't know Jack. With central locations and a loyal/rabid clientele, these stores bustle at all hours with bargain-hunters stocking up on housewares, gifts, appliances, and chocolate bars. They even have groceries, at unbeatable prices. Daily specials, unadvertised to appease suppliers, reward frequent visits. 16 E. 40th St., btw. Madison and Fifth aves. ✆ **212/696-5767.** www.jacks99world.com. Subway: B/D/F/M to 42nd St.; 7 to Fifth Ave. Other locations: *Midtown,* 45 W. 45th St., btw. Fifth and Sixth aves. ✆ **212/354-6888.** Subway: B/D/F/M to 47th–50th sts./Rockefeller Center; 7 to Fifth Ave. *Herald Square,* 110 W. 32nd St., btw. Sixth and Seventh aves. ✆ **212/268-9962.** Subway: B/D/F/M/N/Q/R to 34th St./Herald Sq.; 1/2/3 to 34th St./Penn Station.

Kmart   The words Kmart and inspiring are rarely found in the same sentence, but for me every trip to Astor Place's K is a thrilling reminder of NYC's cultural diversity. Students, yuppies, outer-borough home-makers, and Japanese hipsters all rub shoulders as they prowl the long aisles for cheap clothing, housewares, furniture, and even food. The hardware and paint departments have great deals, and there's an excellent plant section. Direct access to the subway makes it easy to drag your haul home. 770 Broadway, btw. 8th and 9th sts. ✆ **212/673-1540.** www.kmart.com. Subway: 6 to Astor Place; N/R to 8th St. Other location: 250 W. 34th St., btw. Sixth and Seventh aves. ✆ **212/760-1188.** Subway: B/D/F/M/N/Q/R to 34th St./Herald Sq; 1/2/3 to 34th St./Penn Station.

Lot-Less Closeouts   This discounter stretches from Chambers to Reade Street, stocking everything your kitchen, bathroom, closet, or bedroom may be lacking. The prices on clothes, cosmetics, movies, snacks, and salad dressings are as low as they could possibly be. My wife's most recent spree brought home a classy frame ($5), a towel ($6), 5 pairs of Jordache ladies underwear ($5), and set of lovely salad tongs ($2). 97 Chambers St., at Church St. ✆ **212/233-0607.** www.lot-less.com. Subway: A/C or 1/2/3 to Chambers St. Other locations: *Financial District,* 299 Broadway, at Duane St. ✆ **212/233-2146.** Subway: A/C or 1/2/3 or J/Z to Chambers St.; 4/5/6 to Brooklyn Bridge/City Hall; R to City Hall. *Financial District,* 95 Fulton St., btw.

Macy's Flower Show

Outside of sales (which can be great for bargain hunters), the big department stores aren't much help for the budget-minded. For free entertainment, though, they hold their own. Window displays make great theater, and floor after floor of regal goods make for fun browsing. Two weeks around late March/early April bring some serious spectacle when Macy's goes nuts for flowers. The store is transformed by over a million blossoms in 10 gardens. Free 20-minute tours run every half-hour from 11am to 4pm. **www.macys.com**. Flower hot line ℂ **212/494-4495.**

William and Gold sts. ℂ **212/566-8504.** Subway: A/C/J/Z/2/3/4/5 to Fulton St./ Broadway Nassau. Other locations in Queens, Staten Island, and the Bronx.

Macy's (One-Day Sales) Covering 10 stories and an entire city block, this megalith has just about everything, including at any given time a large chunk of the metropolitan shopping population. The key is to buy during the frequent sales. The famous One-Days are the best, usually held on Wednesdays, with the occasional Saturday thrown in. Check the *New York Times* for Macy's full-page advertisements, which sometimes include clip-out coupons for additional 10% to 15% discounts. If you have a Macy's card, they'll sometimes send you coupons via e-mail, or the sales people may throw in an extra discount at the cash register. Herald Sq., W. 34th St. and Broadway. ℂ **212/695-4400.** www.macys.com. Subway: B/D/F/M/N/Q/R to 34th St./Herald Sq.; 1/2/3 to 34th St./Penn Station.

Peachfrog At this housewares-slash-clothing store, you're greeted by complimentary coffee and goods priced so low you wonder why they bothered with a price tag. Upstairs are racks full of designer leftovers and samples. Find Jonathan Adler housewares at 80% off, graphic T's for $9, and Zig-Zag kicks for under $20. 136 N. 10th St., btw. Berry St. and Bedford Ave. ℂ **718/387-3224.** www.peachfrog.com. Subway: L to Bedford Ave.

Pearl River This mini department store couples Chinatown prices with SoHo ambience. The inventory favors Asian classics like paper lanterns, silk pajamas, and sequined slippers. Glazed bowls and other housewares make for inexpensive kitchen outfitting. This is a great spot for cheap gift hunting, too. 477 Broadway, btw. Broome and Grand sts. ℂ **212/431-4770.** www. pearlriver.com. Subway: J/N/Q/R/Z/6 to Canal St.; 6 to Spring St.

5 Dirt Cheap Shopping: A to Z

ANTIQUES/USED FURNITURE

See also "Flea New York," earlier in this chapter.

Film Biz Recycling   Saving the planet one disco ball at a time, the mission of this nonprofit is to keep useful goods out of landfills while promoting creativity. There are recycled props aplenty in their sprawling warehouse, many almost as cheap to purchase as they are to rent. Think $8 IKEA end tables or $35 vintage desk chairs. Should you be shooting or staging a scene that requires a Magnavox entertainment center and a taxi-yellow rotary phone, look no further. (The shop works equally well for apartment furnishing or gift shopping.) 540 President St., btw. Third and Fourth aves., Park Slope, Brooklyn. © **347/384-2336.** Subway: R to Union St.

Fork & Pencil   The twist here is that the proceeds go to charity: A big part of this shop's mandate is to raise awareness about nonprofits and community building. While you're doing some good, you can also fill in the gaps in your home decoration and gift lists. Cool vintage dishes, silverware, lamps, and art fill the petite space. For furniture and larger items, head around the corner to the 18 Bergen St. annex. 221A Court St., at Warren St., Cobble Hill, Brooklyn. © **718/488-8855.** www.forkandpencil.com. Subway: F/G to Bergen St. Other location: 18 Bergen St., between Smith and Court sts. Subway: F/G to Bergen St.

Furnish Green   A suite inside a Broadway office building holds this collection of antique furniture. There's a great eye at work here, with interesting and often elegant pieces on display. Shelves, dressers, desks, and mirrors sell for a fraction of what they would in a conventional antiques shop. The website lists sales and specials, which are the most affordable way to nab some midcentury modern. If you don't want to leave empty-handed, there's also a dollar record rack, and antique glass bottles for $2 to $4. 1261 Broadway, Ste. 505, btw. 31st and 32nd sts. © **917/583-9051.** www.furnishgreen.org. Subway: B/D/F/M/N/Q/R to 34th St./Herald Sq.; 1/2/3 to 34th St./Penn Station.

Green Village Used Furniture & Clothing   The epic junk collection requires some rifling, but the low prices reward your investment in elbow grease. For clothes, find quality on the racks and quantity in the bins—purchase 50 pounds or more and it's $1.50 per pound. Props, costumes, books, dishes, chairs, and miscellaneous antiques round out the 10,000 square feet of possibilities. 276 Starr St., btw. St. Nicholas and Wyckoff aves., Bushwick, Brooklyn. ℂ **718/456-8844**. www.gogreen village.com. Subway: L to Jefferson St.

Junk   The name here isn't exactly self-deprecating: Wares tend to the low-end and you'll have to do some digging. Your reward, however, is solid kitsch at cheap prices. New stock comes in twice a week and turnover is high, so come back often to fill your comic book, needlepoint, and taxidermy needs. 197 N. 9th St., btw. Bedford and Driggs aves., Williamsburg, Brooklyn. ℂ 718/640-6299. Subway: L to Bedford Ave.

RePOP   All manner of stylish furnishings here seek second (and third and fourth) lives in the big city. Chairs, tables, desks, and cabinets can be picked up in pop iterations for prices that are a fraction of those at Manhattan vendors. Pratt proximity brings in artisan crafts, and the events calendar serves up the occasional artist's reception. 68 Washington Ave., btw. Flushing and Park aves., Clinton Hill, Brooklyn. ℂ **718/260-8032**. www.repopny.com. Subway: G to Clinton/Washington aves. Other location: 143 Roebling St., at Metropolitan Ave., Williamsburg, Brooklyn. Subway: L to Bedford Ave.

BIKES

Recycle-A-Bicycle   The organization that runs these shops promotes biking in the city by selling rehabbed bikes at reasonable prices. A top-of-the-line bike could set you back $500 or more, but that's a fraction of its cost new, and your purchase is helping out a worthy cause. 75 Ave. C, btw. 5th and 6th sts. ℂ **212/475-1655**. www.recycleabicycle.org. Subway: L to First Ave.; F to Second Ave. Other location: *DUMBO, Brooklyn,* 35 Pearl St., at Plymouth St. ℂ **718/858-2972**. Subway: F to York St.; A/C to High St.

BOOKS

See the "Word Up: Readings," section on p. 277 for other great sites for literary browsing.

Book-Off   A huge, clean, insanely cheap bookstore in the heart of Midtown may seem like a mirage, but brother, this thing's all real. A Japanese chain, Book-Off retails *manga, anime,* and Tokyo pop bands, along with English-language music, movies, books, and video games. Acres of shelf space are dedicated to $1 and $2 book specials, with plenty of first edition hardcovers represented. More recently arrived books average $5, which is also the median price for CDs. Games and DVDs are generally $7 propositions. FINE PRINT They buy books, too, if you're looking to turn over a home library. 49 W. 45th St., btw. Fifth and Sixth aves. © **212/685-1410.** www.bookoffusa.com. Subway: B/D/F/M to 47th–50th sts./Rockefeller Center.

The Strand   The Strand is as legendary for its 18 miles of books as it is for its 5 inches of aisle space to maneuver in. The big crowds are a testament to the great prices. Review copies of recent books share space with art books at 85% off list and used fiction hardbacks that go for under $5. Bibliophiles with small apartments beware—it's hard to leave empty-handed. 828 Broadway, at 12th St. © **212/473-1452.** www.strand books.com. Subway: L/N/Q/R/4/5/6 to 14th St./Union Sq.

Unoppressive Non-Imperialist Bargain Books   Positioning itself as the anti-B&N, this friendly family-owned shop won't blow you away with the breadth of its selection of Donald Trump autobiographies. It will, however, impress you with its well-chosen bargains in musician biographies, political philosophy, and Eastern religion. Prices start around $2, and great gift ideas abound, especially if there's a Bob Dylan fan in your life. 34 Carmine St., btw. Bleecker and Bedford sts. © **212/229-0079.** www.unoppressivebooks.blogspot.com. Subway: A/B/C/D/E/F/M to W. 4th St./Washington Sq.

Westsider Books   This tiny, charming shop has the best used books Uptown. There's a broad selection of literary and historical works, and the occasional reviewer's copy can also be found, at discounted prices. A separate store holds an amazing collection of vinyl, along with CDs and DVDs. 2246 Broadway, btw. 80th and 81st sts. © **212/362-0706.** www.westsiderbooks.com. Subway: 1 to 79th St. Other location: *Westsider Records,* 233 W. 72nd St., btw. Broadway and West End Ave. © **212/874-1588.** Subway: 1/2/3 to 72nd St.

COSMETICS

Cosmetic Market   Aside from long aisles packed with perfumes and makeup, this little discounter also stocks gifts and housewares. Discontinued products make the crazy-low prices possible—my wife finds her lipstick here for $2.50 (the tube would run $10 at a commercial drugstore). Max Factor, Maybelline, and L'Oréal are among the big names represented. An abbreviated foodstuff selection in back has great prices on oils, vinegars, and Italian coffees. 15 E. 37th St., btw. Fifth and Madison aves. © **212/725-3625.** Subway: 6 to 33rd St.

EDIBLES

Cooking at home is an obvious way of cutting costs, but a trip to the corner deli for fixings can feel like a shakedown by the time you step away from the cash register. Most NYC grocery stores aren't much better, but a few specialty shops offer accessible comestibles.

Deluxe Food Market, Inc.   This market is a mishmash of a bakery, buffet, and grocery store. It's menacingly crowded, but the high-volume turnover keeps things fresh, and the price is right. The steam table in front has fluffy, jumbo-size dumplings (four for $2), along with hot dishes that are priced at two for $3.50 (if you don't speak Chinese, just point). The bakery keeps pastry prices below $1, a premade ham sandwich is $2, and a packaged chef's chicken platter is $3.50. Past the small eat-in section, you'll find a scrum forming around the regular grocery store goods. Fish, meats, and greens are all at rock-bottom prices. You can also load up on frozen specialties, such as big packs of dumplings (the no reselling signs posted all over the shop are a pretty good indicator that you're getting a deal). 79 Elizabeth St., btw. Hester and Grand sts. ℂ **212/925-5766.** Subway: B/D to Grand St.; J/Z to Bowery.

Dowel Quality Products   Many shoppers only know this store for its unrivaled beer selection, conveniently located near the BYOB restaurants of Curry Row. There's a lot more to like here, however, including health and beauty items, incense, teas, and fruits and vegetables. The best savings come on Dowel's own packaged goods, with bulk rice, chutneys, lentils, and curries of every hue among the highlights. 91 First Ave., btw. 5th and 6th sts. ℂ **212/979-6045.** www.dualspecialty.com. Subway: F to Second Ave.

East Village Cheese Store   This discount dairy destination is the perfect starting point for your next party. You can get bread, crackers, pâtés, pickles, and other side items, although the jaw-dropping prices are on the cheeses. In the front refrigerators, goat cheese tubes, and Boursin packages are under $2, and Bries and Camemberts are just $1.50. Behind the counter you'll find a long list of specials on fancy goudas, fetas, and cheddars for $2.99 a pound. The giveaway prices aren't indicative of lower quality. These aren't second-rate goods, just items picked up when some importer added a mistaken zero to an order. Their mistake is your gain. 40 Third Ave., btw. Ninth and Tenth sts. ℂ **212/477-2601.** Subway: 6 to Astor Place; N/R to 8th St.

Essex Street Market When the city squeezed the pushcarts off the Lower East Side 70 years ago, it built a garagelike city market as a replacement. The market evolved into a low-rent grocery store and shopping mall, frequented by Spanish and Chinese locals, who love the prices. (As this is the LES 2.0, gourmet cheeses, pasta, and chocolate can now be found as well—though few of them qualify as dirt cheap.) **Essex Farm** (© 212/533-5609), a huge Korean deli, has taken over the north end of the market. They sell just about everything, but the best deals are on fresh fruit and vegetables. A big container with a blend of gourmet lettuces is just $2.99, fruit salads are around $3, and when the mangoes are ripe they're two for $1. The middle of the market has butchers, fishmongers, and a botanica. In the back you'll find **Batista Grocery** (© 212/254-0796), with great prices on Goya and other dry goods. Cafe tables are available if you want to make a picnic (on nice days you can take your meal down to the East River). Eat-in diners can also take advantage of the legendary **Shopsin's** (© 212/924-5160; www.shopsins.com), relocated here after decades in the West Village. Kenny Shopsin curses like a sailor as he cooks up "Blisters on my Sisters" (a rice/beans/eggs/tortillas combo for $9), along with some 500-plus additional items. Since this is downtown, there's even an art gallery tucked away in the very back (**Cuchifritos;** © 212/598-4124; www.aai-nyc.org/cuchifritos; Tues–Sun noon–6pm). 120 Essex St., btw. Rivington and Delancey sts. © 212/312-3603. www. essexstreetmarket.com. Subway: F to Delancey St.; J/M/Z to Essex St.

May Wah Healthy Vegetarian Food, Inc. Sometimes a vegetarian needs a break from the bean sprout and tofu regimen. The Chinese are fake meat experts, and this little Chinatown shop has a massive selection. A big package of frozen unchicken nuggets is only $4.15, and my personal favorite, citrus spare ribs, are only $3.45. 213 Hester St., btw. Centre St. and Centre Market Place. © 212/334-4428. www.vegieworld. com. Subway: J/N/Q/R/Z/6 to Canal St.

Park Slope Food Coop This Brooklyn legend is as much a lifestyle as a grocery store. Members have to share in hard labor (almost 3 hours every 4 weeks) for the privilege of shopping here, but their reward is the healthiest and most affordable food around. Most produce travels less than 500 miles, and markups are capped at 21%. I'm a member and find the pricing transparency fascinating: You learn that supermarkets aren't so bad on some dairy products, but they

Buying in Bulk for Less at Costco

New York City boasts four Costcos, and the warehouse club finally made its way to Manhattan with great fanfare in 2009. The rest of the country has long headed to Costco for bulk everything, but it takes a little more savvy to get a membership's worth if you're taking your stuff home to a NYC apartment and don't want a giant package of paper towels to replace your couch. What makes the investment (starting at $55 a year) a good one in the city? Some people share the membership with friends, and split their hauls in the parking lot (and some use their Zipcar memberships for trips to stock up at Costco). Others take advantage of the discount pharmacies and opticians in stores, and book their travel on the Costco website. We get all our paper goods and cleaning supplies at our Costco (Long Island City), and take advantage of the deeply discounted coffee, vitamins, and high-quality meats and fish (we might freeze most of a package of a dozen or so boneless, skinless, chicken breasts), and organic milk. Their Kirkland house brand stands up well to the major national brands that are also on the (huge) shelves and is frequently a better bargain. And, there are always tasty samples on offer: which is how we got hooked on the Santa Barbara Mango Salsa with Peach. Costco is also a great place to buy inexpensive but good-quality party foods, ranging from prepared trays of snacks or veggies to cases of beer and soda, chips, dips and fruits and veggies. *Manhattan,* 517 E. 117th St. ℂ **212/896-5873.** Other locations: *Queens,* 32-50 Vernon Blvd., Long Island City. ℂ **718/267-3680.** *Queens:* 61-35 Junction Blvd., Rego Park. ℂ **718/760-6470.** *Brooklyn,* 976 3rd Ave. ℂ **718/965-7603.**

—Kathleen Warnock

really put the screws to you for cheese and spices. (See p. 138 for information on free community lectures and screenings.) 782 Union St., btw. Sixth and Seventh aves., Park Slope, Brooklyn. ℂ **718/622-0560.** www.food coop.com. Subway: R to Union St.; 2/3 to Grand Army Plaza; B/Q to Seventh Ave.

Sahadi's This brightly lit and perennially mobbed Brooklyn grocery store is a great source for Middle Eastern cooking staples. Dozens of varieties of olive oil are available, as are nuts, dried fruits, olives, lentils, chickpeas, and of course top-quality *mahleb* (the Lebanese seasoning made from the insides of cherry pits). 187–189 Atlantic Ave., btw. Court and Clinton sts., Boerum Hill, Brooklyn. © **718/624-4550.** www.sahadis.com. Subway: 2/3/4/5 to Borough Hall; A/C/F/R to Jay St./Metro Tech.

Trader Joe's Few new arrivals in the city have been awaited as breathlessly, by Californians and non-Californians alike, as Trader's. This legendary grocery store sells its own brands, eliminating the middle man and his attendant price premiums. Beyond the great prices are great products, with fresh, often organic ingredients. Somehow the Hawaiian-shirt-wearing staff stays California-friendly, despite the hordes of hard-core New York shoppers. The wine shop next door carries legendary and quite drinkable "Two-Buck Chuck" (though in New York, Charles Shaw's finest runs us 3 bucks). 142 E. 14th St., btw. Third Ave. and Irving Place (wine shop at #138). © **212/529-4612.** www.traderjoes. com. Subway: L to Third Ave.; N/Q/R/4/5/6 to 14th St./Union Sq. Other locations: *Chelsea,* 675 Sixth Ave., btw. 21st and 22nd sts. Subway: F/M to 23rd St. *Upper West Side,* 200 W. 72nd St., at Broadway. © **212/799-0028.** Subway: 1/2/3 to 72nd St. *Cobble Hill, Brooklyn,* 130 Court St., at Atlantic Ave. © **718/246-8460.** Subway: R to Court St.; 2/3/4/5 to Borough Hall. *Forest Hills, Queens,* 90–30 Metropolitan Ave., at 73rd Ave. © **718/275-1791.** Subway: E/F/R to 71st Ave./Forest Hills.

ELECTRONICS

J&R Music World/Computer World I'm constantly surprised how often an online search for discounted electronics brings up J&R as the cheapest supplier out there. Save the shipping cost by coming in to their bustling block-long series of stores. The staff is well informed and not too brusque (at least by New York standards). The prices on cameras, stereos, computers, and software are excellent, and there's good music, film, and houseware shopping as well. Check the paper or the website for dates on the frequent sales. Along Park Row, at Ann St., opposite City Hall Park. © **800/426-6027** or 212/238-9000. www.jandr.com. Subway: 2/3 to Park Place; 4/5/6 to Brooklyn Bridge/City Hall.

FABRICS

Gray Line Linen Savvy seamsters know their way around linen, which has more than double the strength of cotton. Those in-the-know go to this place, which offers rack after colorful rack at crazy-low prices. Linens that high-end stores sell for $30 a yard or more hover in the $9 range here. Considering that Restoration Hardware sells linen curtains for over $100, this is DIY bargain central. 260 W.

39th St., btw. Seventh and Eighth aves. ℂ **212/391-4130.** www.graylinelinen. com. Subway: 1/2/3/7/N/Q/R/S to Times Sq./42nd St.; A/C/E to 42nd St./Port Authority.

Harry Zarin Company   The fabric selection in this old-timer upstairs warehouse goes the whole nine yards, with an overwhelming selection of textures and styles. Deep discounts get even deeper for overruns and closeouts. Downstairs you'll find a recently remodeled conventional furniture store. 318 Grand St., btw. Ludlow and Orchard sts. ℂ **212/ 925-6112.** www.zarinfabrics.com. Subway: B/D to Grand St.; F to Delancey St.; J/M/Z to Essex St.

P & S Fabrics Corp.   Beyond the extensive collection of fabrics, you'll find patterns, trimmings, yarn, and notions at this cluttered downtown shop. Retail accessibility at wholesale prices makes this a great place for fashion DIYers to stock up. Don't miss the clearance rack. 358 Broadway, btw. Franklin and Leonard sts. ℂ **212/ 226-1534.** Subway: J/N/Q/R/Z/6 to Canal St.

GIFTS & ART

★ **Pageant Print Shop**   Some 10,000 antique prints and maps

I Heart New York

The blocks around Times Square and the Empire State Building are littered with cheap souvenir shops. There's nothing wrong with these places (save some deficiencies in the taste department), but for the real bargains your best bet as always is Chinatown. You won't find anything superclassy, but you will find incredibly low prices, allowing you to bring something back for the whole crowd at your next flash mob. **Dollar More** (85 Mulberry St.; ℂ **212/227-0341**) is a great spot if your baggage space is limited. Keychains ($1), shot glasses ($2), and magnets ($2–$2.50) are some options that won't hog too much room. Closer to the Chinatown buses is **New York Music & Gifts** (151 Canal St.; ℂ **646/613-1754**). Although the bulk of the shelves are dedicated to Asian CDs and DVDs, up front you'll find steals on New York–branded merchandise. T-shirts are mostly $4.95 (a few go for $7.95), and there are some good-looking mugs for $3.95 apiece, or three for $10.

are packed into this tiny storefront. You can find great New York City ephemera, as well as images of everything else humans have been interested in during the last century. The owners, who've been in the business their whole lives, pride themselves on having the lowest prices in the city. Don't miss the poster file, with plenty of under-$5 images for combating apartment wall white space. 69 E. 4th St., btw. Second Ave. and Bowery. © **212/674-5296.** www.pageantbooks.com. Subway: F to Second Ave.; 6 to Bleecker St.

SKSK Steve Keene is somewhere between the Henry Ford and the McDonald's of indie art. With his one-man assembly line, he's made over 200,000 paintings. If you're looking to decorate on the cheap, you could do worse than S.K.'s factory outlet in Brooklyn (a part of his studio). There's an array of plywood cutouts, silk-screens, and paintings. A $20 investment will bring you enough to decorate two or three rooms, with change left over. Open Sundays 2 to 6pm, or by appointment. 93 Guernsey St., btw. Norman and Nassau aves., Greenpoint, Brooklyn. No phone. www.stevekeene.com. Subway: G to Nassau Ave.

HOUSEWARES

Broadway Panhandler Pan reviews consistently put this cluttered shop at the top.

> **FREE Get on the Yarn Bus**
>
> Knitters and their ilk can widen their shopping options by trekking up to Westchester on the **Yarn Bus.** The bus connects New Yorkers with the **Flying Fingers Yarn Shop,** which carries those tofu and bamboo yarns you have so much trouble tracking down in Manhattan. The ride to charming Irvington, on the Hudson, takes about a half-hour, and it's totally free. The bus runs twice a day on the weekends, leaving from various spots around Mid- and Uptown. If those times and places aren't convenient, they'll make a custom arrangement for you. Call or e-mail in advance to reserve your place. Look for the blue van with the lamppost-size needles piercing three jumbo yarn balls on the roof. 19 Main St., Irvington, New York. © **877/359-4648.** www.flyingfingers.com.

For restaurant-quality cookware and kitchen tools, you can't find a better combo of selection, price, and service. 65 E. 8th St., at Mercer St. © **212/966-3434.** www.broadwaypanhandler.com. Subway: N/R to 8th St.

Fishs Eddy You can reel in remainders of custom china here. Prices are relatively low, certainly the best you'll do on a plate marked "Blue Plate Special." You can also find retro designs, including soda fountain glasses and vintage-looking flatware. 889 Broadway, at 19th St.

Harvesting the Flower District

Two green thumbs go up for the selection of plant and flower stores on **28th Street between Sixth and Seventh avenues,** and overflowing onto Sixth Avenue. (For those with brown thumbs, a great selection of plastic plants awaits as well.) The stores are a mix of wholesale and retail, with the best prices going to bulk buyers. Small purchasers can also reel in good buys, especially at **Starbright Floral Design** (150 W. 28th St., btw. Sixth and Seventh aves.; ℂ **800/520-8999;** www. starflor.com; subway: 1 or N/R to 28th St.).

ℂ **212/420-9020.** www.fishseddy.com. Subway: L/N/Q/R/4/5/6 to 14th St./ Union Sq. Other location: *Fishs Eddy outlet,* Heartland Village, Staten Island, 2555 Richmond Ave., near Ring Rd. ℂ **718/494-7020.** S61 or S44 local bus to the last stop.

Pearl Paint Pearl Paint has the city's best art supply prices and selection, in a sprawling converted tenement tinted by an air of genial disarray. The company itself is in contraction mode, but their Chinatown location remains an art student requisite. Frames, paints, papers, canvas, and incidentals like day-planners and portfolios all carry the lowest prices in the city. 308 Canal St., btw. Broadway and Mercer St. ℂ **212/431-7932.** www.pearlpaint.com. Subway: A/C/E or 1 to Canal St.

LUGGAGE

Altman Luggage This old-time LES classic has wheeled luggage galore, in addition to businessperson sundries like pens, wallets, and watches. Already deep discounts get even deeper for closeouts and items that have been too long on the showroom floor. FINE PRINT Altman has a lowest-price guarantee for everything they sell. 135 Orchard St., btw. Rivington and Delancey sts. ℂ **212/254-7275.** www.altmanluggage.com. Subway: F to Delancey St.; J/M/Z to Essex St.

MUSIC

Academy Records and CDs Between burning, shredding, and downloading, brick-and-mortar music stores are increasingly imperiled. If you still take your music in tangible form, you can join fellow music junkies at this legendary shop. The secondhand CD shelves are packed with classical, jazz, opera, and rock. Prices are excellent, and the selection is forever in motion as Academy aggressively acquires collections. For vinyl, try **Academy LPs** in the East Village and the Academy Annex in Williamsburg. 12 W. 18th St., btw. Fifth and Sixth aves. ℭ **212/242-3000.** www.academy-records.com. Subway: L/N/Q/R/4/5/6 to 14th St./Union Sq.; F/M to 14th St. *Academy LPs,* 415 E. 12th St., btw. First Ave. and Ave. A. ℭ **212/780-9166.** Subway: L to First Ave. *Academy Annex,* Williamsburg, Brooklyn, 96 N. 6th St., btw. Berry St. and Wythe Ave. ℭ **718/218-8200.** www.academyannex. com. Subway: L to Bedford Ave.

PHOTO EQUPMENT & SUPPLIES

Adorama Photo pros flock to Adorama, which has unbelievably low prices on digital accessories, photo prints, and sundry items like blank cassettes. There's also film and secondhand lenses and SLR bodies, although most of that is headed the way of the eight-track tape. FINE PRINT Closed Friday afternoons, all day Saturday, and Jewish holidays. 42 W. 18th St., btw. Fifth and Sixth aves. ℭ **212/741-0052.** www. adorama.com. Subway: 1 to 18th St.; F/M to 14th St.; L to Sixth Ave.

🔲 Vinyl Haven: The WFMU Record Fair

If you've got an issue with piracy, or album art is a must, old-fashioned vinyl is the way to go. Thrift stores can hook you up with $2 disks, but a modern generation of DJs assure there are slim pickings outside of classical. For record fanatics, the paramount weekend is in late October/early November, when the **WFMU Record Fair** comes to town. WFMU's free-form radio is one of New York's greatest cultural assets, and the record fair brings an incredible array of dealers. The show costs $7 to enter, but that fee includes live bands, screenings in an AV room, and table after table of cheap CDs and vinyl. I ignore the $70 collector disks and head straight for the boxes under the table, where the two-for-$1 disks are most likely to be found. The fair is held at the **Metropolitan Pavilion** (125 W. 18th St., btw. Sixth and Seventh aves.; subway: 1 to 18th St.). For more information, call ℭ **201/521-1416,** or log on to www.wfmu.org/recfair. *Tip:* Sunday afternoon is the best bargain-hunter's time. Buyers are burned out and dealers are doing everything they can to keep from hauling all that obsolete technology back home.

B&H A bustling 35,000-square-foot space holds B&H's massive inventory of digital equipment, lighting, DVD players, home theater systems, and a host of photo-related products. Prices are very competitive, especially for used cameras and accessories. If you don't know exactly what you want, the pros here provide expert advice. FINE PRINT Closed Friday afternoons, all day Saturday, and Jewish holidays. 420 Ninth Ave., btw. 33rd and 34th sts. ℂ **800/606-6969** or 212/444-6615. www.bhphotovideo.com. Subway: A/C/E to 34th St./Penn Station.

PIANOS

Piano Adoption.com FREE Given New Yorkers' limited livable space, it takes a serious level of commitment to dedicate acreage to a set of ivories. If you've got the room and the drive, however, giveaway pianos are surprisingly easy to come by. The Piano Adoption website lists dozens of uprights and baby grands eager for new homes. FINE PRINT These keys are nominally "free," but keep in mind that most all will require at least $100 to get back into tune, on top of whatever the moving costs turn out to be. www.pianoadoption.com.

Toys "R" Them

Among the hideous chains that characterize the new Times Square, **Toys "R" Us** stands out for its free entertainment. The central Ferris wheel, which rises 60 feet in the center of the store, is beloved by the kiddies, who don't begrudge the sometimes long waits. A 5-ton animatronic T-Rex is another crowd pleaser, as is the pink-overload- zone of Barbie's envy-inducing duplex dollhouse. Prices here are good and made better by frequent in-store specials. Demonstrations are fun to watch and usually come with discounts on the product at hand. Even if you don't have a buying agenda, this is an easy place to fill time on a rainy day. 1514 Broadway, at 44th St. ℂ **646/366-8858.** www.toysrus.com. Subway: 1/2/3/7/N/Q/R/S to Times Sq./42nd St.

SALVAGE

Build It Green! NYC As a side-effect of working to save the planet, this nonprofit offers up deeply discounted building materials, which it diverts from landfill languishment. The warehouse holds 75 tons of doors, floors, sinks, and trim. Beyond the contractor-friendly goods, you can also pick up appliances, film props, and even $3 hardback books. For even cheaper stock, come by during a **Stop 'N' Swap** block party (p. 219) and trade up for another man's treasure. Block parties come complete with free music, BBQ, and workshops as well. 3–17 26th Ave., at 3rd St., Astoria, Queens. ✆ **718/777-0132.** www.bignyc.org. Subway: N/Q to Astoria Blvd. Other location: *Gowanus, Brooklyn,* 69 9th St., btw. Second Ave. and Smith St. ✆ **718/725-8925.** Subway: F/G to Smith-9th St.

SWEETS

Economy Candy   The Lower East Side of the 1930s was littered with small specialty shops like this one, which remains a family business 75 years later. With the other shops now defunct, Economy Candy has taken on their responsibilities, selling everything from coffee to nuts to dried fruit. Oh yeah, they also sell a little candy. From floors to rafters, the store is packed with lollipops, gum drops, halvah, gourmet candy bars, bulk chocolate, and pretty much anything else sweet you can think of. Prices are very reasonable, especially when you buy by the pound. 108 Rivington St., btw. Essex and Ludlow sts. ✆ **212/254-1531.** www.economycandy.com. Subway: F to Delancey St.; J/M/Z to Essex St.

6 Free from New York

My apartment would be an exercise in minimalism if it weren't for the generosity of the sidewalks of New York. Lamps, chairs, prints, and even the beveled mirror in the kitchen have all been harvested from the bounty of the curbs. The key is to strike without hesitation because good stuff doesn't lay around the streets for long.

A good place to start is the **Department of Sanitation's** website (**www.nyc.gov/html/dsny**), where you can find out the current collection schedule for any address in any of the boroughs. Unless you're a van owner, you'll probably want to target places that are within close hauling distance. (Trash-picking pros invest in small, wheeled hand trucks.)

Generally, just after the first of the month is the best time to be on the prowl. People have just moved in or out, and they're more likely to be of a disposing bent. Late May, at the end of the school year, is another excellent time. The streets around NYU and Columbia overflow with abandoned student goods. Though much of what you'll see is better suited to a dorm than your swanky digs, with careful culling you can find treasure among another man's trash.

The Art of the Trade

If you're too ashamed of those Spice Girls and Limp Bizkit CDs to bring them to a live swap meet, you could always go the virtual route. **Swap. com** has over a million and a half items itching to ride the consumer carousel. Join for free and then put up some of your less-essential books, games, DVDs, and automobiles for adoption. Even better are the sites **www.paperbackswap.com, www.swapacd.com,** and **www. swapadvd.com**. Unlike Swap, you're trading with the entire membership pool, not just working out a 1-on-1 match. There's also more inventory here—5 million books available on PaperBack Swap alone. Of course that inventory is made up of books people want to get rid of, so you may have to go on a waiting list for more desirable titles. There's no cost to you besides postage (about $3.50 or so per book you ship out). You'll have to post 10 books before they'll let you take in a couple of your own (books are free to receive, as the other person picks up the postage tab for you.) Swapportunities aren't limited to entertainment: The site **MakeupAlley.com** helps facilitate cosmetic exchanges. There's a quarter of a million items to browse through (items get swept away every 3 months), and it's all free beyond the price of your postage. Swap Tokens in Positive, Negative, and Neutral flavors help users determine the trustworthiness of potential partners.

Freecycle NYC `FREE`   This grassroots organization has grown into a serious waste-fighter, with over nine million members worldwide. To connect in NYC, check out their Yahoo Group (**www.groups.yahoo. com/group/freecyclenewyorkcity**), which generates 1,500 leads on free goods every month. There's no cost to join; the main stipulation is that everything offered must be free—not even trading is allowed.

Greencycle Swaps   Greenpoint and Williamsburg represent the cutting edge of New York culture, so it's no surprise to find a local community group there embracing the free market movement. Town Square hosts swaps between 1 and 4pm (usually the second Sat of each month), spread around churches and schools in the two neighborhoods. They ask for a $5 donation and whatever clothes, shoes, bikes, books, and electronics you wish to divest yourself of. Check in at **www.townsquareinc.com** for site addresses and more information.

Stop 'N' Swap FREE For 40-plus years now, **GrowNYC** has been helping keep New York green. Efforts for the environment run from 54 greenmarkets to these all-free shopping fests. The Bronx, Queens, and Build It Green! have all hosted recent events. Entry is free and so are all wares. On the contribution side, they're looking for clean, working, and portable. Furniture is out, but you will find a nice array of clothes, books, and toys. Various locations. © **212/788-7900.** www.grownyc.org.

Swap-O-Rama-Rama Sort through 4,000 pounds of clothes, for free! That's the come-on to this community event, where you dump off some of your own fashion don'ts and then replenish your closet with whatever you find. A small donation never hurts, especially when you're getting both duds and DIY workshops. "Shoppers" can get help with on-the-spot iron-ons, silk-screening, and tailoring. Successful projects are oohed and aahed over at the end-of-the-day fashion show. Check the website for dates and locations, **www.swaporamarama.org**.

Thrift Collective Trading parties are the M.O. of this swap scene, which meets once a month or so to rotate closet fodder. Events tend to have entrance fees (say, $10 in advance or $15 at the door), but that entitles you to browse through gently worn stocks of dresses, pants, T's, scarves, purses, shoes, and more. You're asked to bring some discarded duds of your own (in good condition). Discounted drinks help lower inhibitions about taking home strappy black-leather pumps. To keep up with the swaps (which are usually women-only and for those of legal drinking age), follow on Facebook or **www.thriftcollective.com**.

7 Pet Project

Sure, your loyal, vicious Yorkie saves you thousands of dollars a month in bodyguards and private security, but you don't want to turn around and sink all that cash into an expensive pet-care proposition. Fortunately, New York has places that provide veterinary support at pint-size prices. Don't yet have that mouse-killing tabby in the house? NYC also has pets available at low, low costs.

American Society for the Prevention of Cruelty to Animals Subsidized pet care is available at the Bergh Memorial Animal Hospital & Clinic, run by this legendary group. An appointment for an exam with a vet costs $90, and an emergency visit is $130. They also provide shots, around $25 for rabies or distemper on top of the regular exam fee. If you need to get a pet before you can start worrying about pet care, the ASPCA also has adoption services. Cats and dogs start at around $75 and puppies, kittens, and purebreds go up from there. The cost covers several necessities, including "pet LoJack"—a microchip should your new best friend make a break for freedom. The society also runs five **Mobile Spay/Neuter Clinics,** covering underserved neighborhoods. If you have proof of being on public assistance, the spay/neuter fee is just $5 ($125 otherwise). 424 E. 92nd St., btw. First and York aves. ✆ **212/876-7700.** www.aspca.org. Subway: 4/5/6 to 86th St.

Bideawee The name of this century-old charitable organization derives from the Scottish for "stay awhile," though they'd just as well put cats and dogs through the revolving door as quickly as possible. Adoptions can be had for a processing fee of around $150 (puppies $225), which covers a host of services like spaying, neutering, and microchipping. When it's time for follow-up, Bideawee's veterinary clinic is subsidized and among the most reasonable in the city. 410 E. 38th St., 2nd floor, btw. First Ave. and the FDR. ✆ **866/262-8133.** www.bideawee. org. Subway: 4/5/6/7/S to 42nd St./Grand Central.

The Brooklyn Animal Resource Coalition Love dogs, but not ready for the full-out commitment of daily walking and feeding? Billyburg's BARC will let you test-drive a pooch during morning or evening hours. You'll be helping the shelter out by giving one of their minions some exercise, you'll have a handy conversation-starter, and who knows? Maybe you'll form a bond. Allow a couple of hours if you want to walk or adopt. 253 Wythe Ave., at N. 1st St., Williamsburg, Brooklyn. ✆ **718/486-7489.** www.barcshelter.org. Subway: L to Bedford Ave.

Mayor's Alliance for NYC's Animals Mayor Mike has ambitious plans to make us a no-kill city (we're on track for a 2015 happy conclusion to that story). To that end, his alliance connects low-income residents with low-cost spaying and neutering services. If you're in the pet market, the alliance puts on a series of adoption festivals, including the annual **Adoptapalooza** (www.adoptapaloozanyc.org) spring blowout. In addition to spontaneously falling for an unclaimed cur there, you can hook up your current pets with microchips at a special $25 rate. Mobile microchipping clinics also pay visits to all five boroughs with that same $25 deal. For citywide pet services, the alliance's website is a very helpful clearinghouse. ℃ **212/252-2350.** www.animalalliancenyc.org.

Climb the stairs up to KGB Bar every night of the week to hear some of the best writers in town read their work for free.

ENTERTAINMENT & NIGHTLIFE

New York nights can feel like the exclusive playground of i-bankers and heirs. Velvet ropes mark off champagne bars, stilettos clack down the avenues, and Broadway ticket prices reach heights only a Westchester dowager could ascend to. But that's just one layer of the city's delights. With youth pouring into the area, entertainment for the people has made a serious comeback. It's easy to find top-tier dance, drama, film, and comedy for no more than the price of showing up. Shakespeare in the Park, the Metropolitan Opera, and the Upright Citizens Brigade are among the New York legends that give it away free. On the intimate side, new crowd-sourcing means are opening up all kinds of opportunities for indie theater and dance. Meanwhile, music seeps up from the subway platforms and fills our parks and bars. Everything from jazz to classical to country to rock can be heard in NYC, and a surprising amount of it comes without cost. For those attractions that do charge, discerning patrons can easily keep the cost down in the $5 range. New York is a magnet for talent, and even the performances on the cheap end of the entertainment spectrum can be spectacular. In short, money should be no barrier to experiencing great New York entertainment. It's more an issue of time management.

1 Music Uncovered

New York is in the midst of yet another great rock-'n'-roll scare. A slew of young musicians have rediscovered the jittery energy of New York's '70s and '80s heydays, and they're threatening to become a movement. Phosphorescent, Dirty Projectors, and the National are among the parade of hot new bands putting down Brooklyn roots. It's not just rock, either. Classical, acoustic, salsa, jazz, and even alt-country make a stand in Yankee confines. The only fly in this ointment is capitalism; the bars where groups play also have to pay rent. Most places try to keep the booze flowing, although with a few exceptions New York is not super-uptight about enforcing its drink minimums. The musicians certainly don't care—most of the time they're just happy you're there to listen. You'll find free music waiting 7 nights a week. You might as well embrace the cacophony, because Lord knows it's hard to find a quiet hour in New York City.

FOR THOSE ABOUT TO ROCK

BAMcafé The architecture of the Brooklyn Academy of Music's 1908 HQ is just as impressive inside as out. The arching ceilings in BAMcafé (it was once the building's ballroom) provide both glitz and great acoustics for popular Friday and Saturday night musical performances. The shows are free, presenting a cross section from the spheres of rock, jazz, world, and R&B. Happy hours run 6 to 8pm, with $3 beer and $5 cocktail specials. 30 Lafayette Ave., btw. Ashland Place and St. Felix St. ℂ **718/636-4100.** www.bam.org. Subway: G to Fulton St.; C to Lafayette Ave.; B/D/N/Q/R/2/3/4/5 to Atlantic Ave./Pacific St.

Goodbye Blue Monday `FREE`
This cluttered space under the El serves up live music nightly. With two stages (one indoor, one out), you can find up to seven performances, most every one free. For libations, wine starts at $4 and PBR drafts at $3. They do pass the hat for the musicians. Note that the location isn't exactly Midland City: They're on the Bushwick/Bed-Stuy border, off the hipster beaten track. 1087 Broadway, btw. Dodworth and Lawton sts. ✆ **718/453-6343.** www.good bye-blue-monday.com. Subway: J to Kosciuszko St.; M to Central Ave.

The Living Room A mellow music mecca, the Living Room hosts a slate of live performances every night, biased toward acoustic and otherwise low-key up-and-comers. The occasional national act storms through, and the space is used efficiently, with up to six acts a night. Usually no cover, though they do pass the hat (there's a $10 suggested contribution, as well as a one-drink minimum per set). 154 Ludlow St., btw. Stanton and Rivington sts. ✆ **212/533-7235.** www.livingroomny.com. Subway: F to Second Ave.; J/M/Z to Essex St.

The National Underground A much-needed low-pretense zone is provided by this little pocket of Americana on East Houston. PBR in cans and roots rock soundtracks are the key ingredients for laid-back nights. There are two floors, with live music upstairs, and techno DJs in the basement. Although most of the performers aren't name acts, you won't be dropping money on a cover, either. 159 E. Houston St., btw. Allen and Eldridge sts. ✆ **212/475-0611.** www.thenationalunderground.com. Subway: F to Second Ave.

Parkside Lounge Nestled between projects and East Village tenements, this former brothel brings in an eclectic crowd. Being too far

---

`FREE` **Free & e-zines**

With a city in endless flux and so much stuff going on, it's hard to stay abreast of the best in free and cheap events. My favorite means of keeping up is via electronic newsletters, conveniently e-mailed right to my inbox. Of the e-lists, **Nonsensenyc**'s (www.nonsense nyc.com) is my favorite, specializing in the cheap and offbeat, and providing a comprehensive rundown of the city's many hipster events. (They don't do music; log in to **www.brooklynvegan.com** for that.) Other newsletters worth reading can be found at **www. dailycandy.com**, **http://flavor pill.com/newyork**, and **www. manhattanusersguide.com**.

ENTERTAINMENT & NIGHTLIFE
DOWNTOWN

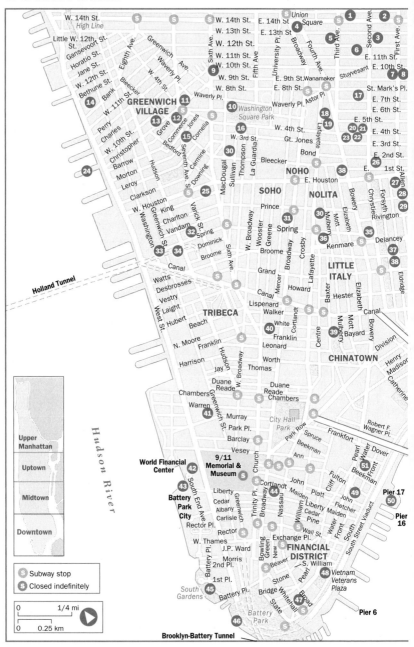

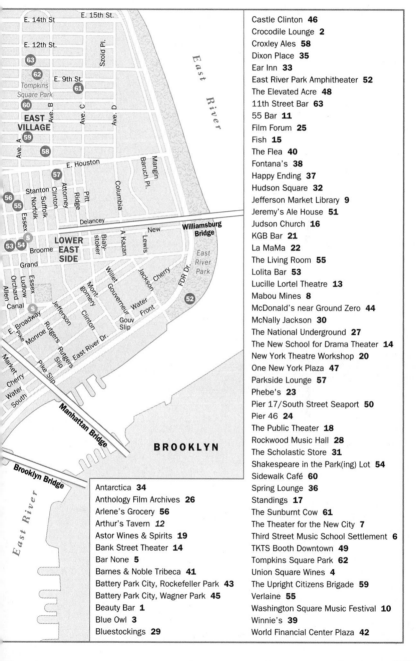

E. 14th St
E. 15th St.
E. 12th St.
Szold Pl.
63
62
Tompkins Square Park
E. 9th St.
61
60
Ave. B
Ave. C
Ave. D
EAST VILLAGE
59
Ave. A
58
E. Houston
Mangin
Baruch Pl.
Columbia
Stanton
Attorney
Pitt
Ridge
56
Suffolk
Clinton
55
Norfolk
Essex
Delancey
New
Williamsburg Bridge
53 **54**
LOWER
EAST
SIDE
Blaystoker
A Kazan
Lewis
Broome
Grand
East River Park
FDR Dr.
Essex
Montgomery
Willet
Gouverneur
Cherry
Jackson
Orchard
Ludlow
Allen
Canal
E. Broadway
Jefferson
Clinton
Monroe
Rutgers
Rutgers Slip
East River Dr.
Water
Front
Gouv Slip
52
Market
Cherry
Water
South
Pike Slip
Manhattan Bridge
BROOKLYN
Brooklyn Bridge
East River
Antarctica **34**
Anthology Film Archives **26**
Arlene's Grocery **56**
Arthur's Tavern **12**
Astor Wines & Spirits **19**
Bank Street Theater **14**
Bar None **5**
Barnes & Noble Tribeca **41**
Battery Park City, Rockefeller Park **43**
Battery Park City, Wagner Park **45**
Beauty Bar **1**
Blue Owl **3**
Bluestockings **29**

Castle Clinton **46**
Crocodile Lounge **2**
Croxley Ales **58**
Dixon Place **35**
Ear Inn **33**
East River Park Amphitheater **52**
The Elevated Acre **48**
11th Street Bar **63**
55 Bar **11**
Film Forum **25**
Fish **15**
The Flea **40**
Fontana's **38**
Happy Ending **37**
Hudson Square **32**
Jefferson Market Library **9**
Jeremy's Ale House **51**
Judson Church **16**
KGB Bar **21**
La MaMa **22**
The Living Room **55**
Lolita Bar **53**
Lucille Lortel Theatre **13**
Mabou Mines **8**
McDonald's near Ground Zero **44**
McNally Jackson **30**
The National Underground **27**
The New School for Drama Theater **14**
New York Theatre Workshop **20**
One New York Plaza **47**
Parkside Lounge **57**
Phebe's **23**
Pier 17/South Street Seaport **50**
Pier 46 **24**
The Public Theater **18**
Rockwood Music Hall **28**
The Scholastic Store **31**
Shakespeare in the Park(ing) Lot **54**
Sidewalk Café **60**
Spring Lounge **36**
Standings **17**
The Sunburnt Cow **61**
The Theater for the New City **7**
Third Street Music School Settlement **6**
TKTS Booth Downtown **49**
Tompkins Square Park **62**
Union Square Wines **4**
The Upright Citizens Brigade **59**
Verlaine **55**
Washington Square Music Festival **10**
Winnie's **39**
World Financial Center Plaza **42**

227

ENTERTAINMENT & NIGHTLIFE IN MIDTOWN

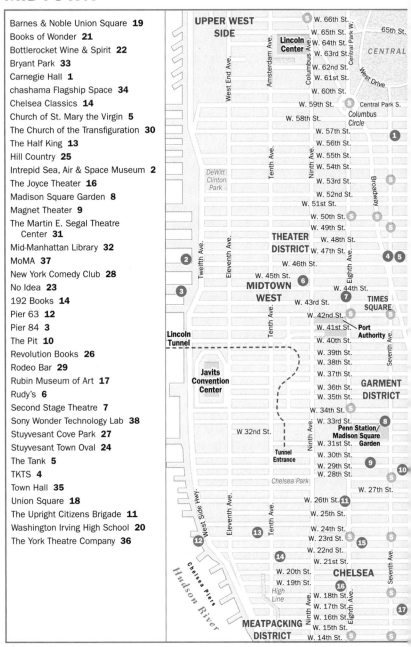

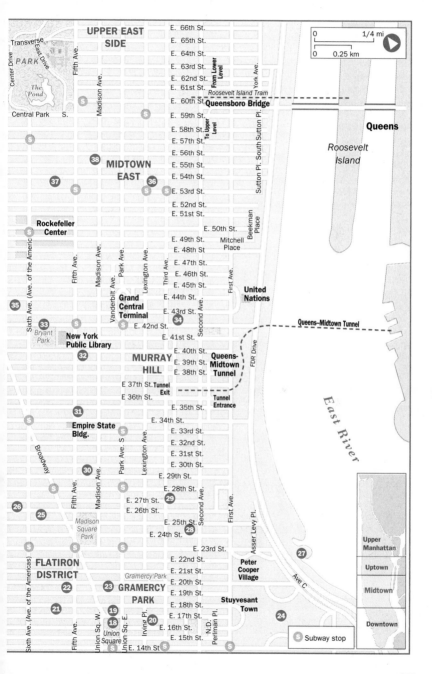

ENTERTAINMENT & NIGHTLIFE UPTOWN

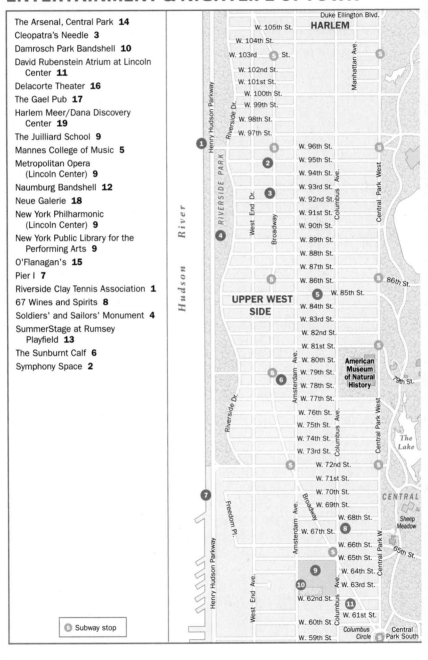

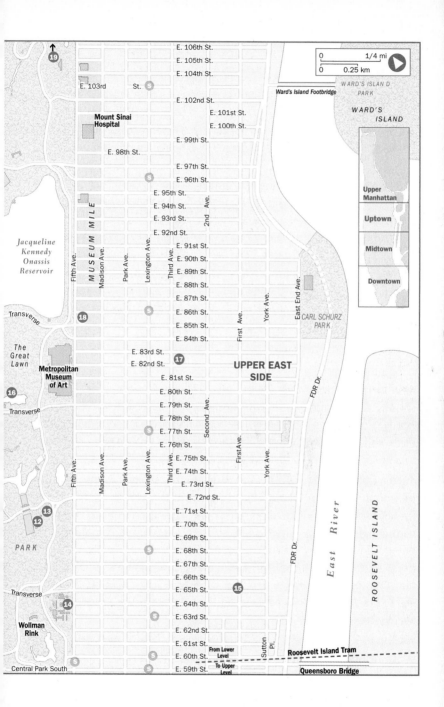

E. 106th St.
E. 105th St.
E. 104th St.
E. 103rd St. Ⓢ
E. 102nd St.
E. 101st St.
E. 100th St.
Mount Sinai Hospital
E. 99th St.
E. 98th St.
E. 97th St.
Ⓢ E. 96th St.
E. 95th St.
E. 94th St.
E. 93rd St.
E. 92nd St.
E. 91st St.
E. 90th St.
E. 89th St.
E. 88th St.
E. 87th St.
Ⓢ E. 86th St.
E. 85th St.
E. 84th St.
E. 83rd St.
E. 82nd St. ⑰
E. 81st St.
E. 80th St.
E. 79th St.
E. 78th St.
Ⓢ E. 77th St.
E. 76th St.
E. 75th St.
E. 74th St.
E. 73rd St.
E. 72nd St.
E. 71st St.
E. 70th St.
E. 69th St.
Ⓢ E. 68th St.
E. 67th St.
E. 66th St.
E. 65th St. ⑮
E. 64th St.
Ⓢ E. 63rd St.
E. 62nd St.
E. 61st St.
E. 60th St.
Ⓢ E. 59th St.

2nd Ave.
Fifth Ave.
MUSEUM MILE
Madison Ave.
Park Ave.
Lexington Ave.
Third Ave.
Second Ave.
First Ave.
First Ave.
York Ave.
York Ave.
East End Ave.

Jacqueline Kennedy Onassis Reservoir

Transverse ⑱

The Great Lawn

Metropolitan Museum of Art

⑯ Transverse

UPPER EAST SIDE

CARL SCHURZ PARK

FDR Dr.

East River

ROOSEVELT ISLAND

⑬
⑫
PARK
Transverse
⑭
Wollman Rink
Central Park South Ⓢ

Sutton Pl.
From Lower Level
To Upper Level
Roosevelt Island Tram
Queensboro Bridge
FDR Dr.

Ward's Island Footbridge
WARD'S ISLAND PARK
WARD'S ISLAND

0   1/4 mi
0   0.25 km

Upper Manhattan
Uptown
Midtown
Downtown

⑲

Todd P. & the Brooklyn Renaissance

With so many bands calling Brooklyn home, it's no surprise to find a thriving live music scene east of the East River. The DIY movement skews young for both fans and performers, and as such the prices are rock bottom. Shows go off without covers (or for $3–$5 a head), and there's cheap booze to go with them. Venues are improvised: An old Masonic lodge, a cheap Mexican restaurant, and above an auto parts store have flared up as music magnets. Impresario **Todd P. (www.todd pnyc.com)** is a major mover, although volatile venue churn has narrowed his focus to the warehouse space at 285 Kent Ave. in Williamsburg. Check in at his website for details. As long as you're in the Williamsburg/Bushwick nabe, you might also check out the free/cheap shows at **Shea Stadium** (www.liveatsheastadium.com), **Death by Audio** (www.myspace.com/deathbyaudioshows), and **Big Snow Buffalo Lodge** (www.bigsnowbk.tumblr.com).

east for most trendroids helps, too. The back room puts on rock shows, with comedy, improv, and burlesque in the mix as well. FINE PRINT If there's a cover, it'll be $5 or so for the band; often a two-drink minimum applies, but it's loosely enforced. 317 E. Houston St., at Attorney St. ✆ **212/673-6270.** www.parksidelounge.net. Subway: F to Second Ave.

Pete's Candy Store FREE   So many quality sounds come through here that you'll feel like a kid in a great music venue. Housed in a friendly former fountain shop, the small stage area in back brings in surprisingly big acts. There's also a rotating selection of nonmusical entertainment, from readings to spelling bees (p. 277). No cover or drink minimum, but the staff encourages contributions to the musicians' tip jar. 709 Lorimer St., btw. Frost and Richardson sts., Williamsburg, Brooklyn. ✆ **718/302-3770.** www.petescandystore.com. Subway: L to Lorimer St.; G to Metropolitan Ave.

Rockwood Music Hall   It took some vision—and a well-developed sense of irony—to conceive of these two postage stamp–size spaces as a "music hall." The close quarters don't seem to scare off the crowds, though, and the intimacy makes for great sound. Local singer-songwriters are interspersed with the occasional touring band, up to

ENTERTAINMENT & NIGHTLIFE IN BROOKLYN

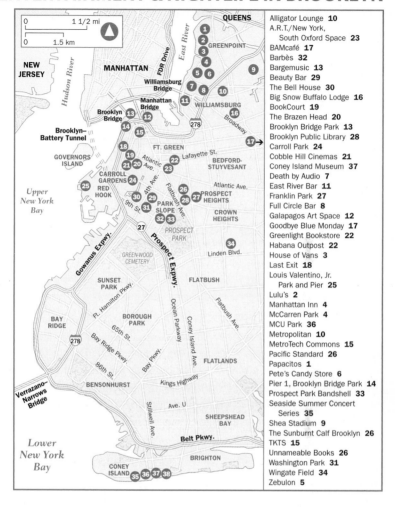

Alligator Lounge **10**
A.R.T./New York,
    South Oxford Space **23**
BAMcafé **17**
Barbès **32**
Bargemusic **13**
Beauty Bar **29**
The Bell House **30**
Big Snow Buffalo Lodge **16**
BookCourt **19**
The Brazen Head **20**
Brooklyn Bridge Park **13**
Brooklyn Public Library **28**
Carroll Park **24**
Cobble Hill Cinemas **21**
Coney Island Museum **37**
Death by Audio **7**
East River Bar **11**
Franklin Park **27**
Full Circle Bar **8**
Galapagos Art Space **12**
Goodbye Blue Monday **17**
Greenlight Bookstore **22**
Habana Outpost **22**
House of Vans **3**
Last Exit **18**
Louis Valentino, Jr.
    Park and Pier **25**
Lulu's **2**
Manhattan Inn **4**
McCarren Park **4**
MCU Park **36**
Metropolitan **10**
MetroTech Commons **15**
Pacific Standard **26**
Papacitos **1**
Pete's Candy Store **6**
Pier 1, Brooklyn Bridge Park **14**
Prospect Park Bandshell **33**
Seaside Summer Concert
    Series **35**
Shea Stadium **9**
The Sunburnt Calf Brooklyn **26**
TKTS **15**
Unnameable Books **26**
Washington Park **31**
Wingate Field **34**
Zebulon **5**

10 acts per night. With success has come more breathing room: an annex now extends back to Orchard Street. Usually no cover, but the tip jar is passed and there's a one-drink minimum. 196 Allen St., btw. Houston and Stanton sts. ℂ **212/477-4155.** www.rockwoodmusichall.com. Subway: F to Second Ave.

Rodeo Bar   This is as country as Manhattan gets, which admittedly isn't saying much. Rodeo's sprawling space doesn't have the feel of an intimate honky-tonk, but the stage area is segregated and more or less self-contained. The cream of the local crop rounds up here, as do a handful of national acts. Mostly Americana and alt-country (whatever that is). There's no cover, usually a one-drink minimum. 375 Third Ave., at 27th St. ☏ 212/683-6500. www.rodeobar.com. Subway: 6 to 28th St.

Sidewalk Café   Having outlived the other live-music spots on Avenue A, the Café serves as a home base for East Village singer-songwriters. A little comedy and open mics get thrown in as well. Each night sees a big bunch of acts. [FINE PRINT] No cover, but a two-drink minimum during performances. 94 Ave. A, at 6th St. ☏ 212/473-7373. www. sidewalkny.com/events/calendar. Subway: F to Second Ave.

JAZZ IT UP

Arthur's Tavern   A West Village relic, Arthur's would be eligible for social security if it were a person and not an amiable, low-rent jazz joint. The music runs the Dixieland-to-trio gamut, and the quality can be spotty, but something's on stage 7 nights a week. [FINE PRINT] No cover, but a one-drink per set minimum. 57 Grove St., btw. Bleecker and W. 4th sts. ☏ 212/675-6879. www.arthurstavernnyc.com. Subway: 1 to Christopher St.

Cleopatra's Needle   Organ trios and quartets highlight the calendar at this Upper West Side neighborhood club. On Wednesday evenings and Sunday afternoons things get even more neighborhoody with open mics. In the wee hours, the floor belongs to jam sessions. Never a cover, though there is a $10 minimum per set. A decent Mediterranean menu provides an alternative to boozing the night away. Usually two sets per night. 2485 Broadway, btw. 92nd and 93rd sts. ☏ 212/769-6969. www.cleopatrasneedleny.com. Subway: 1/2/3 to 96th St.

David Rubenstein Atrium at Lincoln Center FREE   Lincoln Center has really made the most of their box office, supporting it with a high-design public space. You can pick up discount day-of Lincoln Center tickets, or come by on a Thursday night for free music. Target sponsors these 8:30pm concerts, representing genres as diverse as jazz, classical, pop, and world. Shows tend to be well-attended, with the Columbus Avenue entrances often closing early (you can get in on the Broadway side instead). 61 W. 62nd St., btw. Columbus Ave. and Broadway. ☏ 212/875-5350. www.atrium.lincolncenter.org. Subway: 1 to 66th St./Lincoln Center.

Ear Inn FREE   This laid-back old-timer was once a waterfront tavern, although in the course of a couple of centuries, the Hudson has slipped a block or two away. There's solid dinner fare and pints aplenty here, and Monday and Wednesday nights you can enjoy midnight music. Jazz and blues are the usual Ear candy, although country and folk sneak in as well. Sunday evenings at 8pm the Ear Regulars perform jazz variations on trumpet, reed, guitar, and bass. 326 Spring St., btw. Greenwich and Washington sts. ℂ **212/226-9060.** www.earinn.com. Subway: C/E to Spring St.; 1 to Canal St.

55 Bar   Still not entirely recovered from its Prohibition days, 55 Bar has been entertaining the Village on the sly since 1919. The cluttered room brings in top-shelf acts. The cover charges reflect it on some nights, but generally you can slip in for $10 or less, which is a pretty good deal for this level of quality. Tuesday and Sunday nights are your best bets for inexpensive jazz. FINE PRINT Officially, there's a two-drink minimum, but the laid-back staff enforces it loosely. 55 Christopher St., btw. Seventh Ave. S. and Waverly Place. ℂ **212/929-9883.** www.55bar.com. Subway: 1 to Christopher St.

Zebulon FREE   The French owners here manage to blend European sophistication with the low-pretense quotient of greater Brooklyn. Afrobeat, funk, and improv jazz lead the charge. A tin ceiling and jazz posters and album covers add to the charm. Many nights go no-cover (although the hat is passed), and drinks are inexpensive, at least by contemporary standards. 258 Wythe Ave., btw. Metropolitan Ave. and N. 3rd St., Williamsburg, Brooklyn. ℂ **718/218-6934.** www.zebuloncafeconcert.com. Subway: L to Bedford Ave.

CLASSICAL ACTS

Gotham's classical pedigree is hard to knock, as we boast the nation's oldest orchestra (the New York Philharmonic), on top of a couple of venues whose renown just might extend beyond New York Harbor (Carnegie Hall and Lincoln Center leap to mind). The future of music can also be found here, with the nation's most prominent conservatories (think Juilliard) settled on Manhattan schist. Although high prices can accompany the high notes, you aren't obligated to pay through the nose. Schools present a bevy of free shows, big-name venues offer obstructed-view cheap seats, and the Philharmonic and the Metropolitan Opera both gig for free in the summer (see "High Culture for Free," in the "Outdoor Summer Concerts" section, later in this chapter). So weigh your musical options carefully before settling for that Quiet Riot tribute band on Bleecker Street.

Bargemusic FREE   Of all the world's barges dedicated to chamber music, this one is my favorite. Docked just off the Fulton Ferry landing in Brooklyn Heights, the recital room here hosts over a hundred concerts a year. Tickets are generally $35, but at least once a month one concert is given away (usually Sat at 3pm). It's "pot-luck," so you won't know the program until showtime, but it'll be classical, and the performance will be intimate. (There are only 130 seats.) No reservations are taken, so show up before the doors open, which is an hour before showtime. 26 New Dock St., at Water St., at the East River, Brooklyn Heights, Brooklyn. © **718/624-2083.** www.bargemusic.org. Subway: 2/3 to Clark St.; A/C to High St.

The Bronx Symphony Orchestra   With over 6 decades of music making, this entirely democratic group has plenty of experience in bringing Tchaikovsky, Mendelssohn, and Mozart to the masses. All the concerts were once free, but funding constraints have made them a mix of ticketed (still inexpensive, in the $7–$12 range) and complimentary. Check the website for the calendar and locations, which hit all corners of the borough. Various locations around the Bronx. © **718/601-9151.** http://bronxsymphony.com.

Carnegie Hall   A mere Hamilton is all it takes to waltz into Carnegie Hall. Concerts held in the Stern Auditorium or the Perelman Stage are accessible by same-day $10 Rush tickets–even for sold-out shows. The number of available tickets is pretty limited, so you'll want to get there well before the box office opens (11am Mon–Sat, noon on Sun; closed weekends June to late Aug). If you don't mind seeing only half the show, you can also get into Carnegie for half price. Partial-view seats (hey, you're here for the sound anyway) are made available for Stern Auditorium and Perelman Stage shows (Gala and Weill Music Institute events excepted). Carnegie Hall Family Concerts are also excepted, but then they're already a bargain in their own right—targeted to the wee ones, tickets are only $9. Carnegie Hall also takes its show on the road. The **Neighborhood Concert Series** fans out across all five boroughs, bringing everything from classical to jazz to folk. Some 80 shows a year are performed for free—check the website for details. 154 W. 57th St., at Seventh Ave. © **212/247-7800.** www.carnegiehall.org. Subway: A/B/C/D/1 to 59th St./Columbus Circle; N/Q/R to 57th St./Seventh Ave.

The Juilliard School FREE   Juilliard's reputation couldn't be much more burnished, with luminaries like Philip Glass, Yo-Yo Ma, and

FREE Quarter Pounding the Keys

McDonald's and classical music go together like a Big Mac and fries. Er, maybe not. Sunday afternoons see a bizarre cultural collision at the McDonald's nearest Ground Zero. Classical pianist **Andrew Shapiro** and his occasional guests layer lovely New Agey music over the scent of seared meat. Tourists wander in with only an occasional perplexed glance at the grand piano in the window of the second-floor balcony. For erudite music fans, this is probably the calmest it's possible to feel inside a McDonald's. 160 Broadway, btw. Liberty and Cortlandt sts. ✆ **212/385-2063.** www.andrewshapiro.com. Subway: R to Cortlandt St.; A/C/J/Z/2/3/4/5 to Fulton St./Broadway Nassau. Sun sets beginning at noon, 1, 2, and 3pm, season usually runs Nov–June.

Itzhak Perlman among its alums. Since its current students are nominally amateurs, the Lincoln Center school presents most of its concerts for free. Soloists play Morse and Paul Hall, and you can catch the entire orchestra at Alice Tully Hall. Though there is no charge, tickets are required for some shows, available from the box office up to 2 weeks prior to the show (with some standby available same-day; be sure to be on line 1 hr. before curtain). Regular lunchtime concerts keep NYC's morale up; Tuesdays at 12:30pm, an office building atrium at 180 Maiden Lane hosts student performances; and Wednesdays at One programs can be found at Alice Tully Hall. Tuesdays run most of the year, but Wednesdays are limited to the school year. Both are free with no tickets required. The Janet and Leonard Kramer Box Office (Juilliard Box Office), 155 W. 65th St., btw. Broadway and Amsterdam Ave. ✆ **212/769-7406.** www.juilliard.edu. Subway: 1 to 66th St./Lincoln Center.

Manhattan School of Music FREE   With an Art Deco main auditorium (built by the Empire State Building's firm) and six other venues, there's no shortage of places to listen here. Classical music performances are joined by jazz, which snuck into the curriculum after MSM's founding 90 years ago (Yusef Lateef and Harry Connick, Jr., are among the alums). Many shows are free to the public—no ticket required, although reservations are requested for some—as are a series of master classes. Nearby Riverside Park hosts even more performances,

FREE Divine Inspiration: Concerts at the Churches

Even heathens can find entertainment under the city's steeples. Choirs are only the beginning, as recitals and operas also take the altars, often for free. Worker bees downtown love the **Concerts at One** series at St. Paul's Chapel and Trinity Church. Midtowners can enjoy the spring lunchtime concerts at the **Church of the Transfiguration** (better known as the Little Church Around the Corner; 1 E. 29th St. ℂ **212/ 684-4174;** www.littlechurch.org; $5 suggested donation; Tues at 12:30pm). Uptown, the **Interchurch Center,** 475 Riverside Dr. at 120th Street (ℂ **212/870-2200;** www.interchurch-center.org) hosts Wednesday Noonday Concerts at 11:15am. For an evening of polished classical performances, check out the **New York Repertory Orchestra.** Though this all-volunteer group has many amateurs in its ranks, the renditions of Brahms, Mahler, and Stravinsky are all professional. Programming is adventurous, and the shows are free. Usually Saturday nights at 8pm at the Church of St. Mary the Virgin (145 W. 46th St., btw. Sixth and Seventh aves.; ℂ **212/662-8383;** www.nyro.org; subway: B/D/F/M to 47th–50th sts./Rockefeller Center).

at the 116th Street Overlook on mild-weather Sunday afternoons. Most events take place during the school year; check online for a full schedule. 601 W. 122nd St., at Broadway. ℂ **917/493-4428.** www.msmnyc.edu. Subway: 1 to 125th St.

Mannes College of Music FREE During the school year, this 95-year-old institution presents some 400 free concerts. Student groups include baroque chamber, guitar, brass, and opera ensembles. Two concert halls at the college's headquarters host the free shows. There are also remote performances at places like the New School (Mannes merged with it in 1989), where lunchtime performances are followed by receptions. Check the website's calendar for the full listings. 150 W. 85th St., btw. Amsterdam and Columbus aves. ℂ **212/580-0210,** ext. 4817. www.mannes.edu. Subway: B/C to 86th St.

Metropolitan Opera When it comes to opera, the Met is the biggest (240 shows a year, each with seating for nearly 4,000) and the best, with elaborate productions and unrivaled star power. Seats start around $25 and soar from there to over $400. In addition to the free summer shows (see "High Culture for Free," below), standing-room-only tickets can be found. Prices tend to be $22 for orchestra and $17 for family circle (if you buy online, expect a $7.50 surcharge on top of the $2.50 facilities fee). If you can't weather a 4-hour show on your feet, you can vie for **Varis Rush Tickets.** You'll get a seat in the orchestra for just $20 for a Monday-through-Thursday show. Distribution starts at the box office 2 hours before curtain. (For weekend shows, online replaces on line, with $25 tickets made available in a virtual drawing on the Met's website.) Metropolitan Opera at Lincoln Center, btw. W. 62nd and 65th sts. and Columbus and Amsterdam aves. ✆ **212/362-6000.** www. metoperafamily.org. Subway: 1 to 66th St./Lincoln Center.

Naumburg Orchestral Concerts FREE The Naumburg Bandshell in Central Park hosts this short concert series, which sets aside 700 seats for classical music fans (you can also hear the shows from the nearby benches). The series is one of the oldest in the country, with over a century's worth of experience in entertaining New Yorkers. Shows are on four Tuesday nights at 7:30pm, with no rain dates, no tickets or reservations necessary. Midpark, Central Park, just below 72nd St. ✆ **718/340-3018.** www.naumburgconcerts.org. Subway: B/C to 72nd St.; 6 to 68th St./Hunter College.

New York Grand Opera FREE Conductor Vincent La Selva has spent the last 30 years performing the quixotic—or Sisyphean—task of mounting fully staged grand operas for no charge. He's pulled it off, too, with compelling performances that shine despite the occasional lack of polish. Shows are held over 2 or 3 nights in summer at Central Park's Naumburg Bandshell, weather permitting. Naumburg Bandshell, Central Park, midpark, just below 72nd St. ✆ **212/245-8837.** www.new yorkgrandopera.org. Subway: B/C to 72nd St.; 6 to 68th St./Hunter College.

New York Philharmonic The Philharmonic has been satisfying New Yorkers since 1842. The symphony's international fame translates into pricey tickets (usually it's over $100 to sit in the orchestra), but pikers needn't despair. In addition to free summer shindigs in the parks (see "High Culture for Free," below), there are low-priced kid-friendly shows, $12.50 student rush tickets, and the **Open Rehearsal** program. Watching a piece take shape under a conductor's molding is a fascinating process, and it's only $18 (plus a $2 handling fee if you don't stop by the box office) to sit in. Avery Fisher Hall, 10 Lincoln Center Plaza. ✆ **212/875-5900.** www.nyphil.org. Subway: 1 to 66th St./Lincoln Center.

Peoples' Symphony Concerts   A good bet on IBM stock in 1923 is the basis for the endowment of these popular populist concerts. Three separate groupings, the Festival, Mann, and Arens Series, give the people the world-class ensembles they demand. Festival shows are held at Town Hall, and the two others are at Washington Irving High School (with a 1,500-seat capacity and good acoustics, this is not your high school's auditorium). Most single tickets are around $13, but if you invest in a series subscription, the per-show price dips to the $6 to $9 range. Washington Irving High School, 40 Irving Place, at 16th St. ✆ **212/586-4680.** www.pscny.org. Subway: L/N/Q/R/4/5/6 to 14th St./Union Sq. Other location: *Town Hall,* 123 W. 43rd St., btw. Sixth Ave. and Broadway. Subway: B/D/F/M to 42nd St.; N/Q/R/S/1/2/3/7 to 42nd St./Times Sq.

Summer HD Festival `FREE`   The central plaza of Lincoln Center becomes a giant open-air opera house for this August and September series. Although the performances aren't live, they were shot in HD, and both sound and picture quality are excellent. The operas run on 10 consecutive nights, with first-come, first-served seating. Some 3,100 chairs are made available, and another thousand people can join the overflow crowd. Start times are staggered between 7:15 and 8pm; in case of bad weather shows are canceled. Lincoln Center, Broadway btw. 63rd and 64th sts. ✆ **212/362-6000.** www.metoperafamily.org. Subway: 1 to 66th St./Lincoln Center.

Third Street Music School Settlement `FREE`   The oldest community music school in the country, this institution helps reach thousands of students with musical instruction. The talented faculty shows off their own chops at weekly free concerts. Classical pieces predominate, although jazz, folk, and dance are also represented. The Anna-Maria Kellen Auditorium does the hosting, Friday nights at 7pm, September through April, no reservations or tickets necessary. Thursday afternoons in June and July also look for Music in Abe Lebewohl Park, a series of free concerts held at 12:30pm in front of St. Mark's Church-in-the-Bowery (Second Ave. and 10th St.). 235 E. 11 St., btw. Second and Third aves. ✆ **212/777-3240.** www.thirdstreetmusicschool.org. Subway: L to Third Ave.

Wall to Wall at Symphony Space `FREE`   This long-running giveaway is also a long runner, filling the Symphony Space stage with some 12 hours of music. The focus changes from year to year, with one source singled out for comprehensive exploration. The range is extensive, from Bach to Beethoven to Joni Mitchell to Kurt Weill. Performances start at 11am, but folks will line up hours before that. Openings in the general admission seating come in waves, every 3 hours or so. Usually early May; check the website. Symphony Space, 2537 Broadway, at 95th St. ☎ **212/864-5400.** www.symphonyspace.org. Subway: 1/2/3 to 96th St.

OUTDOOR SUMMER CONCERTS

The high season for free music is summer, when cool sounds seem to be coming from every corner of the city. You would think that with so many events the crowds would spread thin, but concerts tend to be consistently well attended. If you're going primarily to see the band, better allow at least an hour to carve out some space. For particularly big names you'll need to get there even earlier. If the scene is more interesting than the sound, however, New York concerts are laid-back enough that you can just wander in and out as the mood strikes you. With shows held at so many spectacular sites, a sunset on the Hudson or late afternoon light on the Brooklyn skyline often come with your (metaphorical) price of admission.

BAM Rhythm & Blues Festival at MetroTech `FREE` MetroTech Commons is as close to a municipal center as Brooklyn gets, and in the summer it's the site of a free lunchtime concert series. As the name suggests, R&B is the focus, though the definition stretches to include blues, reggae, and funk as well. Surprisingly big names like the Neville Brothers and Ohio Players come through. Ten shows are held in all, Thursdays from noon to 2pm, mid-June to mid-August. MetroTech Commons, at Flatbush and Myrtle aves. ☎ **718/636-4100.** www.bam.org. Subway: 2/3 to Hoyt St.; A/C/F/R to Jay St./Metro Tech; B/Q/R to DeKalb Ave.

Battery Park `FREE` Battery Park has the city's most spectacular gardens and shoreline, but its corner-pocket location causes it to be overlooked. Come quitting time, much of the working crowd rushes off to subway cars and ferries, leaving the rest of us more space to enjoy the cultural resources. The River to River Festival cosponsors several summer concerts down here, many of which are underattended by New York standards. The World Financial Center Plaza, Rockefeller Park, and One New York Plaza are among the venues that do the hosting. Check **www.rivertorivernyc.com** for full schedules, and see p. 246 for shows on the Seaport's river. *Rockefeller Park,* at the west end of Chambers and Warren sts. ☎ **212/528-2733.** www.batteryparkcity.org. Subway: 1/2/3 or A/C to

Chambers St. *World Financial Center Plaza,* due east of the North Cove Yacht Harbor. ✆ **212/528-2733.** www.worldfinancialcenter.com. Subway: E to World Trade Center; R to Cortlandt St. *One New York Plaza,* at Water and Whitehall sts. www.rivertorivernyc. com. Subway: R to Whitehall St.; 1 to South Ferry.

Bryant Park FREE   Every year, Bryant Park seems to pack its live music schedule a little tighter. There's a big range of genres, and the park's central location makes it a convenient place to catch some tunes. Broadway's brightest play select summer Thursdays (p. 263). Old-timey piano sounds, as popularized by the likes of Fats Waller, Scott Joplin, and the Gershwins, enliven weekday lunches from 12:30 to 2:30pm (May–Oct). If you're looking for a tuneful segue between your cubicle and a night on the town, check out the After Work concert series, with hot sounds filling the Fountain Terrace from 6 to 7pm on summer Wednesdays. Bryant Park, btw. W. 40th and 42nd sts., along Sixth Ave. ✆ **212/768-4242.** www.bryantpark.org. Subway: B/D/F/M to 42nd St.; 7 to Fifth Ave.

Celebrate Brooklyn!   The Prospect Park Bandshell is a perfect place for a concert, with a festive and friendly crowd. The audio selections are as eclectic as Brooklyn, with acts like Rufus Wainwright, the Spanish Harlem Orchestra, and the Brooklyn Philharmonic. Shows are well attended, so show up early if you want a decent view. Check the website for schedules. The season kicks off at Brooklyn Bridge Park in May, with 3 nights of DJs, dancing, and live music. FINE PRINT A $3 donation is suggested for the band shell shows, with a couple of pricey benefits thrown in. The Prospect Park Bandshell, Park Slope, Brooklyn. ✆ **718/855-7882.** www.bricartsmedia.org. Subway: F or B/Q to Seventh Ave.; 2/3 to Grand Army Plaza. Enter at Prospect Park W. and 9th St. Brooklyn Bridge Park, Pier 1, near Doughty and Furman sts. Subway: A/C to High St.; 2/3 to Clark St.

City Parks Foundation FREE   This group is a major player in New York's free music scene, putting on some hundreds of events in 750 parks across all five boroughs. Check online to see what's playing and when (the same organization runs the legendary SummerStage; see p. 242). One event to keep an eye out for is late August's **Charlie Parker Jazz Festival.** Bird gets honored with shows in two of his neighborhoods, Harlem (where he worked) and the East Village (where he lived). The Harlem show is Saturday afternoon in Marcus Garvey Park. Tompkins Square Park takes over on Sunday. *Marcus Garvey Park,* 18 Mount Morris Park West, at Fifth Ave. ✆ **212/360-1399.** www.cityparks foundation.org. Subway: 2/3 or 4/5/6 to 125th St. *Tompkins Sq.,* btw. 7th and 10th sts. and aves. A and B. Subway: 6 to Astor Place; F to Second Ave.

High Culture for Free

Met Opera in the Parks `FREE`   Critics may sniff that the Metropolitan Opera rests on its laurels, but this institution maintains extremely high standards. Tickets can soar over $400 for shows at the Opera House, but for 2 weeks every summer the fat lady sings for free. Shows are held in parks in all five boroughs. Usually six performances in all. Check the website for exact locations and times; no tickets are required. ✆ **212/362-6000.** www.metoperafamily.org.

New York Philharmonic Concerts in the Parks `FREE`   The New York Philharmonic, one of the world's premier symphonies, gives away some six shows every summer. Composers range from Sibelius to Strauss to Ives. While the atmosphere is more hackey sack than Harnancourt—background for a group picnic rather than an event for the serious music lover—the performances by guest conductors and musicians are often inspired. If the classical music doesn't lure you in, you might stop by just for the free fireworks show afterwards. Performance locations vary, but generally they try to hit all five boroughs (the Staten Island concert is indoors). Check **http://nyphil.org** for exact locations. Outdoor shows start at 8pm, no tickets required. ✆ **212/875-5709.**

Crotona Park Jams `FREE`   Revisiting epic Boogie Down park jams of the '70s, this series celebrates hip-hop culture. A surfeit of spinning DJs, often legends like GrandWizzard Theodore and Kool DJ AJ Scratch, set the tempo. The party is hosted by Tools of War and runs from 4 to 8pm on Thursday nights in July. Check their MySpace for free Harlem grassroots hip-hop events, too. Crotona Park E. and Charlotte St. ✆ **718/378-2061.** www.myspace.com/toolsofwar. Subway: 2/5 to 174th St. Walk south on Boston Rd. to Suburban Place, take a right on Crotona Park E. and then a left onto Charlotte St., where you'll see Indian Lake and the jam.

East River Park Amphitheater `FREE`   This renovated spot on the East River doubles down on beautiful Brooklyn and bridge views with free music programs in summer. Ted Leo and Cat Power have played here in the past, but recent years have seen smaller-profile performers. The amphitheater's capacity is around 1,000 and these shows aren't particularly well publicized, so most times you'll be able to wander in late and still snag a prime seat. Programming is by the City Parks Foundation. 600 Grand St., at the East River. ℭ **212/360-1399.** www. summerstage.org. Subway: F to Delancey St.; J/M/Z to Essex St. Walk along the south side of the Williamsburg Bridge and take the pedestrian bridge over the FDR. Turn left and follow the river down to the amphitheater.

Harlem Meer Performance Festival FREE Latino and African sounds predominate at this *meer*-front festival. The scene is as upbeat as the music, which is usually very danceable. Blankets and picnics are encouraged. Concerts are Sunday afternoons from 2 to 4pm, mid-June through early September, near the Charles A. Dana Discovery Center. Central Park, at 110th St., btw. Fifth and Lenox aves. ℭ **212/860-1370.** www.centralparknyc.org. Subway: 2/3 to Central Park N.

Hudson Square Music & Wine Festival FREE Impresario Michael Dorf has followed the arc of maturity from a grungy music spot (the Knitting Factory) to a refined restaurant and wine bar (City Winery). This festival in his winery's backyard combines Greenmarket goods with fresh grooves, served up by the likes of C. J. Chenier, Popa Chubby, and Naomi Shelton. The event drops Tuesday evenings 5:30 to 7:30pm, from late June through mid-August. FINE PRINT Yes, they serve wine. Hudson Sq.; enter on north side of Spring St., btw. Varick and Hudson sts. ℭ **212/608-0555.** www.citywinery.com. Subway: C/E to Spring St.; 1 to Houston St.

Lincoln Center Out of Doors FREE Lincoln Center is a veritable city of performing arts, and every summer for over 30 years now, the great public square has been home to a diverse series of shows. The breadth is breathtaking, from Chinese opera to Greek dance to cutting-edge jazz to children's story time. Incredibly, it's all free. Check online for exact schedules, covering 2½ weeks from late July to mid-August. *Note:* Several shows take place in the nearby Damrosch Park Bandshell, at West 62nd Street and Amsterdam Avenue. 70 Lincoln Center Plaza, at Broadway and 64th St. ℭ **212/546-2656.** www.lincolncenter.org. Subway: 1 to 66th St./Lincoln Center.

Madison Square Music FREE Madison Square's refurbished park has joined the summer music scrum, with the Oval Lawn Series on Wednesday nights. (A second, the Studio Series, runs on Sat afternoons in the fall.) Radio thrift shop proprietress Laura Cantrell and the ever-soulful Bettye LaVette have been heard here, with the series attracting increasingly big names. If you're looking to picnic you're in luck; the square's main attraction is the Shake Shack (℅ **212/889-6600;** www.shakeshacknyc.com), with $3.55 burgers making for a perfect accompanying picnic. (*Note:* If you're planning on eating from the Shake Shack, allow an extra 8–10 hr. to get through the line, which in nice weather stretches to Maryland.) Madison Square Park, Fifth Ave. at 23rd St. ℅ **212/325-2101.** www.madisonsquarepark.org. Subway: N/R or 6 to 23rd St.

Martin Luther King Jr. Concert Series `FREE`   Jazz, soul, gospel, and old-school rap (MC Hammer!) are some of the genres that can be heard on the Monday night program here. Seating is limited, so you might want to bring your own chair. In case of rain, concerts are postponed to Tuesday. Shows start at 7:30pm. Wingate Field, Winthrop St., btw. Brooklyn and Kingston aves., Brooklyn. ℅ **718/222-0600.** www.brooklynconcerts.com. Subway: 2/5 to Winthrop St.

Music in the Square `FREE`   Union Square invites you to stop by with a blanket and a picnic to enjoy live after-work music. Shows are Thursday evenings at 6pm from mid-June through mid-August, in the South Plaza. Jazz, indie bands, and world music nights provide a diversity of beats. Union Sq. ℅ **212/460-1200.** www.unionsquarenyc.org. Subway: L/N/Q/R/4/5/6 to 14th St./Union Sq.

Music on the Oval `FREE`   The massive housing development that is Stuy Town (some 80 acres hold 25,000 residents) hosts summer music parties on its central green. In June and July, half a dozen Saturday afternoons from 3 to 7pm are dedicated to big-name performers like Blitzen Trapper, Ben Kweller, and Kelly Willis. Note that these shows are nominally reserved for Stuy Town tenants and their guests, although that's all but impossible to enforce. Stuyvesant Town Oval, btw. aves. A and B at 17th St. ℅ **212/420-5000.** www.stuytown.com. Subway: L to First Ave.

RiverRocks `FREE`   I love the festive atmosphere of this concert series. The crowd is friendly, and sunset over the Hudson and the Jersey skyline is inspiring. Roomy Pier 84 does the hosting. If you show up late you won't get very close to the band, but you will find plenty of space for hanging out, or even dancing. Recent performers have been first-rate indie groups like the Antlers and Phosphorescent. Shows are usually Thursday nights; you can find smaller-scale Tuesday and Friday night shows on Pier 45. Pier 84 at W. 44th St. and the Hudson. ℅ **212/627-2121.** www.riverrocksnyc.com. Subway: A/C/E/7 to 42nd St./Port Authority. Walk toward the river.

Riverside Clay Tennis Association Sunset Concert Series FREE This is perhaps the shortest wait ever to get on a tennis court in New York City. Blankets and picnic baskets are encouraged at this Riverside Park shindig, as accompaniment for live jazz, classical, samba, and bluegrass. The setting is lovely, and you can hang around afterward to enjoy the summer night air. Shows are Saturdays from 7 to 9pm, with rain dates set for the same time on Sunday. Riverside Park, the Hudson at 97th St. ✆ **212/978-0277.** www.rcta.info. Subway: 1/2/3 to 96th St.

Seaport Music Festival FREE The South Street Seaport isn't much more than a glorified mall, which is cause enough for most locals to give it a wide berth. In the summer, however, Pier 17 becomes a great draw, with free music. There's not as much as there used to be here, but programming is solid, with memorable recent visits from Animal Collective, Dave Alvin, and Jay Farrar. Events are usually held on Friday nights, with Saturday matinees thrown in. The festival runs late June through mid-July. Also in mid-July, you'll find the *Village Voice*'s free **4Knots Music Festivals,** with up-and-comers holding down outdoor and indoor stages at the Seaport. Pier 17, btw. Beekman and Fulton sts., just east of South St. ✆ **212/SEAPORT** (732-7678). www.seaportmusicfestival.com. Subway: A/C/J/Z/2/3/4/5 to Fulton St./Broadway Nassau.

Seaside Summer Concert Series FREE One of NYC's oldest and largest outdoor concerts, this series is a hit with Coney Island locals, who settle in next to MCU Park for convivial evenings. The booking for this event is borderline scary, with Michael Bolton, Liza Minnelli, and Air Supply playing in recent years. (Shows in '12 included such acts as the Jacksons and Joan Jett.) Concerts begin at 7:30pm on Thursday nights from mid-July to late August. W. 21st St. and Surf Ave., Coney Island, across from MCU Park. ✆ **718/222-0600.** www.brooklynconcerts.com. Subway: D/F/N/Q to Coney Island/Stillwell Ave.

Summergarden FREE For over 40 years, MoMA has been throwing these jazz-inflected summer concerts. The Abby Aldrich Rockefeller Sculpture Garden plays host, so if your mind wanders from the music you have Philip Johnson's elegant layout to enjoy. Juilliard students and groups vetted by Jazz at Lincoln Center do the performing. The shows are on Sundays at 8pm; the garden gates on 54th between Fifth and Sixth avenues open at 7pm, but seating is limited, so show up earlier if you don't want to stand. In case of rain, the concerts move indoors to the Agnes Gund Garden Lobby. 11 W. 53rd St., btw. Fifth and Sixth aves. © **212/708-9400.** www.moma.org. Subway: E/M to Fifth Ave./53rd St.

SummerStage FREE Words like "summer" and "music" and "free" conjure an idyllic picture, especially in the context of Central Park. SummerStage is a crack outfit that brings big-name performers to a stage just off the Rumsey Playfield. To get a seat in the bleachers, better show up a couple of hours before start time. If you're not that patient, you can just wander in at any time, and you should be able to find a spot to stand and/or dance. Since no tickets are required, it's easy to come and go freely unless it's a superpopular show. Acts as varied as James Brown, Sonic Youth, and Hugh Masekela have taken the stage, and recent years have seen film, readings, theater, and comedy added to the mix. Several of the shows are pricey benefits, with tickets retailing for $50 or so, but they're there to keep the free part going. Further supporting the series, donations are solicited as you enter, but no contribution is required. Central Park, at the Rumsey Playfield, near E. 72nd St. © **212/360-2777.** www.summerstage.org. Subway: 6 to 68th or 77th sts.; B/C to 72nd St.

Vans House Parties FREE This series of shows in a massive Greenpoint warehouse is actually indoors, although there's a huge courtyard for open-air mingling. The legendary checkerboard sneaker does the hosting, with a serious sound system making the most of punk-inflected bands. The shows are free and open to all ages, with five billings spread across July and August. It can get pretty sweaty inside, although the crowd is limited by an RSVP system (you'll need to print your confirmation after you sign up online). House of Vans, 25 Franklin St., btw. Meserole Ave. and Quay St., Greenpoint, Brooklyn. www.vans.com. Subway: G to Nassau Ave.

Washington Square Music Festival FREE One of the city's oldest festivals brings classical music (and a little jazz and folk) to the heart of the Village. Usually four pieces are played Tuesday nights in July and early August from 8 to 10pm. The last Tuesday of the month is often set aside for jazz, salsa, or world music. The festival is a mix of inside and out. Alfresco gigs play in the northwest corner of Washington Square Park, in front of the Alexander Lyman Holley Monument. Limited seating is available. Indoor and rainy night dates are at the Church of St. Joseph (371 Sixth Ave., btw. Washington and Waverly places). Near Washington Sq. N., btw. Fifth Ave. and Washington Sq. W. © **212/252-3621.** www.washingtonsquaremusicfestival.org. Subway: A/B/C/D/E/F/M to W. 4th St./Washington Sq.

2 The Reel Cheap World

The film industry loves New York. Blithely ignoring our existing congestion, productions flock to the city to steal our parking spaces and tie up our sidewalks. Gotham-themed films line the video store shelves. Is it because we're a convenient symbol of urban glamour? Or is it simply because New York is the greatest city in the history of the world? Either way, NYC has a lot of cinematic pride, which allows New Yorkers to be extorted with $13 movie tickets, a dearth of cheap afternoon matinees, and new releases sold out by 4pm even on gorgeous sunny days. Fortunately, in New York there are always alternatives. Our libraries are stocked with DVDs, our bars screen in their backrooms, and in the summer we get spectacular film alfresco. Most events are on the house, and those that aren't won't break the bank.

INDIES, CULT CLASSICS & MORE

African Diaspora Ciné-Club `FREE`   The "global Black experience" is the focus of this monthly screening. Films from as far afield as Rwanda, Haiti, and Chad make the cut and help viewers expand their perspective beyond the paltry range of mainstream African and African-American fare. The actual directors often make the post-flick Q&As, and refreshments are served. Screening locations at Teachers College vary, usually Room 263 Macy; films are shown the last Friday of every month at 6pm. Teachers College, Columbia University, 525 W. 120th St., btw. Broadway and Amsterdam Ave. ✆ **212/864-1760.** www.nyadff.org. Subway: 1 to 116th St.; A/B/C/D to 125th St.

Cabaret Cinema   Beneath the Rubin Museum of Art's sparkling galleries is an intimate candlelit screening room. Friday evenings see projections of a terrific lineup of films. When the *Holy Madness* exhibit was up, the museum screened related reels that ranged from *Siddhartha* to *Monty Python's Life of Brian.* Shows come with related commentary from a big-time introducer, like Wallace Shawn answering questions about *My Dinner with Andre.* The movies roll at 9:30pm. There's a $7 bar minimum (purchase a drink or snack upstairs and ask the bartender for a chit, which you'll trade for a free ticket at an adjacent table). 150 W. 17th St., btw. Sixth and Seventh aves. ✆ **212/620-5000.** www.rmanyc.org. Subway: 1/2/3 or F/M to 14th St.; L to Sixth Ave.

chashama `FREE`   The innovative use of multiple spaces is a reinforcement of this arts group's name (it's Farsi for "to have vision").

Storefront windows in scattered locales host free art exhibits, live music, and theatrical productions. In late November or early December, the group sponsors a film festival. The programming follows a theme, like '12's "The Rise of Societies," with docs, shorts, and features all in play. Everything is free, but seats are limited, so make sure to RSVP. Check the website for times and locations. chashama Flagship Space, 217 E. 42nd St., btw. Second and Third aves. ✆ 212/391-8151. www.chafilm fest.com. Subway: 4/5/6/S to 42nd St./Grand Central.

Chelsea Classics   Clearview's Chelsea Cinema keeps the natives from getting too restless by breaking up its regimen of mainstream Hollywood fare with a weekly night of camp classics. Drag darling Hedda Lettuce warms up the room before the early showing. In the programming, Joan Crawford and Bette Davis do not go overlooked. Shows are Thursdays at 7 and 9:30pm, and only $7.50. After the movie, your ticket stub morphs into a free drink if you take it to the nearby **XES Lounge** (www.xesnyc.com). 260 W. 23rd St., btw. Seventh and Eighth aves. ✆ 212/777-FILM (3456). www.clearviewcinemas.com. Subway: 1 or C/E to 23rd St.

Ciné Barbès   In the eclectic spirit of its namesake Parisian neighborhood, Barbès' monthly film series focuses on the quirky and the overlooked. Documentaries on Queens's Willets Point and the life of Candy Darling are recent highlights. FINE PRINT There's a $5 suggested donation, every third Sunday of the month at 5pm. 376 9th St., at Sixth Ave., Park Slope, Brooklyn. ✆ 718/965-9177. www.barbesbrooklyn.com. Subway: F/G to Seventh Ave.

Coney Island Museum   On Saturday nights in summer, the museum screens movies made in the spirit of Coney Island's sideshow past. Expect uplifting cinematic triumphs with the words "bikini" and/or "bandit" in the title. Low-budget productions beget budget prices: Entry is just $6 Saturdays at 8:15pm. In late September, look out for the Coney Island Film Festival. Most programs are only $6 and run through a full weekend of shorts and features. 1208 Surf Ave., 2nd floor, near 12th St. ✆ 718/372-5159. www.indiefilmpage.com. Subway: D/F/N/Q to Coney Island/Stillwell Ave.

Filmwax Film Series   Brooklyn is a hotbed of talent these days, ensuring high levels of quality for this series, which gravitates toward BK filmmakers. Screenings move around the borough, hitting bars, festivals, and the Brooklyn Museum. Documentaries play a central

Members Only: Four Cinemas for Savings

★ **Film Forum**   Does Hollywood still make movies that aren't just flimsy remakes of second-rate television shows? Just when we're ready to give up forever on the medium, the marquee of the **Film Forum** draws us in with some irresistible nugget and we're hooked again. Three screens rotate between revivals, retrospectives, and indies that can't be found elsewhere. The crowd is just as interesting, with big-shot actors and directors often in the house, upping their avant-garde cinematic cred. A 1-year membership to Film Forum is one of the city's best steals. Seventy-five bucks buys you close to half-price movie tickets for all three screens 365¼ days a year. That's $7 instead of $12.50. The next membership level up is an even sweeter deal: $110 entitles you to *two* half-price tickets for every show. Imagine: cheap date opportunities every single day. Membership is good for 1 year from the date of purchase. But wait, there's more. It's also 100% tax deductible (as are the other memberships listed below). Now if only they could make the seats a little more comfortable. 209 W. Houston St., btw. Sixth Ave. and Varick sts. ⓒ **212/727-8110.** www. filmforum.com. Subway: 1 to Houston St.

MoMA   As frustrating as MoMA can be, a membership there carries too many perks for me to resist. On top of complimentary museum admission and sneak previews to new exhibitions, members also get a year's worth of free films. MoMA's programming is excellent and with movies showing in three separate theaters daily, it's hard to run out of

role, although there are also features and shorts. Many nights are free, check the website for details. Various locations. www.filmwax.com.

Neue Galerie `FREE`   This elegant museum tailors its film program to dovetail with the 20th-century German and Austrian masterpieces in the galleries. A recent Otto Dix exhibit was matched with a series of battlefield-themed films that spanned 1930 to 2001. Movies are free Monday afternoons at 4pm in **Café Fledermaus.** 1048 Fifth Ave., at 86th St. ⓒ **212/628-6200.** www.neuegalerie.org. Subway: 4/5/6 to 86th St.

cinematic possibilities (1,500 screenings play each year). Members can also buy half-price tickets for up to five friends (just $5 per ticket) to come along with them. At $85 per year ($140 dual), membership pays for itself after seven flicks. 11 W. 53rd St., btw. Fifth and Sixth aves. ⓒ 212/708-9400. www.moma.org. Subway: E/M to Fifth Ave./53rd St.

The Maysles Cinema Documentaries like *Gimme Shelter* and *Grey Gardens* forged the legend of brothers Albert and David Maysles. Although David has passed on, Albert continues to be an active force in the film world, making documentary film and video accessible to underserved populations from his Harlem HQ. A $50 membership here will get you a year's worth of free screenings. (Most regular shows are $10 suggested admission.) 343 Malcolm X Blvd. (Lenox Ave.), btw. 127th and 128th sts. ⓒ 212/582-6050. www.mayslesinstitute.org. Subway: 2/3 to 125th St.

Anthology Film Archives For over 40 years now, the cinephiles at this totally indie spot have been programming the best of the avant-garde along with cheeky mainstream combos (a recent series called For the Birds covered everything from documentaries to Hitchcock). Your $60 membership ($90 dual) entitles you to free admission for the classic films of the Essential Cinema program, and $6 for all regular shows. 32 Second Ave., at 2nd St. ⓒ 212/505-5181. www.anthology filmarchives.org. Subway: F to Second Ave.

Rooftop Films What began as a lark atop a downtown tenement has now expanded to lawns, parks, and rooftops across Manhattan, Brooklyn, and Queens. On summer nights, God dims the overheads, and indie shorts and features play. Despite screening low-budget productions, Rooftop Films does an incredible filtering job, and quality is impressively high. Film themes run along the lines of "Home Movies" or "Scenes from Texas." Screenings cost $12, but that's a bargain if you value films made by actual human beings and not Hollywood-studio automatons. You may score a free beer, too, as many screenings come

Current Releases for Little Currency

"That $3 theater" became "that $4 theater" and then closed altogether. The Uptown bargain-matinee place got torn down to make way for million-dollar condos. It's becoming harder and harder to find a current release for anything less than the usurious $13 charged for prime-time viewing. If you're in the right neighborhood, though, there are still options left.

Cobble Hill Cinemas   Monday through Friday all shows before 5pm are only $7, as are the first shows of the day on the weekend (as long as they start before 2pm). If matinees don't do it for you, there are also two bargain days, Tuesdays and Thursdays, when all seats for all shows all day and all night are a humble $7. (The only exceptions are special engagements and holidays.) 265 Court St., at Butler St., Boerum Hill, Brooklyn. ℂ **718/596-9113.** www.cobblehilltheatre.com. Subway: F/G to Bergen St.

Kew Gardens Cinemas   First-run films play here, usually more interesting indie fare, with several bargain showtimes. Tuesdays and Thursdays are $7 for all seats all day. Monday, Wednesday, and Friday, all seats are $7 until 5pm, as are seats for the first show before 2pm on Saturdays and Sundays. Holidays and special engagements are excepted for the cheap seats. 81-05 Lefferts Blvd., at Austin St., Kew Gardens, Queens. ℂ **718/441-9835.** www.kewgardenstheatre.com. Subway: E/F to Kew Gardens/Union Turnpike.

Cheap AMs at AMC   Although it's a little ridiculous settling into a theater seat when most folks are still finishing up their first cup of coffee, we should be thankful to American Multi-Cinema for giving us half-price entry to the latest flicks. Just $6 gets you into prenoon shows at their theaters all across the city (weekends and holidays at some theaters, daily at others). See **www.amcentertainment.com**.

with after-party freebies. Check the website for exact locations and times. Movies start after sunset (9pm usually), with live music beforehand. ℂ **718/417-7362.** www.rooftopfilms.com.

Sony Wonder Technology Lab `FREE`   Sony goes to bat for high-def technology by hosting free films in its 73-seat theater. The flicks tend to be well-known Hollywood products of recent vintage. The programming splits between kid and adult fare. Times vary, but generally it's the children at noon on Saturday, and the adults' turn at 3pm. Reservations are recommended; call on Monday morning when a screening is scheduled for later in the week. 550 Madison Ave., at 56th St. © **212/833-8100.** www.sonywondertechlab.com. Subway: 4/5/6 to 59th St.; N/Q/R to Lexington Ave./59th St.

NYC'S DRIVE-IN: OUTDOOR SUMMER SCREENINGS

We may be too cheap for insurance, garages, tickets, tolls, and all the other joys of car ownership, but New Yorkers do know how to enjoy their own kind of drive-in movie. Come summer, the parks roll out the big screens and the locals trundle in with blankets and picnic dinners. Each festival has its own identity, with movies ranging across the decades and the genres, assuring something for every *cinéaste*'s taste. As dusk settles over the city, around 8:30pm or so, the crowd hushes and the reels spin. Lie back and be transported by the magic of the movies under the starry skies. Well, skies.

Central Park Film Festival `FREE`   Central Park has been lending atmosphere to films since 1908 (a silent version of *Romeo and Juliet* was the first movie shot here). The park celebrates its long starring career with this late-summer fest, which puts themed fare on successive nights. *Breakfast at Tiffany's* and *Tootsie* are among past players, many of which have had major scenes filmed here. Admission is free, in the landscape between the Sheep Meadow and the 72nd Street Cross Drive. Usually over 5 nights (Tues–Sat) at the end of August. Gates open at 6:30pm; screenings are at 8pm. Central Park. © **212/310-6600.** www.centralparknyc.org. Subway: 6 to 68th or 77th sts.; B/C to 72nd St.

Films on the Green `FREE`   The Cultural Services department of the French Embassy tries to cut through our reflexive disdain for all things Gallic by giving away these summer flicks. "The green" in the title refers to a rotating selection of parkland (Central, Riverside, Tompkins, and Washington Sq. are the usual suspects). The film series are often themed, like '12's run through French and American literature. Projectors whirl Friday evenings in June and July at sunset (around 8:30pm). `FINE PRINT` Wear your reading glasses, as movies are in French with English subtitles. Various locations. © **212/439-1400.** www. frenchculture.org.

That's the Ticket: Giveaways

To fan the flames of early buzz, some films and plays give seats away early in their runs. If your inbox can handle more junk mail, you can sign on with **New York Show Tickets Inc. (www.nytix.com)** and hope to win big in their daily Broadway ticket lottery. You can also find the occasional giveaway on Craigslist, and there's more on offer at the *Village Voice* and *Time Out New York* websites. Both latter sources have dedicated sections (www.villagevoice.com/promotions/freestuff and the "Free Flix" button at www.timeout.com/newyork/promotions) where you can vie for a movie premiere or two. It's a lottery and the odds are on the long side, but hey, the price is right. A sharp eye can also reward a person with preview seats. Check *Time Out* and the *Village Voice* for advertisements of newly opening productions. In addition to specials on tickets for the first few weeks, sometimes you'll spot an offering for a preview. You'll get something halfway between a dress rehearsal and the final polished show, but it won't cost a cent.

Habana Outpost `FREE` This Fort Greene restaurant is the city's first "eco-eatery," a restaurant dedicated to Earth-friendly practices (you can save a buck on your brunch margarita by powering the bike blender yourself). The converted–parking lot spread couldn't be more laid-back, with a menu of moderately priced Cuban and Mexican food. On Sunday nights from May through October, camp classics *The Last Dragon, Saturday Night Fever,* and *Shaft* are projected on a big back wall. There's no charge or minimum, and it's cheap here ($2 for a hot dog; $2.75 for the famous grilled corn or a draft beer) anyway. Films start at 8pm. 757 Fulton St., at S. Portland St., Fort Greene, Brooklyn. ✆ **718/858-9500.** www.ecoeatery.com. Subway: C to Lafayette St.; G to Fulton St.

Hell Gate Social This arty spot behind an unmarked door ladles on the incentives to get folks to an obscure stretch of Astoria Boulevard. Sunday nights in warmer weather feature BBQ afternoons capped off with free flicks. The corn and grilled meat are all you can eat from 3 to 8pm ($15), and there are two-for-one happy hour drinks. 1221 Astoria Blvd., btw. 12th and 14th sts., Astoria, Queens. ✆ **718/204-8313.** www.hellgate social.com. Subway: N/Q to Astoria Blvd.

HBO Bryant Park Summer Film Festival `FREE` Bryant Park's movies are the most famous and most popular of New York's outdoor talkies. A huge screen goes up along Sixth Avenue across from the library's back porch, and the lawn fills with friendly movie fanatics. Film selections run from kitsch like *Jailhouse Rock* to classics like *The Philadelphia Story* to tripped-out wonders like *2001: A Space Odyssey*. Watching the latter from the grass brings a creepy resonance, given Bryant Park was once a potter's field. The gravel area outside the lawn opens at 4pm, followed by the gates at 5pm. If you want a decent view you should be on-site by then at the latest. Bring a crossword puzzle and a picnic dinner and pretend you're just sitting in the park and not waiting for a show. Latecomers have to watch from way back or the wings. It's not untenable; it's just not as much fun as dancing through the HBO trailer from the heart of the crowd. If you time things right, and the director's done her work, this event is totally worth its logistical impositions. Shows are Monday nights June through August with no rain dates. W. 40th to 41st, on the Sixth Ave. side of Bryant Park. © **212/512-5700.** www.bryantpark.org. Subway: B/D/F/M to 42nd St.; 7 to Fifth Ave.

Movie Nights on the Elevated Acre `FREE` Despite a glowing beacon, a huge swath of open space, and gorgeous harbor views, this downtown park flies well under the radar. Introduce yourself to the spot during free Thursday movie nights in late July and August. Programming focuses on NY classic films (Woody Allen is well represented), paired with indie shorts. The crowd is capped by a ticketing system: Pick up your passes at the ground-level Water Street entrance (two per person) starting at 6pm the evening of the screening. Films begin around 8pm. 55 Water St., at Old Slip. © **212/566-6700.** www.rivertoriver nyc.com. Subway: R to Whitehall; 1 to South Ferry.

Outdoor Cinema Program at Socrates Sculpture Park `FREE` Queens is the most culturally diverse spot on the planet, so it makes sense that a Queens film festival would show off movies from around the world. You'll also find culture-appropriate food vendors, so you can nosh on Italian during *The Bicycle Thief* or Indian while *Monsoon Wedding* plays. The movies flicker at Socrates Sculpture Park in Long Island City, a former dump site resuscitated as an artistic oasis along the East River. There are great skyline sightlines, and they throw in free music and dancing as well, beginning at 7pm. Wednesday nights in July and August, movies start at dusk. 32-01 Vernon Blvd., at Broadway, Astoria, Queens. ℂ 718/784-4520. www.socratessculpturepark.org. Subway: N/Q to Broadway. Walk 8 blocks along Broadway toward the East River.

Red Hook Flicks FREE This neighborhood movie show boasts waterfront sunsets and Statue of Liberty views, on top of screenings of fan favorites like *Bring It On, Highlander,* and *Pee-wee's Big Adventure.* Films go Tuesday nights from mid-July to mid-September, starting around 8:30pm. Louis Valentino, Jr. Park and Pier, near Coffey and Ferris sts., Red Hook, Brooklyn. www.redhookflicks.com. Subway: F/G to Smith/9th St.

RiverFlicks FREE The waters of the Hudson and the Jersey skyline provide the backdrop for RiverFlicks. This is a viewer-friendly scene, with chairs laid out on the pier, free popcorn, and themed films that tend toward crowd-pleasing recent hits. *Legally Blonde, 8 Mile,* and *Gladiator* have all made the cut. This is not actually one of my favorites, as the spot is loud, and overbright lighting makes the screen hard to scan. On the plus side, as a result of the marginal conditions there are usually seats left over (if not, there's blanket-spreading space in back and on the wings). Pier 63 hosts Wednesday nights for adults, and Pier 46 takes Fridays for kids, in July and August. Pier 46, at Charles St. and the Hudson. ℂ 212/627-2121. www.riverflicks.com. Subway: 1 to Christopher St. Walk toward the river. Pier 63, at 22nd St. and the Hudson. Subway: C/E to 23rd St. Walk toward the river.

Solar-Powered Film Series FREE Solar One is New York's first free-standing building to get all of its power not from recycled dinosaurs, but from Helios himself. To celebrate this achievement (and to raise awareness about the inevitable need to live greener in NYC), the building hosts an annual film festival. Over 2 August weekends, projectors running on sun power alone show six well-chosen films, often documentaries that highlight some aspect of our environmental plight. See also p. 272 for the dance series. Stuyvesant Cove Park, 23rd St. and the FDR. ℂ 212/505-6050. www.solar1.org. Subway 6 to 23rd St.; L to First Ave.

Summer Movie Series at the *Intrepid* Sea, Air & Space Museum FREE How 40,000 tons can float is beyond my limited engineering comprehension, but I'm all over any chance to check out a battleship flight deck for free. On select summer Fridays, the *Intrepid* screens a flick on its up-top runway. *Top Gun* plays most every year, along with kid-friendly fare. Doors open at 7:30pm and films start about an hour later; picnics, blankets, and lawn chairs are encouraged (although no booze, to fend off drunken jet-plane joy riding). Pier 86, 46th St. at Twelfth Ave. © **212/245-0072.** www.intrepidmuseum.org. Subway: A/C/E/7 to 42nd St./Port Authority.

Summer on the Hudson: Movies Under the Stars FREE With Trump residential structures rising seemingly overnight, lower Riverside Park is filling out, providing green space for a few thousand newly minted West Siders. For their—and our—entertainment, the park's acreage opens itself up to culture in summer. In addition to sunset music Sundays and other concerts, there's an underrated movie series at 8:30pm on Wednesdays. Curating is usually thematic, with titles like On the Hudson River Waterfront and Terror Through the Decades. Picnics are encouraged, at the end of Pier I. Pier I, the Hudson at 70th St. © **212/408-0219.** www.nycgovparks.org. Subway: 1/2/3 to 72nd St.

SummerScreen FREE Competency with a dash of camp defines the programming at this Brooklyn free film stalwart. *Wayne's World, Jurassic Park,* and *Clueless* are among recent projections. The ball fields at McCarren Park do the hosting, with *L Magazine* working behind the scenes. You'll get a free band thrown in as well. Shows are on

FREE **Watching Between the Lions**

New York's book repositories bear no hard feelings for the many indignities the movies have imposed over the years. Our libraries are so forgiving, in fact, they lend out extensive video collections. It's like Blockbuster, only with less censorship and you don't have to pay for anything. The **New York Public Library for the Performing Arts** (p. 115) holds the massive Reserve Film and Video Collection, with more than 6,000 16mm films, 5,000 VHS tapes, and 1,200 DVDs. Most films circulate for 7 days. You can also make an appointment to watch a film on-site. For documentary and world cinema video, head over to the **Mid-Manhattan Library,** 455 Fifth Ave., at 40th Street (© **212/340-0863;** www.nypl.org; subway: 7 to Fifth Ave., 4/5/6/S to 42nd St./Grand Central, B/D/F/M to 42nd St.).

You can also find screenings at select libraries. The New York Public Library for the Performing Arts (p. 115) is a good place to look, as is the Jefferson Market Library (© 212/243-4334), and the main branch of the Brooklyn Public Library (© **718/230-2100;** www.brooklynpubliclibrary.org).

Wednesday nights from mid-July to mid-August; bring a towel or blanket. McCarren Park, at the corner of Bedford Ave. and N. 12th St., Williamsburg, Brooklyn. ✆ **718/965-6580.** www.summerscreen.org. Subway: L to Bedford Ave.

SyFy Movies With a View `FREE` What could be better than the spectacular sight of the downtown skyline shimmering across the East River? A free movie flickering in front, that's what. Every summer, the Brooklyn riverfront turns into a giant alfresco cinema. This series was once the anti–Bryant Park, with limited attendance, but like its hosting borough it has blown up in recent years and you should arrive early if you want a decent spot. Special bonuses include free valet bike parking, DJs at 6pm, and shorts projected before each feature. Shows are Thursday nights at dusk, in July and August. Pier 1, Harbor View Lawn, Brooklyn Bridge Park, near Doughty and Furman sts. ✆ **718/802-0603.** www.brooklynbridgepark.org. Subway: A/C to High St.; 2/3 to Clark St.

Tribeca Drive-In `FREE` The World Financial Center Plaza shows off the big-budget capabilities of the Tribeca Film Festival. A huge screen and sweet sound make the most of crowd pleasers like *The Goonies* and *Dirty Dancing,* with an accompanying party atmosphere. It takes place in late April, over 3 nights. Check the website for details; gates open at 6pm, programming and giveaways at 6:30pm, and screenings at around 8:15pm. World Financial Center Plaza, Near Vesey St. and North End Ave. ✆ **212/941-2400.** www.tribecafilmfestival.org. Subway: 1 or R to Rector St.; E to World Trade Center; 4/5 to Fulton St.; 2/3 to Park Place.

3 The Theatah

Just as models make their way to California for its surfeit of Beach Girl #4 roles, dramatic actors are drawn to New York City. They're not just waiting on our tables, either. In NYC you can find great performances on every level of theater, from big-time Broadway (with its $100-plus orchestra seats) to $9 Off-Off-Broadway to raw productions in the basements of bars, performed for whatever can be garnered by passing the hat. Cost is not necessarily a barometer of quality. You can drop a few Jacksons to discover the cast of a Broadway blockbuster is just phoning it in, while across town some hungry young talent is drawing tears at a free production of Shakespeare. Other giveaways are offered up by schools, institutions, and work-in-progress programs. If you need something more polished than that, try downtown, where dirt-cheap theaters will get you the dramatic goods for $10 or less.

FREE Rise of the House Ushers

If you have the ability to pass out *Playbill*s, point to seats, and enunciate the phrase "enjoy the show," then you're qualified to see free plays. Many smaller theater companies save money on the cost of ushers by trading your sweat equity for a complimentary seat. You won't be able to do this on Broadway, but almost all the resident nonprofit theaters (Think Playwrights Horizons, Signature) accept volunteer ushers. Each house has a different set of rules, and the number of volunteers needed varies from one to eight per night. Popular productions can have a backlog of a few weeks. The best plan of attack is to find a play you want to see, check the website or call their office to find out if/when they need ushers, and reserve as soon as possible (particularly for hot shows). You'll probably spend the first few minutes pointing out seats to the latecomers, but it's worth it when you settle back in your free seat.

FREE THEATER

FREE WILLIE: SHAKESPEARE ALFRESCO

The Earl of Oxford would probably be gratified to know that all these centuries later his little plays dominate the summer theater scene in the world's capital. Sure, the plays are published under the name of an actor from Stratford, but the passions and conflicts resound just as the Earl wrote them. Troupes love to try their hand at the Bard, and free Shakespeare abounds in the Big Apple. Join your fellow mortals and enjoy the midsummer night dreams.

Boomerang Theatre FREE This Off-Off-Broadway stalwart comes back each year with performances of Shakespeare's plays in parks around New York City. Riverside, Central, and Prospect have all served as stages, usually 3 weekends' worth (Fri nights followed by Sat and Sun matinees). There's also the First Flight program, a series of new play readings, which carries a $5 suggested donation. ✆ **212/501-4096.** www.boomerangtheatre.org.

Gorilla Rep FREE Artistic Director Christopher Carter Sanderson has been pioneering free classical theater for some 2 decades now. His troupe is known for its outdoor performances of *A Midsummer*

Night's Dream, most recently seen shifting around the landmarks of Central Park. Check their website for upcoming productions. ℂ **212/252-5258.** www.gorillarep.org.

Hudson Warehouse `FREE` The neoclassical marble and granite Soldiers' and Sailors' Monument puts a dignified cap on a Riverside Park knoll. For several summers now, it's also served as the backdrop for a rival free-summer-Shakespeare troupe (in a rival park). The players of Hudson Warehouse put on shows in June, July, and August at 6:30pm, Thursday through Sunday, with a work or two of the Bard, plus tangential material like *The Trojan Women* or *Cyrano.* The setting is informal, but the actors work hard to be heard over the ambient sound of park and parkway. Soldiers' and Sailors' Monument, Riverside Park, 89th St. at Riverside Dr. ℂ **917/775-9837.** www.hudsonwarehouse.net. Subway: 1 to 86th St.; 1/2/3 to 96th St.

Inwood Shakespeare Festival `FREE` Inwood Hill Park, with its bald eagles and huge natural forest, is as un-Manhattan as Manhattan gets. The verdant hills here are the backdrop for the Moose Hall Theatre Company's annual takes on Shakespeare. They also branch out to other classic material, like *The Three Musketeers* or *The Hunchback of Notre Dame,* and throw in a children's concert or two. Shows are casual, with a tailgating feel, as local families kick back on blankets. The plays run a dozen times each, Wednesdays through Saturdays at 7:30pm. Inwood Hill Park Peninsula, Isham St. at Seaman Ave. ℂ **212/567-5255.** www.moosehallisf.org. Subway: A to 207th St.; 1 to 215th St.

New York Classical Theatre `FREE` NYCT takes advantage of the natural contours of Central Park to stage its summer Shakespeare productions. Plays begin around 103rd Street and Central Park West, but NYCT's innovation is Panoramic Theatre, which is careful not to cast performers' feet in cement. As scenes shift, the location does as well, furthering the sense of an unfolding story. A second Shakespearean series runs downtown, with Castle Clinton and the World Financial Center as backdrops. No tickets or reservations are required; check the website for showtimes. Central Park. ℂ **212/252-4531.** www.newyork classical.org. Subway: B/C to 103rd St. Battery Park. Subway: 4/5 to Bowling Green; R to Whitehall; 1 to South Ferry. World Financial Center. Subway: E to World Trade Center; R to Cortlandt St.

Shakespeare in the Park `FREE` Shh! Top secret! No one else knows about this amazing cultural giveaway. Every summer a William

Shakespeare play and a non-Shakespeare production, sometimes a musical, is performed in a gorgeous open-air theater in the center of enchanted Central Park. Just show up a couple of minutes before showtime and whisper the password "Birnam Wood." Oh, were it that easy. Some 90,000 people attend the Public Theater/Delacorte Theater's productions every summer, and it's the worst-kept free secret in the city. It takes a lot to justify an hours-long Soviet-style wait for a lousy two-ticket ration, but Joseph Papp's Public Theater rarely comes up short. Design, direction, and acting (often featuring A-list stars) are all world-class. The productions vary from faithful classical interpretations to avant-garde reimaginings. In summer, 1,800-some seats are given out at the Delacorte in Central Park. You'll need some determination for your free Will, as people start lining up 2 or 3 hours early for the 1pm giveaways. For a hot show, you'll find bodies out-side the Delacorte before 8am (in some cases, folks will wait over-night). Just treat the ticket queue, with its natural camaraderie, as part of the experience. If you like your luck, you can vie for tickets from the convenience of a computer. The Virtual Ticketing system (**www.shakespeareinthepark.org**) is a lottery, but with a little persistence you can nab a pair of free seats—I've managed to score in recent years. Iffy weather or a panned production will up your odds of get-ting a ticket. The Public's ticket distribution also goes on the road to Harlem and the four outer boroughs, usually one visit per location per play. Check the Shakespeare in the Park website for the dates.

The season runs June through August and features one or two plays. (In 2012, theatergoers got to see Shakespeare's *As You Like It,* and an eagerly awaited revival of the musical *Into the Woods.*) Delacorte The-ater, Belvedere Castle, near 79th St. and West Dr. © **212/539-8750.** www.public theater.org. Subway: B/C to 81st St.

Shakespeare in the Park(ing) Lot FREE   Central Park is classy and well groomed, with lush grass and trees softening the hard edges of the city. The municipal parking lot on Ludlow Street has none of these charms, but the graffiti-slathered asphalt patch can compete in the realm of Tudor drama. The troupe Drilling CompaNY puts on Shake-speare every summer, with a wealth of energy and wit to make up for the lack of big-name casts and big-budget backdrops. It's a wonder-fully surreal scene, with sword fights and intrigue in the foreground while befuddled neighbors cut through the parking spaces in back.

Seating is first-come, first-served, or bring your own (padding is a must, as that pavement gets hard when you've been parked for a while). There are two plays per summer over 6 weekends (Thurs–Sat) in July and August at 8pm. FINE PRINT Parking is available, and it's very convenient. Ludlow St., btw. Broome and Delancey sts. ✆ 212/873-9050. www.drillingcompany.org. Subway: F to Delancey St.; J/M/Z to Essex St.

Smith Street Stage FREE Smith Street is both friend and foe to this crack troupe, providing space for Shakespearean flights, and also injecting a little distraction in the form of truck and motorcycle background noise. This company knows how to make the most of its environs, integrating itself into Carroll Park. Runs are usually 2 weeks (Wed nights excepted) in late June and early July. BYO seating is encouraged. Carroll Park, Smith St. btw. Carroll and President sts., Carroll Gardens, Brooklyn. www.smithstreetstage.org. Subway: F/G to Carroll St.

MORE ALFRESCO THEATER

Circus Amok FREE Amok rakes muck as it entertains, combining activist sentiments with traditional circus arts. Acrobats, jugglers, and a bearded woman are among the draws. The Circus Amok band often trolls through neighborhoods, gathering an audience for shows performed in local parks. Look for some two dozen shows spread out across the month of September. (Earlier in the year, look for the free programs Works-in-Progress and Circus Sundays, in Williamsburg.) ✆ 646/413-0487. www.circusamok.org.

The Classical Theatre of Harlem FREE This decade-old troupe brings the classics to audiences that aren't exactly inundated with *The Cherry Orchard* or *Waiting for Godot.* They also stretch the definition of classic, as in '08's production of Melvin Van Peebles's musical *Ain't Supposed to Die a Natural Death.* In late July and early August, there are free outdoor performances, with Shakespeare making the rotation. Locations vary; check the website. No tickets or reservations are necessary; shows are mostly Friday and Saturday nights, check the website for details. FINE PRINT Also look for their "Future Classics" reading program, which is free at the Malcolm X and Dr. Betty Shabazz Memorial and Education Center (www.theshabazzcenter.net). ✆ 212/564-9983. www.classicaltheatreofharlem.org.

Piper Theatre Productions FREE This grassroots troupe uses the Old Stone House of Gowanus as a backdrop for its alfresco frolics. An

FREE Tune In to Broadway Revues

Give our regards to theatrical greatest-hits packages. The casts of the Great White Way leave the confines of their stages to flog their shows in Midtown, usually in musical form. Huge stars wander down from their dressing rooms, making these very popular events. And you thought Times Square was crowded already!

Broadway in Bryant Park   Every summer Broadway teases fans with a quick sampler on the Bryant Park stage. *In The Heights, Billy Elliot,* and *Jersey Boys* are among the headliners that have recently performed excerpts for a crowded lawn. Shows are held during Thursday lunch hours (12:30–1:30pm) in July and early August. Behind the Public Library, btw. 40th and 42nd sts. and Fifth and Sixth aves. ℂ **212/768-4242.** www.bryantpark.org. Subway: B/D/F/M to 42nd St.; 7 to Fifth Ave.

Broadway on Broadway   A special stage in Times Square hosts this massive concert on a Sunday in mid-September. At least a baker's dozen of shows make an appearance, including heavy hitters like *The Lion King, Avenue Q,* and *Mamma Mia!* For the finale, enough confetti rains down to give onlookers flashbacks to New Year's Eve. Times Square. ℂ **212/768-1560.** www.broadwayonbroadway.com. Usually around 11:30am. Subway: N/Q/R/S/1/2/3/7 to Times Sq./42nd St.

original focus on adventurous Shakespeare (their *A Midsummer Night's Dream* was set in 19th-c. Coney Island) has shifted to modern crowd pleasers (*The Island of Doctor Moreau* and the musical *Xanadu* in '12). Shows are free, July in Park Slope's renovated Washington Park (formerly J.J. Byrne Park). Washington Park, 3rd St. btw. Fourth and Fifth aves., Park Slope, Brooklyn. ℂ **718/768-3195.** www.pipertheatre.org. Subway: F/G/R to 9th St./Fourth Ave.; R to Union St.

Theatreworks USA FREE   Every summer, this organization puts up a production aimed at rug-rat edification (or at least amusement). The group concentrates on one play per season, usually a modern musical. Tickets are distributed on the day of the performance, with four per adult available 1 hour before curtain time. Shows run one or two times a day, every day but Saturday, mid-July to mid-August. Summer camps usually reserve the bulk of weekday afternoon seats, so your best bet is an evening or Sunday matinee. Lucille Lortel Theatre, 121 Christopher St., btw. Bleecker and Hudson sts. ℂ **212/647-1100.** www.theatreworksusa. org. Subway: 1 to Christopher St.

THEATER WITH CLASS

In the working and reworking of new plays, feedback devices are essential. An audience of warm bodies makes a great barometer for figuring out which scenes are killing and which lines are bombing. With so much untested drama in NYC, it's easy to find showcases, workshops, and readings that are eager for your presence. You'll often be sharing the room with a parcel of pros: agents, producers, and casting directors on the prowl for the next big things. If you don't mind putting up with some unsanded edges, it's a great way to catch a night of free theater.

The Juilliard School `FREE`   The fourth-year students of Juilliard's Drama Division mount full-scale productions to catch the eyes of agents, casting directors, and the press. The general public is invited in as well. Third-years also put on free shows, usually as high-minded as a Shakespearean production. `FINE PRINT` The free tickets go fast. You'll have to wait at the box office the first day they become available, although there's also a same-day standby line. The Janet and Leonard Kramer Box Office (Juilliard Box Office), 155 W. 65th St., btw. Broadway and Amsterdam Ave. ℂ **212/769-7406.** www.juilliard.edu. Subway: 1 to 66th St./Lincoln Center.

LAByrinth Theater Company `FREE`   Staged readings assist in the evolution of new plays in the year-long Barn Series hosted by this Off-Broadway group. Readers can be big-name performers, of the Lili Taylor and Eric Bogosian ilk. Seating is first-come, first-served, so get there at least half an hour early. Bank Street Theater, 155 Bank St., btw. Washington and West sts. ℂ **212/513-1080.** www.labtheater.org. Subway: 1 to Christopher St.

Mabou Mines/Suite `FREE`   Somehow this avant-garde troupe has managed to stay on the cutting edge for over 40 years. A commitment to taking chances and providing opportunities for new voices probably hasn't hurt. Mabou's **Resident Artist Program** presents works in evolution during March and April. Several shows play, multiple times across the first half of the year, and all for free. Call ahead for reservations. 150 First Ave., btw. 9th and 10th sts. ℂ **212/473-1991.** www.maboumines. org. Subway: 6 to Astor Place; L to First Ave.

The Martin E. Segal Theatre Center `FREE` This center is run by CUNY's PhD program in theater, home to a talented crop of scholars, students, actors, and playwrights. The schedule is laden with freebies, including visits from international theatrical heavy-hitters, lecture series, and excerpted plays. In September, check out the Prelude festival (**www.preludenyc.org**), with nearly two dozen performances, readings, and open rehearsals of works in progress. No tickets or reservations are required. 365 Fifth Ave., btw. 34th and 35th sts. © **212/917-1860.** http://web.gc.cuny.edu/mestc. Subway: B/D/F/M/N/Q/R to 34th St./Herald Sq.; 6 to 33rd St.

The New School for Drama `FREE` The New School integrates the arts of acting, directing, and playwriting. The fruits of these synergies can be found during New Voices, an annual playwrights' festival. Six original plays are presented in repertory, showing three times each. The performances are free, but it's best to reserve a seat in advance. The New School for Drama Theater at the Westbeth, 151 Bank St., 3rd floor, btw. Washington St. and the West Side Hwy. © **212/279-4200.** Subway: A/C/E to 14th St.; L to Eighth Ave.

The York Theatre Company `FREE` Inside the tasteful modern confines of St. Peter's Church, the York Theatre trots out unsung new musicals for free performances. The **Developmental Reading Series** has warbled its way through Depression-era Chicago, *fin-de-siècle* Paris, and the present-day Smoky Mountains in recent years. `FINE PRINT` The shows are free but do sometimes "sell out," so reserve early. 619 Lexington Ave., at 54th St. © **212/935-5824,** ext. 524. www.yorktheatre.org. Subway: E/M to Lexington Ave./53rd St.; 6 to 51st St.

DIRT CHEAP THEATER

ALL ABOUT LA MAMA: BIG DRAMA IN SMALL SPACES

Small theater groups are notorious for their shoestring budgets, which means most don't have the luxury of permanent stages. All it takes to make a theater is some matte-black paint, a few gelled lights, and a bunch of folding chairs. Walk-up lofts in Midtown are constantly taking form as Off-Off-Broadway bastions. Downtown, especially the area around East 4th Street, is a locus with more staying power. Several companies work out of the area and most shows have East Village–friendly prices of $15 or less.

★ Dixon Place   Experimentation is the norm at Dixon Place, which bills itself as an "artistic lab with an audience." Since performances are in varied stages of evolution, ticket prices are on the low side, usually $5 to $15, with free and suggested admission events in the mix (membership lowers the price of event tickets and has other perks, ranging from free rehearsal space to invitations to member events). This is the real Downtown New York theater/dance/performance experience. From its humble beginnings in its founder's Bowery walk-up (the sofas doubled as seating) the organization has developed and bought a stand-alone space, with a top-flight theater and a separate lounge that accommodates even more affordable entertainment. They claim to be the only New York theater with a liquor license, and they encourage you to support independent artists by patronizing the bar! 161 Chrystie St., btw. Delancey and Rivington sts. ✆ 212/219-0736. www.dixonplace.org. Subway: J/Z to Bowery; B/D to Grand St.

Galapagos Art Space   This Brooklyn bar began with a mini Temple of Dendur moat in an old Williamsburg mayonnaise factory. In their new DUMBO space, they've built an even bigger lake, which helps cool the structure in summer and warm it in winter. Compelling comedy, theater, music, and film fill the calendar. Most events are in the $10 to $20 range, but plenty of free shows are peppered through the schedule. 16 Main St., btw. Water and Plymouth sts., DUMBO, Brooklyn. ✆ 718/222-8500. www.galapagosartspace.com. Subway: F to York St.; A/C to High St.

La MaMa   This venerable avatar of the avant-garde remains ensconced in the East Village and dedicated to artistic experimentation. Productions are high quality and the ticket prices reflect it—shows can run from $5 to $30. One notable exception is the free **Experiments** readings series, which features in-progress plays read with the writers in attendance, to provide instant-gratification feedback. Look also for the **Coffeehouse Chronicles,** a homecoming of sorts, which recalls the origins of the Off-Off-Broadway world with the original instigators. Those shows are free, although nostalgia is preserved with a passed hat. Check the website for exact days and times. 74 E. 4th St., btw. Second Ave. and the Bowery. ✆ 212/475-7710. www.lamama.org. Subway: F to Second Ave.; 6 to Bleecker St.

The Public Theater   Shakespeare in the Park is only the beginning for the Public Theater, which churns out amazing drama all year long. The **New Work Now!** series presents readings of fresh material by

Theater at the Edge: Fringe NYC

Every August a chunk of the city goes on vacation and the **Fringe Festival** comes rushing in to maintain Gotham's equilibrium. This annual theatrical explosion brings over a thousand performances to downtown spaces. The troupes hail from around the world and range from the baldly amateurish to the highly polished. (As they've pointed out for years, *Urinetown* made its mark at the Fringe before heading uptown to Broadway.) Tickets have a high end of $18 (though you can volunteer in exchange for seeing free shows). You can also purchase festival passes which drop the price of admission depending on how many shows you are determined to see, and $9 tickets if you are a member of the Theatre Development Fund.) Since it's summer in New York City, free outdoor events are all but obligatory. The FringeAL FRESCO series offers up free plays, dance, and even the odd bit of Parkour in locations scattered around downtown. Some events are just teaser versions of longer Fringe shows, but others are the full affair, given away across multiple performances and locations. You can also volunteer in exchange for free admission. Check the website for times and venues. © **212/279-4488.** www.fringenyc.org.

both established dramaturges and up and comers. From December to March, you can catch **PUBLIC LAB,** which puts on bare-bones productions at a price friendly to threadbare budgets. Just $15 gets you into these still-evolving shows. Also check out the **Under the Radar** festivals each winter, held at the Public and other spaces in the East Village, featuring outstanding new experimental work from the U.S. and abroad, with ticket prices topping out at $20. 425 Lafayette St., just below Astor Place. © **212/539-8500.** www.publictheater.org. Subway: 6 to Astor Place; N/R to 8th St.

Spaghetti Dinner   The Great Small Works artists collective is known for its puppetry and "toy theater" shows. Carrying the torch of an East Village tradition, they also host this quirky form of dinner theater. Audience members/diners are treated to performance of every stripe—from puppetry to dance to drama to film—along with a fine vegetarian spaghetti meal. Don't be surprised to find left-wing polemic in the mix as well. Tickets hover around $15, a price that wouldn't have seemed unreasonable when the series started in 1978. Check the website calendar for info about locations and times. Great Small Works. ✆ **718/840-2823.** www.greatsmallworks.org.

The Tank This endlessly inventive theater group has lost spaces to wrecking balls and bad plumbing, but it's hanging on back in Hell's Kitchen. Public affairs are the latest addition to an already strong lineup of comedy, film, music, and theater. Shows can run as high as $15, but much of the calendar stays in the $5 to $10 range. 151 W. 46th St., 8th floor, btw. Sixth and Seventh aves. ✆ **212/563-6269.** www.thetanknyc.org. Subway: N/Q/R to 49th St.; B/D/F/M to 47th–50th sts./Rockefeller Center

The Theater for the New City This alternative theater is known for giving breaks to unknown playwrights. Productions are consistently high quality, though ticket prices are often only $10, with some shows as low as $5. The New City, New Blood reading series gives playwrights the opportunity to absorb audience feedback (readings carry a $5 suggested donation, but there's wine and cheese). Over Memorial Day you can sample dramatics for free during the Lower East Side Festival of the Arts. Theater is only the beginning, as spoken word, cabaret, film, video, and dance performances take over East 10th Street, between First and Second avenues. Events run until after midnight, and everything is free. Also free is the Annual Summer Street Theater, which puts on operettas in a baker's dozen locations spread across five boroughs. 155 First Ave., btw. 9th and 10th sts. ✆ **212/254-1109.** www.theaterforthenewcity.net. Subway: 6 to Astor Place; L to First Ave.

DEEP DISCOUNTS ON BIG-TIME THEATER

Broadway shows—even blockbusters—sometimes have a limited number of cheaper tickets set aside for students and seniors; call the box office directly to inquire. Some popular shows have "lotteries" for cheaper tickets each day; others offer student, general "rush," or "standing room" tickets, which are available only on the day of the show. **Playbill.com** usually keeps a comprehensive list of the rush/student/lottery and other special rates.

Three sites—**Broadway.com** (www.broadway.com), **Playbill Online** (www.playbill.com), and **TheaterMania** (www.theatermania.com)—offer information on Broadway and Off-Broadway shows, and links to their ticket-selling agencies. Each has its own free **online club,** for which you register your e-mail address in exchange for savings on advance-purchase Broadway and Off-Broadway tickets. Discounts range from a few bucks, up to 50% off regular ticket prices. Subscribing to e-mail newsletters also helps you keep track of changing offers.

If you're a total theater maven, consider joining the **Gold Club** at TheaterMania, which costs $99 a year, and entitles you to even more deeply discounted shows, and usually rewards you with a pair of Broadway tickets when you join. Other theater ticket clubs include **Audience Extras,** for $85 a year (www.audienceextras.com), and **Play-by-Play,** for $99 a year (www.play-by-play.com). How deep are the discounts? Well under $20 in many cases, for Broadway or Off-Broadway shows whose tickets can go for $50 to *much* more than that!

For the latest deals, visit **Broadway Box** (www.broadwaybox.com) or **Broadway Offers** (www.broadwayoffers.com) and you can find deals for the shows that need some fannies in the seats . . . act quickly, however: A show that's all but giving away seats before it opens might be sold out if it opens to great reviews.

THE ABCS OF TDF: THE BOOTHS & BEYOND

If you're a full-time student or fit into another designated category (from schoolteacher to retiree to performing arts professional to civil servant to active military, see website for complete listing), you're eligible to join the **Theatre Development Fund** (**www.tdf.org**) for $30 a year. With your TDF membership, you can purchase deeply discounted tickets to events from current Broadway offerings, to dance, classical music, opera, jazz, rock, children's events, and that favorite of the indie theater community: "$9 Off-Off." That's right . . . you can purchase tickets to independent theater for a lot less than the cost of a first-run movie ticket; the entire price of your ticket goes to the company that's offering the ticket, and there's no service charge! (Even if you're not a member, you can purchase the $9 vouchers for off-off).

TDF offers many programs for theater professionals, children, families, and people with disabilities, but the most visible aspect of TDF are "the booths," the three TKTS locations in NYC.

Starting in 1973, in the heart of the Theater District at Father Duffy Square, the organization started selling half-price, same-day tickets for Broadway and Off-Broadway shows. In 1983, TKTS added a downtown branch, and 2008 saw the addition of a TKTS outlet in Brooklyn. Here's the deal:

1. The **Times Square Booth** sells day-of-performance tickets only (and has a "Play Express" line for nonmusical shows).

2. The **South Street Seaport Booth** sells tickets to evening performances on the day of the performance, and matinee tickets the day before.

3. The **Downtown Brooklyn Booth** sells tickets to evening performances on the day of the performance, and matinee tickets the day before, as well as tickets to Brooklyn performing arts events.

All locations sell tickets at 50%, 40%, 30%, and 20% off full-price (plus a $4 per-ticket service charge, which helps support other TDF services and programs). The booths accept credit cards, cash, traveler's checks, or TKTS Gift Certificates.

And you don't even have to trudge to Midtown, South Street Seaport, or MetroCenter to find out what's on the "board." When you subscribe to the **TKTS Today e-mail,** you'll get a daily message listing what's available at the downtown and Brooklyn booths on and Off-Broadway, the curtain time(s), and the daily operating hours. There's also a free smartphone **app** you can download through their website, **www.tdf.org/tkts**.

Of the three booths, Times Square/Father Duffy can have the longest wait, particularly during holidays and other peak tourist seasons (which, really, is every season except winter), so it's definitely worth the trip to get the tickets downtown or in Brooklyn.

4 Let's Dance

Until police started hassling bars, most New Yorkers didn't realize the city had cabaret regulations. Laws regulating public dance had been on the books forever, but it had been many decades since anyone had thought to enforce them. Innocuous tremors and inadvertent hip shakes were suddenly categorized as unlicensed dance expressions. Fortunately, dance in New York has never been limited to clubs and bars. In the parks, on stages, and even in sanctuaries of the city, dance of all levels can be found, legally, and often for free.

Dance Conversations @ The Flea FREE Choreographers present works in progress at this monthly program, usually four per night. It's a discussion series as well, so expect jawing to following the dancing. There are films thrown in as well, usually over a couple of weeks in March. Flea Theater, 41 White St., btw. Broadway and Church St. ℂ 212/226-0051. www.theflea.org. Subway: 1 to Franklin St.

Dance Theater Workshop `FREE` The Judson Memorial Church has been an anchor of the West Village since 1890. The aging church has recently been renovated with a lovely new dance floor ready to host the Dance Theater Workshop's popular Movement Research dance program. Dancers and choreographers vary from week to week, but the emphasis on pushing boundaries remains consistent. No reservations are taken. Performances are seasonal (spring and fall) on Mondays at 8pm; doors open at 7:45pm. DTW also hosts low-cost classes and workshops. Their Open Performance program puts on noncurated experiments and works-in-progress, with a moderated discussion afterward. These are Wednesdays at 8pm, with a suggested donation of $3. Judson Church, 55 Washington Sq. S., btw. Thompson and Sullivan sts. ℂ 212/598-0551. www.movementresearch.org. Subway: A/B/C/D/E/F/M to W. 4th St./Washington Sq. *Open Performance,* A.R.T./New York, South Oxford Space, The Great Room, Ft. Greene, Brooklyn, 138 S. Oxford St., btw. Atlantic Ave. and Fulton St. Subway: C to Lafayette Ave.; B/D/N/Q/R/2/3/4/5 to Atlantic Ave./Pacific St.

Dancing in the Streets `FREE` This arts organization brings site-specific performances to spots across the city. The integration of cityscape and moving bodies is a great way of seeing familiar spaces in a new way. Their signature shows are **Hip Hop Generation Next** and **Breaking Ground—A Dance Charrette.** Check the website for complete performance details; a new permanent home in Hunts Point has put a focus on the South Bronx. www.dancinginthestreets.org.

Downtown Dance Festival `FREE` **Battery Dance Company** showcases both professional and emerging dancers at these outdoor shows. Originality is prized here, as is range—major companies from around the world have joined famed choreographers like Lê Minh Tâm, Paul Taylor, and Mary Anthony. The alfresco setting suggests informality, but the artists take their steps seriously. As the name suggests, sites are usually downtown, 1 week in mid- to late August. Locations vary. ℂ 212/219-3910. www.batterydanceco.com.

Gotham Dance Festival The **Joyce Theater** has been at the forefront of NYC's modern dance scene since 1982. This festival from **Gotham Arts** (www.gothamarts.org) brings 2 weeks of cutting-edge movement to the theater in late May and early June. Tickets are as low as $10. 175 Eighth Ave., at 19th St. ✆ **212/242-0800.** www.joyce.org. Subway: C/E to 23rd St.

MoonDance FREE July and August bring marvelous nights for this dance on Pier 54. Sunday evenings begin with a lesson at 6:30pm and cede to dancing a half-hour later, when you're a full-fledged expert. Dance varieties run from swing to salsa to R&B. Live music from crack bands enhances the lovely riverside setting. Pier 84 on the Hudson, at 44th St. ✆ **212/533-PARK** (7275). www.hudsonriverpark.org. Subway: A/C/E/7 to 42nd St./Port Authority.

Solar-Powered Dance Series FREE An "eco stage" made of recycled materials and a solar-powered sound system support the fancy footwork at this annual series. The environmental advocacy group Solar One does the hosting, with dance films recently added to the mix. In September look for the Sun to Stars festival, an afternoon and evening inspired by all-night concerts along the Ganges. Stuyvesant Cove Park, 23rd St. and the FDR. ✆ **212/505-6050.** www.solar1.org. Subway: 6 to 23rd St.; L to First Ave.

5 Sing, Sing: Karaoke

Maybe it's a side-effect of our blog and Tweet culture, but it seems the old gate-keeping editorial controls have fallen by the wayside. Local music is no exception, with a profusion of live-band karaoke nights allowing amateur lungs to step up to the mic and perform front person duties. Join the caterwauling carousel and do your part to reaffirm the inherent dignity of the human race by drinking way too much tequila and then letting loose on a heartfelt version of "My Humps." More traditional canned-music-and-bouncing-ball karaoke can also be found citywide, often for little more than the price of your boozing. The venues below don't enforce drink minimums, and often karaoke nights are too crowded for anyone to notice if you're not tippling. Then again, doesn't sobriety kind of go against the very spirit of karaoke?

Arlene's Grocery FREE If you've ever wondered where the tri-state has been hiding its best Ozzy Osbourne and David Lee Roth imitators, you've been missing out on the live music karaoke at Arlene's Grocery. Legendary Monday night shows fill 3 hours with the soul-uplifting sounds of '70s classic rock and '80s hair metal. If you sign up and ascend the stage, you'll find the crowd enthusiastic, and nothing beats the thrill of belting out "Black Dog" or "Paradise City" over an ass-kicking band. It's worth a visit just to check out the regulars. Many of them have come all the way from Jersey to show off how well they can work a club full of rabid fans with fingers spread in devil's horns. There's no cover for these covers if you come for Monday night (10pm–1am); Friday's midnight version is $10. 95 Stanton St., btw. Ludlow and Orchard sts. ℂ **212/358-1633.** www.arleneslivekaraoke.com. Subway: F to Second Ave.; J/M/Z to Essex St.

Hill Country `FREE`   The legendary Kreuz Market was the inspiration for this slice of Texas in the big city. The low-ceilinged basement here is a rollicking spot to catch some twang-tinged tunage. On Tuesday nights at 8:30pm, you can add your voice by singing lead with the Wicked Messengers. David Allen Coe makes the set list, but you can also find plenty of hard rock staples. Unfortunately the BBQ don't come free. 30 W. 26th St., btw. Broadway and Sixth Ave. ℂ **212/255-4544.** www. livebandkaraokenyc.com. Subway: F/M to 23rd St.; N/R to 28th St.

Hip Hop Karaoke   We all know the extraordinary levels of talent required to make it in the rap world (just look at the Insane Clown Posse), but that doesn't mean the unpolished among us can't entertain. Hip Hop Karaoke is quickly becoming a phenomenon, with packed shows letting little Biggies rhyme away for a forgiving crowd. (No one will think less of you if you're reading off a crib sheet.) Venues vary, with recent appearances at Mercury Lounge and B. B. King's. Cover is only $5 with flyer ($8 without). Locations vary. www.hiphopkaraoke nyc.com.

Keyboard Karaoke `FREE`   Loser's Lounge keyboardist (and ex–Psychedelic Fur) Joe McGinty tickles the keys for the pleasure of your pipes. His song list hops from Boz Skaggs to Bette Midler, with special guests often joining in. Hosting venues change periodically, although the white grand piano at the Manhattan Inn, where Joe is currently ensconced, will be hard to outdo. It's on Tuesday nights, 10pm to 1am or so. Manhattan Inn, 632 Manhattan Ave., at Nassau Ave. ℂ **718/383-0885.** www.joemcginty.com. Subway: G to Nassau Ave.

O'Flanagan's `FREE`   The Human Karaoke Experience boasts a playlist of over 500 songs, so it shouldn't be hard to find something in your range. Daughter of Brooklyn Pat Benatar (nee Patricia Andrzejewski) has five songs represented, and there's a full complement of Beatles, Stones, and Elvii (both Presley and Costello). The hosting pub, O'Flanagan's on the Upper East Side, is congenial, if a little cookie-cutter. It takes place 2

Thursdays a month, from 9pm to 1:30am. 1215 First Ave., btw. 65th and 66th sts. ✆ **212/439-0660.** www.humankaraoke.com. Subway: F to 63rd St./Lexington Ave.; 6 to 68th St.

Punk Rock Heavy Metal Karaoke   For over a decade, this quartet has been getting heads banging with high-energy rock and the borrowed talents of a revolving door of guest singers. Fifth wheels can choose from almost 300 songs, with arena rock classics heavily represented. Fontana's, on the fringe of Chinatown, is the scene's current home. Gigs are once a month, with a $5 cover. 105 Eldridge St., btw. Broome and Grand sts. ✆ **212/334-6740.** www.punkmetalkaraoke.com. Subway: B/D to Grand St.; F to Delancey St.; J/M/Z to Essex St.

Rock Star Karaoke `FREE`   This hard-working band doesn't let the moss settle, rolling through several gigs a week, sometimes twice a night! The playlist is diverse, covering AC/DC to Britney Spears, with stop-offs at Weezer and Roxette along the way. Look for stops at the National Underground and various Brother Jimmy's BBQs around town. Rock Star Karaoke, various locations. ✆ **917/446-0098.** www.rockstarkaraoke nyc.com.

Winnie's   For actual, old school karaoke, hipsters and Chinatown locals never have enough opportunity to chill together, which is where Winnie's comes in. The place is an ungentrifiable dive, but the savings get passed on to the crooning customer: It's only a buck a song to play along with the hit machine (they're still using laser disks, so don't expect to sing anything more recent than Huey Lewis). It's available daily from 8pm to 4am. 104 Bayard St. ✆ **212/732-2384.** Subway: J/N/Q/R/Z/6 to Canal St.

6 Humor Us: Comedy

There's no shortage of frustrating and surreal experiences in New York, ensuring plenty of fodder for the comedians in our midst. The city is stacked with young comic talent, which means amateur nights are more common than headliner-thick extravaganzas. Alas, amateur nights can also be express trips to the nether regions of stand-up hell. Somehow bad comedy is infinitely more painful than bad tragedy. I advise stepping carefully through the city's improv, open mic, and stand-up minefield. Fortunately, plenty of quick wits can be found in this town. Small investments can lead to big laughs if you hit the right nights. For all the side-splitting and beer-nose-spewing details, see below.

SHOWCASES, IMPROV & OTHER COMEDY ANTICS

Magnet Theater   Three burgeoning improv institutions hold down spaces in Manhattan's 20s. This entry learned its comedic lessons in Chicago and at the UCB (Upright Citizens Brigade, see below). Emphasizing a more theatrical feel than its neighbors, the shows here attract student, resident, and pro players, generating laughs 7 nights a week. Look to Wednesday and Thursday for $7 evenings, where one entry gets you 5 hours of LOLing. Most shows are $5, some are free, there's no drink minimum, and you can enjoy $2 PBRs during select performances. 254 W. 29th St., btw. Seventh and Eighth aves. ✆ 212/244-8824. www.magnettheater.com. Subway: 1 to 28th St.

New York Comedy Club `FREE`   Most nights the comedy here is $15 and a two-drink minimum, but you can get in for free at an open mic. Sunday, Monday, and Friday at 6pm are the slots, part of the longest-running open mic in New York. There's no drink minimum, and although it's statistically unlikely, it is possible to see an overlooked talent just breaking in. For aspiring comedians (most everyone in the audience), it's $5 for 6 minutes on stage and a drink. (Thurs nights, SuperEgo Comedy also hosts an open mic, $5 cover for performers, plus a one-drink minimum for all, 6:30–8:30pm.) 241 E. 24th St., btw. Second and Third aves. ✆ 212/696-LAFF (5233). www.newyorkcomedyclub.com. Subway: N/R or 6 to 23rd St.

The Pit   This upstart has yet to reach the UCB's level of improv evolution (see below), but they're headed in the right direction. The Peoples Improv Theater's primary mission is as a school, with an ex-SNL writer and Second City alum among the faculty. Many shows involve student performers and are priced accordingly (lots of freebies slotted in to the calendar). Regular tickets run between $5 and $8. Two separate stages mean some 10 shows to choose from nightly. 123 E. 24th St., btw. Park and Lexington aves. ✆ 212/563-7488. www.thepit-nyc.com. Subway: 6 or N/R to 23rd St.

The Upright Citizens Brigade   The UCB brings Chicago-style long-form improv comedy to the Big Apple. With founders that can be found on SNL and in the movies, the talent level is high, which is crucial in the hit-or-miss medium of improvisation. Plus, the complete lack of scripts saves you money. Sunday night sees two performances of ASSSSCAT 3000. The extra *Ss*? For savings: The 7:30pm show is $10, but the 9:30pm version is free! Tickets for the latter are distributed at 8:15pm, but it's popular (Amy Poehler is a cast member) so try to get there at least an hour early. Shows on Monday and Wednesday at 11pm are also free, as is the midnight Friday show. The rest of the schedule runs between $5 and $10 (mostly $5), which is still a steal. The Harold Night's two $5 shows (Tues at 7 and 9pm) are especially noteworthy, with some rapier wits putting the old Harold technique through its paces. A second theater (UCB East, or "the Beast") is now open under Two Boots in the East Village. You'll find similar fare, with free jams and open mics alongside shows for $5 to $10. Upright Citizens Brigade Theatre, 307 W. 26th St., btw. Eighth and Ninth aves. ℭ **212/366-9176.** www.ucbtheatre.com. Subway: C/E to 23rd St. Other location: *East Village,* 153 E. 3rd St., btw. aves. A and B. ℭ **212/366-9231.** Subway: F to Second Ave.; 6 to Astor Place; N/R to 8th St.

7 Game Night

Too damn smart? Bars (and other public spaces) across the city offer trivia nights, an excuse to meet new people and show off the fruits of all those wasted hours learning to differentiate between Arnold Snarb and Arnold Strong. Gather up some compatriots, or join a team of fellow-stragglers, and convert that synaptic alacrity into bragging rights and bar tabs.

The Gael Pub FREE This standard-issue Irish pub distinguishes itself with a hugely popular trivia night. Tuesday nights at 8:30pm you can find six categories, with audio and visual rounds shuffled in to the mix. Winners get a $50 gift certificate. Losers hope to get lucky on a $20 tab raffle. 1465 Third Ave., btw. 82nd and 83rd sts. ℭ **212/517-4141.** www. thegaelpubnyc.com. Subway: 4/5/6 to 86th St.

Last Exit Pop Quiz @ Last Exit isn't free, but the $5 cover can be considered an investment. The cash goes into a pot for the eventual winner. Groups of four compete, and if you show up short-handed, they'll make a team for you. Categories include Canadian or Not Canadian? and Bodega Price Is Right. *Warm up:* Who wrote *Last Exit to Brooklyn?* Trivia nights are on the first and third Mondays of the month, from 9 to 11pm. Register around 8:30pm and bring a pen or pencil. *Answer:* The late Hubert Selby, Jr. Every third Tuesday check out the Slurring Bee, a $5 spelling competition. 136 Atlantic Ave., btw. Clinton and Henry sts., Brooklyn Heights, Brooklyn. ℭ **718/222-9198.** www.lastexit bar.com. Subway: R/2/3/4/5 to Borough Hall; F/G to Bergen St.

Pacific Standard FREE   As the name suggests, there's a chill West Coast undertone here, with Cali expats often in attendance. Sunday night quizzes can get more boisterous with teams of six packed in, but a projector ensures everybody gets a fair chance to glean the questions. A free round of drinks goes to the winners, weekly at 8pm. 82 Fourth Ave., btw. St. Marks Place and Bergen St., Park Slope, Brooklyn. ℭ **718/858-1951.** www.pacificstandardbrooklyn.com. Subway: B/D/N/Q/R/2/3/4/5 to Atlantic Ave./Pacific St.

Pete's Candy Store   At Pete's Wednesday Quizz-Off, categories range from general knowledge to music to top 10s, with prizes for the top three finishers. The action starts at 7:30pm. The first Monday of every month you can revisit ancient humiliations with a spelling bee. At 7:30pm, trip over words like *roriferous* and *keratic.* (Or is it *kerratic?*) That's why the **Williamsburg Spelling Bee (www.nycbee.com)** operates on a gentle three-strike basis. All games are free, though there's a loosely enforced two-drink minimum. 709 Lorimer St., btw. Frost and Richardson sts., Williamsburg, Brooklyn. ℭ **718/302-3770.** www.petescandy store.com. Subway: L to Lorimer St.; G to Metropolitan Ave.

8 Word Up: Readings

New York has always been a city of writers, and modern Gotham has no shortage of literary lights. Undiscovered hopefuls, midlist strivers, and huge names with cultlike followings all find their way to lecterns across the city. Bars, galleries, libraries, bookstores, and schools do the hosting. With eight million other stories unfolding in the Naked City, most people don't take the time to be read to, and I usually find literary events are pleasantly underattended. There are exceptions— voices of the moment and package nights that bring in a bunch of big names at once—but generally you have a better chance to see a big-time writer up-close than you'll get with any actress, athlete, or musician. And almost always you'll get to do it for free.

AT BOOKSTORES

Bookshops are good spots for getting a hit of that sweet, sweet literature, and getting it for free. Some stores offer regular readings, and some just signings, but either way on a quiet night you may get the chance to talk up a favorite author.

Barnes & Noble `FREE` The Union Square location gets the biggest names and most frequent readings. Literary stars like David Sedaris, Helen Fielding, and Michael Chabon come through to read from their works or participate in conferences and discussions. The seating area is large, but you should show up early for the best-sellers because it does get crowded. For children's story times, look to the TriBeCa branch and Saturday mornings. 33 E. 17th St., btw. Broadway and Park Ave. S. ✆ **212/253-0810.** www.bn.com. Subway: L/N/Q/R/4/5/6 to 14th St./Union Sq. Other location: *TriBeCa*, 97 Warren St., at Greenwich St. ✆ 212/587-5389. Subway: 1/2/3/A/C to Chambers St.

Bluestockings `FREE` A DIY ethos is in full effect at this newly expanded radical bookstore, fair trade cafe, and activist center. Frequent readings of a feminist and lesbian bent intersperse with seminars and meetings. The readings and many lectures/discussions are free; other events can ask for suggested donations of $5 to $10. The **Dyke Knitting Circle** meets the third Sunday of every month from 4 to 6pm. It's open to all levels of knitting skill; bring yarn and needles. 172 Allen St., btw. Rivington and Stanton sts. ✆ **212/777-6028.** www.bluestockings. com. Subway: F to Second Ave.; J/M/Z to Essex St.

BookCourt `FREE` For over 3 decades now, this Cobble Hill favorite has been a clean and well-lighted place for literary fans. The local authors section is comprehensive, which is impressive considering how many writers are calling the area home. In-store readings, signings, book clubs, and lectures bring in important new voices. 163 Court St., btw. Dean and Pacific sts., Cobble Hill, Brooklyn. ✆ **718/875-3677.** www.book court.org. Subway: F/G to Bergen St.; R to Court St.; 2/3/4/5 to Borough Hall.

Books of Wonder `FREE` The agenda here is books for the kiddies. Readings are held on Fridays at 4pm and Sundays at noon. Publication parties and workshops are also thrown into the mix, often with light refreshments served. 18 W. 18th St., btw. Fifth and Sixth aves. ✆ **212/989-3270.** www.booksofwonder.com. Subway: L/N/Q/R/4/5/6 to 14th St./Union Sq.

Greenlight Bookstore `FREE` With the path of destruction wreaked by big retailers, Amazon, and e-readers, it's a wonder that any community bookstores have survived at all. Shopping at this indie Fort Greene newcomer feels downright wholesome, with a neighborly staff and a stellar selection. There's a dense slate of readings, with Jhumpa Lahiri, Matthew Modine, and Jeffrey Eugenides among the bold-faced names that have appeared here. For the little ones, Saturdays at 11am are story times; a baby and toddler edition comes 11am Sundays. 686 Fulton St., at S. Portland St., Fort Greene, Brooklyn. ℭ **718/246-0200.** www.greenlight bookstore.com. Subway: C to Lafayette Ave.

McNally Jackson `FREE`   This big, sophisticated bookshop counters the trend of every last retail inch of SoHo and NoLita being dedicated to overpriced boutiques. McNally Jackson (nee Robinson) thrives with an independent spirit and a knowledgeable staff. A full slate of readings, discussions, and signings can be found. Fridays at 4pm and Saturdays at 11:30am are dedicated to the wee ones. Grownups should try to catch **Real Characters,** an excellent monthly storytelling performance. 50 Prince St., btw. Lafayette and Mulberry sts. ℭ **212/274-1160.** www.mcnallyjackson.com. Subway: 6 to Spring St.; N/R to Prince St.

192 Books `FREE`   This lovely shop brings in authors for 7pm readings. Night of the week varies, and seating is limited so call ahead for reservations, especially if it's Ethan Hawke reading Mayakovsky. (Mary Gaitskill, Mark Strand, and A. M. Homes have also graced this intimate space.) Check the website for the schedule. 192 Tenth Ave., at 21st. ℭ **212/255-4022.** www.192books.com. Subway: C/E to 23rd St.

Revolution Books `FREE`   The revolution will be televised, and it will also make its way into print. Alternative viewpoints are aired during in-store readings and screenings right in the heart of the Machine. 146 W. 26th St., btw. Sixth and Seventh aves. ℭ **212/691-3345.** www.revolutionbooks nyc.org. Subway: N/R/1 to 28th St.

The Scholastic Store `FREE`   The retail outlet for the children's publisher Scholastic has books and toys and a full schedule of in-store events. Every Tuesday, Wednesday, and Thursday at 11am is story time, plus there are book signings and special events scattered across the schedule. Most everything is free, although craft workshops can have a small materials fee. 557 Broadway, btw. Prince and Spring sts. ℭ **212/343-6166.** www.scholastic.com/sohostore. Subway: N/R to Prince St.

Unnameable Books `FREE`   A response to a lawsuit over an innocuous former name was the inspiration behind this odd moniker. The selection here is well curated, and there are great prices on lightly used literature. (Look for the $1 bargain rack out front.) Check the Facebook of "Unnameable Boox" for frequent free readings at the shop. 600 Vanderbilt Ave., at St. Marks Ave., Prospect Heights, Brooklyn. ℭ **718/789-1534.** www.uncalledforreadings.blogspot.com. Subway: B/Q to Seventh Ave.

AT BARS & CAFES

What better way to advertise the intelligent conversation your coffee shop or booze hall induces than by associating yourself with articulate new voices? Reading series have cropped up in bars and cafes (and even laundromats) across the city, and the informal settings encourage more showmanship than a bookshop lectern. With extreme readings added to the mix, these venues are likely spots to be entertained while listening to an author intone.

Earshot Reading Series   This monthly Thursday night reading series provides opportunities for MFA students to be heard. Although that means less polished material, it gives you a great chance to catch a real up-and-comer. Established writers also make appearances, usually five writers in all. The show does come with a $5 cover, but then it also comes with a free drink. Lolita Bar on the Lower East Side does the hosting. 266 Broome St., btw. Allen and Orchard sts. ✆ **212/966-7223.** www. earshotnyc.com. Subway: F to Delancey St.; J/M/Z to Essex St.; B/D to Grand St.

Franklin Park Reading Series `FREE`   This converted garage in Crown Heights is long on ramshackle charm. Culture comes around monthly, with the second Monday dedicated to literature, and the third Monday to films (see Filmwax on p. 249). Both events start at 8pm, but they're popular, so take advantage of seating at 7:30pm. Look for up to five writers on the reading series nights. 618 St. John's Place, btw. Franklin and Classon aves., Crown Heights, Brooklyn. ✆ **718/975-0196.** www.franklinparkbrooklyn.com. Subway: 2/3/4/5 to Franklin Ave.

The Half King `FREE`   *The Perfect Storm* author Sebastian Junger is a co-owner of this bustling Chelsea bar. He's also an occasional reader on literary nights here. There are about 50 events a year, often found

---

`FREE` Rooftop Refrains

The **Academy of American Poets** sets up a poesy idyll every summer on the roof of the arsenal in Central Park. High above the city bustle, find four sessions of declaiming versifiers. Lovely views accompany, select Thursday nights at 6:30pm. (The readings move inside in case of rain.) 830 Fifth Ave., at 64th St. ✆ **212/408-0100.** www.poets.org. Subway: F to 63rd St./Lexington Ave.; 6 to 68th St.

on Monday nights. 505 W. 23rd St., near Tenth Ave. ℂ **212/462-4300.** www.the halfking.com. Subway: C/E to 23rd St.

Happy Ending `FREE`   This Chinatown lounge, whose name advertises a salient detail about the services of the former tenant (a massage parlor), is home to ambitious reading and storytelling series. Readings start at 8pm; check the calendar for monthly visits from groups as disparate as Southern writers and sex workers. 302 Broome St., at Forsythe St. ℂ **212/334-9676.** www.happyendinglounge.com. Subway: B/D to Grand St.; F to Delancey St.; J/M/Z to Essex St.

KGB Bar `FREE`   Hidden away in a former speak-easy on the second floor of an East Village tenement, KGB has the most comprehensive reading series in the city. Sunday night brings fiction, Monday poetry, Tuesday nonfiction, and some Wednesdays feature the fantastic, in the form of sci-fi authors. *Drunken! Careening! Writers!* (third Thurs) is a long-running series with the ethos of presenting 1) good writers, 2) who read their work well, and 3) something in it makes people laugh. And 15 minutes tops. The bar was once the clubhouse of the Ukrainian Labor Home, and the commie kitsch adorning the walls completes the literary atmosphere. Most readings start at 7pm. 85 E. 4th St., near Second Ave. ℂ **212/505-3360.** www.kgbbar.com. Subway: F to Second Ave.; 6 to Bleecker St.

Secret Science Club `FREE`   With the whole dying-planet thing going on these days, science is enjoying a resurgence in the popular imagination. This monthly series attracts physicists, mathematicians, and even Nobel Prize–winning biologists. In addition to a free lecture, there's music, Q&As, and science-themed cocktails. It happens once a month at 8pm, doors open at 7:30pm, and the limited seats go fast. The Bell House, 149 7th St., btw. Second and Third aves., Park Slope, Brooklyn. ℂ **718/643-6510.** www.secretscienceclub.blogspot.com. Subway: F/G to Smith/9th St.; F/G/R to 9th St./Fourth Ave.

Triptych Readings `FREE`   These poetry nights evolved from the long-running Reading Between A&B series. Emerging poets are the focus, usually three per night. The neighborhood bar that hosts couldn't be more congenial. The readings are held monthly at 7pm; check the calendar. 510 E. 11th St., btw. aves. A and B. ℂ **212/982-3929.** www. readab.com. Subway: L to First Ave.

9 Talking Points

New York's most famous television shows are incredibly popular, and waits of 6 months or longer are commonplace (to see *The View,* you'd better break out your appointment book a year or two in advance). Often you'll have to send a postcard or e-mail with your relevant info and preferred dates. (Tickets to a taping make a great cheap birthday present, by the way.)

For those who arrive without tickets, it is possible to get standbys on the day of the show. Usually they'll only give one ticket per standee, so everyone in the party has to be assembled. Even then it's no guarantee, since standby status only kicks in if there are enough no-shows among the regular ticket holders. Of course, if you're not choosy about what you want to see, plenty of shows that tape in New York are always looking for audience members. The NYCVB has more details on tapings (© **212/484-1222;** www.nycvb.com), with some two dozen potential shows represented.

The Colbert Report `FREE` Stephen Colbert's nightly "news" program has reached the cult status of *The Daily Show,* which spun it off in the fall of '05. Colbert's studio is *The Daily Show*'s cramped former home, making it a harder ticket to nab than its progenitor. Comedy Central has an online ticket request system, but it's usually booked up solid. Your best bet is to follow the Twitter feed (**twitter.com/#!/Daily tix**), which pops up with spare tickets a few times a day. For standby seating, you can hope for a no-show by going to the studio door. Tapings are Mondays through Thursdays at 7pm, but to have a shot for a standby you should get there by 4pm. You'll increase your chances if there isn't a big-name guest on the docket, or if the weather is iffy. Audience members must be at least 18. No bears. 513 W. 54th St., btw. Tenth and Eleventh aves. © **212/767-8600.** www.comedycentral.com. Subway: A/B/C/D/1 to 59th St./Columbus Circle.

The Daily Show with Jon Stewart `FREE` There's been no drought of mockable material in the news recently, which helps Jon Stewart's satirical news/talk show remain a water-cooler conversation staple. In addition to biting analysis of current events, if you attend a taping you'll be treated to a few minutes of personable conversation with Jon himself. Though the show is more popular than ever, it's filmed in a new and larger studio, so tickets aren't impossible to come by. Tapings are Monday through Thursday with doors open at 5pm, though they want you there an hour early. Finding a ticket online is best done through the Twitter feed shared with *The Colbert Report* (Twitter feed: **twitter.com/#!/Dailytix**). If you're vying for a standby seat, be there by 2:30pm. The minimum age is 18. 733 Eleventh Ave., btw. 51st and 52nd sts. ✆ **212/767-8600.** www.thedailyshow.com. Subway: A/B/C/D/1 to 59th St./ Columbus Circle.

Good Morning America FREE   If seeing the face of George Stepha-nopoulos first thing in the morning is actually an enticing prospect for you, join the live audience in ABC's studio right on Broadway. There are no tickets, but you can feel free to join the throng outside the Broadway and 44th Street studio window. Around the 8am hour there's a lot of outdoor filming, but you'll need to have staked out your place well before then. In the summers, big-name performers (think LMFAO or Demi Lovato) come to Rumsey Playfield in Central Park for the **Good Morning America Summer Concert Series.** Those shows are free and require no tickets, running from 7 to 9am (but get there by 6am). ABC Studios, 1500 Broadway, at 44th St. ✆ **212/930-7855.** Subway: N/Q/R/S/1/2/3/7 to Times Sq./42nd St.

Late Night with Jimmy Fallon FREE   Former host Conan O'Brien may have received some shabby treatment, but the honeymoon continues for Jimmy Fallon. The best plan for tickets here is to call about a month in advance and request up to four tickets. For last-minute openings, check the Late Night Twitter feed (@**latenightjimmy**), or try for a standby. Starting at 9am outside 30 Rockefeller Plaza—the GE Building—under the NBC Studios awning on the 49th Street side, you can get one ticket per person, with no guarantee of entry. The third option is entering the **Band Bench lottery** (www.fallonbandbench. com). If you're rabid about a particular group, these are great seats if you get lucky (and if you just want in, enter "ANY" as your lottery code). You must be 17 to attend tapings. NBC Studios, 30 Rockefeller Plaza, 49th St., btw. Fifth and Sixth aves. ✆ **212/664-3056.** www.nbc.com. Subway: B/D/ F/M to 47th–50th sts./Rockefeller Center; N/Q/R to 49th St.

The Late Show with David Letterman FREE   And the number-one hottest New York TV taping ticket is . . . yeah, it's still Letterman. Though it's not what it was in the '80s, the show has really picked it up lately, with our favorite Hoosier squeezing the most out of his regulars, and Paul and the band keeping things energetic. Tapings are Monday through Thursday usually at 5:30pm, sometimes with a second taping

Thursday at 8pm. You can request tickets online (it's a lottery and usually a 6-month wait) or you can stop by the theater in person. The lobby handles walk-ins Monday through Thursday from 9:30am to noon, and weekends from 10am to 6pm. If you're feeling lucky, you can also try calling in for a same-day standby seat. The phone line opens at 11am. Be patient and use your redial button liberally. Also bone up on your Letterman trivia because you may need to pass a test to get the tickets (which aren't actually tickets but are spots on the standby line, should anything open up and should you have correctly identified Biff Henderson's real first name as James). You must arrive an hour and a quarter before tape time, be 18 or older, and be ready to show some ID. Ed Sullivan Theater, 1697 Broadway, btw. 53rd and 54th sts. ✆ **212/247-6497.** www.cbs. com/latenight/lateshow (click on "Get Tickets"). Subway: B/D/E to Seventh Ave.

The Today Show `FREE` Watching NBC's morning mainstay is free and easy; just show up outside *Today*'s glass-walled studio at Rockefeller Center, on the southwest corner of 49th Street and Rockefeller Plaza. Tapings are Monday through Friday from 7 to 10am, but if you want to be up front, 7am is way too late to be rushing over with your goofy hat and hand-painted sign. In the summer, *Today* holds a series of concerts in Rockefeller Center, generally on Friday mornings at 7am. It's always big names playing (that is, Usher or Bieber), and they attract commensurate huge crowds so don't get there any later than 6am. Southwest corner of 49th St. and Rockefeller Plaza. ✆ **212/664-3056.** www. today.msnbc.msn.com. Subway: B/D/F/M to 47th–50th sts./Rockefeller Center; N/Q/R to 49th St.

Who Wants to Be a Millionaire `FREE` Millionaires miss out on all the fun listed in this book, but you can look on with condescending pity should anyone run the table against Meredith Vieira. Tapings are usually Monday through Wednesday at 2:30 and 4pm when the show is in production. Note that they'll want you there 2 hours early and the show can take 2 hours or longer to tape, so make sure you're fed and watered before you go in (and be warned that as posh as the set looks on television, those benches are hard). Requests for tickets can be made online; you must be 18 or older to attend. ABC at 30 W. 67th St., btw. Columbus Ave. and Central Park West. ✆ **212/479-7755.** www.millionairetv. com. Subway: 1 to 66th St./Lincoln Center.

10 Big Leagues, Little Prices

It's said that it's now cheaper to be an opera fan than to follow a professional sports team, and with big league ticket prices racing well ahead of inflation it's easy to believe. The NFL long ago climbed into the stratosphere, and with new stadiums the Mets and Yankees seem eager to follow suit. Premium Knicks seats? Prices top out over $330. And this for a team that hasn't played a second-round playoff game since the last millennium and let Jeremy Lin go to *Houston*? Fortunately, outside of the occasional bout of Linsanity, athletics can be accessed for not too much scratch in NYC. (To get out on a field of play yourself, see p. 168 in chapter 5, "Local Living.")

The Amazin' Mets   Citi Field has replaced mostly charmless Shea, but Yankee-level crowds have yet to materialize. That doesn't make this a cheap ticket, but "dynamic pricing" will let you in to Promenade Outfield seats for less-popular matchups for as little as $12. That's just on the official website—for better bargaining head right to **StubHub** (www.stubhub.com). This reseller lets the market set the value of tickets, and you'll see folks ditching their seats for as little as $4 a pop. This is a strategy that often works with early season games, or games against cellar-dwelling opponents. Citi Field, 126th St., at Roosevelt Ave., Flushing, Queens. ☏ **718/507-8499.** www.mets.com. Subway: 7 to Mets/Willets Point.

Baby Bombers   The **Staten Island Yankees** have a waterfront stadium just a few steps from the ferry terminal. Running from $13 to $22, tickets are slightly easier to come by than the Cyclones', although they're scarce and pricey when the two rivals play. Gluttons in groups can take advantage of $22 all-you-can-eat specials. Richmond County Bank Ballpark, Staten Island. ☏ **718/720-9200.** www.siyanks.com. Subway: R to Whitehall St.; 1 to South Ferry, take the ferry to Staten Island and follow the signs.

B-Ball in Brooklyn   Brooklyn got its own NBA team in 2012 when the Nets headed over from Jersey to the brand new Barclays Center, in downtown BK. It remains to be seen whether they'll sell out or stink up the joint, but it'll cost you a minimum of $30 (ouch) for the cheapest ticket at the box office, though we found some for $10 on StubHub. Barclays Center, 620 Atlantic Ave., Brooklyn. ☏ **718/933-3000.** www. nba.com/nets. Subway: 2/3, 4/5, B, D, N/Q/R to Atlantic Ave.

Playing the Horses

Horse racing has seen its bottom line repeatedly gouged by the dumb luck of state lotteries. With fewer fans trekking out to the track, Belmont and the Big A will be happy to see you when you go. So happy, in fact, that they'll let you in for only a nominal charge (or no charge at all). While it's possible to lose some real money on the ponies, I have a system. Always pick the first horse off the rail that's wearing red, or any horse whose name begins with *B*. You can't miss.

Aqueduct Racetrack FREE Thoroughbred racing runs from late October or early November to late April or early May. 110th St. and Rockaway Blvd., Rockaway Beach, Queens. ✆ **718/641-4700.** www.nyra.com. Clubhouse and Skyline Club admission is free, parking is $2. Closed Mon–Tues. Subway: A to North Conduit.

Belmont Park When the season ends at Aqueduct (see above), the ponies run here, from May through July, and September through October. Hempstead Ave., Belmont, Long Island. ✆ **516/488-6000.** www.nyra.com. Tickets $3–$5, with free parking. Closed Mon–Tues. Train: LIRR Belmont Express from Penn Station or Flatbush Ave.

Damn Yankees The new Yankee Stadium has been derided as a "mallpark" rather than a ballpark, but there's no disputing the time and effort put into all those smooth finishes. Despite the pricey build-out (and the pricey virtual all-star squad that plays there), you can find a few ways to get in the building for cheap. The Yankee website will lead you to $15 outfield seats, which is as cheap as you'll get. As with the Mets, the better option is StubHub, especially early in the season, when the Yankees are out of the playoff race, or not facing an arch-rival. Yankee Stadium, 1 E. 161st St., at River Ave., the Bronx. ✆ **718/293-6000.** www.yankees.com. Subway: B/D/4 to 161st St./Yankee Stadium.

Knicks & Cut-Rate Seats Ten-dollar Knicks seats are about as elusive as Knicks playoff victories. They do exist, but they're in the nosebleed sections and they tend to sell out quickly. If you don't pick them up in September when they first go on sale, your best bet is to check StubHub, where season-ticket holders unload their spares at list (or below) after another disappointing season. Madison Square Garden, 4 Pennsylvania Plaza, Seventh Ave., at 34th St. ✆ **212/465-6741.** www.nba.com/knicks. Subway: A/C/E/1/2/3 to 34th St./Penn Station.

★ **Mini Mets** No one confuses the **Brooklyn Cyclones** for "dem bums" of old, but the newish stadium near the Atlantic Ocean and the Coney Island boardwalk has fast become a borough fave. Box seats are $14 to $17. General admission and reserved bleacher seats will only set you back $9 ($10 on game day). Though some of the sheen is off the stadium, tickets still go quickly. And you see both the Parachute Jump and the Atlantic Ocean just past the outfield fence! MCU Park, 1904 Surf Ave., at W. 19th St., Coney Island, Brooklyn. ✆ **718/449-8497.** www.brooklyncyclones.com. Subway: D/F/N/Q to Coney Island/Stillwell Ave.

Rumble on the River FREE Practitioners of the sweet science assemble every summer on the Hudson at this offshoot of the Church Street Boxing Gym's legendary amateur bouts. There's a full-on ring and no punches pulled as a series of pugilists go three rounds apiece. The event takes place at Pier 84, usually on a Thursday night in mid-summer. Pier 84, at W. 44th St. and the Hudson. ✆ **212/533-7275.** www.hudsonriverpark.org. Subway: A/C/E/7 to 42nd St./Port Authority. Walk toward the river.

Sweet Land of Liberty The Liberty are an NYC team in name only at the moment; summer renovations of Madison Square Garden have sent All-Star Cappie Pondexter and crew across the river to the Prudential Center in Newark, New Jersey, until their old digs are refurbished. Though prices go as high as $250, you can find a fair number of tickets for as little as $10, and discounts (often including food and drink) abound. Prudential Center, 25 Lafayette St., Newark, NJ. Tickets: ✆ **212/465-6766.** www.wnba.com/liberty. Accessible by PATH train and NJ Transit.

11 Into the Drink

FREE WINE TASTINGS

The intricacies of wine are endless, which is excuse enough to try as much of the stuff as possible. The wine shop tasting experience can be frustrating because you're only getting sips, but if you've come for edification and not to catch a cheap buzz, there's little chance of going away disappointed. Besides, many shops throw in free snacks for your trouble.

Astor Wines & Spirits NOHO `FREE` Astor's ginormous space in the basement of the De Vinne Press Building hosts free tastings pretty much every weeknight, with another one thrown in on Saturday afternoon. Look for artisanal champagnes, liquor, and sakes among the offerings, with the booze in question usually discounted 15%. Regular prices are great here, too, making this my top stop for stocking up. 399 Lafayette St., at E. 4th St. ℭ **212/674-7500.** www.astorwines.com. Subway: 6 to Bleecker St.; B/D/F/M to Broadway/Lafayette St.

Bottlerocket Wine & Spirit FLATIRON `FREE` This Flatiron shop works hard to maintain its neighborly reputation. Wine giveaways certainly don't hurt. Look for tastings on Thursdays, Fridays, or Saturdays, usually 5 to 8pm. 5 W. 19th St., btw. Fifth and Sixth aves. ℭ **212/929-2323.** www.bottlerocketwine.com. Subway: N/R to 23rd St.; F/M to 14th St.; L to Sixth Ave.

67 Wines and Spirits UPPER WEST SIDE `FREE` Rotating hosts walk guests through wine tastings at this shop, highlighting the fruits of a particular country or region. The schedule is extensive, with tastings running most every weeknight, plus a 4pm Saturday slot. The bottles being sampled go for 10% off. 179 Columbus Ave., btw. 67th and 68th sts. ℭ **212/724-6767.** www.67wine.com. Subway: 1 to 66th St.

Union Square Wines UNION SQUARE `FREE` The new larger digs of this neighborhood shop mean more counter space for uncorking the fruit of the vine. Tastings are held several nights a week, with as many as two dozen different wines in rotation. (Whiskey, vodka, and sake show up as well.) Look for 20% discounts on sampled vintages. 140 Fourth Ave., at 13th St. ℭ **212/675-8100.** www.unionsquarewines.com. Subway: L/N/Q/R/4/5/6 to 14th St./Union Sq.

12 Free & Cheap Pub Grub

There's nothing like a salty treat to keep the beer orders flowing: Witness the ubiquity of pretzels and peanuts in proximity to barstools. Several New York bars get more elaborate with their snacks, offering up bagels, wings, and pizza pies. Discounts can be deep—in many cases all the way down to $0—although most places expect you to spring for a drink or two, since they're running bars and all.

Alligator Lounge WILLIAMSBURG This lounge took over a former pizza joint to exploit an existing wood-burning oven. The result is remarkably good pies, *free* with the purchase of a drink. That's right—a free personal pizza with your beer. Toppings are $1 a pop. The pies roll from 6pm on the weekdays and 3pm on the weekends, and they don't stop until a bleary-eyed 3:30am. 600 Metropolitan Ave., btw. Leonard and Lorimer sts., Williamsburg, Brooklyn. ✆ **718/599-4440.** Daily 3pm–4am. Subway: L to Lorimer St.; G to Metropolitan Ave.

The Brazen Head BOERUM HILL, BROOKLYN Sharing a name with Dublin's oldest pub, this low-key neighborhood spot rolls out the welcome wagon with dining and drink specials. Monday nights see free chicken wings (and thighs) from 5pm on, Wednesday evenings there's complimentary cheese, and Sunday afternoons bring bagels, fixin's, and $5 Bloody Marys and mimosas. 228 Atlantic Ave., btw. Court St. and Boerum Place, Boerum Hill, Brooklyn. ✆ **718/488-0430.** www.brazenheadbrooklyn.com. Tues–Sat noon–4am; Sun–Mon noon-2am. Subway: F/G to Bergen St.; A/C/G to Hoyt-Schermerhorn.

Crocodile Lounge EAST VILLAGE This Alligator Lounge spinoff may not win any prizes for its pizzas, but it's hard to beat for price ($0) and convenience (especially for NYU students). The lure of one free pizza per drink attracts a young and hungry crowd. Crocodile kitsch and free Skee-Ball complete the atmosphere. 325 E. 14th St., btw. First and Second aves. ✆ **212/477-7747.** Daily noon–4am. Subway: L to First Ave.

Croxley Ales EAST VILLAGE This pub represents something between the death of a once-proud indie 'hood and a breath of unpretentious relief in a trendier-than-thou zone. Croxley puts games on its televisions and offers specials at the bar. If you're drinking, you're entitled to 20¢ wings on Saturdays from noon to 5pm, and all day and night on Sundays. That price goes down to 10¢ on Monday, Tuesday, Wednesday, and Thursday nights from 5pm to 1am (Thurs's iteration features boneless wings). You get to choose from four sauces, and if hot's not hot enough for you, $2 nets "Cry Like a Baby Sauce." 28 Ave. B, btw. 2nd and 3rd sts. ✆ **212/253-6140.** www.croxley.com. Mon–Fri 4pm–2am; Sat–Sun noon–2am. Subway: F to Second Ave.

East River Bar WILLIAMSBURG East of the East River is the site of this paint factory turned biker bar turned casual South Williamsburg hang. Industrial chic corrugated metal adorns the outdoor patio, which holds a real, live barrel drum barbecue pit. That, and three smaller grills, provide the fire for BYOBBQ nights (as in Bring Your Own). Call ahead to reserve charcoal space. 97 S. 6th St., btw. Bedford Ave. and Berry St. ℂ 718/302-0511. www.eastriverbar.com. Sun–Thurs 5pm–2am; Fri–Sat 5pm–4am. Subway: J/M/Z to Marcy Ave.

Fish WEST VILLAGE   This restaurant is a decent facsimile of a sea-food shack, with a lively crowd and walls cluttered with old water-front photos and buoys. Though the sit-down prices aren't cheap, you can net a great deal at the bar. Just $8 covers a half-dozen clams or oysters along with a PBR or a glass of house wine. Available at all hours, 7 days a week, and perfect for date nights. 280 Bleecker St., at Jones St. ℂ 212/727-2879. www.fishrestaurantnyc.com. Sun–Thurs noon–11pm; Fri–Sat noon–midnight. Subway: 1 to Christopher St.; A/B/C/D/E/F/M to W. 4th St./Washington Sq.

Full Circle Bar WILLIAMSBURG   Billyburg takes its lumps for being a land of prolonged adolescence, but there are times that call for unabashed youthful fun. This Grand Street bar fits the bill, with Skee-Ball in back, and cheap drinks at the rail. Tuesdays and Thursdays bring free Skee plus free hot dogs and jumbo pretzels. (Happy hours with $4 Genny Cream Ale plus a dog or pretzel run weeknights 5–9pm and weekends 2–9pm.) For even cheaper access to Genesees, come the last Thursday of the month for a free Genny bar from 11am to 1pm. 318 Grand St., btw. Havemeyer St. and Marcy Ave. ℂ 718/388-7577. www.fullcirclebar.com. Mon–Fri 5pm–4am; Sat–Sun 2pm–4am. Subway: J/M/Z to Marcy Ave.; L to Lorimer St.; G to Metropolitan Ave.

Lulu's GREENPOINT   Like its siblings Alligator Lounge and Croco-dile Lounge, this bar has made its reputation on the dispensing of free pizza. Every drink you buy entitles you to a crisp thin-crust pie that's way tastier than it needs to be. Over a dozen toppings are available, for just a buck each. The bar itself sprawls comfortably over three floors, with free rock shows thrown in for your entertainment. The only misstep? They should have named it Cayman Lounge. 113 Franklin St., at Greenpoint Ave. ℂ 718/383-6000. Mon–Fri 1pm–4am; Sat–Sun 2pm–4am. Subway: G to Greenpoint Ave.

Metropolitan WILLIAMSBURG   When the weather turns forgiving, the grill at this gay Williamsburg haunt turns to wings, dogs, and veggie burgers. The patio setting is spectacular, with lots of space beneath the creeping vines. A cheerful crowd gets even friendlier the more they're plied with cheap drinks ($7 pitchers of Bud) and free meat (or fake meat, as the case may be). Start time is around 4pm on Sunday afternoons. Also look for two-for-one happy hours, $3 well drinks, and $1 PBR nights scattered through the schedule. 559 Lorimer St., btw. Metropolitan Ave. and Devoe St. ✆ **718/599-4444.** www.metropolitan barny.com. Daily 3pm–4am. Subway: L to Lorimer St.; G to Metropolitan Ave.

Papacitos GREENPOINT   This ramshackle Brooklyn spot offers not one, not two, but *three* happy hours. The first runs on weekdays between 11am and 4pm, with discount tacos and $2 Tecates and Modelo Especials. At 4pm, happy hour number two kicks in: the same cheap cans, plus $5 margaritas, discount nachos, and other drink specials. The third happy hour fills the last hour of the night and includes $5 drink specials and all-you-can-eat popcorn. 999 Manhattan Ave., btw. Huron and Green sts. ✆ **718/349-7292.** www.papacitosbrooklyn.com. Mon–Thurs 11am–1am; Fri–Sat 11am–2am; Sun 11am–midnight. Subway: G to Greenpoint Ave.

Phebe's EAST VILLAGE   When this corner was occupied by a Bowery saloon you could get a worker's lunch for 40¢. On Monday and Wednesday nights that same outlay will get you four chicken wings— they're just a dime apiece with the purchase of a pitcher. Tuesday from 8pm until midnight it's two-for-one burgers, and there are happy hour discounts from 4 to 8pm every weeknight. A recent spruce-up has made for a comfortable scene, popular with NYU students and postcollegiate partyers. 361 Bowery, at E. 4th St. ✆ **212/358-1902.** www.phebes nyc.com. Daily 11am–4am. Subway: 6 to Astor Place; N/R to 8th St.

Rudy's MIDTOWN WEST   The pig that stands sentry outside this Hell's Kitchen dive is there to prime your appetite for hot dogs. *Free* hot dogs. After a quarter-century of tube-steak dispensing, they've recently upgraded to Hebrew National, too. Rudy's Blonde Ale is just $7 a pitcher ($2.50 a pint), should you feel like luxuriating with a cold one in a duct-taped booth. 627 Ninth Ave., btw. 44th and 45th sts. ✆ **646/707-0890.** www.rudysbarnyc.com. Mon–Sat 8am–4am; Sun noon–4am. Subway: A/C/E/7 to 42nd St./Port Authority.

Spring Lounge SOHO   A profusion of stuffed sharks provides the alternative name ("the Shark Bar") for this long-running corner spot. The place dates back to the 1920s and an illegal beer bucket-to-go operation. Its current iteration features a trim and mostly tourist crowd. Wednesday nights at 5pm, take advantage of free hot dogs, cooked in a beer of the week. On Sundays at noon grab a free bagel and fixin's with your eye-opener. 48 Spring St., at Mulberry St. 🕐 212/965-1774. www.thespringlounge.com. Mon–Sat 8am–4am; Sun noon–4am. Subway: 6 to Spring St.; N/R to Prince St.

Standings EAST VILLAGE   The EVill's evolution away from its gritty alternative status is complete enough to now accommodate sports bars. This is an amiable one, with eight plasma screens and happy hour specials that run weeknights from 5 to 7pm. Come on a Friday night and you'll get free pizza—they treat the entire bar starting at 8pm until it runs out. There are also free atomic wings to sate devotees of the church of Monday Night Football. 43 E. 7th St., btw. Second and Third aves. 🕐 212/420-0671. www.standingsbar.com. Mon–Fri 5pm–2am; Sat noon–2am; Sun noon–midnight. Subway: 6 to Astor Place; N/R to 8th St.

13 Liquid Assets (Happiest Hours!)

Despite the rise of the $18 cocktail, an entire paycheck isn't required for a night on the town. Recession pressures have opened up happy hours across town, and two-for-one and $1-off specials are all but ubiquitous. Even sweeter deals can be found, especially in the cheap drinker's mecca of the East Village.

Bar None EAST VILLAGE   For the longest happy hours in the city the choice is, without exception, Bar None. You have to wait until noon, but then you'll get $3 Bud and Bud Light pints and $4 wells and other drafts until 8pm. Stick around until 11pm and you can take advantage of Power Hour, 60 minutes of $3 Buds and Bud Lights. Miscellaneous drink specials run from Sunday through Thursday evening, too. The environs are divey, but it's perfectly amiable, and the prices can't be beat. 98 Third Ave., btw. 12th and 13th sts. 🕐 212/777-6663. www.barnonenyc.com. Daily noon–4am. Subway: L to Third Ave.

Blue Owl EAST VILLAGE   It's gotten hard to swing a cat in NYC without knocking over a tray full of fancy cocktails. Most purveyors charge up the yin-yang for their mixology, but hit a happy hour at Blue Owl and you'll be sipping in style for just $6. The cocktail specials run weeknights from 5 to 8pm, extended to 10pm on Wednesdays.

Get Pretty Nailed at Beauty Bar

Beer goggles aren't the only way you'll look better in a barroom. **Beauty Bar**'s famed Martinis & Manicures happy hours connect stiff drinks and prettified fingernails. Get a cocktail (a Blue Wash, say, with Curaçao) and a number from the barkeep and then wait your turn for an able manicurist. The combo runs just $10, although after all the attention lavished on your cuticles, you'll be wanting to tip as well. Weeknights 6 through 11pm, weekends 7 until 11pm. 231 E. 14th St., btw. Second and Third aves. ℂ **212/539-1389.** www.thebeautybar. com. Subway: L to Third Ave.; L/N/Q/R/4/5/6 to 14th St./Union Sq. Other location: *Park Slope, Brooklyn,* 249 Fifth Ave., btw. Garfield Place and Carroll St. ℂ **718/788-8867.** Subway: R to Union St.

Classic Mondays see half-price vintage cocktailing until midnight. 196 Second Ave., btw. 12th and 13th sts. ℂ **212/505-2583.** www.blueowlnyc.com. Sun–Thurs 5pm–2am; Fri–Sat 5pm–4am. Subway: L to First or Third aves.

Jeremy's Ale House FINANCIAL DISTRICT   When you need to show a tourist real New Yorkers, you can't do much better than the über-authentic Jeremy's. A mix of blue and white collars hangs out beneath a burgeoning collection of liberated ties and bras. The house is known for its huge Styrofoam cups, which hold a full *quart* of beer. A Coors is $5. After-work happy hours (weekdays 4–6pm) feature half-price well drinks, $4 Coors and Coors Light buckets, and $1.50 junior burgers. With the fish market departed from South Street there are fewer takers, but construction workers and film students can still avail themselves of the Eye Opener, $1.75 for a bucket of Coors, available Monday through Friday from 8 to 10am. 228 Front St., btw. Peck Slip and Beekman St. ℂ **212/964-3537.** www.jeremysalehouse.com. Mon–Fri 8am–midnight; Sat 10am–midnight; Sun noon–11pm. Subway: A/C/J/Z/2/3/4/5 to Fulton St./Broadway Nassau.

Moo Life Group   The chainlet begun with the SPF-deprived Sunburnt Cow is as friendly and fun-loving as you'd expect an Aussie production to be. Dinners are convivial enough, but the real action

What's in a Name? Free Drinks!

If you're one of those people who has a name, you can drink for zero dollars and zero cents at bars **No Idea** and **Antarctica.** There is one small catch: Your name has to sync up with the name of the night. Each bar posts a different monthly list, and although there are some oddball monikers, there are also plenty of occasions to hang out with fellow Meghans, Joshes, and Jessicas. Open-tab Name Night runs 5 to 11pm Monday through Saturday (at Antarctica Sat Name Night is 8pm–1am). Check www.noideabar.com and www.antarcticabar.com to see when you're up. FINE PRINT They're not running a booze charity; the idea is to drag along some friends and let them run up the tab while you hobnob with a roomful of fellow Vartans. If you show up alone they may not let you play along. *No Idea:* 30 E. 20th St., btw. Park Ave. and Broadway. ✆ **212/777-0100.** Subway: 6 or N/R to 23rd St. *Antarctica:* 287 Hudson, at Spring St. ✆ **212/352-1666.** Subway: C/E to Spring St. Note that at press time, Antarctica was in the process of trying to renew its lease.

here is at weekend brunch. All four locations are notorious for their generous pours on Moo Marys, Screwdrivers, Greyhounds, or—most famously—Moomosas. Take your choice from any brunch item and pair it with all the booze you care to drink and you're looking at a $25 commitment. FINE PRINT They're cash-only in the daylight hours. The Sunburnt Cow, East Village, 137 Ave. C, btw. 8th and 9th sts. ✆ **212/529-0005.** www.moolifegroup.com. Subway: F to Second Ave.; L to First Ave. Mon–Fri 4pm–2am; Sat–Sun 11am–2am. Other locations: The Sunburnt Calf, Upper West Side, 226 W. 79th St., btw. Broadway and Amsterdam Ave. ✆ **646/823-9255.** Subway: 1 to 79th St. The Sunburnt Calf Brooklyn, Prospect Heights, Brooklyn, 611 Vanderbilt Ave., btw. Bergen St. and St. Marks Ave. ✆ **347/915-1000.** Subway: C to Clinton-Washington Aves.; B/Q to Seventh Ave.; 2/3 to Bergen St.

Verlaine LOWER EAST SIDE   Finding a dive that'll hook you up with a cheap happy hour is no great sleight, but a sleek spot that'll discount you 7 nights a week? Verlaine's house specials are a litchi martini, just $5 between 5 and 10pm, joined by $5 sangrias, Vietnamese Bloody Marys, basic cocktails, and house wine. Hops heads can knock back $3 Yuenglings. The space is a little generic, but it's stylish, and you don't have to pad yourself with cocktail napkins to avoid sticking to the surfaces. 110 Rivington St., btw. Essex and Ludlow sts. © **212/614-2494.** www.verlainenyc.com. Sun–Mon 5pm–1am; Tues–Wed 5pm–2am; Thurs–Sat 5pm–4am. Subway: F to Delancey St.; J/M/Z to Essex St.

*Trinity Churchyard, at the foot of Manhattan, is a quiet stop on one of our Free &
Cheap Itineraries.*

FREE & DIRT CHEAP DAYS

Though New York is happy to gouge visitors for $40 bus tours and boat cruises, a person can scope out a lot of city for no money at all. The city's close quarters mean you can hit a huge range of sights without putting excessive mileage on your soles. A tour of the Financial District will walk you through 350 years of essential American history. NYC's unparalleled subway system can take you back in time (to Coney Island) and to another country (Brighton Beach) without even an hour's commitment to riding the rails. Or you can propel yourself: A stroll across the Brooklyn Bridge provides stunning skyline views and intriguing history on the far side. You don't even need to pack—Gotham's corner stores are already storing your provisions for you.

Itinerary 1: Coney Island

Where	Coney Island, Brooklyn.
How to Get There	D/F/N/Q to Stillwell Avenue/Coney Island. The subway ride is about 50 minutes from downtown Manhattan. You can also use the B/Q at Brighton Beach.
How Long to Spend There	It's easy to amuse yourself along the boardwalk and environs for 2 or 3 hours. Anything longer probably requires a beach towel and a page-turner.
What to Bring	If you're planning on a dip, a bathing suit and towel are the obvious needs. There are public restrooms, cabanas for changing, and showers for shedding salt water. Even if you're going to keep to the streets, bring sunscreen because there's light aplenty reflecting off the sand and sea.
Best Times to Go	Morning's calm is nice. Midday summer days can be brutal and hectic. Late afternoons the crowds start to disperse and the light is lovely.
Tip	The big holiday weekends bring in special events, but they also bring the biggest crowds. If you're not in the mood for the crush, go on a weekday, or keep to the fringes, which are less populated. In the nonsummer months, the amusement parks are closed and the boardwalk is almost empty, but the experience can be peaceful and replenishing.

After a few weeks or months of city living, trapped in the concrete canyons, it's easy to forget that New York City grew high and fast because of its access to water. New York Harbor stays close to the public consciousness, but too many overlook the Atlantic Ocean, which is just a subway ride away. When you feel like traveling to a distant place but don't want to invest more than a couple of Metrocard swipes, Coney Island is hard to beat. In summer, the area becomes a blue-collar resort, with salsa bands and volleyball games and screaming kids on the rides. As with all of Brooklyn, it's the furthest thing from monolithic. Tourists, hipsters, and elderly immigrant locals all overlap on the beachfront benches. Giuseppe Cautela wrote in 1925, "When you bathe in Coney, you bathe in the American Jordan. It is holy water. Nowhere else in the United States will you see so many races mingle in a common purpose for a common good." Yes, there's a major spruce-up taking place to go with a new $250-million subway terminal, but Coney is still a long ways away from shedding its diverse and gritty charm.

① The Beach

The Atlantic up close is hard to beat and the broad beaches here are a nice spot to start a tour. Get good and hot in the sun and then go for a dip. The water is not the cleanest, but just follow the lead of the other souls out there bobbing

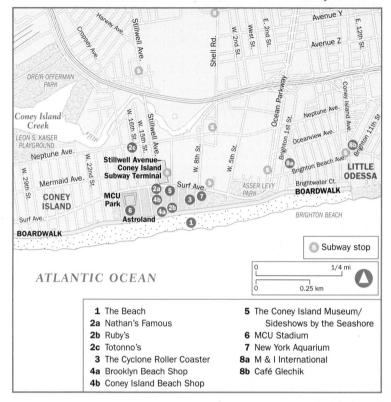

1 The Beach
2a Nathan's Famous
2b Ruby's
2c Totonno's
3 The Cyclone Roller Coaster
4a Brooklyn Beach Shop
4b Coney Island Beach Shop

5 The Coney Island Museum/
  Sideshows by the Seashore
6 MCU Stadium
7 New York Aquarium
8a M & I International
8b Café Glechik

in the waves. On a hot day it's particularly refreshing. A few blocks to the east of the former Astroland and the subway station, the bodies thin out quickly and you can find wide-open stretches. If you're unwilling to track sand back in your shoes, a stroll along the boardwalk offers endless tattoo-admiring entertainment.

② Mealtime

The options for cheap beach food in Coney Island are almost limitless. Fried clams, fried dough,

french fries, and soft-serve ice cream are among the highlights.

● On July 4th at high noon, hefty Americans and rail-thin Japanese fight it out in the annual Coney Island Hot Dog Eating Contest. For $3.75 a pop you can hold your own minicontest at **Nathan's Famous** (ⓒ **718/946-2202;** www.nathansfamous.com), which still sells some million dogs a year here. The stand at 1310 Surf Ave., at Stillwell Avenue, is still on the same spot

Coney Island Costs

Free	
Sun, sand, and sea	$0
Dirt Cheap	
A day at the beach + fireworks + a Nathan's hot dog	$3.75
Add-Ons for Spendthrift Millionaires	
Cyclone Roller Coaster or Wonder Wheel	$6–$8
+ Half a pizza	$8
+ Sideshow	$10

where Nathan Handwerker originated the business in 1916. (A second location is on the boardwalk.)

● **Ruby's,** 1213 Boardwalk West, near Stillwell Avenue (© **718/ 372-9079;** www.rubysconey island.com), a louche bar that dates back to 1934, recently survived an eviction scare. They've refurbished their family-run beachfront bar, with $4 burgers and $5 beers highlighting the menu.

● As appealing as fried food on a picnic table just off the beach can be, it's worth noting that one of New York's best **pizzas** is just a few blocks away. At 1524 Neptune Ave., between 15th and 16th streets, **Totonno's** (© **718/372-8606**) is an old-school, family-run operation that serves up top pies (no slices). The fresh mozzarella and crisp crusts haven't lost a step through 85 years of operation. Small plain pies are $16.50, larges $19.50. They're closed Mondays and Tuesdays.

③ The Legendary Cyclone

The **Cyclone Roller Coaster** (© **718/372-0275;** www.astroland. com) is the granddaddy of Coney Island amusements. Accelerating heart rates since 1927, it's the oldest and most-imitated roller coaster in the world. It's also a quota-starved insurance underwriter's nightmare, with engineering limited to a pulling chain and gravity, but still managing to get those rickety cars up to 60 mph. The supporting rails and wooden boards look mighty untrustworthy, but of course that's the thrill (and in truth, the safety record here is excellent). Rides are $8 a pop ($5 for a re-ride) for 1 minute and 50 seconds of action, so it's not exactly dirt cheap, though it's definitely memorable.

The Coney Island Skyline

Parachute jumps were developed as military-training devices, but leave it to America to convert them to fun. Coney Island's parachute jump started out as a ride at the 1939 World's Fair in Queens before packing up for Brooklyn, where it served thrill-seekers until 1964. The skeletal form that remains has an unexpected elegance. A recent design contest was the first step in installing an architecturally ambitious new base, complete with a restaurant and visitor center. The jump has been designated a historic landmark and it's the pride of the local skyline, so much so that it's sometimes called the Eiffel Tower of Brooklyn.

The Eiffel Tower of Paris was the motivator for George Washington Gale Ferris, an engineer who took up the challenge for America to respond to the Frenchies' innovations in steel. The famous wheels still bear his name and Coney Island's version, the 1920s **Wonder Wheel** (*©* **718/372-2592;** www.wonderwheel.com), is one of the world's tallest at 150 feet. From the ground it looks like a gentle spin, but as the cars slide on lateral rails they create a somewhat stomach-churning effect. For panoramic views of the city and sea it's worth it (and if you opt for a white car you'll be spared the swinging). The $6 cost to ride, however, is a matter of individual budgetary discretion.

④ Souvenirs

Although not dirt cheap, if you're looking to bring back a memento the **Brooklyn Beach Shop** may be just your speed. Newly installed at 1223 Boardwalk West, near Stillwell Avenue, this offshoot of the **Coney Island Beach Shop** (*©* **718/333-1110;** www.coney islandbeachshop.com) has a nice set of Coney-themed T's ($12–$20). Coney taffy is $5.99 a box, or two for $10.

⑤ The Coney Island Museum & Sideshows

The **Coney Island Museum** (*©* **718/372-5159;** www.coney island.com) stands in proud opposition to the history-shrouding changes planned for the area. A $5 admission provides entry to an evolving second-floor space. Funhouse mirrors, old signage, and a creepy baby's coffin (complete with baby skeleton) exemplify the collection. Rotating

Make a Date with Your Coney Island Baby

Coney Island after hours can be even seedier than the daylight spectacle, but that doesn't impede on the potential for a great cheap date. The sight of the dark swells of the Atlantic and the cleared-out beach is pretty grand. The only thing that could improve on it is free **fireworks,** which come around 9:30pm every Friday night from mid-June to late August (and also a few Sat, thanks to the Cyclones). After the fireworks if you've got money to burn, check out Sideshows by the Seashore's **Burlesque by the Beach.** Troupes from around the city come down to shake various body parts. Campy costumes and fire-eating round out the experience. Shows are Thursday nights at 9pm and Friday nights at 10pm; tickets cost $12 to $15.

On Saturday nights, the same Sideshow folk unfold chairs in the **Coney Island Museum** so they can project campy films (p. 249). Coney Island–themed fare and other B-movie obsessions are the norm, and it's only $6. 1208 Surf Ave., 2nd floor. ✆ **718/372-5159.** www.indiefilmpage.com. Sat 8:15pm.

Time it right and you can save that $6. On Monday nights at dusk in July and early August, crowd-pleaser films show on a 40-foot screen on the boardwalk at West 10th Street. New York's tourist bureau joins with **Rooftop Films** (www.nycgo.com/rooftopfilms) to do the hosting.

temporary exhibits reflect the love this organization has for Coney Island's vanished heyday.

Just around the corner you'll find **Sideshows by the Seashore,** run by the same people. It's the nation's last 10-in-1 freak show; step right up to see illustrated men and women, fire-eating, albino-serpent handling, and even beds of nails. The theater is small and run-down, but there's 45 minutes of entertainment for $10 adults,

$5 kids 12 and under. If you're patient, you may hear the barker hustle up some empty seats at a discount. Shows run from Easter through mid-September. Shows are between 1 and 8pm, weekends only early in the season, moving to daily in mid-June.

⑥ MCU Stadium

The return of baseball to Brooklyn certainly hasn't diminished local pride, and tickets to Mets farmhands, the **Brooklyn Cyclones**

(✆ **718/449-8497;** www.brooklyn cyclones.com), aren't that easy to come by. If the game you're aching to see sells out, keep in mind that some standby seats are made available on game day outside the boardwalk stadium. Seats are pretty cheap for professional sports: $9 to $17.

⑦ New York Aquarium

If you've really got your timing down, you can enjoy a cheap visit to the city's only aquarium: After 3pm on Fridays it's "pay what you wish." See p. 107 for more details.

⑧ Bonus Round: Brighton Beach

If you want to leave America but neglected to pack a passport, there is a close-by option. A quick trip east on the boardwalk will put you in the heart of **Little Odessa** in Brighton Beach. Between the strolling Russian émigrés, the Cyrillic signs, and the clunky design on the sidewalk cafes, you'll be forgiven for thinking you've walked into a Black Sea resort town. The cafes are surprisingly pricey, but there's plenty of cheap street fare a block inland. Take a left and walk toward the El, which runs above Brighton Beach Avenue, a bustling street dotted with caviar shops and street vendors.

For total immersion in a foreign land, check out the **M & I**

International (✆ **718/615-1011**) supermarket at 249 Brighton Beach Ave. You can stock up for the trip home, or enjoy Russian pastries or smoked fish in the upstairs cafe. Prices are all outerborough low.

To enjoy a more sit-down experience, join the foodies making a pilgrimage to **Café Glechik** (✆ **718/616-0766;** glechik.com) at 3159 Coney Island Ave. This petite Ukrainian restaurant is known for its dumplings, served in two supple varieties (*pelmeni*, folded like tortellini, and *vereniki*, which resemble pirogi). There are also excellent soups, salads, and kabobs, and most everything comes in well under $10.

Special Events

- With body paint and beads, plus a few strategic scraps of fabric to keep things legal, the avatars of New York's retroculture scene transform themselves into mermaids and Neptunes at the annual ★ **Mermaid Parade,** Surf Avenue from West 21st to West 10th streets (✆ **718/372-5159;** www.coney island.com/mermaid.shtml). Classic cars join the procession as it works its way east on Surf Avenue, dispersing when the participants dash down the beach to the ageless Atlantic. It takes place on a Saturday around the summer solstice.

Itinerary 2: From Brooklyn Bridge to DUMBO

How to Get There	To reach the Brooklyn Bridge in Manhattan, take the J/Z to Chambers Street or the 4/5/6 to Brooklyn Bridge–City Hall. Return from DUMBO on the F train at York Street, or walk about 15 minutes to Brooklyn Heights to catch the A/C train at High Street, or the 2/3 train at Clark Street.
How Long to Spend There	The walk across the bridge takes 30 minutes or so, and it's easy to spend an hour walking around on the Brooklyn side. Adding galleries, meals, and park time can stretch out the visit to 2 or 3 hours.
Best Times to Go	A sunny afternoon is ideal, but it's all good. Late at night it gets pretty sparse around the bridge and DUMBO, which can have its own appeal. It's more disconcerting than it is dangerous..
Tip	If you're interested in the galleries, check in advance to see which ones have exhibits up. Note that galleries in DUMBO keep different hours than those in Manhattan; many are closed midweek, but open on Sundays.

❶ The Bridge

The Brooklyn Bridge is one of New York's great treasures, and as such, it's not a very well kept secret. Tourists, bikers, joggers, and commuters jam the planks on sunny days. The dizzying rigging, stunning views, and towering Gothic charm leave a person feeling like they're within the sanctuary of an inside-out cathedral. The bridge's official romance with New York began in 1883, and from Walt Whitman through Hart Crane, the love has only grown. When you reach the first tower, stop for a while so you can admire the Manhattan views. The assorted plaques here are a mix of the ceremonial and the informative.

❷ The Brooklyn Side: DUMBO & Its Galleries

On the far side of the bridge, the pathway slants downward and divides. Staying to the right takes you to Downtown Brooklyn and Brooklyn Heights, and veering to the left will put you beneath an overpass. Walk down the stairs, hang a left, and head toward the water. You'll find yourself among the cobblestones and broad-shouldered buildings that characterize **DUMBO.** DUMBO (Down Under the Manhattan Bridge Overpass) is a surprisingly well-preserved patch of old industrial New York. Artists have infiltrated the area, and their touches can be seen on and around many of the loft structures.

ITINERARY 2: FROM BROOKLYN BRIDGE TO DUMBO

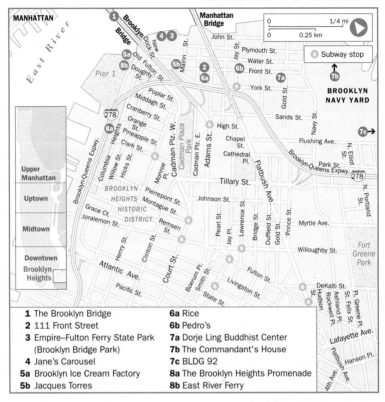

1 The Brooklyn Bridge
2 111 Front Street
3 Empire–Fulton Ferry State Park
   (Brooklyn Bridge Park)
4 Jane's Carousel
5a Brooklyn Ice Cream Factory
5b Jacques Torres
6a Rice
6b Pedro's
7a Dorje Ling Buddhist Center
7b The Commandant's House
7c BLDG 92
8a The Brooklyn Heights Promenade
8b East River Ferry

For a closer look, check out some of the galleries. (Even if you don't like the art, many of the spaces have killer views.) The **1st Thursdays DUMBO Gallery Walk** (✆ **718/222-2500;** www.brooklyn artproject.com) is a great way to sample the goods, augmented with free music and artists' talks. If you don't feel like much of a schlep, 111 Front St., between Washington and Adams streets, hosts several fine institutions, including:

- **A.I.R. Gallery** `FREE` This gallery has made a name for itself as an advocate for women in visual arts. Suite #228. ✆ **212/255-6651.** www.airgallery.org. Wed–Sun 11am–6pm.

- **BAC Gallery** `FREE` The gallery arm of the Brooklyn Arts Council is particularly good for group shows. Suite #218. ✆ **718/625-0080.** www.brooklynartscouncil. org. Mon–Fri 10am–5pm.

Brooklyn Bridge/DUMBO Costs

Free	
Historic walk, art galleries, afternoon in the park	$0
Dirt Cheap	
Walk, art, park, plus a ride on a historic carousel	$2
Add an ice-cream cone or hot chocolate	$3.25–$4
Add-Ons for Spendthrift Millionaires	
Cuban sandwich at Pedro's	$6.50
Brunch at Rice	$12

● **DUMBO Arts Center** Innovative art shows take place here, with a $2 suggested donation. Suite #218. ② **718/694-0831.** www.dumboartscenter.org. Wed–Sun noon–6pm.

③ Park It

One of the biggest changes to NYC's waterfront has occurred along the DUMBO shoreline. The former **Empire–Fulton Ferry State Park** has been folded into the new **Brooklyn Bridge Park** (www.brooklynbridgepark nyc.org), which now offers up 85 acres for the cooling of jets. In the heart of DUMBO, at the end of Old Dock Street, you'll find a grassy swath on the site of the former landing of the Manhattan ferry. Amazingly, the ferry ran until 1924, despite competition from the Brooklyn Bridge. The landscaped segment to the north was a parking lot until it was decided that billion-dollar views of the city, the water, and the bridges might be better appreciated by human beings than panel trucks. The boat traffic and skyline are both hypnotizing, and this is one of my favorite places to chill in the entire city. On the south side of the Brooklyn Bridge, six industrial piers beneath the Brooklyn Promenade are being reborn as additional open space.

④ Go Around

The focal point between the Brooklyn and Manhattan bridges is newly anchored by ★ **Jane's Carousel** (② **718/222-2502;** www. janescarousel.com). Built in 1922 by the Philadelphia Toboggan Company, the ride is fresh off a 25-year restoration, which has returned the luster to steeds, scenery panels, and dual chariots. A ride is $2, or you can just enjoy the views for free—the carousel is housed in a modernist glass box reminiscent of an Apple store. It's especially striking at dusk.

Crossing Over (The Other Bridges)

New York's two other East Village crossings are more utilitarian approaches to Brooklyn, but they're excellent alternatives if you've already done the Brooklyn Bridge to death. The Williamsburg Bridge is newly refurbished, with walk- and bikeways to connect Billyburg with the Lower East Side. The Manhattan Bridge's pathway is narrow and the subway can be near deafening, but the views are unimpeachable. On the Manhattan end you get ancient tenements cutting razor-sharp lines through Chinatown, at midpoint you overlook the stunning full span of the Brooklyn Bridge, and on the far side you can spy on the parks of DUMBO.

5 Treat Yourself

- A post-stroll cool down can be found at the **Brooklyn Ice Cream Factory** (✆ **718/246-3963;** www.brooklynicecreamfactory. com) on the Fulton Ferry Landing Pier. The ice cream is made in Brooklyn in small batches, and it's as pleasurable as the views ($4 for a cup or cone). If the line outside the shop's historic fireboat house is daunting, you can usually find a Blue Marble ice cream vendor just to the south, on Pier 1.

- A little further inland, chocolatier extraordinaire **Jacques Torres** (✆ **718/875-9772;** www. mrchocolate.com) operates a factory at 66 Water St. Though the chocolates themselves could never be confused with dirt cheap, once they take liquid form they become affordable.

Order a hot chocolate and you're basically drinking a candy bar. Opt for the "wicked" version, with its subtle hints of hot pepper, and enjoy extra warmth. This rich treat is a relative steal at $3.25.

6 Mealtime

- Asian fusion fave **Rice** (✆ **718/ 222-9880;** www.riceny.com), at 81 Washington St., brings its exotic grains to Brooklyn, from Thai black to Bhutanese red. Starches are accompanied by curries, salads, and satays. Entrees run $9 to $12; brunch is served noon to 4pm on the weekends. There's a great side garden, should the weather accommodate.

- Nearby **Pedro's** (✆ **718/797- 2851**) occupies a ramshackle basement at 73 Jay St. that feels taken straight from a David Lynch flick. Dominican and Mexican standards are served, with a big plate of pork, rice, and beans for only $9. Tables at street level allow for leisurely alfresco dining (with cheap margaritas).

⑦ Vinegar Hill

If you're up for more exploring of the area, DUMBO is quick to traverse (91 buildings comprise the historic district, representing NYC's best surviving cluster of industrial architecture, from ante-bellum brick counting houses to early-20th-century factories). Walk up Front Street, keeping the water to your left. When you reach Gold Street, peek through the yellow cement blocks on the corner at no. 98. The compound inside belongs to the **Dorje Ling Buddhist Center** (© **718/522-6523;** www.jonang.org). When Front Street dead-ends, take a left and enter my favorite forgotten neighborhood in New York, Vinegar Hill. The well-preserved mid-19th-century buildings are oddly juxtaposed with a field of electrical transformers. The neighborhood is only 4 square blocks. Taking a right on Evans Street will bring you to a cul-de-sac, where you'll see an elegant white **house** behind a gate. Between 1806 and 1966 this is where the Navy Yard commandant hung his hat, while keeping watch over the outfitting of ships to fight everything from Barbary pirates to Nazis. The residence is now in private hands. Another half a mile of walking will bring you to more on the Navy Yard. If you walk up Navy Street and turn left onto Nassau Street (it becomes Flushing Ave.), you'll pass what remains of the derelict Second Empire structures that made up Admiral's Row. At Carlton Avenue you'll find the Navy Yard's fascinating free museum, **BLDG 92** (p. 89).

Dim Sum Good Eats

The entrance to the Brooklyn Bridge is just behind City Hall, which is just behind Chinatown, which is the cheapest place around to fuel up for a hearty walk. At dim sum brunches, carts full of dumplings, duck feet, and other delights are wheeled around the big banquet halls of Chinatown restaurants (p. 49). It's easy to pack away a lot of food for no more than $10.

Make a Date on the Brooklyn Bridge

The Brooklyn Bridge at night is one of the most romantic spots in the city. You can take in the Manhattan skyline, plus the shimmering lights of Brooklyn, plus the mystery of the dark water below, plied by tugs and ferries. In the hours after dusk there's still plenty of foot traffic on the bridge so there's no menace, but it's much more secluded and sedate than at the rush hour or high noon peaks. If you've done a little planning, you can crank up the romance level a few notches by timing your visit with the moonrise, creeping up over the Brooklyn skyline. Check the paper or a weather website for the exact time and allow an extra 20 minutes or so for the satellite to clear the rooflines. If you're really organized, make the date for the full moon—it's the best free show the city's got.

Special Events

- Thursday nights in July and August, walk over the Brooklyn Bridge and then reward yourself with a free flick. The **Brooklyn Bridge Park SyFy Movies With a View summer film series** projects just south of the bridge at Pier 1. (See p. 258 in "Entertainment & Nightlife" for a full review.)

- One weekend in late September (Fri–Sun) you can get the entire DUMBO arts scene at once. During the **Dumbo Arts Festival** (© **718/488-8588;** www. dumboartsfestival.com), galleries and artists' studios open their doors for some 150,000 gawkers. There's also live music, film, performance art, and installations adorning the streets.

8 Homeward Bound

If your dogs are barking too much to hoof it back on the Brooklyn Bridge, you have three subway lines to choose from. The F train accesses DUMBO proper at the York Street station (corner of Jay St.). Just up the hill on the other side of the Brooklyn Bridge lies Brooklyn Heights. The neighborhood is staid, but the historic building stock is astounding. The fruit streets (Pineapple St., Orange St., and Cranberry St., running east-west) are especially nice to stroll through. The **Brooklyn Promenade** along the Hudson has brilliant views of the Manhattan skyline. The A/C trains run to nearby High Street station, and the 2/3 goes to central Clark Street. Or skip the underground and leave by water. The **East River Ferry** (© 800/533-3779; www.nywaterway.com) connects DUMBO at Old Fulton and Furman streets with terminals in Brooklyn, Queens, and Manhattan. A one-way ticket is $4.

Itinerary 3: The Secrets of Lower Manhattan

Where	Broadway's bottom mile, ending at New York Harbor.
How to Get There	The area is very well covered by trains. The tour starts near City Hall, which can be accessed by the 4/5/6 to Brooklyn Bridge/City Hall; the A/C or 1/2/3 or J/Z to Chambers St.; or the R to City Hall.
How Long to Spend There	A straight walk can be done in an hour. To get your fill of museums add 2 more hours, and a round-trip on the ferry clocks in at another hour.
Best Times to Go	The ferry's views of downtown and the Statue of Liberty are great at night, and incomparable at dusk. On the weekends Lower Manhattan feels deserted, with tourists the only signs of life. Quiet streets in New York are a great luxury, but many of the museums and almost all of the stores and restaurants are closed. To really get a feel for the area, hit it on a weekday.
Advance Planning	The Federal Reserve Bank, the gallery of the American Numismatic Society, City Hall, Tweed Courthouse, and the 9/11 Memorial can all be visited for free, but advance reservations are required.

New York City's post–Native American life began on Manhattan's southern tip. The oddly shaped streets here attest to organic urban planning, with the names reflecting ancient exports (Beaver St.), resources (Pearl St.), and fortifications (Wall St.). New York is notorious for paving over its own history, but the Financial District is home to some unlikely survivors. The layers of history here tell the story of New York, and with it the story of the United States. From Dutch colony to national capital to financial leviathan to 9/11, the heritage is densely clustered, and easily reached by a short walk down Broadway. Much of it is approachable, too. George Washington's pew, desk, and inauguration Bible can all be found here for free. Look past the $153 billion that changes hands daily at the New York Stock Exchange, and check out these historic giveaways.

❶ African Burial Ground National Monument

Construction of the Federal Office Building at 290 Broadway (at Duane St.) revealed a hidden and mostly forgotten layer of New York City history. The **African Burial Ground National Monument** (© 212/637-2019; www.nps.gov/afbg) memorializes the 6²⁄₃-acre cemetery that stretches beneath the city's

ITINERARY 3: THE SECRETS OF LOWER MANHATTAN

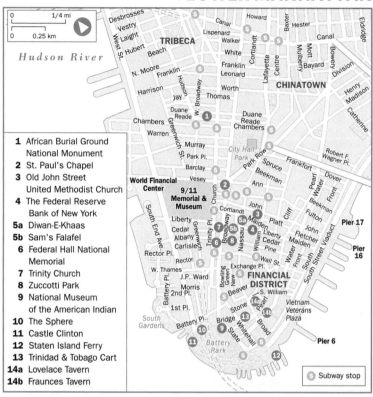

0 — 1/4 mi
0 — 0.25 km

Hudson River

Desbrosses
Vestry
Laight
West St.
Hubert
Beach
N. Moore
Franklin
Harrison
Jay
Hudson
W. Broadway
Duane
Reade
Chambers
Greenwich St.
Warren
Murray
Park Pl.
Barclay
Vesey

TRIBECA

Canal
Lispenard
Walker
White
Franklin
Leonard
Worth
Thomas
Duane
Reade
Chambers

Howard
Canal
Lafayette
Centre
Cortlandt

Hester
Baxter
Mulberry
Mott
Bayard
Bowery
Division

Eldridge
Canal

CHINATOWN

Henry
Madison
Catherine

City Hall Park
Robert F. Wagner Pl.
Park Row
Frankfort
Spruce
Beekman
Ann

World Financial Center

9/11 Memorial & Museum

South End Ave.
Greenwich
Trinity
Church
Broadway
Liberty
Cedar
Albany
Carlisle
Rector Pl.
Rector
W. Thames
J.P. Ward
Morris
2nd Pl.
1st Pl.
South Gardens
Battery Pl.
Battery Park

Cortlandt
John
Platt
Maiden
Liberty
Cedar
Nassau
Pine
William
Wall St.
Exchange Pl.
FINANCIAL DISTRICT
New
Beaver
S. William
Stone
Broad
Whitehall
State
Bridge

Cliff
John
Fletcher
Maiden
Fulton
Pearl
Water
Front
South
South Street Viaduct

Pier 17
Pier 16
Pier 6

Vietnam
Veterans
Plaza

Pearl
Water
Front
Dover

Subway stop Ⓢ

1 African Burial Ground National Monument
2 St. Paul's Chapel
3 Old John Street United Methodist Church
4 The Federal Reserve Bank of New York
5a Diwan-E-Khaas
5b Sam's Falafel
6 Federal Hall National Memorial
7 Trinity Church
8 Zuccotti Park
9 National Museum of the American Indian
10 The Sphere
11 Castle Clinton
12 Staten Island Ferry
13 Trinidad & Tobago Cart
14a Lovelace Tavern
14b Fraunces Tavern

municipal center. Starting in the 1690s, some 15,000 Africans were laid to rest here. Undulating mounds and a granite memorial make somber markers for the 419 bodies reinterred here. There's a small interactive visitor center, where you can find out more about the monument. To your left on Chambers Street you'll see Tweed Courthouse, and behind it City Hall, which keeps George Washington's desk in its Governor's Room. At select times you can get free tours of these buildings; see p. 128 and 126.

② St. Paul's Chapel

On the far side of City Hall Park, at Vesey Street, you'll find this satellite chapel (℃ **212/233-4164;** www.saintpaulschapel.org) of Trinity Church. Completed in 1766, this is the oldest continuously used public building in the city. The interior is surprisingly cheerful and colorful. Even the 9/11 exhibits have an upbeat and

Lower Manhattan Walk Costs

Free	
A museum, three churches, three national monuments, and a round-trip ferry ride	$0
Dirt Cheap	
The museum, monuments, ferry, and a Caribbean lunch	$5
Add-Ons for Spendthrift Millionaires	
Historic tavern museum	$7

healing tone, although a self-congratulatory note does seep in. On the north side of the chapel you can see the pew used by George Washington when New York was the official seat of the U.S. government. Over the pew is a 1795 painting of the Great Seal, in one of its earliest renditions. Out back is a little country graveyard, which miraculously survived the rain of debris on 9/11. Standing amid the ancient tombstones and looking up at the rising 1 World Trade Center will give you a sense of the neighborhood's long historical scope.

3 Old John Street United Methodist Church

Head 1 block south and make a left onto John Street. Just past Nassau Street you'll reach a quiet little plot that's been dedicated to Methodism since 1768, when the first American congregation began meeting in a humble chapel here. In the tiny, free museum (© **212/269-0014;** www.johnstreetchurch.org) you'll find a wooden pulpit and altar from the original building, along with a still-working clock given by John Wesley himself. The paintings and memorabilia are on the musty side, but it's an interesting history—Harlem's Mother A.M.E. Zion Church had its origins among freed slaves here. The current church dates to 1841, as reflected in the understated Italianate sanctuary upstairs.

4 The Federal Reserve Bank of New York

One block south on Nassau Street, between Maiden Lane and Liberty Street, you'll reach the Florentine Renaissance hulk of the Federal Reserve Bank (see p. 91 for a full review). The **American Numismatic Society** (© **212/571-4470,** ext. 112; www.numismatics.org) keeps a gallery here. Among the cowrie shells and currency you'll find a 1933 Double Eagle, a gold coin purchased for 400,000 times the value printed on its face. Due to increased security, you'll need to make an appointment to visit.

⑤ Meal Break

Right around the corner at 53 Nassau St. is a small shop with fresh, delicious Indian food. **Diwan-E-Khaas** (℃ 212/571-7676) serves rich *palak paneer* for $6.50 and chicken *tikka masala* for $7.50. Entrees include a choice of rice or naan. A second location is at 26 Cedar St. (℃ 212/480-0697).

Also nearby is downtown legend **Sam's Falafel,** run from a cart on the northeast corner of Cedar Street and Broadway. The long line will tip you off to the quality of the food here. Portions are huge and prices are tiny ($4 for a sandwich, $6 for a platter).

⑥ Federal Hall National Memorial

Keep walking south on Nassau Street and in 3 blocks you'll reach Wall Street. At this corner is **Federal Hall** (℃ 212/825-6888; www.nps.gov/feha), which is not a heavily trafficked site, probably because the really interesting stuff happened in predecessor structures. The current building was built in 1842 to serve as a U.S. custom house, and it's now a Park Service museum. Exhibits touch on Washington's inauguration, the drafting of the Bill of Rights,

Take a Free Ride

The Alliance for Downtown New York's Downtown Connection offers a free bus service that provides easy access to downtown destinations, including Battery Park City, the World Financial Center, and South Street Seaport. The buses, which run daily, every 10 minutes or so, from 10am to 7:30pm, make dozens of stops along a 5-mile route from Chambers Street on the west side to Beekman Street on the east side. For schedules and more information, call the **Downtown Connection** at ℃ **212/566-6700,** or visit www.downtownny.com.

and the first stirring of rebellion against British authority, all of which occurred right here. The building itself is a preeminent example of Greek Revival architecture, with an impressive rotunda, and the 1767 Bible used by George Washington for his 1789 presidential inauguration is on display. Otherwise, there's not much to see beyond a comprehensive collection of New York brochures. The vertiginously steep stairs outside are a popular spot to spy on the chaos that surrounds the **New York Stock Exchange.** The 1903 classical structure that houses it is just in front of you, at 18 Broad St.

7 Trinity Church

One block to the west is Broadway, where **Trinity Church** (© **212/602-0800;** www.trinitywallstreet.org) wedges in at the intersection of Wall Street. They've been ministering Episcopal-style on this spot since 1698. The current Gothic Revival church was built in 1846, under architect Richard Upjohn, and was the city's tallest building for over 4 decades. The interior is dark and somber. The churchyard is also of interest, with its ancient headstones (Alexander Hamilton is one of the boldface names buried here) somehow surviving in the shadow of mammon.

8 Zuccotti Park

Head back out to Broadway and turn north for a couple of blocks. At Cedar Street you'll see **Zuccotti Park** (© **212/442-4500**), made famous by the Occupy Wall Street encampment. Grab a spot in the shade if you'd like to impersonate a member of the 99%. If you've reserved passes to the **9/11 Memorial** (p. 96), keep on Cedar Street for 2 blocks until it ends at Greenwich Street. Just to your left, at Albany Street, is the entrance. Try to avoid the siren song call of legendary discounter **Century 21** (p. 201), another block up at 22 Cortlandt St.

9 National Museum of the American Indian

When you get back to Broadway, make your way south. The enigmatic markers in the sidewalk commemorate ticker tape parades held in this "Canyon of Heroes." Across from 26 Broadway you'll see Arturo Di Modica's bronze *Charging Bull,* which in an act of guerilla art was snuck into the neighborhood in 1989. Behind it is **Bowling Green,** Manhattan's oldest public park. It was here or very close by that Peter Minuit, director general of New Netherland, traded the legendary $24 in beads for Manhattan. Just a few feet away the Smithsonian maintains the **National Museum of the American Indian** (© **212/514-3700;** www.americanindian.si.edu), which shows off the unparalleled craftsmanship of Native American art. Even if the walls were bare, the building itself, the former U.S. custom house, would be worthy of a visit. It was completed in 1907 to the specifications of Beaux Arts master Cass Gilbert (he also did the nearby Woolworth Building), and the central rotunda by Raphael Guastavino is a structural marvel.

10 The Sphere

In Native American times, Broadway was a trading route known as the Wiechquaekeck Trail. Its southern terminus is Battery Park. If you follow the promenade that begins at the intersection of State Street and Battery Place (headed toward Castle Clinton), you'll pass a 9/11 memorial. Fritz Koenig's sculpture **The Sphere** stands behind an eternal flame lit on the first anniversary of the terrorist attacks. Koenig designed *The Sphere* as a symbol of world peace and for 30 years it adorned the plaza at the World Trade Center. The sculpture was salvaged from the rubble and placed here, where the shoreline would have been in 1625 New Amsterdam. Though battered and abused, *The Sphere* is surprisingly intact, with 1 World Trade Center visible behind it. There's a metaphor in there someplace, I hope. Through 2012, there was a long-running battle about moving the sculpture to accommodate a running path. Some want it moved to the 9/11 Museum. At press time, it was still at Battery Park, but do check before you come to see if it's been relocated elsewhere.

🕚 Castle Clinton

Continuing down to New York Harbor, you'll reach **Castle Clinton** (✆ **212/344-7220;** www.nps.gov/cacl), a Napoleonic-era fort. Although this battery has undergone several renovations,

from theater hall to aquarium, the original 1811 walls are still intact. Castle Clinton once served as New York's immigration station, and one out of every six Americans can trace their ancestry through here. The New York Classical Theatre employs the fort during summer Shakespeare performances (p. 260). The battery's day job is mostly as the ticket station for the Statue of Liberty and Ellis Island ferries. You can save $17 and get out into New York Harbor for free by following Battery Park around to the south and east to the Whitehall Terminal.

🕛 Staten Island Ferry

The poor man's Circle Line, the **Staten Island Ferry** (✆ **718/815-BOAT** [2628]) is one of my all-time favorite NYC freebies. From Manhattan to St. George and back again takes a little more than an hour, with inspiring views all the way. The ferry's new terminal rises exuberantly over the water at the end of Whitehall and State streets. Find a seat on the right-hand side of the boat as you enter. You'll have great vantages of the downtown skyline. About halfway through the ride, you'll spot Lady Liberty from the same western windows. On the Staten Island side, there's isn't all that much

Paying Your Respects at 9/11 Memorial Plaza

Ten years and a day after the two hijacked planes brought down the twin towers of the World Trade Center, and close to 3,000 people were killed, a memorial to that fateful day finally opened to the public. Since its opening, it has become the most-visited attraction in New York City, with over 4.5 million visiting the memorial since it opened. The centerpiece within the 8-acre Memorial Plaza is the two reflecting pools and waterfalls, located in the 1-acre footprints of the individual towers. Each reflecting pool is surrounded by a brass parapet where the names of the victims of both the 9/11 and February 1993 bombings are engraved and arranged in an order as to where they worked, close to their coworkers or friends, or wherever their families thought they could best be located. Despite the cacophony of incessant drilling and construction work that surrounds the Memorial (the Freedom Tower; the skyscraper to replace the Twin Towers, is still under construction, as are other adjacent buildings), the experience is a moving one and a reminder of not only the horror of that tragic day, but of the valor of those who gave their lives to save others. Admission is free, but to visit, you must make a (free) online reservation at **www.911memorial.org/visitor-passes.** Same-day visits are available at the Memorial's Preview Site: 20 Vesey St. (at Church St.) beginning at 9:00am, the NYC & Co. kiosk at City Hall, and the NY Water Taxi booth at the South Street Seaport (limited to four passes per person on a first-come, first-served basis). Security, as you can imagine, is tight. You and your bags will be scanned/searched. For more information visit the Memorial's website: **www.911memorial.org.**

to do without a further bus or train ride. The **Staten Island Museum** (© **718/727-1135;** www.statenislandmuseum.org) is not quite worth the walk, let alone the $3 suggested admission. You'll find a four-legged chicken in a jar, a hairball from a cow's stomach, an intriguing Native American carved head, and not much else. More compelling are the neighborhood's Sri Lankan restaurants. **SanRasa** (© **718/420-0027;** www.sanrasa.com) is just a few blocks from the terminal at 226 Bay St., and well worth a pilgrimage. Come on a Sunday and you can enjoy an all-you-can-eat buffet table ($11), laden with mutton curry, buttery *papadum* flatbread, and a spicy eggplant dish that's the best use of the vegetable I've ever found. Inexpensive minor league baseball games (p. 302) are also just a few steps from the terminal.

⓭ Meal Break II

Food carts are a classic part of the New York scene, and a big part of the downtown worker diet. You'll see sidewalks lined with them all through the Financial District, although many are just variations on a falafel-and-mystery-meat theme. If you're up for some Caribbean home cooking, check out **Trinidad and Tobago Cart** (© 646/436-9974), on the south side of Whitehall Street between Pearl and Bridge streets. There's usually a line and items sell out on the early side, but that's a reflection of the high quality and low price. Just $5 nets a small-size luncheon, with rice and beans, a veggie side, and stewed, curried, or jerked proteins. *Roti,* an India-inspired flatbread, wraps $5 to $6 sandwiches, with the meat inside cooked until it's falling off the bone. Scotch bonnet hot sauce provides a nice sharp complement, but it's only for the brave.

⓮ Bonus Round: Historic Taverns

If you bypass the ferry, you can find a couple of bonus sites just to the north and east of Battery Park. One block up is Broad Street, where a massive office building sits at no. 85. Under the colonnade, you'll see a brass railing over glass flooring. Peer into the ground and you'll be looking at stones laid in 1670. During construction of this skyscraper, the foundations of **Lovelace Tavern** were discovered. You can also see the foundations of successor structures, and a support beam for the eyesore high-rise overhead. A more famous tavern is across the street, just to the south at 54 Pearl. This is definitely an optional stop because it comes with a $7 admission charge. **Fraunces Tavern** (© 212/425-1778; www.frauncestavern museum.org) has impressive historical credentials. The building's origins date to 1719, and George Washington gave his farewell speech to his officers in the Long Room upstairs. Unfortunately, multiple fires and remodels have made the current version something less than authentic. Among the more interesting relics under glass is a lock of George's hair, which will be absolutely essential when it comes time to clone the father of our country.

The subway might not cost a nickel anymore, but here are some useful listings and information that can help you enjoy the free & dirt cheap lifestyle.

NYC BASICS FROM A TO Z

1 Information Centers

The city runs six information centers, which are stocked with free maps and brochures, as well as discount coupons for tourist-friendly fare. Check with **www.nycgo.com** for information, or call ✆ **212/484-1222,** which is also the number for the centers below unless otherwise noted.

Gateway to America: Discover New York Harbor Visitor Information Center   Federal Hall (Financial District), 26 Wall St., at Broad St. ✆ **212/825-6990.** Mon–Fri 9am–5pm. Subway: 2/3/4/5 to Wall St.

Official Visitor Information Kiosk—Chinatown   At the triangle of Canal, Walker, and Baxter sts. Daily 10am–6pm; holidays 10am–3pm. Subway: J/N/Q/R/Z/6 to Canal St.

Official Visitor Information Kiosk—City Hall Broadway and Park Row. Mon–Fri 9am–6pm; Sat–Sun 10am–5pm; holidays 9am–3pm. Subway: 2/3 to Park Place; R to City Hall; 4/5/6 to Brooklyn Bridge/City Hall; A/C/J/Z to Fulton St./Broadway Nassau.

Official Visitor Information Center—Harlem Studio Museum, Harlem, 144 W. 125th St., btw. Lenox Ave. and Adam Clayton Powell Blvd. ℂ **212/222-1014.** Mon–Fri noon–6pm; Sat–Sun 10am–6pm. Subway: 2/3 to 125th St.

Official NYC Information Center—Midtown 810 Seventh Ave., btw. 52nd and 53rd sts. Mon–Fri 8:30am–6pm; Sat–Sun 9am–5pm; holidays 9am–3pm. Subway: B/D/E to Seventh Ave.; N/Q/R to 57th St.; 1 to 50th St.

Official NYC Information Center—Times Square Alliance 1560 Broadway (the east side of Seventh Ave. btw. 46th and 47th sts.). ℂ **212/768-1560.** Daily 8am–8pm. Subway: N/Q/R to 49th St.; 1/2/3/7/N/Q/R/S to 42nd St./Times Sq.

Information at the Libraries New York's public libraries are founts of information, and real live librarians will answer your brief *factual* questions (this service is of little utility for existential concerns). The Bronx, Staten Island, and Manhattan residents can call ℂ **917/ASK-NYPL** (917/275-6975), Monday to Saturday 9am to 6pm. You can also text, IM, or e-mail for answers (there's a form you can fill out online, and they'll e-mail your reply). Check **www.nypl.org/ask-nypl/phone-us** for more numbers for specialized questions. In Brooklyn, call ℂ **718/230-2100,** option 5 (Mon–Thurs 9am–6pm, Fri–Sat 10am–6pm). There's also a 24/7 online chat service, which the Queens Library participates in as well. The Queens InfoLine is ℂ **718/990-0728** (Mon and Wed–Thurs 9am–8:45pm, Tues 1–8:45pm,

> ## Current Events
>
> The city does a decent job of providing the latest scoop on goings-on around town. **NYC & Company** keeps a 24-hour information hot line (ℂ **800/NYC-VISIT** [692-8474] or 212/397-8222). For listings of music, theater, museum, and other events, check online at www.nycgo.com. An even better source is **NewYorkology** (www.newyorkology.com), an indie New York travel guide with city basics and attraction and event listings. See below for other sources.

Fri–Sat 9am–6:45pm, Sun noon–4:45pm). Brooklyn and Queens also provide answers via e-mail.

Internet Access for Free or Cheap   The city's Wi-Fi zones are constantly expanding. The South Street Seaport, Bryant Park, City Hall Park, Union Square, and Penn Station are among the areas covered by free wireless connections. (The entire outdoor part of DUMBO is now covered, thanks in part to **www.nycwireless.net**.) Many hotels have gotten onboard, and lobbies like the Ace Hotel (20 W. 29th St.; © **212/679-2222**) are good spots to log in. Check **www.openwifinyc. com** for an index. Many public libraries are Wi-Fi friendly, in addition to the free computers they provide for Internet connections. Check online for more information (**www.nypl.org** in the Bronx, Manhattan, and Staten Island; **www.queenslibrary.org** or **www.brooklynpublic library.org**). Many cafes and fast-food establishments also offer Internet access; the Wi-Fi connections at McDonald's and Starbucks are free and easy to access. The **ING DIRECT Café** at 968 Third Ave., between 57th and 58th streets (© **212/752-8432;** cafes.ingdirect. com), offers free Internet-connected computers (and cheap and tasty coffee) on weekdays from 7am to 6pm, and Saturdays 10am to 6pm.

2 Getting There & Getting Around

GETTING THERE

By Plane

New York City is served by three major airports: **LaGuardia Airport** (© **718/533-3400**), **John F. Kennedy (JFK) International Airport** (© **718/ 244-4444**), and **Newark International Airport** (© **973/961-6000**) in New Jersey. Newark sometimes has the best cheap flight deals, and during high-traffic hours it can be the most accessible to and from Manhattan. For transportation information for all three airports, call **Air-Ride** (© **800/247-7433**).

Getting into Town from the Airports

JFK   **AirTrain JFK** (© **877/JFK-AIRTRAIN** [535-2478]; www.panynj. gov) has been running for almost a decade now, and it's my favorite pick for airport travel. The cost is only $5 (on top of the subway or Long Island Railroad fare to get within AirTrain range), the ride is smooth, and monorails come around often enough that you won't be in a panic over missing your flight. JFK terminals connect with the E/J/Z trains at Sutphin Boulevard/Archer Avenue, the LIRR at Jamaica Station, and the A train at Howard Beach. For the latter, make sure you catch an A to Far Rockaway, not to Lefferts Boulevard. The train runs 24/7. Allow about an hour for the subway and monorail once you've left Manhattan.

LaGuardia   The **M60 bus** ($2.25) serves all LaGuardia terminals, connecting to the Upper West Side of Manhattan. Bus rides from 106th Street and Broadway average 1 hour to the airport, though traffic will cause that time to vary. The **Q48** in Queens also makes LaGuardia runs, taking about half an hour for the trip from the 7 train at Flushing/Main Street. For the complete schedule, call ℂ **718/330-1234** or log on to www.mta.info/nyct/service/airport.htm.

Newark   The **AirTrain Newark** (ℂ **888/EWR-INFO** [397-4636]) is a smooth ride, but it's a little pricey at $12.50 one-way. It takes 20 minutes to get from Penn Station in Manhattan to the airport monorail. The cheapest trip is to take the **PATH train** (ℂ **800/772-2222;** www.njtransit.com) from Manhattan to Newark ($2). At Newark Penn Station you can catch the **62 bus,** which makes several stops but will get you to the airport for only $1.50. On the downside, it's all but impossible to make that combined trip in under an hour.

Carpooling Alternatives   God bless the interwebs for bringing people together. Emerging online services are gearing up to help you save money on cabs and black cars via carpool hookups. **Fare/Share** (**www.faresharenyc.com**) uses an iPhone app to connect riders while **CabCorner** (**www.cabcorner.com**) facilitates shares online. **Ride Amigos** (**www.rideamigos.com**) takes a broader approach, opening its ride board for events and commutes.

By Interstate Bus

Busing to and from New York City from major East Coast cities has become the single most cost-effective way to get into town. Originally, these were cheap bus services created by Chinese-Americans as a means of getting between New York City and Boston, Philadelphia, and Washington, D.C. Budget travelers discovered the bus lines, and a number of companies offer frequent, regular service between most of the major cities in the East (and as far west as Buffalo and

Toronto) for a fraction of what you'd pay by train or plane. Although the Chinatown buses remain the cheapest, we'd recommend that you check out the newer, larger services, which are more comfortable and offer amenities such as Wi-Fi, as well as a safer ride.

From Philadelphia, the average ride might range from $10 to $20; for the other two cities you'll pay $15 to $30, but there are times when specials reduce the fares to just $1.

You'll probably wait for the bus to pick you up or depart from a street corner, rather than a bus station, which some people might count as a bonus if you're not fond of bus stations.

For individual company websites, visit

- **Megabus** (© **877/GO2-MEGA** [462-6342]; www.megabus.com)

- **Boltbus** (© **877/BOLTBUS** [265-8287]; www.boltbus.com)

- **Vamoose** (© **877/393-2828**; www.vamoosebus.com)

- **DC2NY** (© **888/888-DCNY** or 202/332-2691; www.dc2ny.com)

GETTING AROUND TOWN
By Subway & City Bus

The **MTA** (© **511,** out of region **877/690-5116;** www.mta.info) cooked its books and put the screws to subway and bus riders—$2.25 is now the price of a single ride, and they've cut back service to boot. Until straphangers are called upon for our next bloodletting, there are a couple of discounts. When you spend $10 or more on a pay-per-ride **MetroCard,** you get a 7% bonus. Unlimited rides are available in 7-day ($29) and 30-day ($104) formats. Children under 44 inches tall ride free.

By Boat

The **Staten Island Ferry** (© **718/815-BOAT** [2628]; www.siferry.com; subway: R to Whitehall St., 4/5 to Bowling Green, 1 to South Ferry) is hard to beat for scenic satisfaction, with great views of the Statue of Liberty, Ellis Island, and Governors Island. The boat runs 24/7, leaving from the new terminal at Whitehall, on the southeastern tip of Manhattan. On the far side you can enjoy the distractions of St.

George, Staten Island (such as they are—see p. 315), or you can follow the boat-loading sign and circle back across the harbor. Other **ferry services** (www.nywaterway.com) and the **New York Water Taxi** (www.nywatertaxi.com) also offer great views, but it's hard to compete with free. Staten Island ferries leave every 15 to 30 minutes on weekdays, less frequently during off-peak and weekend hours.

BY CAR

New York's spectacular public transportation and surfeit of taxis should be enough to dissuade you from city driving, but I can add a few cautions. Traffic can be miserable, and at weird hours, too (mile-long backup to get across the Brooklyn Bridge at 3am, anyone?). Parking is difficult: Lots charge king's ransoms, and street parking can be impossible to find. If you leave your car too close to a hydrant (or another infraction) you're looking at least at a $100 ticket in Manhattan, or a visit to the tow pound. Driving in the city is doable, but with so much that can be accessed by foot power alone, why risk the hassle?

ON FOOT

This town is built for walking. The dense clustering of neighborhoods makes for great overlaps and cultural collisions, which are best enjoyed at a pedestrian's pace. You can get a taste of the city's diversity within just a few blocks. For example, standing on the corner of Grand and Broadway downtown, you're less than a 10-minute walk from Chinatown, TriBeCa, SoHo, NoHo, the West Village, the East Village, Little Italy, and the Lower East Side. Supplement with a train ride here or there, and you can enjoy plenty of city without resorting to more complicated (and expensive) modes of motion.

BY BIKE

Under the Bloomberg administration, the city has become exponentially more bike friendly. Swaths of asphalt are now reserved for the pedaling crowd, in bike lane, shared lane, and bike path form. The latter category is buffered against vehicular traffic, and all three types provide extensive city access. The free **NYC Cycling Map** has all the details, along with bike shop and bike rental coordinates. Libraries and bicycle shops are among the map distributors, or you can call and request one for free (© **311,** or 212/NEW-YORK (639-9675) outside of the city). To download the map as a PDF, see **www.nyc.gov**.

By Taxi

My senior citizen mother gets all around the city by foot, train, and bus. She considers resorting to taxis "unsporting." Now I wouldn't think less of you for not making your way as ruggedly as a little old lady, but cabs aren't cheap, and if you're traveling at anything close to a peak hour it's much slower than zipping under clogged streets on the train. A taxi costs $2.50 at entry, plus 50¢ for every fifth of a mile, 50¢ for every minute of idling, 50¢ more between 8pm and 6am, and a $1 more for rush hour. If it's an odd hour, or you're in an unfamiliar place, by all means hail a cab, but it's my least favorite way of traveling.

3 Free & Dirt Cheap Resources A to Z

Disability Services The mayor maintains an office (✆ **212/788-2830**) that provides free advice to visitors with disabilities on how to get around the city. The major subway stations have elevators, but city buses are better prepared for those with disabilities. Every city bus is equipped to carry a wheelchair.

Emergencies The number for emergency police, fire, and ambulance service is, of course, ✆ **911.** For nonemergencies and just about any city government function you can think of, call ✆ **311** (out of town callers can use 212/NEW-YORK [639-9675]). Other emergency numbers include the **AIDS Helpline** (✆ 800/AIDS-NYC [243-7692]), **Animal Bites** (✆ 212/676-2483), **Poison Control** (✆ 800/222-1222 or 212/764-7667), **Suicide Prevention** (✆ 212/673-3000), **Traveler's Aid JFK** (✆ 718/656-4870), and **Safe Horizon** (formerly Victim Services; ✆ 212/577-7700). Among the city's 24-hour emergency rooms are **Bellevue Hospital Center** (462 First Ave.; ✆ 212/562-1000), **New York Downtown Hospital** (170 William St.; ✆ 212/312-5000), **St. Luke's/Roosevelt Hospital** (425 W. 59th St.; ✆ 212/523-4000), and **St. Luke's Hospital** (1111 Amsterdam Ave.; ✆ 212/523-4000).

GLBT Resources The **Lesbian, Gay, Bisexual & Transgender Community Center** (208 W. 13th St., btw. Seventh and Eighth aves.; ✆ **212/620-7310;** www.gaycenter.org) is a meeting place for more than 400 organizations. Most of the online calendar lists events with charges, but there are a few freebies, like the free lending library and archive. GLBT information can also be found in the free monthly *Next* (www.next magazine.com) for gay men, *GO Magazine* (www.gomag.com), aimed at a lesbian audience, and the free weekly *Gay City News* (www.gay citynews.com). You can find copies stacked up in bars, clubs, stores, and sidewalk boxes throughout town. If you don't want to risk getting a little ink on your fingertips, their websites are also good sources of information. The **Gay and Lesbian National Hot Line** (© **888/THE-GLNH** [843-4564]; www.glnh.org) offers peer counseling and information on upcoming events. It's open Monday through Friday 4pm to midnight, Saturday noon to 5pm. Also see p. 153 for the **Gay Men's Health Crisis;** their hot line is © **800/AIDS-NYC** (243-7692).

Legal Aid   Any person familiar with cop shows knows that in the U.S., an accused person has "the right to consult with an attorney and to have that attorney present during questioning, and that, if he or she is indigent, an attorney will be provided at no cost to represent her or him." Another freebie! See p. 155 for **Legal Services NYC** (© **646/442-3600;** www.legalservicesnyc.org).

Moving   "Man with a Van" signs are ubiquitous on city streetlamps and bulletin boards. For small moves, I find that's as good a way as any to go. For the online version of those streetlamp flyers, **www.citymove.com** is a helpful site. Movers bid against each other so you get decent prices, and movees critique the jobs so you know which companies to avoid.

Newspapers & Magazines   New York has three major dailies. The *New York Times* is the legendary paper of record, and the *Daily News* and *New York Post* are tabloid style and always entertaining. Two free daily papers, *AM-New York* and *Metro,* can be found near subways in the mornings. *The New Yorker, New York Magazine,* and *Time Out New York* are weekly glossies with extensive information on city goings-on.

Pharmacies   Duane Reades are ubiquitous in NYC, with some 250 branches. Locations with 24-hour pharmacies include 1279 Third Ave. (© **212/744-2668**), 250 W. 57th St. (© **212/265-2101**), and 2522 Broadway (© **212/663-1580**). Two of the city's Rite Aids also offer 24-hour service: 301 W. 50th St. (© **212/247-8384**) and 408 Grand St. (© **212/529-7115**).

Post Offices   The **Main Post Office,** at Eighth Avenue and 33rd Street (© **212/967-8585**), is open 24 hours a day, 7 days a week. Check www.usps.com for other city locations; note that New York post offices generate long lines—try to time your visit with a morning or afternoon lull, or make use of the automated machines.

Smoking Laws   New York's legendary tolerance does not extend to smokers. You can light up on the sidewalks, but smoking on public transportation and in hotel lobbies, taxis, shops, and parks is prohibited. Most bars and restaurants ban smoke as well, although their outdoor areas are generally exceptions. Buy cigarettes before you hit the city: A pack will set you back around $13 now.

Telephone Service   Several small companies have come into the New York phone market, significantly undercutting AT&T and Verizon. Prices start low, but once the Man slaps on his $20 or so in monthly taxes and surcharges, it may not seem quite so cheap. If you're already paying for broadband, you can get around the gummint by signing up with a company like **Vonage** (www.vonage.com). Monthly rates start low: $11.99 for basic (300 free min. of local and long-distance), up to $24.99 for all-you-can-yak. Usually you can keep your existing number, too. The next broadband telecommunications wave is to turn your PC into a phone. **Skype** (www.skype.com) will let you talk free with other Skype users worldwide. You'll need a mic and headphones, but those are cheap enough, and the program downloads quickly. (For calls outside the Skype system, rates start at around 2.3¢ per min., or 1.2¢ per min. with a subscription.) **Yahoo!** is another entrant into this field. Their rates start at nothing (PC to PC via Yahoo! Messenger), and vary widely for PC to phone. Long-distance starts around 2¢ per minute. For 60¢ a minute you can get caught up with your college buddies in Antarctica. Check www.voice.yahoo. com for the latest offers. If you're only interested in long-distance savings by traditional means, compare rates online at **www.lowermy bills.com**. (The site also offers rate comparisons on everything from cellphones to insurance to mortgages.) Also, if you're still paying for directory assistance for businesses, stop. Google has a completely free text service (send to Ⓒ **GOOGL** [46645]) for use with cellphones.

Tipping   Despite the cheapness advocated on these pages, I consider good tipping to be essential for my financial karma. Typically in New York, we leave 20% for our waiters/waitresses/waitrons (less for poor service), 10% for food delivery guys (more if it's pouring or freezing), 10% for cabdrivers, 10% or so for bartenders, around 15% for hairdressers, and $1 per bag for bellhops.

For Further Reading

The same era that's coined the words *frugalista* and *recessionista* has also spawned a host of cheap living material on the interwebs. Our colleague **Broke-Ass Stuart** maintains a great website, with an army of columnists providing tips on how to live more for less (www.broke assstuart.com). **Cheapism** (www.cheapism.com) is almost a *Consumer Reports* for the price-conscious, with product overviews and sample costs. Coupon codes can be plucked from **www.retailmenot.com**, and group-rate specials are churned out daily at **www.groupon.com**. Locally, **Brokelyn** (www.brokelyn.com) runs a well-researched and fun-to-read site about all things cheap in Brooklyn. To keep up with New York's music scene (free and not free), check out **Brooklyn Vegan** (www.brooklynvegan.com) and **Oh My Rockness** (www.ohmyrock ness.com). **Nifty NYC** (www.niftynyc.com) has a helpful website, as well as a meaty daily e-mail blast. **The skint** (www.theskint.com) is another excellent resource, with both daily e-mails and online listings. When I'm not toiling for Frommer's, I moonlight as the NYC listings editor for **BlackBook** (www.blackbookmag.com)—check the website or free iPhone app for tons more on New York City shops, bars, restaurants, and hotels.

Toilets   For free public toilets, you can take advantage of the efforts of people with way too much time on their hands by logging on to **www.thebathroomdiaries.com** and browsing the lists of facilities. Many city parks have comfort stations, though they're usually not the cleanest. **Bryant Park** is an exception, with neat facilities in the northeast corner of the park along 42nd, between Fifth and Sixth avenues. Transit hubs are good bets. The downstairs **Dining Concourse at Grand Central** recently added a second set of facilities on the west end. Until everyone else figures it out, they're not nearly as crowded as the east end. **Penn Station** has public restrooms on the Main Concourse near the ticket windows. **Port Authority** is not nearly as scary as it used to be, and restrooms are located all over the terminal. The main restrooms, on the Main Concourse of the South Wing and on the second floor between the North Wing and the South Wing, are clean enough and heavily trafficked by commuters. Bookstores with cafes are almost always equipped with restrooms. **Barnes & Noble** has locations across the city. Other merchants worth noting are department stores and retailers like **Old Navy, Kmart,** and **Bed Bath & Beyond.** Large hotels are also great options. Times Square is a particularly unfriendly area for restrooms, but the **New York Marriott Marquis** (1535 Broadway, at 46th St.) has nice facilities in its eighth-floor lobby. Also good is the **Official NYC Information Center** on Seventh Avenue between 46th and 47th streets.

INDEX